The Saga of Gunnlaug Serpent-Tongue

Original Text, Translations, and Word Lists

Translated by
Matthew Leigh Embleton

Copyright ©2025 Matthew Leigh Embleton. All rights reserved.

The Saga of Gunnlaug Serpent-Tongue

The Saga of Gunnlaug Serpent-Tongue (*Old Norse*) 4
The Saga of Gunnlaug Serpent-Tongue (*Old Icelandic*) 76
Word List *(Norse to English)* 144
Word List *(English to Norse)* 190

Cover: Old Norse text over an outline of Iceland. Author's design.

The original Old Icelandic and Old Norse texts are in the public domain.
These translations ©2021 Matthew Leigh Embleton
©2025 Matthew Leigh Embleton (This Edition)

Acknowledgments

I have long been fascinated by languages and history, and I am very grateful to the special people in my life who have supported and encouraged me in my work. Thank you for believing in me. You know who you are.

Introduction

The Saga of Gunnlaug Serpent-Tongue (Gunnlaugs Saga Ormstungu) is the story of a promising young man named Gunnlaug who achieves fame for his bravery and poetry in the courts of kings and earls throughout the Norse world. However, a prophetic dream foretells a love rivalry, betrayal, and tragedy. The rich tradition of Icelandic literature survived by oral tradition over several centuries before being written down in the 13th Century.

Old Norse is a North Germanic language spoken by inhabitants of Scandinavia from about the 7th to the 15th centuries. Old Icelandic is a variety of Old West Norse that emerged during the Norse settlement of Iceland in the second half of the 9th century.

The meaning of the word 'saga' (plural: 'sǫgur' or 'sögur') translates as 'that which is said', or more widely: a 'saying', 'statement', 'story', 'tale', or 'narrative'.

This book contains:
- The Saga of Gunnlaug Serpent-Tongue (Old Norse Version)
- The Saga of Gunnlaug Serpent-Tongue (Old Icelandic Version)

The texts are presented in their original Norse, with a literal word-for-word line-by-line translation, and a Modern English translation, all side-by-side. In this way, it is possible to see and feel how the Norse language worked and how it has evolved. Also included is a word list with 3,019 Norse words translated in to English, and 1,846 English words translated into Norse.

This book is designed to be of use and interest to anyone with a passion for the Old Norse or Old Icelandic language, Norse history, or languages and history in general.

The Saga of Gunnlaug Serpent-Tongue (Old Norse)

The Saga of Gunnlaug Serpent-Tongue (Old Norse)

Old Norse	Literal	English
1	1	1
Þorsteinn hét maðr.	Thorstein was-named a-man	There was a man named Thorstein
Hann var Egilsson, Skalla-Grímssonar, Kveld-Úlfssonar hersis ór Nóregi, en Ásgerðr hét móðir Þorsteins ok var Bjarnardóttir.	He was son-of-Egil, son-of-Skalla-Grim, son-of-Kveld-Ulf local-leader from Norway, and Asgerd was-named mother Thorstein's and was daughter-of-Bjorn.	He was the son of Egil, the son of Skalla Grim, son of Kveld Ulf the local leader from Norway, and Thorstein's mother was named Asgerd, the daughter of Bjorn.
Þorsteinn bjó at Borg í Borgarfirði.	Thorstein lived at Borg in Borgafjord.	Thorstein lived at Borg in Borgafjord.
Hann var auðigr at fé ok höfðingi mikill, vitr maðr ok hógværr ok hófsmaðr um alla hluti.	He was rich of wealth and leader great, wise man and humble and moderate-man about all things.	He was rich in wealth and a great leader, a wise man and humble and moderate in all things.
Engi var hann afreksmaðr um vöxt eða afl sem Egill, faðir hans, en þó var hann it mesta afarmenni ok vinsæll af allri alþýðu.	None was he accomplished about growth or strength as Egil, father his, and thought was he the most outstanding-man and popular of all people.	He was not as accomplished in size or strength as his father Egil, and he was thought of as the most outstanding and popular man of all people.
Þorsteinn var vænn maðr, hvítr á hár ok eygr manna bezt.	Thorstein was handsome man, white of hair and eyes man's best.	Thorstein was a handsome man, with white hair and the best of eyes of men.
Hann átti Jófríði Gunnarsdóttur, Hlífarsonar.	He married Jofrid daughter-of-Gunnar, son-of-Hlífar.	He married Jofrid, the daughter of Gunnar, the son of Hlifar.
Hana hafði átt fyrr Þóroddr, sonr Tungu-Odds, ok var þeira dóttir Húngerðr, er þar fæddist upp at Borg með Þorsteini.	She had married before Thorod, son Tunga-Odd's, and was their daughter Hungerd, was there fostered up at Borg with Thorstein.	She had previously married Thorod, son of |Tunga-Odd, and their daughter was Hungerd, who was fostered by Thorstein at Borg.
Jófríðr var skörungr mikill.	Jofrid was noble great.	Jofrid was very much noble.
Þau Þorsteinn áttu margt barna, en þó koma fá við þessa sögu.	Then Thorstein had many children, but though coming few with this saga.	Then Thorstein had many children, but only a few come into this saga.

The Saga of Gunnlaug Serpent-Tongue (Old Norse)

Old Norse	Literal	English
Skúli var ellstr sona þeira, annarr Kollsveinn, þriði Egill.	Skuli was oldest son theirs, another Kollsveinn, third Egil.	Skuli was their oldest son, the second was Kollsveinn, the third was Egil.
2	2	2
Eitt sumar, er þat sagt, at skip kom af hafi í Gufuárósi.	One summer, was it said, that ship came out-of sea in Gufua.	One summer it was said that a ship came ashore in Gufua.
Bergfinnr er nefndr stýrimaðr fyrir skipinu, norrænn at ætt, auðigr at fé ok heldr við aldr.	Bergfinn was named steersman for ship, Norwegian by descendents, rich in wealth and rather with age.	The captain of the ship was named Bergfinn, a Norwegian by ancestry, rich in wealth and old aged.
Hann var vitr maðr.	He was wise man.	He was a wise man.
Þorsteinn bóndi reið til skips ok réð jafnan mestu, hver kaupstefna var, ok svá var enn.	Thorstein farmer rode to ships and decided usually most, whose trading-posts were, and so was then.	Thorstein the farmer rode to the ships and usually decided most of where trading posts were, and it was the same this time.
Austmenn vistuðust, en Þorsteinn tók við stýrimanni, fyrir því at hann beiddist þangat.	Easterners found-a-place, and Thorstein took with steersman, for because that he invited there.	The easterners found themselves lodgings, and Thorstein took in the captain, because he had invited him there.
Bergfinnr var fátalaðr of vetrinn, en Þorsteinn veitti honum vel.	Bergfinn was quiet about winter, and Thorstein provided-for him well.	Bergfinn was quiet during the winter, and Thorstein provided for him well.
Austmaðrinn hendi mikit gaman at draumum.	Eastern-man hand much enjoyment of dreams.	The easterner was very interested in dreams.
Um várit einn dag ræddi Þorsteinn um við Bergfinn, ef hann vildi ríða með honum upp undir Valfell.	About spring one day discussed Thorstein about with Bergfinn, if he wished ride with him up to Valfell.	One day in the spring, Thorstein discussed with Bergfinn, if he would like to ride with him up to Valfell.
Þar var þá þingstöð þeira Borgfirðinga.	There was then assembly-post theirs Borgafjord-people.	There was an assembly of the Borgafjord people.
En Þorsteini var sagt, at fallnir væri búðarveggir hans.	Then Thorstein was said, that fallen were booth-walls his.	Then Thorstein said that the walls of his booth had fallen in.

The Saga of Gunnlaug Serpent-Tongue (Old Norse)

Old Norse	Literal	English
Austmaðrinn kveðst þat vilja, ok riðu þeir heiman of daginn þrír saman ok húskarl Þorsteins, þar til er þeir koma til bæjar þess, er at Grenjum heitir.	Eastern-man said that willed, and rode they home about days three together and servant Thorstein's, there until when they came to farm this, is that Grenjar called.	The easterner said that he would like to go, and they rode from his home for about three days, together with Thorstein's servant, until they came to the farm that is named Grenjar.
Þar bjó einn maðr félítill, er Atli hét.	There lived one man poor, was Atli named.	There lived a poor man who was named Atli.
Hann var landseti Þorsteins, ok beiddi Þorsteinn Atla, at hann færi til starfs með þeim ok hefði pál ok reku.	He was tenant Thorstein's, and asked Thorstein Atli, that he journey to work with them and have hoe and shovel.	He was a tenant of Thorstein's, and Thorstein asked Atli, that he journey to work with them and bring a hoe and a shovel.
Hann gerði svá.	He did so.	He did so.
Ok er þeir koma upp undir Valfell til búðartóftanna, þá tóku þeir til starfs allir ok færðu út veggina.	And when they came up to Valfell to booth-ruins, then took they to work all and went out-of walls.	And when they came up to Valfell to the booth ruins, then they took to work digging out the walls.
Veðrit var heitt af sólu, ok varð þeim Þorsteini ok Austmanni erfitt.	Weather was hot of sun, and became they Thorstein and Eastern-man difficult.	The weather was hot with the sun, and, and it became difficult for Thorstein and the easterner.
Ok er þeir höfðu út fært veggina, þá settist Þorsteinn niðr ok Austmaðr í búðartóftina, ok sofnaði Þorsteinn ok lét illa í svefni.	And when they had out-of gone walls, then sat Thorstein down and easterner in booth, and slept Thorstein and lay badly in sleep.	And when they had finished digging out the booths, Thorstein and the easterner sat down in the booth, and Thorstein slept, but his sleep was uneasy.
Austmaðr sat hjá honum ok lét hann njóta draums síns, ok er hann vaknaði, var honum erfitt orðit.	Easterner sat beside him and let him enjoy dreams his, and as he awoke, was he difficult of-words.	The easterner sat beside him and let him enjoy his dreams, and as he awoke, he found it hard to speak.
Austmaðr spurði, hvat hann hefði dreymt, er hann lét svá illa í svefni.	Easterner asked, what he had dreamt, as he lay so badly in sleep.	The easterner asked what he had dreamt, since he lay so badly in his sleep.
Þorsteinn svaraði: "Ekki er mark at draumum".	Thorstein answered: "Nothing is proof of dreams".	Thorstein answered: "Dreams don't mean anything".

The Saga of Gunnlaug Serpent-Tongue (Old Norse)

Old Norse	Literal	English
Ok er þeir riðu heim um kveldit, þá spyrr Austmaðr, hvat Þorstein hefði dreymt.	And as they rode home about evening, then asked easterner, what Thorstein had dreamt.	And as they rode home that evening, then the easterner asked what Thorstein had dreamt.
Þorsteinn segir: "Ef ek segi þér drauminn, þá skaltu ráða hann, sem hann er til".	Thorstein said: "If I say to-you dream, then shall-you advise it, as it was to".	Thorstein said: "If I say to you what I dreamt, you must advise what it really means".
Austmaðr kveðst á þat hætta mundu.	Easterner said of that risk would.	The easterner said he would risk it.
Þorsteinn mælti þá: "Þat dreymði mik, at ek þóttumst heima vera at Borg ok úti fyrir karldurum, ok sá ek upp á húsin ok á mæninum álft eina væna ok fagra, ok þóttumst ek eiga ok þótti mér allgóð.	Thorstein spoke then: "That dreamed me, that I thought home was at Borg and out before man-door, and looked I up of house and of roof-ridge swan one kind and fair, and thought I owned and thought me all-good.	Thorstein then spoke: "I dreamt that I thought I was home at Borg, standing by the main door, and I looked up at the house, and I saw a fine, beautiful swan up on the roof ridge, and I thought that I owned her, and I was very pleased with her.
Þá sá ek fljúga ofan frá fjöllunum örn mikinn.	Then saw I flying over from the-mountains eagle great.	Then I saw a great eagle flying over from the mountains.
Hann fló hingat ok settist hjá álftinni ok klakaði við hana blíðliga, ok hon þótti mér þat vel þekkjast.	He flew here and sat beside the-swan and chattered with her happily, and she thought to-me that well familiar.	He flew here and sat beside the swan and chatted with her happily, and she seemed to be pleased with that.
Þá sá ek, at örninn var svarteygr ok járnklær váru á honum.	Then looked I, that eagle was black-eyed and iron-claws were of him.	Then I looked at the eagle, and it had black eyes and iron claws.
Vaskligr sýndist mér hann.	Bold seemed to-me him.	He seemed to me to be very bold.
Því næst sá ek fljúga annan fugl af suðrætt.	Because next saw I flying another bird of the-south.	Because next I saw another bird flying from the south.
Sá fló hingat til Borgar ok settist á húsin hjá álftinni ok vildi þýðast hana.	Saw flying here to Borg and sat on house beside the-swan and wished join her.	I saw it fly here to Borg, and sit on the house beside the swan, and it wanted to join her.
Þat var ok örn mikill.	That was and eagle great.	It was a great eagle.

The Saga of Gunnlaug Serpent-Tongue (Old Norse)

Old Norse	Literal	English
Brátt þótti mér sá örninn, er fyrir var, ýfast mjök, er hinn kom til, ok þeir börðust snarpliga ok lengi, ok þat sá ek, at hvárumtveggja blæddi.	Soon thought to-me looked eagle, that before was, ruffled much, that he came towards, and they fought sharply and long, and that saw I, that either-side bled.	It soon looked to me like the eagle that came before was very much ruffled, and came towards him, and they fought viciously for a long time, and they were both bleeding.
Ok svá lauk þeira leik, at sinn veg hné hvárr þeira af húsmæninum, ok váru þá báðir dauðir, en álftin sat eftir hnipin mjök ok daprlig.	And so ended their sport, that they fell sank where they of house-roof-ridge, and were then both dead, and swan sat remaining dejected much and sad.	And so ended their sport, that they both fell from the roof of the house, and then they were both dead, and the swan remained sitting, dejected and very sad.
Ok þá sá ek fljúga fugl ór vestri.	And then saw I flying bird from the-west.	And then I saw a bird flying from the west.
Þat var valr.	That was falcon.	That was a falcon.
Hann settist hjá álftinni ok lét blítt við hana, ok síðan flugu þau í brott bæði samt í sömu ætt, ok þá vaknaða ek.	He sat beside the-swan and lay gently with her, and after flew they to away both together in same direction, and then woke I.	He sat beside the swan and he was gentle towards her, and afterwards they both flew away together in the same direction, and then I woke up.
Ok er draumr þessi ómerkiligr", segir hann, "ok mun vera fyrir veðrum, at þau mætast í lofti ór þeim ættum, er mér þótti fuglarnir fljúga".	And was dream this un-marked-like", said he, "and should be therefore winds, that they meet in the-sky from their directions, that to-me thought the-birds flying".	And this dream was unremarkable", he said, "and must be to do with the winds, which meet in the sky from different directions, that the birds were flying from".
Austmaðr segir: "Ekki er þat mín ætlan", segir hann, "at svá sé".	Easterner said: "Not is that my supposing", said he, "that so see".	The easterner said: "I don't think that's what it's about", he said, "as I see it".
Þorsteinn mælti þá: "Ger af drauminum, slíkt er þér sýnist líkligast, ok lát mik heyra".	Thorstein spoke then: "Make of the-dream, such as to-you seem likely, and let me hear".	Thorstein then spoke: "Make of the dream what you think is likely, and let me hear".
Austmaðr mælti: "Fuglar þeir munu vera manna fylgjur".	Easterner spoke: "Birds they would be men followers".	The easterner spoke: "The birds must be the followers of important men".

The Saga of Gunnlaug Serpent-Tongue (Old Norse)

Old Norse	Literal	English
En húsfreyja þín er eigi heil, ok mun hon fæða meybarn frítt ok fagrt, ok munt þú unna því mikit.	When housewife yours is not well, and should she give-birth baby-girl free and beautiful, and shall you love therefore much.	When your housewife is with child, she will give birth to a baby girl, free and fair, and you will love her very much".
En göfgir menn munu biðja dóttur þinnar ór þeim ættum, sem þér þóttu ernirnir fljúga at, ok leggja á hana ofrást ok berjast of hana ok látast báðir af því efni.	Then noble men shall propose-to daughter yours from those directions, as to-you thought the-eagles flew from, and lay to her love and fight about her and die both of therefore prospects.	Then noble men shall propose to your daughter from those directions, that you thought the eagles flew from, and propose to her, and fight over her, and both of them shall die".
Ok því næst mun inn þriði maðr biðja hennar ór þeiri ætt, er valrinn fló at, ok þeim mun hon gift verða.	And therefore next should then third man propose to-her from there direction, that falcon flew from, and then should she married become.	And then next a third man will propose to her from the direction that the falcon flew from, and then shall she become married.
Nú hefi ek þýddan draum þinn ok hygg eftir munu ganga".	Now have I translated dream yours and think after shall go".	Now I have translated your dream, and I think that is how it will go".
Þorsteinn svarar: "Illa er draumr ráðinn ok óvingjarnliga", sagði hann, "ok munt þú ekki drauma ráða kunna".	Thorstein answered: "Badly is dream determined and unfriendly", said he, "and shall you not dreams advise to-know".	Thorstein answered: "Your interpretation of the dream is bad and unfriendly", he said, "and you cannot know to advise".
Austmaðr svarar: "Þú munt at raun um komast, hversu eftir gengr".	Easterner answered: "You shall but see about comes, how-so after goes".	The easterner answered: "You shall see how it comes about, with what goes after".
Þorsteinn lagði fæð á Austmanninn, ok fór hann á brott um sumarit, ok er hann nú ór sögunni.	Thorstein took-to sadness of Eastern-man, and fared he of away about summer, and is he now out-of the-saga.	Thorstein began to dislike the easterner, and he travelled away in the summer, and he is now out of the saga.

3   3   3

The Saga of Gunnlaug Serpent-Tongue (Old Norse)

Old Norse	Literal	English
Um sumarit bjóst Þorsteinn til þings ok mælti til Jófríðar húsfreyju, áðr hann fór heiman: "Svá er háttat", segir hann, "at þú ert með barni, ok skal þat barn út bera, ef þú fæðir meybarn, en upp fæða, ef sveinn er".	About summer prepared Thorstein to the-assembly and spoke to Jofrid housewife, before he travelled-from home: "So is the-way", said he, "that you are with child, and shall that child out born, if you give-birth-to baby-girl, then up give-birth, if boy is".	About summertime, Thorstein prepared to go to the assembly, and spoke to his wife Jofrid, before he travelled from home: "So it will be", said he, "that you are with child, and if the child born is a baby girl, then it must be given up to die, but if it is a boy, it will be brought up".
Ok þat var þá siðvanði nökkurr, er land var allt alheiðit, at þeir menn, er félitlir váru, en stóð ómegð mjök til handa, létu út bera börn sín, ok þótti þó illa gert ávallt.	And that was then custom something-of, when land was all all-heathen, that the people, who poor were, and stood without much to hand, laid out born children theirs, and thought though badly done always.	And that was the custom, when the land was all heathen, that people who were poor without much to hand, laid outside their born children, though it was always thought a bad thing to do.
Ok er Þorsteinn hafði þetta mælt, þá svarar Jófríðr: "Þetta er óþínsliga mælt", segir hon, "slíkr maðr sem þú ert, ok mun þér eigi sýnast þetta at láta gera, svá auðigr maðr sem þú ert".	And when Thorstein had this said, then answered Jofrid: "This is unhealthily spoken", said she, "such man as you are, and should you not appear this to let be-done, so wealthy man as you are".	And when Thorstein had said this, then Jofrid answered: "This is most unworthily said", she said, "that a man such as you, should appear to allow this to be done, wealthy man that you are".
Þorsteinn svarar: "Veizt þú skaplyndi mitt", segir hann, "at eigi mun hlýðisamt verða, ef af er brugðit".	Thorstein answered: "Know you temper mine", said he, "that not should obedient be, if out-of is brought".	Thorstein answered: "You know my temper", he said, "if obedience is brought out".
Síðan reið hann til þings, en Jófríðr fæddi meðan meybarn ákafa fagrt.	Afterwards rode he to assembly, and Jofrid bore meanwhile baby-girl extremely beautiful.	Afterwards he rode to the assembly, and meanwhile Jofrid gave birth to an extremely beautiful baby girl.

The Saga of Gunnlaug Serpent-Tongue (Old Norse)

Old Norse	Literal	English
Konur vildu þat bera at henni, en hon kvað þess litla þörf ok lét þangat kalla smalamann sinn, er Þorvarðr hét, ok mælti hon: "Hest minn skaltu taka ok leggja söðul á ok færa barn þetta vestr í Hjarðarholt Þorgerði Egilsdóttur ok bið hana upp fæða með leynd, svá at Þorsteinn verði eigi varr við, ok þeim ástaraugum renni ek til barns þessa, at víst eigi nenni ek, at þat sé út borit.	Women wanted that carry to her, and she said this little need and had from-there call shepherd theirs, was Thorvard named, and spoke she: "Horse mine shall-you take and lay saddle of and take child this west to Hjardarholt Thorgerd daughter-of-Egil and ask her up foster with secrecy, so that Thorstein will-be not where with, and they lovely-eyes run I to child this, that know not care I, that that saw out carried.	The women wanted to carry the child to Jofrid, but she said there was little need, and had her shepherd whose name was Thorvard, brought to her, and she spoke: "You shall take my horse and saddle it, and take this child west to Hjardarholt, to Thorgerd, daughter of Egil, and ask her to foster her in secrecy, so that Thorstein will not be not be aware of it, and my loving eyes look over the child, such that I care not to carry it out to die.
En hér eru þrjár merkr silfrs, er þú skalt hafa at verkkaupi, en Þorgerðr skal fá þér fari vestr þar ok vist um haf".	Then here are three marks silver, that you shall have to spend, and Thorgerd shall have you fare west there and provisions about the-sea".	Now here are three marks of silver for you to spend, and Thorgerd shall help you travel west and provide for your voyage by sea".
Þorvarðr gerði sem hon mælti.	Thorvard did as she spoke.	Thorvard did as she spoke.
Síðan reið hann vestr í Hjarðarholt með barnit ok fekk Þorgerði í hendr, en hon lét upp fæða landseta sína, er bjuggu inn á Leysingjastöðum í Hvammsfirði.	Afterwards rode he west to Hjardarholt with child and got Thorgerd to hand, and she had up foster tenants hers, as lived then of Leysingastadir in Hvammsfjord.	Afterwards he rode west to Hjardarholt with the child and gave it to Thorgerd, she had it brought up by her tenants, that lived in Leysingastadir in Hvammsfjord.
En hon tók Þorvarði fari norðr í Steingrímsfirði í Skeljavík ok vist of haf, ok fór hann þar útan, ok er hann nú ór sögunni.	Then she took Thorvard going north in Steingrimsfjord in Skeljavik and provisions about the-sea, and fared he there out-of, and is he now out-of the-saga.	She also took Thorvard going north in Steingrimsfjord in Skeljavik, and provisions for the sea, and he travelled abroad from there, and he is now out of the saga.
Ok er Þorsteinn kom heim af þingi, þá sagði Jófríðr honum, at barnit er út borit, sem hann hafði fyrir mælt, en smalamaðr var í brott hlaupinn ok stolit í brott hesti hennar.	And when Thorstein came home of assembly, then said Jofrid to-him, that child was out carried, as he had before said, and shepherd was to away run and stole to away horse hers.	And when Thorstein came home from the assembly, Jofrid said to him that the child had been carried out, as he had said before, and the shepherd stole the horse and ran away.

The Saga of Gunnlaug Serpent-Tongue (Old Norse)

Old Norse	Literal	English
Þorsteinn kvað hana hafa vel gert ok fekk sér smalamann annan.	Thorstein said she had well done and got himself shepherd another.	Thorstein said she had done well, and he got himself another shepherd.
Nú liðu svá sex vetr, at þetta varð ekki víst.	Now passed so six winters that this became not known.	Now six winters passed, without this becoming known.
Ok þá reið Þorsteinn til heimboðs vestr í Hjarðarholt til Óláfs pá, mágs síns, Höskuldssonar, er þá þótti vera með mestri virðingu allra höfðingja vestr þar.	And then rode Thorstein to home-invitation west in Hjardarholt to Olaf Peacock's, brother-in-law his, son-of-Hoskuld, were they thought to-be with most worthy all chieftains west there.	And then Thorstein rode to a home invitation west in Hjardarholt to Olaf Peacock, his brother in law, son of Hoskuld, and they were thought to be the most worthy of all chieftains there.
Þorsteini var þar vel fagnat, sem líkligt var.	Thorstein was there well welcomed, as likely was.	Thorstein was well welcomed there, as was expected.
Ok einnhvern dag at veizlunni, er þat sagt, at Þorgerðr sat á tali við Þorstein, bróður sinn, í öndvegi, en Óláfr átti tal við aðra menn.	And one day at feast, was it said, that Thorgerd sat of talking with Thorstein, brother hers, in foremost, while Olaf had talked with other men.	And one day at the feast, it was said, that Thorgerd sat talking with her brother Thorstein, on the front benches, while Olaf had talked with other men.
En yfir gegnt þeim á bekkinum sátu meyjar þrjár.	Then across opposite them a group sitting girls three.	There was a group of three girls sitting opposite.
Þá mælti Þorgerðr: "Hversu lízt þér, bróðir, á stúlkur þessar, er hér sitja gegnt okkr?"	Then spoke Thorgerd: "How appears to-you, brother, of girls these, are here sitting opposite us?"	Then Thorgerd spoke: "Brother, how do you these girls seem to you, who are sitting opposite us?"
Hann svarar: "Allvel", segir hann, "ok er þó ein fegrst miklu, ok hefir hon vænleik Óláfs, en hvíti ok yfirbragð várt Mýramanna".	He answered: "All-well", said he, "and was though one fair much, and has she likeness Olaf's, and white and complexion our Myrar-folk".	He answered: "Very well", he said, "And though one of them is very fair, with the likeness of Olaf, and white in complexion like our Myrar folk".
Þorgerðr svarar: "Víst er þat satt, er þú segir, bróðir, at hon hefir hvíti ok yfirbragð várt Mýramanna, en eigi vænleik Óláfs pá, því at hon er eigi hans dóttir".	Thorgerd answered: "Certain is that true, as you said, brother, that she has white and complexion ours Myrar-folk, and not likeness Olaf Peacock's, because that she is not his daughter".	Thorgerd answered: "It is certainly try as you say, brother, that she has a white complexion of our Myrar folk, but not a likeness of Olaf Peacock, because she is not his daughter".

The Saga of Gunnlaug Serpent-Tongue (Old Norse)

Old Norse	Literal	English
"Hversu má þat vera?" segir Þorsteinn, "en þó sé hon þín dóttir".	"How-so may that be?" said Thorstein, "but though so she your daughter".	"How can that be?", said Thorstein, "since she is your daughter?"
Hon svarar: "Með sannendum at segja þér, frændi", kvað hon, "þá er þessi þín dóttir, en eigi mín, in fagra mær", ok segir honum síðan allt, sem farit hafði, ok biðr hann fyrirgefa sér ok konu sinni þessi afbrigði.	She answered: "With truth to say to-you, kinsman", said she, "then is this your daughter, and not mine, the fair girl", and said she since all, as went had, and asked he forgive her and wife his this deviation.	She answered: "To say truthfully to you, kinsman", she said, "then this the fair girl is your daughter, and not mine", and afterwards she said all of what had happened, and asked him to forgive her and his wife for this deviation.
Þorsteinn mælti: "Ekki kann ek ykkr at ásaka um þetta, ok veltr þangat, sem vera vill, um flesta hluti, ok hafið þit vel yfir slétt vanhyggju mína.	Thorstein spoke: "Nothing can I you to forsake about this, and depend there, so be will, about most things, and have you well across smoothed carelessness mine.	Thorstein spoke: "I cannot blame you for any of this, and as it often is, what will be will be, and you have smoothed across my carelessness well".
Lízt mér svá á mey þessa, at mér þykkir mikil gifta í at eiga jafnfagrt barn, eða hvat heitir hon?"	Appears to-me so of girl this, that to-me consider much gift to that have equally-beautiful child, but what called she?"	It appears to me that it is a great gift to have such a beautiful child, but what is her name?"
"Helga heitir hon", segir Þorgerðr.	"Helga named she-is", said Thorgerd.	"Her name is Helga", said Thorgerd.
"Helga in fagra", segir Þorsteinn.	"Helga the fair", said Thorstein.	"Helga the Fair", said Thorstein.
"Nú skalt þú búa ferð hennar heim með mér".	"Now shall you prepare journey her home with me".	"Now you shall prepare her to journey home with me".
Hon gerði svá.	She did so.	She did so.
Þorsteinn var þaðan út leiddr með góðum gjöfum, ok reið Helga heim með honum ok fæddist þar upp með mikilli virðing ok ást af föður ok móður ok öllum frændum.	Thorstein was from-there back led with good gifts, and rode Helga home with him and fostered there up with much honour and love of father and mother and all kinsmen.	Thorstein was given splendid gifts there, and Helga rode home with him and was brought up there with much honour and the love of her father and mother and all kinsmen.
4	4	4

The Saga of Gunnlaug Serpent-Tongue (Old Norse)

Old Norse	Literal	English
Í þenna tíma bjó uppi á Hvítársíðu á Gilsbakka Illugi svarti Hallkelsson, Hrosskelssonar.	In those times lived up of Hvitarsida of Gilsbakka Illugi the-Black son-of-Hallkel, son-of-Hrosskel.	In those times, Illugi the Black, son of Hallkel, son of Hrosskel, lived in Hvitarsida in Gilsbakka.
Móðir Illuga var Þuríðr dylla, dóttir Gunnlaugs ormstungu.	Mother Illugi's was Thurid Dylla, daughter Gunnlaug Serpent-Tongue's.	Illugi's mother was Thurid Dylla, the daughter of Gunnlaug Serpent-Tongue.
Illugi var annarr mestr höfðingi í Borgarfirði en Þorsteinn Egilsson.	Illugi was second greatest leader in Borgafjord but-for Thorstein son-of-Egil.	Illugi was the second greatest leader in Borgafjord, after Thorstein Egilsson.
Illugi svarti var stóreignamaðr ok harðlyndr mjök ok helt vel vini sína.	Illugi the-Black was large-property-man and hardy much and held well friends his.	Illugi the Black was a big property owner, and very much hardy, and stood by his friends.
Hann átti Ingibjörgu, dóttur Ásbjarnar Harðarsonar ór Örnólfsdal.	He married Ingibjorg, daughter Asbjarnar son-of-Hardar's from Ornolfsdal.	He married Ingibjorg, daughter of Asbjarnar, son of Hardar from Ornolfsdal.
Móðir Ingibjargar var Þorgerðr, dóttir Miðfjarðar-Skeggja.	Mother Ingibjorg's was Thorgerd, daughter Midfjorder-Skeggi's.	Ingibjorg's mother was Thorgerd, daughter of Midfjorder Skeggi.
Börn Ingibjargar ok Illuga váru mörg, én fá koma við þessa sögu.	Children Ingibjorg's and Illugi's were many, and few coming with this saga.	Ingibjorg and Illugi had many children, but few of them come into this saga.
Hermundr hét sonr þeira, en annarr Gunnlaugr.	Hermund named son theirs, and another Gunnlaug.	Their son was named Hermund, the second was Gunnlaug.
Báðir váru þeir efniligir menn ok þá frumvaxta maðr.	Both were they promising men and then prime-grown men.	Both were promising men, and they were grown in their prime.

The Saga of Gunnlaug Serpent-Tongue (Old Norse)

Old Norse	Literal	English
Svá er sagt frá Gunnlaugi, at hann var snemmendis bráðgerr, mikill ok sterkr, ljósjarpr á hár, ok fór allvel, svarteygr ok nökkut nefljótr ok skapfelligr í andliti, miðmjór ok herðimikill, kominn á sik manna bezt, hávaðamaðr mikill í öllu skaplyndi ok framgjarn snemmendis ok við allt óvæginn ok harðr ok skáld mikit ok heldr níðskár ok kallaðr Gunnlaugr ormstunga.	So is said from Gunnlaug, that he was precocious quick, great and strong, light of hair, and fared all-well, black-eyes and some-what ugly-nose and pleasant in face, medium-narrow and hardy-much, becoming of himself man best, a-loud-man much in all temper and ambitious precocious and with all ruthless and hard and poet great and rather abusive and called Gunnlaug Serpent-Tongue.	So it is said of Gunnlaug, that he was precocious, great and strong, with light hair, well travelled, with black eyes, and a somewhat ugly nose, with a pleasant face, medium narrow and very much hardy, becoming the best man he could, a loud man of mood, stubborn and ruthless and hard in his ambition, he was a gifted poet, but sometimes an abusive one, and he was called Gunnlaug Serpent-Tongue.
Hermundr var þeira vinsælli ok hafði höfðingjabragð á sér.	Hermund was of-them more-popular and had chieftaincy about him.	Hermund was the more popular of them, and had an air of chieftaincy about him.
Ok er Gunnlaugr var tólf vetra gamall, bað hann föður sinn fararefna, ok kvaðst hann vilja fara útan ok sjá sið annarra manna.	And when Gunnlaug was twelve winters old, asked he father his travel-goods, and said he willed travel out and see traditions other people.	And when Gunnlaug was twelve winters old, he asked his father for some travel goods, and said that he wanted to travel abroad and see the traditions of other people.
Illugi bóndi tók því seinliga, kvað hann eigi mundu þykkja góðan í útlöndum, er hann þóttist trautt mega semja við hann þar heima, sem hann vildi.	Illugi farmer took therefore reluctance, saying he not would be-valued good in other-lands, for he thought scarcely able-to negotiate with him there home, as he wished.	Illugi the farmer took reluctance to this, saying that he would not be appreciated in other lands, because he thought that he was scarcely able to negotiate with him at home as he wished.
Ok einnhvern morgin var þat alllitlu síðar, at Illugi bóndi gekk út snemma ok sá, at útibúr hans var opit, ok váru lagðir út vörusekkar nökkurir á hlaðit sex ok þar lénur með.	And one morning was it very-little afterwards, that Illugi farmer went out early and saw, that out-house his was opened, and were laying out sacks some of farmyard six and there laying along.	Soon after this, Illugi went out early one morning, and saw that his outhouse was open, and there were six sacks laying outside the farmyard.
Hann undraðist þetta mjök.	He was-surprised this much.	He was very surprised at this.

The Saga of Gunnlaug Serpent-Tongue (Old Norse)

Old Norse	Literal	English
Þar gekk þá at maðr ok leiddi fjögur hross, ok var þar Gunnlaugr, sonr hans, ok mælti: "Ek hefi sekkana út lagit", segir hann.	There went then by man and led four horses, and was there Gunnlaug, son his, and spoke: "I have sacks out laid", said he.	Then went a man also leading four horses, and it was his son Gunnlaug, and he spoke: "I have laid out the sacks", he said.
Illugi spyrr, hví hann gerði svá.	Illugi asked, why he did so.	Illugi asked why he had done so.
Hann sagði, at þat skyldi vera fararefni hans.	He said, that it should be travel-goods his.	He said that it should be his travel goods.
Illugi mælti; "Engi ráð skalt þú taka af mér ok fara hvergi, fyrr en ek vil", ok kippði inn aftr vörusekkunum.	Illugi spoke; "None authority shall you take of me and travelling neither, before that I wish", and dragged then back ware-sacks.	Illugi spoke: "You shall not take away from my authority, or travel either, before I say so", and dragged the sacks of wares back.
Gunnlaugr reið þá í brott þaðan ok kom um kveldit ofan til Borgar, ok bauð Þorsteinn bóndi honum þar at vera, ok þat þiggr hann.	Gunnlaug rode then to away from-there and came about evening over to Borg, and invited Thorstein farmer him there to be, and that accepted he.	Gunnlaug then rode away from there and arrived at Borg in the evening, and Thorstein the Farmer invited him to stay there, and he accepted.
Gunnlaugr segir Þorsteini, hversu farit hafði með þeim feðgum.	Gunnlaug said Thorstein, howso gone had with them father-and-son.	Gunnlaug said to Thorstein how it had gone between them, father and son.
Þorsteinn bað hann þar vera þeim stundum, sem hann vildi, ok þar var hann þau missari ok nam lögspeki at Þorsteini, ok virðist öllum mönnum þar vel til hans.	Thorstein invited him there to-be them awhile, as he wished, and there was he then a-season and took lawspeaking by Thorstein, and worthied all people there well to him.	Thorstein invited him to stay there for a while, as long as he wished, and he was there for a season, and took to learning lawspeaking from Thorstein, and all the people there thought well of him.
Jafnan skemmtu þau Helga sér at tafli ok Gunnlaugr.	Equally entertained then Helga privately at board-games and Gunnlaug.	Gunnlaug and Helga entertained each other privately by playing board games.
Lagði hvárt þeira góðan þokka til annars bráðliga, sem raunir bar á síðan.	Took either-way they good charm to each-other soon, as experience bore out since.	They took to charming each other as events later bore out.

The Saga of Gunnlaug Serpent-Tongue (Old Norse)

Old Norse	Literal	English
Þau váru mjök jafnaldrar.	They were much equal-aged.	There were very much the same age.
Helga var svá fögr, at þat er sögn fróðra manna, at hon hafi fegrst kona verit á Íslandi.	Helga was so fair, as that was said wise men, that she had fairest woman been of Iceland.	Helga was so fair, so say wise men, that she had been the fairest woman of all Iceland.
Hár hennar var svá mikit, at þat mátti hylja hana alla, ok svá fagrt sem gull barit, ok engi kostr þótti þá þvílíkr sem Helga in fagra í öllum Borgarfirði ok víðara annars staðar.	Hair hers was so great, as that may cover her all, and so fair as gold beaten, and none credited thought they like as Helga in fairness in all Borgafjord and wider other places.	Her hair was so great, that it covered all of her, and was as fair as beaten gold, and no one thought there was anyone like Helga in fairness, in Borgafjord and in places further afield.
Ok einnhvern dag, er menn sátu í stofu at Borg, þá mælti Gunnlaugr til Þorsteins: "Einn er sá hlutr í lögum, er þú hefir eigi kennt mér, at fastna mér konu".	And one day, were men sitting in main-room at Borg, then spoke Gunnlaug to Thorstein: "One is seen part of law, that you have not taught me, to propose myself wife".	Now one day, men were sitting around the main room at Borg, then Gunnlaug spoke to Thorstein: "There is one part of the law, that you have not taught me, how to propose to a wife".
Þorsteinn segir: "Þat er lítit mál", ok kenndi honum atferli.	Thorstein said: "That is little matter", and taught him procedure.	Thorstein said: "That is a small matter", and taught him the procedure.
Þá mælti Gunnlaugr: "Nú skalt þú vita, hvárt mér hafi skilizt, ok mun ek nú taka í hönd þér ok láta sem ek festa mér Helgu, dóttur þína".	Then spoke Gunnlaug: "Now shall you know, whether to-me have understood, and should I now take in hand to-you and have as I to-propose me Helga, daughter yours".	Then Gunnlaug spoke: "Now to know, whether I have understood, I should now take your hand, and act as thought I am proposing to Helga, your daughter".
Þorsteinn segir: "Þarfleysi ætla ek þat vera", segir hann.	Thorstein said: "Needless intend I that to-be", said he.	Thorstein said: "I don't see any need for that", he said.
Gunnlaugr þreifaði þá þegar í hönd honum ok mælti: "Veit mér nú þetta", segir hann.	Gunnlaug felt then there in hand him and spoke: "Know me now this", said he.	Gunnlaug then felt for his hand and spoke: "Now know this of me", he said.
"Ger sem þú vill", segir Þorsteinn, "en þat skulu þeir vita, er hjá eru staddir, at þetta skal vera sem ómælt ok þessu skulu engi undirmál fylgja".	"Do as you like", said Thorstein, "and that should they know, that beside are standing, that this shall be as not-spoken and this should none under-speech follow".	"Do as you like", said Thorstein, "and they should know, those who are standing here, that this shall not be as spoken, and this should have no hidden meaning".

The Saga of Gunnlaug Serpent-Tongue (Old Norse)

Old Norse	Literal	English
Síðan nefndi Gunnlaugr sér vátta ok fastnaði sér Helgu ok spurði síðan, hvárt þá mætti svá nýta.	Then named Gunnlaug himself witnesses and betrothed himself Helga and asked then, whether they may so use.	Then Gunnlaug named his witnesses and betrothed himself to Helga, and he asked them whether they may use.
Hann kvað svá vera mega, ok varð mönnum mikit gaman at þessu, þeim sem við váru staddir.	He said so be able-to, and became people much enjoyment at this, them as with were standing.	He said it may be, and people were much joyed at this, those who were standing there.
5	5	5
Önundr hét maðr, er bjó suðr at Mosfelli, Hann var auðmaðr inn mesti ök hafði goðorð suðr þar um nesin.	Onund was-named a-man, that lived south at Mosfell, he was rich-man then most and had godord south there about the-headland.	There was a man named Onund, that lived in the south at Mosfell, he was the richest man and held the position of godord in the south around the headland.
Hann var kvángaðr maðr, ok hét Geirný kona hans Gnúpsdóttir, Molda-Gnúpssonar, er nam suðr Grindavík.	He was married man, and named Geirny wife his daughter-of-Gnup, son-of-Molda-Gnup, that took-land south Grindavik.	He was a married man, and his wife was named Geirny, daughter of Gnup, son of Molda Gnup, that took land south Grindavik.
Þeira synir váru þeir Hrafn ok Þórarinn ok Eindriði.	Their sons were they Hrafn and Thorarin and Eindridi.	Their sons were Hrafn and Thorarin and Eindridi.
Allir váru þeir efniligir menn, en þó var Hrafn fyrir þeim í hvívetna.	All were they promising men, and thought was Hrafn before them in everything.	They were all promising men, and it was thought that Hrafn was the best of them at everything.
Hann var mikill maðr ok sterkr, manna sjáligastr ok skáld gott, ok er hann var mjök rosknaðr, þá fór hann landa á milli ok virðist hvervetna vel, þar sem hann kom.	He was great man and strong, man most-visible and poet good and when he was much mature then travelled he lands in between and seemed everywhere well there where he went.	He was a great and strong man, worth looking at, and a good poet, and when he had matured, he travelled between lands and was will thought of wherever he went.
Þá bjó suðr á Hjalla í Ölfusi þeir Þóroddr inn spaki Eyvindarson ok Skafti, sonr hans, er þá var lögsögumaðr á Íslandi.	They lived south of Hjalli in Olfus they Thorod the Wise son-of-Eyvind and Skafti, son his, that then was lawspeaker of Iceland.	Thorod Eyvindarson the Wise, and his son Skafti lived at Hjalli in Olfus in those days, then Skafti was lawspeaker in Iceland.

The Saga of Gunnlaug Serpent-Tongue (Old Norse)

Old Norse	Literal	English
Móðir Skafta var Rannveig, dóttir Gnúps Molda-Gnúpssonar, ok váru þeir systrasynir Skafti ok Ónundarsynir.	Mother Skafti's was Rannveig, daughter-of Gnup son-of-Molda-Gnup, and were they cousins Skafti and Onund's-sons.	Skafti's mother was Rannveig, daughter of Gnup, son of Molda Gnup, and so Skafti and Onund's sons were cousins.
Var þar vinátta mikil með frændsemi.	Was there friendship much with kinship.	There was much friendship and kinship.
Þá bjó út at Rauðamel Þorfinnr Sel-Þórisson ok átti sjau sonu, ok váru allir efniligir menn.	They lived out at Raudamel Thorfinn son-of-Sel-Thori and had seven sons, and were all promising men.	Thorfinn Seal-Thorisson then lived at Raudamel, and he had seven sons, and all were promising men.
Þeir hétu svá: Þorgils, Eyjólfr ok Þórir, ok váru þeir mestir menn út þangat.	They-were named so: Thorgils, Eyolf and Thorir, and were they best men out there.	They were named: Thorgils, Eyolf, and Thorir, and they were the best men out there.
Ok þessir menn, er nú eru nefndir, váru allir uppi á einn tíma.	And these men, that now were mentioned, were all up at one time.	All these men that are mentioned were living at this time.
Ok þessu nær urðu þau tíðendi, er bezt hafa orðit hér á Íslandi, at landit varð allt kristit, ok allt fólk hafnaði fornum átrúnaði.	And this near became then news, the best having word here of Iceland, that land became all Christian, and all people rejected ancient religion.	And it was about this time, the best thing ever to have happened here in Iceland, that all the land became Christian, and all the people rejected ancient religion.
Gunnlaugr ormstunga, er áðr var frá sagt, var nú ýmisst at Borg með Þorsteini eða Illuga, feðr sínum, á Gilsbakka, sex vetr, ok var hann þá átján vetra, ok samðist þá mikit með þeim feðgum.	Gunnlaug Serpent-Tongue, as before was from said, was now either at Borg with Thorstein or Illugi's, father his, of Gilsbakka, six winters, and was he then eighteen winters, and agreed they much with them father-and-son.	Gunnlaug Serpent-Tongue, as was mentioned before, was now either at Borg with Thorstein or his father Illugi's, at Gilsbakka, for six winters, and he was then eighteen winters old, and father and son agreed with each other very much.
Maðr hét Þorkell svarti.	A-man was-named Thorkell the-Black.	There was a man named Thorkell the Black.
Hann var heimamaðr Illuga ok náfrændi ok hafði þar upp vaxit.	He was house-man Illugi's and near-kin and had there up grown.	He was a houseman of Illugi's and a kinsman, and he had grown up there.

The Saga of Gunnlaug Serpent-Tongue (Old Norse)

Old Norse	Literal	English
Honum tæmðist arfr norðr í Vatnsdal í Ási, ok beiddi hann Gunnlaug fara með sér, ok hann gerði svá, ok riðu norðr tveir saman í Ás ok fengu féit, ok greiddu þeir féit af höndum, er varðveitt höfðu, með atgöngu Gunnlaugs.	He came-into inheritance north in Vatnsdal in As, and asked he Gunnlaug travel with him, and he did so, and rode north two together in As and got wealth, and paid they wealth of hands, as preserved had, with to-going Gunnlaug.	He came into inheritance at As in Vatnsdal in the north, and asked Gunnlaug to go with him, and he did so, and the two rode north together to As, and collected the wealth, and they paid the wealth from the hands of those who had preserved, going to Gunnlaug.
Ok er þeir riðu norðan, gistu þeir í Grímstungum at auðigs bónda, er þar bjó.	And as they rode from-north, guested they in Grimstungur at wealthy farmer, who there lived.	As they rode from the north, they were guests of Grimstungur, a wealthy farmer who lived there.
Ok um morgininn tók smalamaðr hest Gunnlaugs, ok var þá sveittr mjök, er þeir fengu.	And about morning took shepherd horse Gunnlaug's, and was then sweat much, when they got.	And about morning, a shepherd took Gunnlaug's horse, which was then very sweaty, when they got it back.
Gunnlaugr laust smalamanninn í óvit.	Gunnlaug loosed the-shepherd to senseless.	Gunnlaug struck the shepherd senseless.
Bóndi vildi eigi svá búit hafa ok beiddi bóta fyrir.	Farmer wished not so to-settle have and asked compensation for.	The farmer did not want to settle, and asked for compensation for this.
Gunnlaugr bauð at gjalda bónda mörk.	Gunnlaug offered to pay farmer a-mark.	Gunnlaug offered to pay the farmer a mark.
Bónda þótti þat of lítit.	Farmer thought that about little.	The farmer thought little of this.
Gunnlaugr kvað vísu:	Gunnlaug said verse:	Gunnlaug said a verse:
Mörk bauðk mundangs sterkum manni, tyggja ranna. Grásíma skaltu góma glóðspýtis þat nýta. Iðrask munt, ef yðrum allráðr flóða ór sjóði lætr eyðanda líða linns samlagar kindar.	Mark invited middle strong, man, chew lodgings. Grey-wire shall-your gums, fire that use. sea-serpent should, if your all-ruling flood from funds has destroyed passing serpents same-lying sheep.	A mark offered the middle strong, Man, chewing lodgings, Grey-wire shall your gums, Fire that, use, Sea-serpent should, if your All-ruling flood from funds, Has destroyed passing, Serpents lying together with sheep.

The Saga of Gunnlaug Serpent-Tongue (Old Norse)

Old Norse	Literal	English
Þessi varð sætt þeira, sem Gunnlaugr bauð, ok riðu þeir suðr heim við svá búit.	This became settlement theirs, which Gunnlaug offered, and rode they south home with such settled.	Thus became their settlement, which Gunnlaug had offered, and when it was settled they rode home south.
Ok litlu síðar beiddi Gunnlaugr föður sinn fararefna í annat sinn.	And little afterwards asked Gunnlaug father his travel-goods a second-time his.	And a little while later, Gunnlaug asked his father for travel goods a second time.
Illugi segir: "Nú skal vera sem þú vill", segir hann.	Illugi said: "Now shall be as you will", said he.	Illugi said: "Now it shall be as you wish", he said.
"Hefir þú nú heldr samit þik ór því, sem var".	"Have you now held agreement you of before, than was".	"Now that you are more agreeable than you were before".
Reið Illugi þá heiman skjótt ok keypti skip hálft til handa Gunnlaugi, er uppi stóð í Gufuárósi, at Auðuni festargram.	Rode Illugi then home quickly and bought ship half to hand Gunnlaug, was up stood in Gufua, at Audun's Festargram.	Illugi then rode from home quickly and bought a half share of a ship to give to Gunnlaug, that was stood in Gufua, at Audun's Festargram.
Þessi Auðunn vildi eigi útan flytja sonu Ósvífrs ins spaka eftir víg Kjartans Óláfssonar, sem segir í Laxdæla sögu, ok varð þat þó síðar en þetta.	This Audun willed not to-out carry sons Osvif's the Wise after killing Kjartan son-of-Olaf, as said in Laxdardal saga, and became that though later than this.	This was the same Audun who would not take the sons of Osvif the Wise abroad after the killing of Kjartan Olafsson, as said in Laxardal saga, which happened later though than this.
Ok er Illugi kom heim, þá þakkaði Gunnlaugr honum vel.	And as Illugi came home, then thanked Gunnlaug him well.	And as Illugi came home, he then thanked Gunnlaug well.
Þorkell svarti réðst til ferðar með Gunnlaugi, ok var fluttr varnaðr þeira til skips, en Gunnlaugr var at Borg, meðan þeir bjuggu skipit, ok þótti glaðara at tala við Helgu en vera í starfi með kaupmönnum.	Thorkell the-Black rode to travel with Gunnlaug, and were transferred wares theirs to ship, and Gunnlaug was at Borg, while they prepared ship, and thought gladder to talk with Helga than be in work with trading-men.	Thorkell the Black travelled with Gunnlaug, and their wares were transferred to their ship, when Gunnlaug was at Borg, while they prepared the ship, and he was happier to talk with Helga than be at work with trading men.
Einnhvern dag spurði Þorsteinn Gunnlaug, ef hann vildi ríða til hrossa með honum upp í Langavatnsdal.	One day asked Thorstein Gunnlaug, if he wished ride to horses with him up in Langvatnsdal.	One day Thorstein asked Gunnlaug, if he would like ride up to his horses with him up to Langvatnsdal.

The Saga of Gunnlaug Serpent-Tongue (Old Norse)

Old Norse	Literal	English
Gunnlaugr kvaðst þat vilja.	Gunnlaug said that willed.	Gunnlaug said that he would like to.
Nú ríða þeir tveir saman, þar til er þeir koma til selja Þorsteins, er heita á Þorgilsstöðum, ok váru þar stóðhross, er Þorsteinn átti, fjögur saman ok váru rauð at lit.	Now rode they two together, there towards as they came to shelter Thorsteins, was called of Thorglisstadir, and were there stud-horses, that Thorstein had, four together and were red in colour.	Now the two rode together, until there they came to Thorstein's shelters, where Thorstein's horses were, and they were a stud of four red horses.
Hestr var allvænligr ok lítt reyndr.	Horse was promising and little experienced.	The horse was a promising creature, but little experienced.
Þorsteinn bauð at gefa Gunnlaugi hrossin, en hann kvaðst eigi hrossa þurfa, er hann ætlaði af landi.	Thorstein offered to give Gunnlaug horses, and he said not horses needed, that he intended out-of land.	Thorstein offered to give Gunnlaug his horses, but he said he did not need horses, but he intended to travel abroad.
Ok þá riðu þeir til annarra stóðhrossa.	And then rode they to other stud-horses.	And then they rode to another stud of horses.
Var þar hestr grár með fjórum merum, ok var sá baztr í Borgarfirði, ok bauð Þorsteinn at gefa þann Gunnlaugi.	Was there horse grey with four mares, and was seen best in Borgafjord, and invited Thorstein to give then Gunnlaug.	There was a grey horse with four mares, and he was the best horse in Borgafjord, and Thorstein offered to give him to Gunnlaug.
Hann svarar: "Eigi vil ek þessi heldr en hin, eða hví býðr þú mér eigi þat, er ek vil þiggja?"	He answered: "Not will I this rather as others, but why invite you me not that, which I wish receive?"	He answered: "I do not want this horse any more than the others, but why don't you offer me something I will accept?"
"Hvat er þat?" segir Þorsteinn.	"What is that?" said Thorstein.	"What is that?" said Thorstein.
Gunnlaugr mælti: "Helga in fagra, dóttir þín".	Gunnlaug spoke: "Helga the fair, daughter yours".	Gunnlaug spoke: "Your daughter, Helga the Fair".
Þorsteinn svarar: "Eigi mun þat svá skjótt ráðast", segir hann ok tók annat mál, ok riðu heimleiðis ofan með Langá.	Thorstein answered: "Not should that so quickly arranged", said he and took another matter, and rode home-way over with Langa.	Thorstein answered: "That will not be so quickly arranged", he said, and changed the subject, and they rode home over the Langa river.

The Saga of Gunnlaug Serpent-Tongue (Old Norse)

Old Norse	Literal	English
Þá mælti Gunnlaugr: "Vita vil ek", segir hann, "hverju þú vill svara mér um bónorðit".	Then spoke Gunnlaug: "Know wish I", said he, "how you will answer me about marriage-proposal".	Then Gunnlaug spoke: "I wish to know", he said, "how you will answer my marriage proposal".
Þorsteinn svarar: "Ekki sinni ek hégóma þínum", segir hann.	Thorstein answered: "No mind I vanity yours", said he.	Thorstein answered: "I will give no mind to your vanity", he said.
Gunnlaugr mælti: "Þetta er alhugi minn, en eigi hégómi".	Gunnlaug spoke: "This is all-mind mine, and not vanity".	Gunnlaug: "This is all my mind and no vanity".
Þorsteinn svarar: "Vita skyldir þú fyrst, hvat þú vildir.	Thorstein answered: "Know should you first, what you will.	Thorstein answered: "You should know first, what you want.
Ertu eigi ráðinn til útanferðar ok lætr þó sem þú skylir kvángast? Er þat ekki jafnræði með ykkr Helgu, meðan þú ert svá óráðinn, ok mun því ekki verða á litit".	Are-you not determined to out-travel and have thought that you seek marriage? Is that not equally with you Helga, meanwhile you are so undecided, and should therefore not be of considering".	Are you not determined to go abroad and you have thoughts about getting married? It is not suitable for you and Helga, while you are so undecided, and therefore I shall not consider it".
Gunnlaugr mælti: "Hvar til ætlar þú um gjaforð dóttur þinnar, ef þú vill eigi gifta syni Illuga svarta, eða hvar eru þeir í Borgarfirði, er meira háttar sé en hann?"	Gunnlaug spoke: "Where to intend you about give daughter yours, if you will not gift son-of Illugi the-Black, and where are they in Borgafjord, are more such so than he?"	Gunnlaug spoke: "Where do you intend to find a match for your daughter, if you will not give her to the son of Illugi the Black, and where are there in Borgafjord, people as important as him?"
Þorsteinn svarar: "Ekki fer ek í mannjöfnuð", segir hann, "en værir þú slíkr maðr sem hann, þá myndi þér eigi frá vísat".	Thorstein answered: "Nothing go I in men-comparing", said he, "and be you such man as he, then would to-you not from turn".	Thorstein answered: "I do not go in for comparing men", he said, "and if you were such a man as him, then you would not be turned away".
Gunnlaugr mælti: "Hverjum vill þú heldr gifta dóttur þína en mér?"	Gunnlaug spoke: "Who will you rather gift daughter yours than to-me?"	Gunnlaug spoke: "Who would you rather give your daughter to than me?"
Þorsteinn svarar: "Margt er hér gott mannval.	Thorstein answered: "Many are here good men-choice.	Thorstein answered: "There are many good men to choose from.

The Saga of Gunnlaug Serpent-Tongue (Old Norse)

Old Norse	Literal	English
Þorfinnr at Rauðamel á sjau sonu ok alla vel mannaða".	Thorfinn at Raudamel of seven sons and all well manly".	Thorfinn at Raudamel has seven sons, and they are all very manly".
Gunnlaugr svarar: "Hvárrgi þeira Önundar né Þorfinns er jafnmenni föður míns, því at þik skortir sýnt við hann, eða hvat hefir þú í móti því, er hann deildi kappi við Þorgrím goða Kjallaksson á Þórsnesþingi ok við sonu hans ok hafði einn þat, er við lá?"	Gunnlaug answered: "Neither they Onund nor Thorfinn is equal-man father mine, because as you short seemed with him, but what have you to meet therefore, as he dealt warrior with Thorgrim the-Good son-of-Kallak of Thorsnes-Assembly and with sons his and had one that was with had?"	Gunnlaug answered: "Neither Onund nor Thorfinn are equal to my father, even you fall short of him, and what have you therefore to match him, as he dealt with the warrior Thorgrim Kjallakson the godi and his sons at the Thorsnes Assembly by himself and came away with everything that was to be had?"
Þorsteinn svarar: "Ek stökkða í brott Steinari, syni Önundar sjóna, ok þótti þat heldr mikilræði".	Thorstein answered: "I drove to away Steinar, son-of Onund Sjoni, and thought that rather great-issue".	Thorstein answered: "I drove away Steinar, the son of Onund Sjoni, and that was thought of as a great achievement".
Gunnlaugr svarar: "Egils nauztu at því, föður þíns, enda mun þat fám bóndum vel endast at synja mér mægðar".	Gunnlaug answered: "Egil next-to that since, father yours, an-end should that get farmer well ended that refuses me marriage".	Gunnlaug answered: "You had your father Egil to help you then, and such an end a farmer would get if they refused me marriage".
Þorsteinn svarar: "Hafðu í frammi kúgan við þá uppi við fjöllin, en þat kemr þér fyrir ekki hér úti á Mýrunum".	Thorstein answered: "Have-you to from bullying with those up within hills, and that comes to-you for nothing here out of the-moors".	Thorstein answered: "Have your bullying with the people in the hills, and nothing will come of that for you here in the moorlands".
Um kveldit koma þeir heim.	About evening came they home.	About evening came they home.
Ok um morgininn ríðr Gunnlaugr upp á Gilsbakka ok bað föður sinn ríða til kvánbæna með sér út til Borgar.	And about morning rode Gunnlaug up of Gilsbakka and asked father his ride to marriage-proposal with himself out to Borg.	And about morning, Gunnlaug rode up to Gilsbakka and asked his father to ride back to Borg with him to make a marriage proposal.

The Saga of Gunnlaug Serpent-Tongue (Old Norse)

Old Norse	Literal	English
Illugi svarar: "Þú ert óráðinn maðr, þar sem þú ert ráðinn til útanferðar, en lætr nú sem þú skulir starfa í kvánbænum, ok veit ek, at slíkt er ekki við skaplyndi Þorsteins".	Illugi answered: "You are undecided man, there as you are determined to out-travel, and have now that you should work to marriage-proposal, and know I, that such is nothing with temper Thorsteins".	Illugi answered: "You are an unsettled man, there as you are determined to go abroad, and now you have you should strive for a marriage proposal, and I know that this does nothing for Thorstein's temper".
Gunnlaugr svarar: "Ek ætla þó útan allt eins, ok líkar mér ekki, útan þú fylgir þessu".	Gunnlaug answered: "I intend though out-of all one and like I nothing, out-of you following this".	Gunnlaug answered: "I intend though abroad, and I like nothing outside of you following me in this".
Síðan reið Illugi heiman með tólfta mann ofan til Borgar, ok tók Þorsteinn vel við honum.	Since rode Illugi home with twelve men over to Borg, and took Thorstein well with him.	Then Illugi rode to Borg with twelve men, and Thorstein received him well.
Um morgininn snemmaræddi Illugi til Þorsteins: "Ek vil tala við þik".	About morning early decided Illugi to Thorsteins: "I wish speak with you".	Early in the morning, Illugi said to Thorstein: "I would like to speak with you".
Þorsteinn svarar: "Göngum upp á Borgina ok tölum þar".	Thorstein answered: "Go-we up to Borg and talk there".	Thorstein answered: "Let's go up to Borg and talk there".
Ok svá gerðu þeir.	And so did they.	And so they did.
Gunnlaugr gekk með þeim.	Gunnlaug went with them.	Gunnlaug went with them.
Þá mælti Illugi: "Gunnlaugr, frændi minn, kveðst hafa vakit bónorð við þik fyrir sína hönd, at biðja Helgu, dóttur þinnar, en nú vil ek vita, hvern stað eiga skal málit.	Then spoke Illugi: "Gunnlaug, kinsman mine, said has awoken proposal with you for her hand, to propose Helga, daughter yours, and now wish I know, how stands owned shall matter.	Then Illugi spoke: "My kinsman Gunnlaug said he has brought up a marriage proposal with you for the hand of your daughter Helga, and now I wish to know how the matter stands".
Er þér kunnig ætt hans ok fjáreign vár.	Is to-you known descendents his and wealth being.	His descendants and wealth are known to you.
Skal hvárki til spara af várri hendi staðfestu né mannaforráð, ef þá er nær en áðr".	Shall neither to save of provisions to-hand established nor looked-after, if then is nearer than before".	It shall neither be sparing of provisions to hand, nor overlooked, if this brings it nearer than before".

The Saga of Gunnlaug Serpent-Tongue (Old Norse)

Old Norse	Literal	English
Þorsteinn svarar: "Þat eitt finn ek Gunnlaugi, at mér þykkir hann vera óráðinn", segir hann, "en ef hann væri þér líkr í skaplyndi, þá mynda ek lítt seinka".	Thorstein answered: "That one find I Gunnlaug, that to-me think he was undecided", said he, "but if he was to-you like in temper, then would I little delay".	Thorstein answered: "The one finding I have with Gunnlaug, is that he seems unsettled to me", he said, "but if he was more like you in temperament, then I would little delay".
Illugi svarar: "Þetta mun okkr verða at vinslitum, ef þú synjar okkr feðgum jafnræðis".	Illugi answered: "This should our be it friendship, if you refuse we father-and-son equally".	Illugi answered: "This would be our friendship, if you refuse us father and son equally".
Þorsteinn svarar: "Fyrir þín orð", segir hann, "ok okkra vingan þá skal Helga vera heitkona Gunnlaugs, en eigi festarkona, ok bíða þrjá vetr.	Thorstein answered: "For your words", said he, "and our friendship then shall Helga be promised-woman Gunnlaug, and not engaged-woman, and wait three winters.	Thorstein answered: "For your words", he said, "and our friendship, Helga will be promised to Gunnlaug, but not betrothed, and shall wait three winters.
En Gunnlaugr skal fara útan ok skapa sik eftir góðra manna siðum, en ek skal lauss allra mála, ef hann kemr eigi svá út eða mér virðist eigi skapferði hans".	Then Gunnlaug shall travelling out-of and create himself after good man customs, and I shall lose all matter, if he comes not so back-from or me seems not temperament his".	Then Gunnlaug shall travel abroad and make himself after the customs of good men, and I shall loose any obligation, if he does not come back so, or if to me his temperament is not worthy".
Ok við þetta skilja þeir.	And with this separated they.	And with this they separated.
Ríðr Illugi heim, en Gunnlaugr til skips.	Rode Illugi home, and Gunnlaug to ships.	Illugi rode home, and Gunnlaug to his ships.
Ok er þeim gaf byr, létu þeir í haf ok kómu skipi sínu norðr við Nóreg ok sigldu inn eftir Þrándheimi til Niðaróss ok lágu þar í lægi ok skipuðu upp.	And were they given fair-wind, left they in sea and came ships theirs north with Norway and sailed then past Trondheim to Nidaros and low there in lay and ships up.	And when they were given a fair wind, they headed to sea, and their ships came north to Norway, and they sailed past Trondheim to Nidaros, there they had the ship laid up.
6	6	6
Í þenna tíma réð fyrir Nóregi Eiríkr jarl Hákonarson ok Sveinn, bróðir hans.	In those times ruled along Norway Erik earl son-of-Hakon and Svein, brother his.	In those times Erik Hakonarson and his brother Svein ruled Norway.

The Saga of Gunnlaug Serpent-Tongue (Old Norse)

Old Norse	Literal	English
Eiríkr jarl hafði þá atsetu inn á Hlöðum at föðurleifð sinni ok var ríkr höfðingi.	Erik earl had then to-seat then of Lade at estate his and was kingdom leader.	Earl Erik had an estate in Lade, and was a powerful leader.
Skúli Þorsteinsson var þá með jarli ok var hirðmaðr hans ok vel metinn.	Skuli son-of-Thorstein was then with earl and was court-man his and well appreciated.	Skuli Thorsteinsson was there with him, and was one of his court men, and he was well appreciated.
Þat er frá sagt, at þeir Gunnlaugr ok Auðunn festargramr gengu tólf menn saman inn á Hlaðir.	That is from said, that they Gunnlaug and Audun Festargram went twelve men together then of Lade.	It is said from this, that Gunnlaug and Audun Festargram went with ten other men went to Lade.
Gunnlaugr var svá búinn, at hann var í grám kyrtli ok í hvítum leistbrókum.	Gunnlaug was so prepared, that he was in grey tunic and in white breeches.	Gunnlaug was dressed in a grey tunic and white breeches.
Sull hafði hann á fæti niðr á ristinni.	Boil had he of foot down of instep.	He had a boil in the instep of his foot.
Freyddi ór upp blóð ok vágr, er hann gekk við.	Rose from up blood and opened, as he walked with.	Blood rose up from it and it opened as he walked.
Ok með þeim búningi gekk hann fyrir jarlinn ok þeir Auðunn, ok kvöddu hann vel.	And with them clothes went he before earl and they Audun, and greeted him well.	And with those clothes, he went before the earl with Audun, and greeted him well.
Jarl kenndi Auðun ok spyrr hann tíðenda af Íslandi, en Auðunn sagði slík, sem váru.	Earl knew Audun and asked him news of Iceland, and Audun said such, as was.	The earl knew Audun and asked him for news from Iceland, and Audun said as such there was.
Jarl spyrr Gunnlaug, hverr hann væri, en hann sagði honum nafn sitt ok ætt.	Earl asked Gunnlaug, who he was, and he said to-him name his and descendents.	The earl asked Gunnlaug who he was, and he said to him his name and descendants.
Jarl mælti: "Skúli Þorsteinsson", sagði hann, "hvat manna er þessi á Íslandi?"	Earl spoke: "Skuli son-of-Thorstein", said he, "what man is this of Iceland?"	The earl spoke: "Skuli Thorsteinsson", he said, "what man is this of Iceland?"
"Herra", segir hann, "takið honum vel, hann er ins bezta manns sonr á Íslandi, Illuga svarta af Gilsbakka, ok fóstbróðir minn".	"Lord", said he, "take him well, he is the best man's son of Iceland, Illugi the-Black of Gilsbakka, and foster-brother mine".	"Lord", he said, "take him well, he is the best man's son of Iceland, Illugi the Black of Gilsbakka, and my foster brother".

The Saga of Gunnlaug Serpent-Tongue (Old Norse)

Old Norse	Literal	English
Jarl mælti: "Hvat er fæti þínum, íslendingr?"	Earl spoke: "What is foot yours, Icelander?"	The earl spoke: "What is with your foot, Icelander?"
"Sullr er á, herra", sagði hann.	"Boil is it lord", said he.	"Boil is it lord", said he.
"Ok gekk þú þó ekki haltr?"	"And walked you though not limping?"	"And though you walked limping?"
Gunnlaugr svarar: "Eigi skal haltr ganga, meðan báðir fætr eru jafnlangir".	Gunnlaug answered: "Not shall limp walk, while both feet are equally-long".	Gunnlaug answered: "One shall not walk with a limp, while both feet are equally long".
Þá mælti hirðmaðr jarls, er Þórir hét: "Þessi remb-ist mikit, íslendingrinn, ok væri vel, at vér freistaðim hans nökkut".	Then spoke court-man earl's, was Thorir named: "This haughty much, Icelander, and would-be well, that we test him somewhat".	Then one of the earl's court men who was named Thorir spoke: "This Icelander is rather haughty, and we should test him somewhat".
Gunnlaugr leit við honum ok mælti:	Gunnlaug looked to him and spoke:	Gunnlaug looked at him and spoke:
"Hirðmaðr es einn, sá 's einkar meinn. Trúið hánum vart, hann 's illr ok svartr".	"Court-man which one, So was especially painful. Believe him hardly, He was ill and black".	"A certain court man, So especially horrible, Believe him hardly, He's evil and black".
Þá vildi Þórir grípa til öxar.	Then willed Thorir gripped to axe.	Then Thorir wanted to grip his axe.
Jarl mælti: "Lát vera kyrrt", segir hann, "ekki skulu menn gefa at slíku gaum,	Earl spoke: "Let be still", said he, "nothing should men give to such heed,	The earl spoke: "Let's be calm", he said, "it's nothing for men to give such heed to,
eða hvé gamall maðr ertu, Íslendingr?"	but how old man are-you, Icelander?"	but how old are you, Icelander?"
Gunnlaugr svarar: "Ek em nú átján vetra", segir hann.	Gunnlaug answered: "I am now eighteen winters", said he.	Gunnlaug answered: "I am now eighteen winters", he said.
"Þat læt ek um mælt", segir jarl, "at þú verðir eigi annarra átján".	"That have I about say", said earl, "that you will-be not another eighteen".	"About that I have to say", said the earl, "that you will not be another eighteen".

The Saga of Gunnlaug Serpent-Tongue (Old Norse)

Old Norse	Literal	English
Gunnlaugr mælti ok heldr lágt: "Bið mér engra forbæna", segir hann, "en bið þér heiðr".	Gunnlaug spoke and rather low: "Bid me none afflictions", said he, "but bid to-you honour".	Gunnlaug spoke rather low: "Bid me no afflictions", he said, "but bid to your honour".
Jari mælti: "Hvat sagðir þú nú, Íslendingr?"	Earl spoke: "What said you now, Icelander?"	The earl spoke: "What did you saw just now, Icelander?"
Gunniaugr svarar: "Svá, sem mér þótti vera eiga, at þú bæðir mér engra forbæna, en bæðir sjálfum þér hallkvæmri bæna".	Gunnlaug answered: "So, as to-me thought was owned, that you bid me none afflictions, and bid yourself to-you more-effective prayer".	Gunnlaug answered: "So as I deemed fit, that you should not bid me afflictions, and bid for yourself more effective prayer".
"Hverra þá?" segir jarl.	"What then?" said the-earl.	"What then?" said the earl.
"At þú fengir eigi þvílíkan dauðdaga sem Hákon jarl, faðir þinn".	"That you get not what death-day as Hakon Earl, father yours".	"That you do not meet your death as your father Earl Hakon did".
Jarl setti svá rauðan sem blóð ok bað taka fól þetta skjótt.	Earl put so red as blood and asked take fool this quickly.	The earl went as red as blood and asked for this fool to be taken away quickly.
Þá gekk Skúii fyrir jarl ok mælti: "Gerið fyrir mín orð, herra, ok gefið manninum grið, ok fari hann á brott sem skjótast".	Then went Skuli before earl and spoke: "Do for my words, lord, and give this-man mercy, and go him to away as quickest".	Then Skuli went before the earl and spoke: "Lord, please do as I ask, and give this man mercy, and let him go away as quickly as possible".
Jarl mælti: "Verði hann á brottu sem skjótast, ef hann vill griðin hafa, ok komi aldri í mitt ríki síðan".	Earl spoke: "Will-be he of away as quickest, if he will mercy have, and come never in mine kingdom since".	The earl spoke: "Let him be away as quickly as possible, if he will have mercy, and never come to my kingdom after".
Þá gekk Skúli út með Gunnlaugi ok ofan á bryggjur.	Then went Skuli out-of with Gunnlaug and over of quay.	Then Skuli went out with Gunnlaug outside and down to the quay.
Þar var Englandsfar albúit til útláts,	There was England-voyage prepared to out-let,	There was an England voyage prepared to head out,
ok þá tók Skúli Gunnlaugi far ok Þorkatli, frænda hans.	and then took Skuli Gunnlaug travel and Thorkell, kinsman his.	And then Skuli took Gunnlaug to travel, and his kinsman Thorkell.

The Saga of Gunnlaug Serpent-Tongue (Old Norse)

Old Norse	Literal	English
En Gunnlaugr fekk Auðuni skip sitt til varðveizlu ok fé sitt, þat er hann hafði eigi með sér.	Then Gunnlaug got Audun's ship his to custody and wealth his, that as he had not with himself.	Then Gunnlaug gave custody of his ship to Audun, and all that which he did not have with him.
Nú sigla þeir Gunnlaugr í Englandshaf ok kómu um haustit suðr við Lundúnabryggjur ok réðu þar til hlunns skipi sínu.	Now sailed they Gunnlaug in England's-sea and came about autumn south with London-town and rode there to point ships theirs.	Now Gunnlaug sailed to the English sea and came at about autumn to London town and drew their ship up there.
7	7	7
Þá réð fyrir Englandi Aðalráðr konungr Játgeirsson ok var góðr höfðingi.	Then ruled along England Æthelred king son-of-Edgar and was good leader.	Then England was ruled by King Æthelred, son of Edgar, and he was a good leader.
Hann sat þenna vetr í Lundúnaborg.	He sat that winter in London-town.	He sat that winter in London town.
Ein var þá tunga á Englandi sem í Nóregi ok í Danmörku.	One was then tongue of England as in Norway and in Denmark.	Then the language of England was one with that in Norway and in Denmark.
En þá skiptust tungur í Englandi, er Vilhjálmr bastarðr vann England.	Then they exchanged tongue in England, when William Bastard won England.	Then they changed language in England, when William the Bastard conquered England.
Gekk þaðan af í Englandi valska, er hann var þaðan ættaðr.	Went from-there of in England French, as he was from-there descended.	French went from then on in England, as he was from there descended.
Gunnlaugr gekk bráðliga fyrir konung ok kvaddi hann vel ok virðuliga.	Gunnlaug went soon before king and greeted him well and worthily.	Gunnlaug soon went before the king and greeted him well and worthily.
Konungr spurði, hvaðan af löndum hann væri.	King asked, where of lands he was.	The king asked which land he was from.
Gunnlaugr segir sem var, "en því hefi ek sótt á yðvarn fund, herra, at ek hefi kvæði ort um yðr, ok vilda ek, at þér hlýddið kvæðinu".	Gunnlaug said as was, "Then because have I sought of yours meeting, lord, that I have poem worded about you, and will I, that to-you listen poem".	Gunnlaug said as it was, "Then because I have sought to meet you, lord, that I have worded a poem about you, and I would like you to listen to the poem".
Konungr kvað svá vera skyldu.	King said so was should.	The king said so it should be.

The Saga of Gunnlaug Serpent-Tongue (Old Norse)

Old Norse	Literal	English
Gunnlaugr flutti fram kvæðit vel ok sköruliga, en þetta er stefit í:	Gunnlaug brought from poem well and boldly, and this is staved in:	Gunnlaug performed the poem well and boldly, and it has this stave.
"Herr sésk allr enn örva Englands sem goð þengil. Ætt lýtr grams ok gumna *gunnbráðs Aðalráði".*	"Army see all still excitement England's as good angel. descendents bow warrior and men war-swift Æthelred".	"All the army are still in awe, At England's good angel, Descendents bow warrior men, war-swift Æthelred".
Konungr þakkaði honum kvæðit ok gaf honum at bragarlaunum skarlatsskikkju skinndregna inum beztum skinnum ok hlaðbúna í skaut niðr ok gerði hann hirðmann sinn,	King thanked him poem and gave him as character-reward scarlet-cloak skinned in best skins and loaded in hem down and made he court-man his,	The king thanked him for the poem and gave him to reward his character a scarlet cloak, skinned in the best skins, and with an embroidered band down to the hem, and he made him his court man.
ok var Gunnlaugr með konungi um vetrinn ok virðist vel.	and was Gunnlaug with king about winter and seemed well.	And Gunnlaug was with the king all winter, and was well thought of.
Ok einn dag um morgininn snemma þá mætti Gunnlaugr þrem mönnum á stræti einu, ok nefndist sá Þórormr, er fyrir þeim var.	And one day about morning early then met Gunnlaug three people on street one, and named that Thororm, was before them was.	And early one morning Gunnlaug met three men in the street, and the one before them was named Thororm.
Hann var mikill ok sterkr ok furðu torvelligr.	He was great and strong and surprisingly difficult.	He was big and strong, and surprisingly difficult.
Hann mælti: "Norðmaðr", segir hann, "sel mér fé nökkut at láni".	He spoke: "Northman", said he, "sell me wealth some to loan".	He spoke: "Northman", he said, "lend me some money".
Gunnlaugr svarar: "Ekki mun þat ráðligt at selja fé sitt ókunnum mönnum".	Gunnlaug answered: "Not should that advised to sell wealth one's unknown people".	Gunnlaug answered: "It's not well advised to lend one's wealth to unknown people".
Hann svarar: "Ek skal gjalda þér at nefndum degi".	He answered: "I shall pay to-you that named day".	He answered: "I shall pay you on the named day".
"Þá skal á þat hætta", segir Gunnlaugr.	"Then shall of that risk", said Gunnlaug.	"Then I shall take that risk", said Gunnlaug.

The Saga of Gunnlaug Serpent-Tongue (Old Norse)

Old Norse	Literal	English
Síðan seldi hann honum féit.	Afterwards sold he him wealth.	Afterwards he lent him wealth.
Ok litlu síðar fann Gunnlaugr konunginn ok segir honum fjárlánit.	And little afterwards found Gunnlaug king and said to-him-of fee-loan.	A little while afterwards, Gunnlaug met the king and told him about the loan.
Konungr svarar: "Nú hefir lítt til tekizt.	King answered: "Now have little to take.	The king answered: "Now have things less taken.
Þessi er inn mesti ránsmaðr ok víkingr, ok eig ekki við hann, en ek skal fá þér jafnmikit fé".	This is the most robber-man and viking, and own not with him, and I shall get to-you equal wealth".	This is the most notorious robber and viking, have nothing to do with him, and I shall get you the same money".
Gunnlaugr svarar: "Illa er oss þá farit", segir hann, "hirðmönnum yðrum, göngum upp á saklausa menn, en láta slíka sitja yfir váru, ok skal þat aldri verða".	Gunnlaug answered: "Badly are us then going", said he, "court-men yours, go-we up of sake-less men, and let such sitting over wares, and shall that never be".	Gunnlaug answered: "We are going badly", he said, "your court men, we go above helpless men, and let such a man sit over our heads, and that shall never be.
Ok litlu síðar hitti hann Þórorm ok heimti féit af honum, en hann kvaðst eigi gjalda mundu.	And little afterwards met he Thororm and claimed wealth of him, and he said not pay would.	And little afterwards he met Thororm and claimed back the money, but he said he would not pay.
Gunnlaugr kvað þá vísu þessa:	Gunnlaug said then verse this:	Gunnlaug then said this verse:
Meðalráð es þér, Móði	Among-advice which to-you, Móði	"You are ill advised, Modi,
malma galdrs, at halda,	metals spell, to keep,	It is bad for wealth, to keep,
att hafið ér við prettum	to have that with trick	That you have with deceived,
oddrjóð, fyr mér hoddum.	point-reddener, before me hoard.	Point reddener, before me hoarding.
Vita mátt hitt, at heitik,	know might other, that named,	Know may also, that promised,
hér sék á því færi,	here see of because opportunity,	Here to see is opportunity,
þat fekksk nafn af nökkvi,	that received name of given-name,	That received name of something,
naðrstunga, mér ungum.	venomous-sting, me young.	Venomous sting, from my youth.

The Saga of Gunnlaug Serpent-Tongue (Old Norse)

Old Norse	Literal	English
"Nú vil ek bjóða þér lög", segir Gunnlaugr, "at þú gjalt mér fé mitt eða gakk á hólm við mik ella á þriggja nátta fresti".	"Now will I offer to-you law", said Gunnlaug, "that you expenses to-me wealth mine or go of duel with me otherwise of three nights from-now".	"Now I will offer to you the law", said Gunnlaug, "that you pay me my money, or otherwise go to a duel with me three nights from now".
Þá hló víkingrinn ok mælti: "Til þess hefir engi oröit fyrri en þú at skora mér á hólm, svá skarðan hlut sem margr hefir fyrir mér borit, ok em ek þess albúinn".	Then laughed viking and spoke: "to this had none become before as you that challenged me of duel, so wronged lot as many have before me carried, and am I this all-ready".	Then the viking laughed and spoke: "No one has challenged me to a duel before, so many have suffered at my hands, and I am ready for this".
Ok við þat skilðu þeir Gunnlaugr at sinni.	And with that separated they Gunnlaug to them.	And with that Gunnlaug parted.
Gunnlaugr segir konungi svá búit.	Gunnlaug said king so settled.	Gunnlaug told the king how it was settled.
Hann svarar: "Nú er komit í allóvænt efni.	He answered: "Now has come in all-not-expected prospects.	He answered: "Now have come unexpected prospects.
Þessi maðr deyfir hvert vápn.	This man blunts any weapon.	This man blunts any weapon.
Nú skaltu mínum ráðum fram fara, ok er hér sverð, er ek vil gefa þér, ok með þessu skaltu vega, en sýn honum annat".	Now shall-you my advice from going, and is here sword, that I wish give to-you, and with this shall-you fight, and show him another".	Now shall you go from my advice, here is a sword that I wish to give you, and you shall fight with this, but show him another".
Gunnlaugr þakkaði konungi vel.	Gunnlaug thanked king well.	Gunnlaug thanked the king well.
Ok er þeir váru til hólms búnir, þá spyrr Þórormr, hvernig sverð þat væri, er hann hafði.	And when they were to duel ready, then asked Thororm, which sword that is, that he had.	And when they were ready to duel, then Thororm asked what sword it was that he had.
Gunnlaugr sýnir honum ok bregðr, en hafði lykkju um meðalkafla á konungsnaut ok dregr á hönd sér.	Gunnlaug showed him and drew, and had loop about average-head of king's-gift and drew of hand himself.	Gunnlaug showed him and drew, but had a loop about the middle section of the king's gift, and dragged it over his hand.

The Saga of Gunnlaug Serpent-Tongue (Old Norse)

Old Norse	Literal	English
Berserkrinn mælti, er hann sá sverðit: "Ekki hræðumst ek þat sverð", segir hann ok hjó til Gunnlaugs með sverði ok af honum mjök svá skjöldinn allan.	Berserker spoke, as he looked sword: "Nothing afraid I that sword", said he and struck to Gunnlaug with sword and of him much so shield all.	The berserker spoke as he looked at the sword: "No fear do I have at that sword", he said and struck towards Gunnlaug with his sword, and much of his shield was off.
Gunnlaugr hjó þegar í mót með konungsnaut, en berserkrinn stóð hlífarlauss fyrir ok hugði, at hann hefði it sama vápn ok hann sýndi, en Gunnlaugr hjó hann þegar banahögg.	Gunnlaug struck then to meet with king's-gift, and the-berserker stood helpless before and thought, that he had the same weapon and he showed, then Gunnlaug struck him then death-blow.	Gunnlaug struck to meet him with the king's gift, and the berserker stood helpless before him and thought that he had the same weapon that he showed him, then Gunnlaug struck him his death blow.
Konungr þakkaði honum verkit, ok af þessu fekk hann mikla frægð í Englandi ok víða annars staðar.	King thanked him the-work, and of this got he much fame in England and widely other places.	The king thanked him for the work, and of this he got much fame in England and widely among other places.
Um várit, er skip gengu milli landa, þá bað Gunnlaugr Aðalráð konung orlofs at sigla nökkut.	About spring, were ships going between lands, then asked Gunnlaug Æthelred king leave to sail some.	About spring, there were ships travelling between lands, and then Gunnlaug asked Æthelred for leave to go sailing.
Konungr spyrr, hvat hann vildi þá.	King asked, what he wished then.	The king asked him what he wanted to do.
Gunnlaugr svarar: "Ek vilda efna þat, sem ek hefi heitit,"- ok kvað vísu þessa:	Gunnlaug answered: "I will carry-out that, as I have promised", and said verse this:	Gunnlaug answered: "I would like to carry out a promise I have made", and said this verse:
Koma skalk vistar vitja viggs döglinga þriggja, því hefk hlutvöndum heitit hjarls ok tveggja jarla. Hverfkak aftr, áðr arfi,	Come shall surely visit slayers of-the-dead three, because have bond called earldoms and two earls. Districts return, before inheritance,	I shall come to surely visit, Three slayers of the dead, As promised worthy men, And two earls of lands. Districts return, before inheritance,
auðveitir gefr rauðan orma beð fyr ermar, odd-Gefnar mér stefni.	wealth-provides give red serpent bed for sleeves, point-given me summoned.	Wealth provides giving red, Serpent bed for sleeves, Point given me summoned.

The Saga of Gunnlaug Serpent-Tongue (Old Norse)

Old Norse	Literal	English
"Svá skal ok vera, skáld", segir konungr ok gaf honum gullhring, er stóð sex aura, "en því skaltu heita mér", segir konungr, "at koma aftr til mín at öðru hausti, fyrir því at ek vil eigi láta þik fyrir sakar íþróttar þinnar".	"So shall and be, poet", said king and gave him gold-ring, which stood six ounces, "and because shall-you call me", said king, "to come back to me to another autumn, for because that I wish not leave you for sake as-vigorous yours".	"So shall it will be, poet", said the king and gave him a gold ring, which stood at six ounces, "and therefore you shall call me", said the king, "to come back another autumn, because I do not wish to lose as vigorous a man as you".
8	8	8
Síðan siglir Gunnlaugr af Englandi með kaupmönnum norðr til Dyflinnar.	Then sailed Gunnlaug of England with trading-men north to Dublin.	Then Gunnlaug sailed north with trading men to Dublin.
Þá réð fyrir Írlandi Sigtryggr konungr silkiskegg, sonr Óláfs kvárans ok Kormlaðar dróttningar.	Then ruled along Ireland Sigtrygg king Silk-Beard, son Olaf's Kvarans and Kormlod queen.	Then Ireland was ruled by King Sigtrygg Silk-Beard, the son of Olaf Kvaran and Queen Kormlod.
Hann hafði þá skamma stund ráðit ríkinu.	He had then short while ruling kingdom.	He had only been ruling for a short while then.
Gunnlaugr gekk fyrir konung ok kvaddi hann vel ok virðuliga.	Gunnlaug went before king and called him well and worthily.	Gunnlaug went before the king and greeted him worthily.
Konungr tók honum sæmiliga.	King took him same-like.	The king received him in the same way.
Gunnlaugr mælti: "Kvæði hefi ek ort um yðr, ok vilda ek hljóð fá".	Gunnlaug spoke: "Poem have I worded about you, and will I listen have".	Gunnlaug spoke: "I have worded a poem about you, and I would like it to have a hearing".
Konungr svarar: "Ekki hafa menn til þess orðit fyrri at færa mér kvæði, ok skal víst hlýða".	King answered: "Nothing have men to this word before that bring me poem, and shall certain listen".	The king answered: "I have not had men wording me a poem before, and I shall certainly listen".
Gunnlaugr kvað þá drápuna, ok er þetta stefit í:	Gunnlaug said then drapa, and is this staved in:	Gunnlaug then said a drapa, and it has this stave in it:
Elr sváru skæ Sigtryggr við hræ.	Nourishes swears askew Sigtrygg with corpses.	Nourishes the sorceress's wolf, Sigtrygg with corpses.
Ok þetta er þar:	And this is there:	And this is also there:

The Saga of Gunnlaug Serpent-Tongue (Old Norse)

Old Norse	Literal	English
Kann ek máls of skil, / *hvern ek mæra vil* / *konungmanna kon,* / *hann 's Kvárans son.* / *Muna gramr við mik,* / *venr hann gjöfli sik,* / *þess mun grepp vara,* / *gollhring spara.* / *Segi hildingr mér,* / *ef hann heyrði sér* / *dýrligra brag,* / *þat es drápulag.*	Can I speak about understand, / Each I praise wish / King-descendents man, / He was Kvaran's son. / Should warrior with me, / Custom he gifts him, / This should poet wares, / Gold-ring save. / Say war-king to-me, / If he heard himself / Glorious poetry, / That which drapa-layer.	I know how to speak of, / Who I wish to praise, / Descendants of kings, / He was Kvaran's son. / Should the king with me, / His custom give gifts, / This should poet wares, / Gold ring save, / Say war king to me, / If he heard himself, / Glorious poetry, / That is a drapa layer.
Konungr þakkaði honum kvæðit ok kallaði til sín féhirði sinn ok mælti svá: "Hverju skal launa kvæðit?"	King thanked him poem and called to his fee-servant theirs and spoke so: "How shall repay poem?"	The king thanked him for the poem and called to his fee servant, and spoke so: "How shall I repay the poem?"
Hann svarar: "Hverju vilið þér, herra?" segir hann.	He answered: "How will to-you, lord?" said he.	He answered: "How would you like to, lord?" he said.
"Hversu er launat", segir hann, "ef ek gef honum knörru tvá?"	"How is repaid", said he, "if I give him knorrs two?"	"How is he repaid", he said, "if I give him two knorrs?"
Féhirðir svarar: "Of mikit er þat, herra", segir hann.	Fee-servant answered: "About much is that, lord", said he.	The fee servant answered: "That would be of too much, lord", he said.
"Aðrir konungar gefa at bragarlaunum gripi góða, sverð góð eða gullhringa góða".	"Other kings give as character-reward treasure good, sword good or gold-ring good".	"Other kings give as character reward good treasure, a good sword, or a good gold ring".
Konungr gaf honum klæði sín af nýju skarlati, kyrtil hlaðbúinn ok skikkju með ágætum skinnum ok gullhring, er stóð mörk.	King gave him clothing theirs of new scarlet, tunic laden and cloak with wonderful skins and gold-ring, which stood mark.	The king have him his clothing of scarlet, laden with tunic, and a cloak with wonderful skins, and a gold ring, which weighed a mark.
Gunnlaugr þakkaði honum vel ok dvaldist þar skamma stund ok fór þaðan til Orkneyja.	Gunnlaug thanked him well and dwelled there short while and fared from-there to Orkney.	Gunnlaug thanked him well and stayed there a short while, and travelled from there to Orkney.
Þá réð fyrir Orkneyjum Sigurðr jarl Hlöðvisson.	Then ruled along Orkneys Sigurd earl son-of-Hlodvi.	Then Sigurd Hlodvisson ruled along the Orkneys.

The Saga of Gunnlaug Serpent-Tongue (Old Norse)

Old Norse	Literal	English
Hann var vel til íslenzkra manna.	He was well to Icelander men.	He thought well of Icelander men.
Gunnlaugr kvaddi jarl vel ok sagði sik hafa at færa honum kvæði.	Gunnlaug greeted earl well and said he had of brought him poem.	Gunnlaug greeted the earl well and said that he had brought him a poem.
Jarl kvaðst hlýða vilja kvæði hans, svá stórra manna sem hann var á Íslandi.	Earl said listen willed poem his, so great man as he was of Iceland.	The earl said he wanted to hear his poem, as he was a great man of Iceland.
Gunnlaugr flutti kvæðit, ok var þat flokkr ok vel ortr.	Gunnlaug performed poem, and was that flokk and well worded.	Gunnlaug performed the poem, and it was a flokk that was well worded.
Jarl gaf honum breiðöxi, silfrrekna alla, at kvæðislaunum ok bauð honum með sér at vera.	Earl gave him broad-axe, silver-inlay all, as poem's-reward and invited he with him to be.	The earl gave him a broad axe, with silver inlay, as a poem's reward, and he invited him to stay with him.
Gunnlaugr þakkaði honum gjöfina ok boð it sama, en kveðst verða at fara austr til Svíþjóðar ok gekk síðan á skip með kaupmönnum, þeim er sigldu til Nóregs, ok kómu um haustit austr við Konungahellu.	Gunnlaug thanked him gift and bid to same, and said be that travelling east to Sweden and went since of ship with trading-men, they were sailed to Norway, and came about autumn east with Kungalf.	Gunnlaug thanked him for the gift and for the invitation, and said that he was travelling east to Sweden, then he went to ship with trading men, and they sailed to Norway, and they arrived at Kungalf in the east.
Þorkell, frændi hans, fylgði honum jafnan.	Thorkell, kinsman his, followed him equally.	His kinsman Thorkell followed him as usual.
Ór Konungahellu fengu þeir leiðtoga upp í Gautland it vestra, ok kómu fram í kaupstað þeim, er í Skörum heitir.	Out-of Kungalf got they guide up in Geatland the West, and came from in trading-station they, as in Skarar named.	Out of Kungalf they got a guide in West Geatland, and came to a market town that was named Skarar.
Þar réð fyrir jarl sá, er Sigurðr hét ok var við aldr.	There ruled along earl so, was Sigurd named and was with age.	There ruled there an earl named Sigurd, who was with age.
Gunnlaugr gekk fyrir hann ok kvaddi hann vel ok kvaðst kvæði hafa ort um hann.	Gunnlaug went before him and greeted him well and said poem had worded about him.	Gunnlaug went before him and greeted him well, and said a poem that he had worded about him.
Jarl gaf gott hljóð til.	Earl gave good hearing to.	The earl gave good hearing to.

The Saga of Gunnlaug Serpent-Tongue (Old Norse)

Old Norse	Literal	English
Gunnlaugr kvað kvæðit, ok var þat flokkr.	Gunnlaug said poem, and was it flokk.	Gunnlaug said the poem, and it was a flokk.
Jarl þakkaði honum ok launaði honum vel ok bauð honum með sér at vera um vetrinn.	Earl thanked him and rewarded him well and invited him with him to be about winter.	The earl thanked him and rewarded him well and invited him to stay about winter.
Sigurðr jarl hafði jólaboð mikit um vetrinn.	Sigurd earl had Yule-invitation much about winter.	Earl Sigurd held a great Yule feast about the winter.
Ok atfangadag jóla koma þar sendimenn Eiríks jarls norðan af Nóregi, tólf saman.	And eve-day Yule came there sending-men Erik's earl north of Norway, twelve together.	And on the eve of Yule, messengers of Earl Erik arrived, from Norway in the north, there were twelve of them together.
Þeir fóru með gjöfum til Sigurðar jarls.	They travelled with gifts to Sigurd earl's.	They travelled to Earl Sigurd with gifts.
Jarlinn fagnaði þeim vel ok skipaði þeim um jólin hjá Gunnlaugi.	Earl celebrated them well and directed them about Yule beside Gunnlaug.	The earl received them well and directed them to the Yule festival beside Gunnlaug.
Þar var ölteiti mikil.	There was unrest much.	There was much unrest.
Gautar ræddu um, at engi jarl væri meiri ok frægri en Sigurðr.	Geatlanders discussed about, that none earl was better and more-famous than Sigurd.	The Geatlanders discussed about, that no earl was better and more famous than Sigurd.
Nóregsmönnum þótti Eiríkr jarl miklu framar.	Norwegian-men thought Erik earl much above.	The Norwegian men thought Earl Erik was high above.
Ok um þetta þrættu þeir, ok tóku Gunnlaug til órskurðarmanns hvárirtveggju um þetta mál.	And about this quarrelled they, and took Gunnlaug to deciding-person either-side about this matter.	And they quarrelled about this, and took to Gunnlaug as the deciding person either way about this matter.
Gunnlaugr kvað þá vísu þessa:	Gunnlaug said then verse this:	Gunnlaug then said this verse:
Segið ér frá jarli, oddfeimu stafir, þeima, hann hefir litnar hávar, hárr karl es sá, bárur. Sigreynir hefir sénar sjalfr í miklu gjalfri	Saying that from earl, Spear-sister stave, them, He had colours high, Has man who saw, waves. Triumphs has seen Himself in much gifts	You speak of the earl, Staves of the spear sisters, He had colours high, Has the man seen, waves, Triumphs has seen, Himself in much gifts,

The Saga of Gunnlaug Serpent-Tongue (Old Norse)

Old Norse	Literal	English
austr fyr unnar hesti Eiríkr bláar fleiri.	Eastern for won horse Erik blue more.	Eastern for won horse, Erik blue more.
Hvárirtveggju unðu vel við órskurðinn, en betr Nóregsmenn.	Either-side won well with decision, and better Norwegian-men.	Either side were pleased with the decision, especially the Norwegians.
Sendimenn fóru þaðan eftir jólin með fégjöfum, er Sigurðr jarl sendi Eiríki jarli.	Sending-men travelled from-there after Yule with fee-gifts, that Sigurd earl sent Erik earl.	Messengers travelled from there after Yule with gifts of wealth, that Sigurd had sent Earl Erik.
Sögðu þeir nú Eiríki jarli órskurðinn Gunnlaugs.	Said they now Erik earl ruling Gunnlaug's.	They said to Earl Erik about Gunnlaug's summary.
Jarli þótti Gunnlaugr hafa sýnt við sik einurð ok vináttu ok lét þau orð um fara, at Gunnlaugr skyldi þar friðland hafa í hans ríki.	Earl thought Gunnlaug had showed with him fairness and friendliness and lay then words about travelling, that Gunnlaug should there peace-land have in his kingdom.	The earl thought Gunnlaug had showed fairness and friendliness with him, and had word travel, that Gunnlaug should have peace there in his kingdom.
Þat frétti Gunnlaugr síðan, hvat jarl hafði um mælt.	That heard Gunnlaug since, what earl had about said.	Gunnlaug heard of this afterwards, what the earl had said about it.
Sigurðr jarl fekk Gunnlaugi leiðtoga austr í Tíundaland í Svíþjóð, sem hann beiddi.	Sigurd earl got Gunnlaug guide eastern in Tiundaland in Sweden, as he asked.	Earl Sigurd got Gunnlaug a guide to take him east into Tiundaland in Sweden, as he had asked.
9	9	9
Í þenna tíma réð fyrir Svíþjóð Óláfr konungr sænski, sonr Eiríks kontmgs sigrsæla ok Sigríðar innar stórráðu, dóttur Sköglar-Tósta.	In those times ruled along Sweden Olaf king Swede, son Erik's king victorious and Sigrid the ambitious, daughter Forest-Tostig.	In those times King Olaf the Swede ruled Sweden, son of King Erik the Victorious, and Sigrid the Ambitious, daughter of Forest Tostig.
Hann var ríkr konungr ok ágætr, metnaðarmaðr mikill.	He was powerful king and fine, ambitious-man great.	He was a powerful king and fine king, and a man of great ambition.

The Saga of Gunnlaug Serpent-Tongue (Old Norse)

Old Norse	Literal	English
Gunnlaugr kom til Uppsala nær þingi þeira Svía um várit, ok er hann náði konungs fundi, kvaddi hann konunginn.	Gunnlaug came to Uppsala near assembly theirs Sweden about spring, and as he caught king meeting, called he king.	Gunnlaug came to Uppsala near to the time of their assembly about springtime, and when he caught the king's attention, he greeted the king.
Hann tók honum vel ok spyrr, hverr hann væri.	He took him well and asked, who he was.	He received him well and asked who he was.
Hann kvaðst vera íslenzkr maðr.	He said was Icelander man.	He said he was an Icelander man.
Þar var þá með Óláfi konungi Hrafn Önundarson.	Then were they with Olaf king Hrafn son-of-Onund.	Then Hrafn Onundarson was with the king.
Konungr mælti: "Hrafn", segir hann, "hvat manna er hann á Íslandi?"	King spoke: "Hrafn", said he, "what man is he of Iceland?"	The king spoke: "Hrafn", he said, "what kind of man of Iceland is he?"
Maðr stóð upp af inum óæðra bekk, mikill ok vaskligr, gekk fyrir konung ok mælti: "Herra", segir hann, "hann er innar beztu ættar ok sjálfr inn vaskasti maðr".	Man stood up of in lower bench, great and bold, went before king and spoke: "Lord", said he, "he is the best noble and himself the boldest man".	A large and bold man stood up from the lower bench, went before the king and spoke: "Lord", he said, "he is the best noble and the boldest man".
"Fari hann þá ok siti hjá þér", sagði konungr.	"Go he then and sit beside to-you", said king.	"Let him go and sit next to you", said the king.
Gunnlaugr mælti: "Kvæði hefi ek at færa yðr", sagði hann, "ok vilda ek, at þér hlýddið ok gæfið hljóð til".	Gunnlaug spoke: "Poem have I that brought you", said he, "and will I, that to-you listen and give hearing to".	Gunnlaug spoke: "I have brought you a poem", he said, "and I would like that you listen and give hearing to".
"Gangið fyrst ok sitið", sagði konungr,	"Go first and sit", said king,	"Go first and sit", said the king,
"ekki er nú tóm til yfir kvæðum at sitja".	"not is now time to across poem to sitting".	"now is not the time to sit over poems".
Þeir gerðu svá.	They did so.	They did so.
Tóku þeir þá tal með sér, Gunnlaugr ok Hrafn.	Took they then talking with themselves, Gunnlaug and Hrafn.	Gunnlaug and Hrafn then took to talking among themselves.

The Saga of Gunnlaug Serpent-Tongue (Old Norse)

Old Norse	Literal	English
Sagði hvárr öðrum frá ferðum sínum.	Said where others from voyage theirs.	They said to each other about their travels.
Hrafn kvaðst farit hafa áðr um sumarit af Íslandi til Nóregs ok öndverðan vetr austr til Svíþjóðar.	Hrafn said travel had back about summer of Iceland to Norway and before winter eastern to Sweden.	Hrafn said that he had left Iceland for Norway the summer before, and before winter east to Sweden.
Þar gerist brátt vel með þeim.	There was soon well with them.	They soon became friends.
Ok einn dag, er liðit var þingit, váru þeir báðir fyrir konungi, Gunnlaugr ok Hrafn.	And one day, when ended was assembly, were they both before king, Gunnlaug and Hrafn.	And one day, when the assembly had ended, Gunnlaug and Hrafn were both before the king.
Þá mælti Gunnlaugr: "Nú vilda ek, herra", segir hann, "at þér heyrðið kvæðit".	Then spoke Gunnlaug: "Now will I, lord", said he, "that you hear poem".	Then Gunnlaug spoke: "Now I would like, lord", he said, "for you to hear the poem".
"Þat má nú", segir konungr.	"That may now", said king.	"That may be now", said the king.
"Nú vil ek flytja kvæði mitt, herra", segir Hrafn.	"Now wish I carry poem mine, lord", said Hrafn.	"Now I would like to perform my poem, lord", said Hrafn.
"Þat má vel", segir hann.	"That may well", said he.	"That may well be", he said.
"Þá vil ek flytja fyrr kvæði mitt, herra", segir Gunnlaugr, "ef þér vilið svá".	"Then will I carry before poem mine, lord", said Gunnlaug, "if you will so".	"Then I would like to perform my poem first, lord", he said, "if you will it so".
"Ek á fyrr at flytja, herra", segir Hrafn, "er ek kom fyrr til yðvar".	"I to before that carry, lord", said Hrafn, "as I came before to you".	"I should go before, lord", said Hrafn, "as I came to you first".
Gunnlaugr mælti: "Hvar kómu feðr okkrir þess", segir hann, "at faðir minn væri eftirbátr föður þíns, hvar nema alls hvergi? Skal ok svá með okkr vera".	Gunnlaug spoke: "Where came father yours this", said he, "that father mine was aftermath father yours, where taken all either? Shall and so with us be".	Gunnlaug spoke: "Where did our fathers come from," he said, "that my father was your father's follower, where but nowhere at all? So it shall be with us".
Hrafn svarar: "Gerum þá kurteisi", segir hann, "at vér færim þetta eigi í kappmæli, ok látum konung ráða".	Hrafn answered: "Let-us-be then courteous", said he, "that we able this not in contest, and let king decide".	Hrafn answered: "Let us then be courteous", he said, "that we do not contest this, and let the king decide".

The Saga of Gunnlaug Serpent-Tongue (Old Norse)

Old Norse	Literal	English
Konungr mælti: "Gunnlaugr skal fyrri flytja, því at honum eirir illa, ef hann hefir eigi sitt mál".	King spoke: "Gunnlaug shall before carry, because that he spares badly, if he has not his matter".	The king spoke: "Gunnlaug shall perform before, because he has it badly, if he does not have his own way".
Þá kvað Gunnlaugr drápuna, er hann hafði orta um Óláf konung,	Then said Gunnlaug drapa, that he had worded about Olaf king,	Then Gunnlaug performed the drapa that he had worded about King Olaf,
ok er lokit var drápunni, þá mælti konungr:	And when ended was drapa, then spoke king:	And when the drapa was ended, then the king spoke:
"Hrafn", sagði hann, "hversu er kvæðit ort?"	"Hrafn", said he, "how is poem worded?"	"Hrafn", he said, "how is the poem worded?"
"Vel, herra", sagði hann,	"Well, lord", said he,	"Well, lord", he said,
"þat er stórort kvæði ok ófagrt ok nökkut stirðkveðit, sem Gunnlaugr er sjálfr í skaplyndi".	"It is large poem and ugly and somewhat stiff-spoken, as Gunnlaug is himself in temper".	"It is a large poem, and ugly, and somewhat stiff spoken, as Gunnlaug is himself in temper".
"Nú skaltu flytja þitt kvæði, Hrafn", segir konungr.	"Now shall-you carry your poem, Hrafn", said king.	"Now you shall perform your poem, Hrafn", said the king.
Hann gerir svá.	He did so.	He did so.
Ok er lokit var, þá mælti konungr:	And when ended was, then spoke king:	And when it was finished, then the king spoke:
"Gunnlaugr", segir hann, "hversu er kvæði þetta ort?"	"Gunnlaug", said he, "how is poem this worded?"	"Gunnlaug", he said, "How is this poem worded?"
Gunnlaugr svarar: "Vel, herra", segir hann,	Gunnlaug answered: "Well, lord", said he,	Gunnlaug answered: "Well lord", he said,
"þetta er fagrt kvæði, sem Hrafn er sjálfr at sjá, ok yfirbragðslítit.	"This is beautiful poem, as Hrafn is himself to see, and little-appearance.	"This is a beautiful poem, as Hrafn is himself to look at, and of little appearance.
Eða hví ortir þú flokk um konunginn", segir hann, "eða þótti þér hann eigi drápunnar verðr?"	But why worded you flokk about king", said he, "or thought you he not drapa worth?"	"But why did you compose a flokk about the king", he said, "but did you not think he was worth a drapa?"

The Saga of Gunnlaug Serpent-Tongue (Old Norse)

Old Norse	Literal	English
Hrafn svarar: "Tölum þetta eigi lengr,	Hrafn answered: "Talk this not longer,	Hrafn answered: "Let us not talk about this longer,
til mun verða tekit, þótt síðar sé", segir hann, ok skilðu nú við svá búit.	To should be taken, though afterwards so", said he, and separated now with so settled.	It should be taken up afterwards", he said, and with that they separated.
Litlu síðar gerðist Hrafn hirðmaðr Óláfs konungs ok bað hann orlofs til brottferðar.	Little afterwards became Hrafn court-man Olaf's king and asked he leave to away-travel.	A little afterwards, Hrafn was made one of King Olaf's court men, and he asked for leave to travel.
Konungr veitti honum þat.	King supported him that.	The king supported his request.
Ok er Hrafn var til brottferðar búinn, mælti hann til Gunnlaugs: "Lokit skal nú okkarri vináttu, fyrir því at þú vildir hræpa mik hér fyrir höfðingjum.	And as Hrafn was to away-travel prepared, spoke he to Gunnlaug: "Ended shall now our friendliness, for because that you willed down me here before chiefs.	And as Hrafn was preparing to travel away, he spoke to Gunnlaug: "Our friendship is now ended, because you wanted to do me down before the court.
Nú skal ek einhverju sinni eigi þik minnr vanvirða en þú vildir mik hér".	Now shall I any this not you less disrespect as you willed me here".	Now I shall give you no less disrespect than you willed me here".
Gunnlaugr svarar: "Ekki hryggja mik hót þín", segir hann, "ok hvergi munum vit þess koma, at ek sé minna virðr en þú".	Gunnlaug answered: "Nothing back me threat yours", said he, "and neither should with this come, that I so less worth than you".	Gunnlaug answered: "Nothing of your threats holds me back", he said, "and neither will become of this that I am thought of as a lesser man than you".
Óláfr konungr gaf Hrafni góðar gjafar at skilnaði, ok fór hann í brott síðan.	Olaf king gave Hrafn good gifts to separate, and travelled he to away since.	King Olaf gave Hrafn good gifts when they separated, and after that he travelled away.
Hrafn fór austr um várit ok kom til Þrándheims ok bjó skip sitt ok sigldi til Íslands um sumarit ok kom skipi sínu í Leiruvág fyrir neðan Heiði, ok urðu honum fegnir frændr ok vinir, ok var hann heima þann vetr með föður sínum.	Hrafn travelled east about spring and came to Trondheim and prepared ship his and sailed to Iceland about summer and came ship theirs in Leiruvog before below Heath, and became he celebrated kinsmen and friends, and was he home then winter with father his.	Hrafn travelled east in the spring and came to Trondheim, and prepared his ship, and sailed to Iceland in the summer, and his ship came to Leiruvog, below the heath, and he became celebrated with his kinsmen and friends, and he was them home in the winter with his father.

The Saga of Gunnlaug Serpent-Tongue (Old Norse)

Old Norse	Literal	English
Ok um sumarit á alþingi fundust þeir frændr, Skafti lögmaðr ok Skáld-Hrafn.	And about summer of assembly found they kinsmen, Skafti lawman and Poet-Hrafn.	And at the assembly in the summer Hrafn the Poet met his kinsman Skafti the Lawspeaker.
Þá mælti Hrafn: "Þitt fullting vilda ek hafa til kvánbænar við Þorstein Egilsson, at biðja Helgu, dóttur hans".	Then spoke Hrafn: "Your help will I have to propose with Thorstein son-of-Egil, to propose Helga, daughter his".	Then Hrafn spoke: "I would like to have your help to propose with Thorstein Egilsson, a proposal to his daughter Helga".
Skafti svarar: "Er hon eigi áðr heitkona Gunnlaugs ormstungu?"	Skafti answered: "Is she not before promised-woman Gunnlaug Serpent-Tongue's?"	Skafti answered: "Hasn't she already been promised to Gunnlaug Serpent-Tongue?"
Hrafn svarar: "Er eigi liðin sú stefna nú", segir hann, "sem mælt var með þeim? Enda er miklu meiri hans ofsi en hann muni nú þess gá eða geyma".	Hrafn answered: "Is not passed that agreement now", said he, "as said was with them? Ended is much better his vehemence than he should now this give or retain".	Hrafn answered: "Hasn't that agreement passed now", he said", as was said with them? In the end, his is so proud these days, he won't now care about this".
Skafti svarar: "Gerum sem þér líkar".	Skafti answered: "Let-us-be as to-you like".	Skafti answered: "Let it be as you like".
Síðan gengu þeir fjölmennir til búðar Þorsteins Egilssonar.	Since went they crowded to booth Thorsteins son-of-Egil.	Afterwards they crowded to the booth of Thorstein Egilsson.
Hann fagnaði þeim vel.	He received them well.	He received them well.
Skafti mælti: "Hrafn, frændi minn, vill biðja Helgu, dóttur þinnar, ok er þér kunnig ætt hans ok auðr fjár ok menning góð, frændaafli mikill ok vina".	Skafti spoke: "Hrafn, kinsman mine, will propose Helga, daughter yours, and as you know descendents his and rich wealth and culture good, kinsmen great and friends".	Skafti spoke: "Hrafn, my kinsman, wishes to propose to your daughter Helga, and as you know his descendants and wealth and good culture, great kinsmen and friends".
Þorsteinn svarar: "Hon er áðr heitkona Gunnlaugs, ok vil ek halda öll mál við hann, þau sem mælt váru".	Thorstein answered: "She is before promised-woman Gunnlaug, and wish I keep all matter with he, then as said was".	Thorstein answered: "She is already a promised woman to Gunnlaug, and I wish to keep this matter with him, as was said".
Skafti mælti: "Eru nú eigi liðnir þrír vetr, er til váru nefndir með yðr?"	Skafti spoke: "Were now not passed three winters, as to were mentioned with you?"	Skafti spoke: "Haven't those three winters now already passed, as were promised with you?"

The Saga of Gunnlaug Serpent-Tongue (Old Norse)

Old Norse	Literal	English
"Já", sagði Þorsteinn, "en eigi er sumarit liðit, ok má hann enn til koma í sumar".	"Yes", said Thorstein, "but not is summer passed, and may he still to come in summer".	"Yes", said Thorstein, "but this summer is not yet passed, and he may still come home this summer".
Skafti svarar: "En ef hann kemr eigi til sumarlangt, hverja ván skulum vér þá eiga þessa máls?"	Skafti answered: "And if he comes not to summer-long, what hope shall we then own this matter?"	Skafti answered: "And if he does not come back in the summer, what hope shall we then have in this matter?"
Þorsteinn svarar: "Hér munum vér koma annat sumar, ok má þá sjá, hvat ráðligast þykkir, en ekki tjár nú þetta at tala lengr at sinni".	Thorstein answered: "Here should we come next summer, and may then see, what advice-lies seems, and not force now this that speak longer to this".	Thorstein answered: "We shall come here next summer, and we may then see, what decision seems best, and not force it now by talking about it any longer".
Ok við þat skilðu þeir, ok riðu menn heim af þingi.	And with that separated they, and rode men home of assembly.	And with that they separated, and men rode home from the assembly.
Ekki fór þetta tal leynt, at Hrafn bað Helgu.	Nothing went this talked secret, that Hrafn asked Helga.	Nothing about this was talked about as a secret, that Hrafn asked Helga.
Eigi kom Gunnlaugr út á því sumri.	Not came Gunnlaug out of before summer.	Gunnlaug did not come back that summer.
Ok annat sumar á alþingi fluttu þeir Skafti bónorðit ákafliga, kváðu þá Þorstein lausan allra mála við Gunnlaug.	And next summer of assembly moved they Skafti marriage-proposal extremely, saying then Thorstein lost all matter with Gunnlaug.	And next summer at the assembly, Skafti petitioned for the marriage proposal vociferously, saying then that Thorstein had lost the agreement with Gunnlaug.
Þorsteinn svarar: "Ek á fár dætr fyrir at sjá, ok vilda ek gjarna, at engum manni yrði þær at rógi.	Thorstein answered: "I of few daughters therefore that see, and will I gladly, that no men should therefore then slander.	Thorstein answered: "I have few daughters to see for, and I wish that no men should slander before them".
Nú vil ek finna fyrst Illuga svarta".	Now will I find first Illugi the-Black".	Now I wish first to find Illugi the Black".
Ok svá gerði hann,	And so did he,	And so he did.

The Saga of Gunnlaug Serpent-Tongue (Old Norse)

Old Norse	Literal	English
Ok er þeir fundust, þá mælti Þorsteinn: "Þykkir þér ek eigi lauss allra mála við Gunnlaug, son þinn?"	And as they met, they spoke Thorstein: "Seems to-you I not lost all matter with Gunnlaug, son yours?"	And as they met, then Thorstein spoke: "Does it seem to you that I have lost all agreement with your son Gunnlaug?"
Illugi mælti: "Svá er víst", segir hann, "ef þú vill.	Illugi spoke: "So is certain", said he, "if you will.	Illugi spoke: "So it is certain", he said, "If you wish.
Kann ek hér nú fátt til at leggja, er ek veit eigi gerla efni sonar míns, Gunnlaugs".	Can I here now few to that have, as I know not completely prospects son mine, Gunnlaug".	I can add little to that here, as I don't completely know my son Gunnlaug's prospects".
Þorsteinn gekk þá til Skafta, ok keyptu þeir svá, at brúðlaup skyldi vera at vetrnáttum at Borg, ef Gunnlaugr kæmi eigi út á því sumri, en Þorsteinn lauss allra mála við Hrafn, ef Gunnlaugr kæmi til ok vitjaði ráðsins.	Thorstein went then to Skafti's, and kept they so, to wedding should be at winter-nights at Borg, if Gunnlaug came not out-of of before summer, then Thorstein lost all matter with Hrafn, if Gunnlaug came to and visited council.	Then Thorstein went back to Skafti, and they settled matters so that, if Gunnlaug did not come back that summer, Hrafn and Helga's marriage should take place at Borg at the Winter Nights, but that Thorstein would be without any obligation to Hrafn if Gunnlaug were to come back and go through with the wedding.
Eftir þat riðu menn heim af þinginu, ok frestaðist tilkváma Gunnlaugs, en Helga hugði illt til ráða.	After that rode men home of assembly, and postponed till-came Gunnlaug, and Helga thought ill to decision.	After the men rode home from the assembly, and Gunnlaug's return was still delayed, and Helga thought badly of the decision.
10	10	10
Nú er þat at segja frá Gunnlaugi, at hann fór af Svíþjóðu þat sumar til Englands, er Hrafn fór til Íslands, ok þá góðar gjafar af Óláfi konungi at skilnaði þeira.	Now is that to say from Gunnlaug, as he fared of Sweden that summer to England, that Hrafn fared to Iceland, and then good gifts of Olaf king as separated they.	Now it is to say of Gunnlaug that he travelled from Sweden to England that summer, when Hrafn travelled to Iceland, and was given good gifts from King Olaf as they separated.
Aðalráðr konungr tók við Gunnlaugi allvel, ok var hann með honum um vetrinn með góðri sæmð.	Æthelred king took with Gunnlaug all-well, and was he with him about winter with good honour.	King Æthelred received Gunnlaug well, and he was with him over the winter with good honour.

The Saga of Gunnlaug Serpent-Tongue (Old Norse)

Old Norse	Literal	English
Í þenna tíma réð fyrir Danmörku Knútr inn ríki Sveinsson ok hafði nýtekit við föðurleifð sinni ok heitaðist jafnan at herja til Englands, fyrir því at Sveinn konungr, faðir hans, hafði unnit mikit ríki á Englandi, áðr hann andaðist vestr þar.	In Those times ruled along Denmark Canute then kingdom son-of-Svein and had newly-taken with estate his and was-called equally that army to England's, for because that Svein king, father his, had won much kingdom of England, before he died west there.	In those times the ruler of Denmark was Canute the Great, son of Svein, and he had newly taken with his estate and was always promising to invade England, because King Svein his father had conquered much of England, before he died there in the west.
Ok í þann tíma var mikill herr danskra manna vestr þar, ok var sá höfðingi fyrir, er Hemingr hét, sonr StrútHaralds jarls ok bróðir Sigvalda jarls, ok helt hann þat ríki undir Knút konung, er Sveinn konungr hafði áðr unnit.	And in those times was great band Danish men west there, and was seen leader for, was Heming named, son-of Strut-Harald earl and brother-of Sigvalda earl, and held he that kingdom to Canute king, which Svein king had before won.	And in those times there was a great band of Danish men, whose leader was Heming, the son of Earl Strut-Harald and the brother of Earl Sigvalda, and he held the kingdom under Canute that Svein had conquered before.
Um várit bað Gunnlaugr konunginn sér orlofs til brottferðar.	About spring asked Gunnlaug king himself leave to away-travel.	During the spring, Gunnlaug asked the king for leave to travel away.
Hann svarar: "Eigi samir þér nú at fara frá mér, til slíks ófriðar sem nú horfir hér í Englandi, þar sem þú ert minn hirðmaðr".	He answered: "Not so to-you now to travel from me, to such un-peace as now looks here in England, there as you are my court-man".	He answered: "It is not so now for you to travel from me, while such war looks likely here in England, as you are my court man".
Gunnlaugr svarar: "Þér skuluð ráða, minn herra, ok gef mér orlof at sumri til brottferðar, ef Danir koma eigi".	Gunnlaug answered: "You should advise, mine lord, and give me leave at summer to away-travel, if Danish come not".	Gunnlaug answered: "You shall decide, my lord, and give me leave in the summer if the Danes don't come".
Konungr svarar: "Sjám vit þá".	King answered: "We-see with then".	The king answered: "We'll see then".
Nú leið þat sumar ok vetrinn eftir, ok kómu Danir eigi.	Now passed that summer and winter remaining, and came Danish not.	Now passed the summer and the following winter, and the Danes did not come.

The Saga of Gunnlaug Serpent-Tongue (Old Norse)

Old Norse	Literal	English
Ok eftir mitt sumar fekk Gunnlaugr orlof til brottferðar af konungi, ok fór Gunnlaugr þaðan austr til Nóregs ok fann Eirík jarl í Þrándheimi á Hlöðum, ok tók jarl honum þá vel ok bauð honum þá með sér at vera.	And after mid summer got Gunnlaug leave to away-travel of king, and fared Gunnlaug from-there eastern to Norway and found Erik earl in Trondheim of Lade, and took earl him then well and invited him then with himself to be.	After mid summer Gunnlaug was given leave to travel away from the kind, and Gunnlaug travelled east from there to Norway, and found Earl Erik at Lade in Trondheim, and the earl received him well and invited him to stay there with him.
Gunnlaugr þakkar honum boðit ok kveðst þó vilja fara fyrst út til Íslands á vit festarmeyjar sinnar.	Gunnlaug thanked his offer and said though willed travelling first out to Iceland of with intended-maiden his.	Gunnlaug thanked him for his kind offer, and said that first he wanted to travel out to Iceland to his promised maiden.
Jarl mælti: "Nú eru öll skip brottu, þau er til Íslands bjuggust".	Earl spoke: "Now are all ships away, they are to Iceland prepared".	The earl spoke: "Now all the ships that were prepared to go to Iceland have gone".
Þá mælti hirðmaðr einn: "Hér lá Hallfreðr vandræðaskáld í gær út undir Agðanesi".	Then spoke court-man one: "Here lying Hallfred Troublesome-Poet in yesterday out-of to Agdanes".	Then one of the court men spoke: "Hallfred the Troublesome Poet was lying out in Agdanes yesterday".
Jarl svarar: "Svá má vera", segir hann.	Earl answered: "So may be", said he.	The earl answered: "So may it be then", he said.
"Hann sigldi heðan fyrir fimm náttum".	"He sailed hence before five nights".	"He sailed from there five nights ago".
Eiríkr jarl lét þá flytja Gunnlaug út til Hallfreðar, ok tók hann við honum með fagnaði, ok gaf þegar byr undan landi, ok váru vel kátir.	Erik earl had then taken Gunnlaug out to Hallfred, and took he with him with celebrated, and gave then fair-wind under land, and was well merry.	Earl Erik then had Gunnlaug taken out to Hallfred, and he received him and celebrated him well, and then they were given fair wind offshore, and they were very merry.
Þat var síð sumars.	That was later summer.	That was later summer.
Hallfreðr mælti til Gunnlaugs: "Hefir þú frétt bónorðit Hrafns Önundarsonar við Helgu ina fögru?"	Hallfred spoke to Gunnlaug: "Had you news marriage-proposal Hrafn's son-of-Onund with Helga the Fair?"	Hallfred spoke to Gunnlaug: "Have you heard the news about Hrafn Onundarson's marriage proposal with Helga the Fair?"

The Saga of Gunnlaug Serpent-Tongue (Old Norse)

Old Norse	Literal	English
Gunnlaugr kveðst frétt hafa ok þó ógerla.	Gunnlaug said news had and thought insignificant.	Gunnlaug said that he had not heard the news, and that he thought it was insignificant.
Hallfreðr segir honum slíkt, sem hann vissi af, ok þat með, at margir menn mæltu þat, at Hrafn væri eigi óröskvari en Gunnlaugr.	Hallfred said him such, as he knew of, and that with, that many men spoke that, to Hrafn was not less-brave than Gunnlaug.	Hallfred told him as much as he knew about it, and with that many men spoke that Hrafn was no less brave than Gunnlaug.
Gunnlaugr kvað þá vísu:	Gunnlaug said then verse:	Gunnlaug then said a verse:
Rækik lítt, þótt leiki, létt veðr es nú, þéttan austanvindr at öndri andness viku þessa.	Care little, though toyed, Light weather as now, dense East-wind that second Against-headland week this.	With little care, though toyed, Light weather as now, dense, East wind, that second, Against the headland, this week.
Meir séumk hitt, en hæru hoddstríðandi bíðit, orð, at eigi verðak jafnröskr taliðr Hrafni.	More see other, and grey-hair Hoard-warrior bid, Words, that not worth Equally spoke-of Hrafn.	More seeing other, and grey hair, Hoard warrior bid, Words, that not worth, Equally spoke of Hrafn".
Hallfreðr mælti þá: "Þess þyrfti, félagi, at þér veitti betr en mér málin við Hrafn.	Hallfred spoke then: "This need, companion, that to-you provided-for better than me matters with Hrafn.	Hallfred then spoke: "Companion, you will need to have better matters than me, that I had with Hrafn".
Ek kom skipi mínu í Leiruvág fyrir neðan Heiði fyrir fám vetrum, ok átti ek at gjalda hálfa mörk silfrs húskarli Hrafns, ok helt ek því fyrir honum.	I came ships mine in Leiruvog for below Heath for few winters, and had I to pay half mark silver housekeeper Hrafn's, and held I because before him.	I came with my ship to Leiruvog below Heath a few winters ago, and I had to pay half a mark of silver to Hrafn's housekeeper, and I held it for him.
En Hrafn reið til vár með sextigu manna ok hjó strengina, ok rak skipit upp á leirur ok búit við skipbroti.	Then Hrafn rode to spring with sixty men and struck strings, and drove ship up of clays and settled with shipwreck.	Then in the spring Hrafn rode with sixty men and cut the ropes, and the ship drove up on the clays and settled shipwrecked.
Varð ek þá at selja Hrafni sjálfdæmi, ok galt ek mörk, ok eru slíkar mínar at segja frá honum".	Became I then to shelter Hrafn self-judgement, and paid I mark, and was silver mine to say from him".	It became that I granted Hrafn self-judgement, and I paid him a mark of silver, and that is all I have to say about him".

The Saga of Gunnlaug Serpent-Tongue (Old Norse)

Old Norse	Literal	English
Ok þá var þeim eintalat um Helgu, ok lofaði Hallfreðr mjök vænleik hennar.	And then were they only-spoken about Helga, and praised Hallfred much kindness hers.	And then they were only talking about Helga, and Hallfred praised her kindness very much".
Gunnlaugr kvað þá vísu þessa:	Gunnlaug said then verse this:	Gunnlaug then said this verse:
Munat háðvörum hyrjar hríðmundaðar Þundi hafnar hörvi drifna hlýða jörð at þýðask, þvít lautsíkjar lékum lyngs, es várum yngri, alnar gims á ýmsum andnesjum því landi.	Should-not slander fire While-formed thunder Wary linen drive Listen earth to attach, To drape-oneself played Headlands, which we younger, Measured noble of various Headlands therefore land.	The slander fire should not, While formed the thunder, Weary linen driven, Listen to the earth court, To drape oneself played, Headlands, which we younger, Measured of various noble, Headlands therefore the land.
"Þetta er vel ort", segir Hallfreðr.	"This is well worded", said Hallfred.	"That is well worded", said Hallfred.
Þeir tóku land norðr á Melrakkasléttu í Hraunhöfn hálfum mánaði fyrir vetr ok skipuðu þar upp.	They took land north of Melrakkasletta in Hraunhofn half month before winter and ships there up.	They took land north of Melrakkasletta in Hraunhofn half a month before winter, and unloaded the ship.
Þórðr hét maðr.	Thord was-named a-man.	There was a man named Thord.
Hann var bóndason þar á Sléttunni.	He was farmer's-son there of the-plains.	He was a farmer's son there on the plains.
Hann gekk í glímur við þá kaupmennina, ok gekk þeim illa við hann.	He went in wrestling with then trading-men, and went they badly with him.	He went wrestling with the trading men, and they fared badly with him.
Þá var komit saman fangi með þeim Gunnlaugi.	Then were come together received with them Gunnlaug.	Then they came together with Gunnlaug.
Ok um nóttina áðr hét Þórðr á Þór til sigrs sér,	And about night before called Thord of Thor to victory himself,	And during the night before Thord called upon Thor to gain victory,
ok um daginn, er þeir fundust, tóku þeir til glímu.	and about day, were they found, took they to wrestling.	and in the day, they met, and took to wrestling.

The Saga of Gunnlaug Serpent-Tongue (Old Norse)

Old Norse	Literal	English
Þá laust Gunnlaugr báða fætrna undan Þórði ok felldi hann mikit fall, en fótrinn Gunnlaugs stökk ór liði, sá er hann stóð á, ok fell Gunnlaugr þá með Þórði.	Then swept Gunnlaug both feet under Thord and fell he greatly falling, and foot Gunnlaug jumped from body, so as he stood to, and fell Gunnlaug then with Thord.	Then Gunnlaug swept both feet away from under Thord, and he fell a great fall, but Gunnlaug's foot jumped out of his body, the one he was standing on, and Gunnlaug then fell with Thord.
Þá mælti Þórðr: "Vera má", segir hann, "at þér vegni eigi annat betr".	Then spoke Thord: "Be-it may", said he, "that to-you going not else better".	Then Thord spoke: "Maybe", he said, "that there is nothing going better for you".
"Hvat þá?" segir Gunnlaugr.	"What then?" said Gunnlaug.	"What do you mean?" said Gunnlaug.
"Málin við Hrafn, ef hann fær Helgu innar vænu at vetrnóttum, ok var ek hjá í sumar á alþingi, er þat réðst".	"Matters with Hrafn, if he can Helga inside kind at winter-nights, and was I beside in summer of assembly, as that decided".	"The matter with Hrafn, if he gets Helgi in good spirits on winter nights, and I was with him this summer at the Assembly, when it was decided."
Gunnlaugr svarar engu.	Gunnlaug answered nothing.	Gunnlaug gave no answer.
Þá var vafiðr fótrinn ok í liðinn færðr ok þrútnaði allmjök.	Then was wrapped foot and in passed brought and swollen all-very.	Then his foot was wrapped and joint reset and it was very swollen.
Þeir Hallfreðr riðu tólf menn saman ok kómu suðr á Gilsbakka í Borgarfirði þat laugarkveld, er þeir sátu at brúðlaupinu at Borg.	There Hallfred rode twelve men together and came south of Gilsbakka in Borgafjord that Saturday-night, were they sitting at wedding-feast at Borg.	Hallfred and Gunnlaug rode south with ten other men and came south of Gilsbakka in Borgarfjord that Saturday night, they were sitting at the wedding feast at Borg.
Illugi varð feginn Gunnlaugi, syni sínum, ok hans förunautum.	Illugi became relieved Gunnlaug, son his, and his companions.	Illugi became relieved to see his son Gunnlaug and his companions.
Gunnlaugr kvaðst þá þegar vilja ofan ríða til Borgar.	Gunnlaug said they then willed over ride to Borg.	Gunnlaug said that he wanted to ride over to Borg there and then.
Illugi kvað þat ekki ráð, ok svá sýndist öllum nema Gunnlaugi.	Illugi said that nothing advice, and so seemed all taken Gunnlaug.	Illugi said that was not advisable, and so thought all except Gunnlaug.

The Saga of Gunnlaug Serpent-Tongue (Old Norse)

Old Norse	Literal	English
En Gunnlaugr var þó ófærr fyrir fótarins sak-ar, þótt hann léti ekki á sjást, ok varð því ekki af ferðinni.	But Gunnlaug was thought incapable for foot's sake, though he let not of see, and became because not of travelling.	But Gunnlaug was thought incapable for the sake of his foot, though he did not let it show, and it became that he did not travel.
Hallfreðr reið heim um morgininn til Hreðuvatns í Norðrárdal.	Hallfred rode home about morning to Hreduvatn in Norduradal.	Hallfred rode home about morning to Hreduvatn in Norduradal.
Þar réð fyrir eignum þeira Galti, bróðir hans, ok var vaskr maðr.	There managed before owned their Galti, brother his, and was bold man.	There his brother Galti managed his brother's property there, and was a bold man.

11

Nú er at segja frá Hrafni, at hann sat at brúðlaupi sínu at Borg, ok er þat flestra manna sögn, at brúðrin væri heldr döpr, ok er þat satt, sem mælt er, at lengi man þat, er ungr getr, ok var henni nú ok svá,	Now as to say from Hrafn, that he sat at wedding theirs at Borg, and was the best man said, that bride was rather sad, and was that true, as said was, that long remembered that, which young can, and was her now and so,	Now it is to say of Hrafn, that he sat at their wedding feast at Borg, and it was said by most people, that the bride was rather sad, and that was true as it was said, that things learned young last longest, and that was certainly the case with her then.
Þat varð til nýlundu þar at veizlunni,, at sá maðr bað Húngerðar Þóroddsdóttur ok Jófríðar, er Svertingr hét ok var Hafr-Bjarnarson, Molda-Gnúpssonar, ok skyldu þau ráð takast um vetrinn eftir jól uppi at Skáney.	So became to newcomer there at feast, that saw man asked Hungerd daughter-of-Thorodd and Jofrid, was Sverting named and was son-of-Hafur-Bjarni, son-of-Molda-Gnup, and should they advice take about winter after Yule up at Skaney.	It so happened that a newcomer there at the feast, a man named Sverting, the son of Goat Bjorn, the son of Molda Gnup, asked for the hand of Hungerd, daughter of Thorod and Jofrid, and the wedding was to take place about winter after Yule up at Skaney.
Þar bjó Þorkell, frændi HúngerSar, sonr Torfa Valbrandssonar.	There lived Thorkell, kinsman Hundergar's, son Torfi son-of-Valbrand.	There lived Thorkell, a kinsman of Hungerd, the son of Torfi Valbrandsson.
Móðir Torfa var Þórodda, systir Tungu-Odds.	Mother Torfi was Thorodd, sister Tunga-Odd's.	Torfi's mother was Thorodd, sister of Tunga Odd.
Hrafn fór heim til Mosfells með Helgu, konu sína.	Hrafn fared home to Mosfell with Helga, wife his.	Hrafn travelled home to Mosfell with Helga, his wife.

The Saga of Gunnlaug Serpent-Tongue (Old Norse)

Old Norse	Literal	English
Ok er þau höfðu þar skamma stund verit, þá var þat einn morgin, áðr þau risu upp, at Helga vakir, en Hrafn svaf, ok lét hann illa í svefni.	And as then had there short while been, then was it one morning, before they rose up, that Helga woke, and Hrafn slept, and lay he badly in sleep.	And when they had been there a short while, then one morning before they rose up, Helga woke, and Hrafn slept, and he lay badly in his sleep.
Ok er hann vaknaði, spyrr Helga, hvat hann hefði dreymt.	And as he awoke, asked Helga, what he had dreamt.	And as he awoke, Helga asked what he had dreamt.
Hrafn kvað þá vísu:	Hrafn said then verse:	Hrafn then said a verse:
Hugðumk orms á armi ý döggvar þér höggvinn, væri, brúðr, í blóði beðr þinn roðinn mínu,	Though serpent of arms By dew to-you cut-down, Was, brother, in blood Bedding yours reddened mine,	As though of serpents on arms, By dew yours, cut down, Was, brother, in blood, Bedding yours, was reddened by mine,
knættit endr of undir ölstafns Njörun Hrafni, líka getr þat lauka lind, höggþyrnis binda.	Bowl end about to Ale-staff Njörun Hrafn, Like can it leek Linden, shock-thorn bind.	Bowl end about to, Ale-staff Njörun Hrafn, Like can that leek, Linden, shock thorn bind.
Helga mælti: "Þat mun ek aldri gráta", segir hon, "ok hafið þér illa svikit mik, ok mun Gunnlaugr út kominn".	Helga spoke: "That should I never weep", said she, "and have you badly tricked me, and should Gunnlaug out becoming".	Helga spoke: "I shall never weep over that", he said, "and you have badly tricked me, and should Gunnlaug be coming out".
Ok grét Helga þá mjök.	And wept Helga then much.	And then Helga wept much.
Ok litlu síðar fluttist útkváma Gunnlaugs.	And little afterwards returned out-coming Gunnlaug.	And little afterwards came the news of Gunnlaug's return.
Helga gerðist þá svá stirð við Hrafn, at hann fekk eigi haldit henni heima þar, ok fóru þau þá heim aftr til Borgar, ok nýtti Hrafn lítit af samvistum við hana.	Helga became then so stiff with Hrafn, that he got not stayed her home there, and travelled they then home returning to Borg, and use Hrafn little of together-staying with her.	Helga then became so stiff with Hrafn, that he could not keep her at home, and so they want back to Borg, and Hrafn had little of staying together with her.
Nú búast menn til boðs um vetrinn.	Now prepared men to settle about winter.	Now men prepared to settle for the winter.
Þorkell frá Skáney bauð Illuga svarta ok sonum hans.	Thorkell from Skaney invited Illugi the-Black and sons his.	Thorkell from Skaney invited Illugi the Black and his sons.

The Saga of Gunnlaug Serpent-Tongue (Old Norse)

Old Norse	Literal	English
Ok er Illugi bóndi bjóst, þá sat Gunnlaugr í stofu ok bjóst ekki.	And was Illugi farm prepared, then sat Gunnlaug in main-room and readied not.	And as Illugi's farm was prepared, then Gunnlaug sat in the main room and did not get ready.
Illugi gekk til hans ok mælti: "Hví býst þú ekki, frændi?"	Illugi went to him and spoke: "Why prepared you not, kinsman?"	Illugi went to him and spoke: "Why are you not prepared, kinsman?"
Gunnlaugr svarar: "Ek ætla eigi at fara".	Gunnlaug answered: "I intend not at travel".	Gunnlaug answered: "I do not intend to travel".
Illugi mælti: "Fara skaltu víst, frændi", segir hann, "ok slá ekki slíku á þik, at þrá eftir einni konu, ok lát sem þú vitir eigi, ok mun þik aldri konur skorta".	Illugi spoke: "Travelling shall-you certain, kinsman", said he, "and strike not such of you, that desire after one wife, and let as you know not, and should you never women shortage".	Illugi spoke: You shall certainly travel, kinsman", he said, "and don't strike so much of you to desire one wife, behave as though you don't know, and you should never be short of women".
Gunnlaugr gerði sem faðir hans mælti, ok kómu þeir til boðsins, ok var þeim Illuga ok sonum hans skipat í öndvegi, en þeim Þorstein'i Egilssyni ok Hrafni, mági hans, ok sveitinni brúðguma í annat öndvegi gegnt Illuga.	Gunnlaug did as father his spoke, and came they to invitation, and were they Illugi and sons his directed in foremost, and they Thorstein son-of-Egil and Hrafn, son-in-law his, and party bridegroom's in other foremost opposite Illugi.	Gunnlaug did as his father had spoken, and they came to the feast, and Illugi and his sons were given one high seat at the front, and Thorstein Egilsson, his son in law Hrafn and the bridegroom's group in the other front opposite Illugi.
Konur sátu á palli, ok sat Helga in fagra næst brúðinni ok rendi oft augum til Gunnlaugs, ok kemr þar at því, sem mælt er, at eigi leyna augu, ef ann kona manni.	Women sitting of platform, and sat Helga the Fair next bride and ran often eyes to Gunnlaug, and came there that because, as said is, that not hiding eyes, if love a-woman man.	The women were sitting at a cross bench, and Helga the Fair sat next to the bride, and often ran her eyes to Gunnlaug, and so it came, as it is said, that if a woman loves a man, her eyes won't hide it.
Gunnlaugr var þá vel búinn ok hafði þá klæðin þau in góðu, er Sigtryggr konungr gaf honum, ok þótti hann þá mikit afbragð annarra manna fyrir margs sakar, bæði afls ok vænleiks ok vaxtar.	Gunnlaug was then well prepared and had then clothes there in good, as Sigtrygg king gave him, and thought he then much outstanding other men for many's sake, both strength and good-looks and build.	Gunnlaug was then well prepared with good clothes, that King Sigtrygg gave him, and he seemed very much outstanding compared to other men, in both strength, good looks, and build.

The Saga of Gunnlaug Serpent-Tongue (Old Norse)

Old Norse	Literal	English
Lítil var gleði manna at boðinu.	Little were glad people to invitation.	There was little gladness at the feast.
Ok þann dag, er menn váru í brottbúningi, þá brugðu konur göngu sinni ok bjuggust til heimferðar.	And that day, when men were in leaving-prepared, then brought women going theirs and prepared to home-travel.	And that day, when men were preparing to leave, then the woman prepared to travel home.
Gunnlaugr gekk þá til tals við Helgu, ok töluðu lengi, ok þá kvað Gunnlaugr vísu:	Gunnlaug went then to talk with Helga, and talked long, and then said Gunnlaug verse:	Gunnlaug then went to talk with Helga, and they talked for a long time, and then Gunnlaug said a verse:
Ormstungu varð engi allr dagr und sal fjalla hægr, síz Helga en fagra Hrafns kvánar réð nafni.	Serpent-Tongue's were none All day under hall mountain Right, since Helga but fair Hrafn's wife decided name.	For Serpent-Tongue were none All days under the hall mountain Right, since Helga but Fair Hrafn's wife decided took the name.
Lítt sá hölðr enn hvíti hjörþeys faðir meyjar, gefin vas Eir til aura ung, við minni tungu.	Little saw handled still white Faced father girl's, Given was Eir to ounces Young, with less tongue.	Little saw handled still white Faced father girl's, Given was Eir to ounces Young, with less tongue.
Ok enn kvað hann:	And still said he:	And still he said:
Væn, ák verst at launa, vín-Gefn, föður þínum, fold nemr flaum af skaldi flóðhyrs, ok svá móður, því at gerðu bil borða bæði senn und klæðum, herr hafi hölðs ok svarra hagvirki, svá fagra.	Fair, that worst to repay, Wine-given, father yours, Ground taken flame of poet Flood-deer, and so mother, Because to make space bore Both they under clothed, Band had flesh and answer Advantage, so fair.	Fair, the worst to repay, Wine-given, father yours, Ground taken flame of poet, Flood-deer, and so mother, Because to make space bore Both they under clothed, Band had flesh and answer Advantage so fair.
Ok þá gaf Gunnlaugr Helgu skikkjuna Aðalráðsnaut, ok var þat gersimi sem mest.	And then gave Gunnlaug Helga cloak Æthelred-gift, and was that treasured as most.	And then Gunnlaug gave Helga the cloak that Æthelred had given him, and that was treasured most.
Hon þakkaði honum vel gjöfina.	She thanked him well gift.	She thanked him well for the gift.

The Saga of Gunnlaug Serpent-Tongue (Old Norse)

Old Norse	Literal	English
Síðan gekk Gunnlaugr út, ok váru þá komin hross ok hestar söðlaðir ok margir allvænligir ok bundnir heima á hlaðinu.	Afterwards went Gunnlaug out, and were then coming horses and stallions saddled and many all-promising and bound home of farmyard.	Afterwards Gunnlaug went outside, and there were horses and stallions saddled, many of them promising, and bound home at the farmyard.
Gunnlaugr hljóp á bak einhverjum hesti ok reið á skeið eftir túninu ok at þangat, er Hrafn stóð fyrir, ok varð Hrafn at hopa undan.	Gunnlaug jumped of back somebody's horse and rode of sheathed-sword after the-field and that there, as Hrafn stood before, and was Hrafn to avoid under.	Gunnlaug jumped on the back of somebody's horse and rode with sheathed sword to the field where Hrafn was standing, Hrafn had to avoid him.
Gunnlaugr mælti: "Ekki er at hopa undan, Hrafn", segir hann, "fyrir því at enga ógn býð ek þér at sinni, en þú veizt, til hvers þú hefir unnit".	Gunnlaug spoke: "Nothing is that avoid under, Hrafn", said he, "for because that none threat offer I to-you at once, and you know, to what you had deserved".	Gunnlaug spoke: "Nothing is that to avoid, Hrafn", he said, "because I offer you no threat at once, but you know, to what you deserve".
Hrafn svarar ok kvað vísu:	Hrafn answered and said verse:	Hrafn answered and said a verse:
Samira okkr of eina, Ullr benloga, Fullu, frægir folka Ságu, fangs í brigð at ganga. Mjök eru margar slíkar, morðrunnr, fyr haf sunnan, ýtik sævar Sóta, sannfróðr, konur góðar.	Same we about one, Ullr bone-flying, full, Famous folk saw, Embrace in trickery to go. Much were many silver, Murder-running, for the-sea south, out seas sought, true-knowledge, women good.	We are one and the same, Ullr bone flying, full, Famous folk saw, Embrace in trickery to go, Much were many silver, Murder running, for the south sea, Out seas sought, True knowledge, good women.
Gunnlaugr svarar: "Vera má", segir hann, "at margar sé, en eigi þykkir mér svá".	Gunnlaug answered: "be-it may", said he, "that many so, but not seemed me so".	Gunnlaug answered: "It may be", he said, "that there are many, but it does not seem to me".
Þá hljópu þeir Illugi at ok Þorsteinn, ok vildu ekki, at þeir ættist við.	Then ran they Illugi to and Thorstein, and willed not, that they come-together with.	Then Illugi and Thorstein ran over to them, and did not wan them to come together.
Þá kvað Gunnlaugr vísu:	Then said Gunnlaug verse:	Then Gunnlaug said this verse:
Gefin vas Eir til aura ormdags en litfagra,	Given was Eir to ounces Serpent-days and fair-colour,	Given was Eir to ounces, Serpent days and fair colour,

The Saga of Gunnlaug Serpent-Tongue (Old Norse)

Old Norse	Literal	English
þann kveða menn né minna minn jafnoka, Hrafni, allra nýztr meðan austan Aðalráðr farar dvalði, því es menrýris minni málgráðr, í gný stála.	Then greeted men not less Mine equal, Hrafn, All new meanwhile east Æthelred travel dwelled, Because was men-equal less Degree, in rage steel.	Then greeted men not less My equal, Hrafn, All new meanwhile east, Æthelred travel dwelled, Because were men less equal, Degree, in rage steel.
Ok eftir þetta riðu menn heim hvárirtveggju, ok var allt kyrrt ok tíðendalaust um vetrinn.	And after this rode men home either-side, and was all still and news-less about winter.	After this men rode home each way, and all was still and without news over the winter.
Nýtti Hrafn ekki síðan af samvistum við Helgu, þá er þau Gunnlaugr höfðu fundizt.	Use Hrafn not since of together-staying with Helga, then as then Gunnlaug had found.	Hrafn had no use to stay together with Helga, once Gunnlaug had found her.
Ok um sumarit riðu menn fjölmennir til þings, Illugi svarti ok synir hans með honum, Gunnlaugr ok Hermundr, Þorsteinn Egilsson ok Kollsveinn, sonr hans, Önundr frá Mosfelli ok synir hans allir, Svertingr Hafr-Bjarnarson.	And about summer rode men crowded to the-assembly, Illugi the-Black and sons his with him, Gunnlaug and Hermund, Thorstein Egilsson and Kollsveinn, son his, Onund from Mosfell and sons his all, Sverting son-of-Hafur-Bjarni.	And about summer men rode and crowded to the assembly, Illugi the Black with his sons, Gunnlaug and Hermund, Thorstein Egilsson and his son Kollsveinn, Onund from Mosfell and all his sons, and Sverting son of Hafur Bjarni.
Skafti hafði þá enn lögsögu.	Skafti had then still lawspeaker.	Skafti still had the job of lawspeaker.
Ok einn dag á þinginu, er menn gengu fjölmennir til Lögbergs ok er þar var lykt at mæla lögskilum, þá kvaddi Gunnlaugr sér hljóðs ok mælti: "Er Hrafn hér Önundarson?"	And one day of assembly, as men went crowded to Law-Rock and as there was smell of business legal-settlement, they called Gunnlaug himself be-heard and spoke: "Is Hrafn here son-of-Onund?"	And one day at the assembly, as men crowded to the Law-Rock, and as there was the smell of the business of legal settlement, they called that Gunnlaug himself be heard, and he spoke: "Is Hrafn Onundarson here?"
Hann kveðst þar vera.	He said there was.	He said that he was there.
Gunnlaugr ormstunga mælti þá: "Þat veizt þú, at þú hefir fengit heitkonu minnar ok dregst til fjandskapar við mik.	Gunnlaug Serpent-Tongue spoke then: "That know you, as you had caught wife mine and drawn to hostility with me.	Gunnlaug Serpent-Tongue then spoke: "You know as you caught my intended wife, that you have drawn hostility from me.

The Saga of Gunnlaug Serpent-Tongue (Old Norse)

Old Norse	Literal	English
Nú fyrir þat vil ek bjóða þér hólmgöngu hér á þinginu á þriggja nátta fresti í Öxarárhólmi".	Now for that will I bid to-you duel here of assembly of three nights from-now in Oxararholm".	Now for that I will bid you to duel here at the assembly three nights from now in Oxararholm".
Hrafn svarar: "Þetta er vel boðit, sem ván var at þér", segir hann, "ok em ek þess albúinn, þegar þú vill".	Hrafn answered: "This is well bid, as looked was that to-you", said he, "and am I this all-ready, when you will".	Hrafn answered: "This is well bid, as is expected from you", he said, "and I am all ready for this, when you will".
Þetta þótti illt frændum hvárstveggja þeira, en þó váru þat lög í þann tíma at bjóða hólmgöngu, sá er vanhluta þóttist verða fyrir öðrum.	This thought ill kinsmen either-side they, and though was that law in that time that bid duel, looked that party thought becoming before other.	This the kinsmen on either side thought was bad, but though it was the law in that time, that a duel could be bid, if it seemed that one party had been wronged by another.
Ok er þrjár nætr váru liðnar, bjuggust þeir til hólmgöngu, ok fylgði Illugi svarti syni sínum til hólmsins með miklu fjölmenni, en Skafti lögsögumaðr fylgði Hrafni ok faðir hans ok aðrir frændr hans.	And when three nights were passed, prepared they to duel, and followed Illugi the-Black son his to duel-his with much followers, and Skafti law-speaker-man followed Hrafn and father his and others kinsmen his.	And when the three nights were passed, they prepared to duel, and Illugi the Black went to the island with his son, with many followers, and Skafti the Lawspeaker followed Hrafn, his father, and other kinsmen.
Ok áðr Gunnlaugr gengi út í hólminn, þá kvað hann vísu þessa:	And before Gunnlaug went out in duel, then said he verse this:	And before Gunnlaug went out into the duel, then he said this verse:
Nú emk út á eyri alvangs búinn ganga, happs unni goð greppi gört, með tognum hjörvi. Hnakk skalk Helgu lokka, haus vinnk frá bol lausan loks með ljósum mæki ljúfsvelgs, í tvau kljúfa.	Now am-I out-of of island Field prepared go, Luck love good grasp Be, with extended sword. Saddle shall Helga lure, House win from trunk lost Finally with lights sword Sweet-swallower, in two cleave.	Now I am out on an island, Field prepared to go, Luck love good grasp, Be, with extended sword. Saddle shall Helga lure, House win from trunk lost Finally with lights sword Sweet swallower, in two cleave.
Hrafn svarar ok kvað þetta:	Hrafn answered and said this:	Hrafn answered and said this:
Veitat greppr, hvárr greppa gagnsæli hlýtr fagna. Hér 's bensigðum brugðit, búin es egg í leggi.	Provided grasp, where grasp Benefit-happier get welcomes. Here was wound-sickles brought-out, Done which ridge in leg.	Provided grasp, where grasp Benefit happier gift welcomes. Here was the sickle's wound brought out, Done which ridge in leg.

The Saga of Gunnlaug Serpent-Tongue (Old Norse)

Old Norse	Literal	English
Þat mun ein ok ekkja ung mær, þótt vér særimsk, þorna spöng af þingi þegns hugrekki fregna.	That should one and widow Young girl, though we wound, Thorn arch of assembly Citizen courage news.	That should one and widow Young girl, though we wound, Thorn arch of assembly Citizen courage news.
Hermundr helt skildi fyrir Gunnlaug, bróður sinn, en Svertingr Hafr-Bjarnarson fyrir Hrafn.	Hermund held shield for Gunnlaug, brother his, and Sverting son-of-Hafur-Bjarni for Hrafn.	Gunnlaug's brother Hermund held his shield, and Sverting son of Hafur Bjarni did for Hrafn.
Þrem mörkum silfrs skyldi sá leysa sik af hólminum, er sárr yrði.	Three marks silver should so resolve him of duel, as wound should.	Three marks of silver should resolve he who was wounded in the duel.
Hrafn átti fyrr at höggva, er á hann var skorat, ok hjó hann í skjöld Gunnlaugs ofanverðan, ok brast sverðit þegar sundr undir hjöltunum, er til var höggvit af miklu afli.	Hrafn had before to strike, as that he was challenged, and struck he in shield Gunnlaug above, and burst sword then asunder to hilt, as to was struck of much strength.	Hrafn was to strike first, as it was him that had been challenged, and he struck at Gunnlaug's shield, and the blow was so mighty that the sword broke to the hilt.
Blóðrefillinn hraut upp af skildinum ok kom í kinn Gunnlaugi ok skeindist hann heldr en eigi.	Point-of-sword jumped up of shield and came in cheek Gunnlaug and scratched him rather but not.	The point of the sword jumped from the shield and struck Gunnlaug's cheek, scratching him slightly.
Þá hljópu feðr þeira þegar í millim ok margir aðrir menn.	Then ran father theirs then in between and many other men.	Then their fathers ran between them, along with many other men.
Þá mælti Gunnlaugr: "Nú kalla ek, at Hrafn sé sigraðr, er hann er slyppr".	Then spoke Gunnlaug: "Now call I, that Hrafn so defeated, as he that escapes".	Then Gunnlaug spoke: "Now I declare that Hrafn is defeated, as he has escaped".
"En ek kalla, at þú sér sigraðr", segir Hrafn, "er þú ert sárr orðinn".	"And I call, that you yourself defeated", said Hrafn, "as you are wounded have-become".	"And I declare that you yourself are defeated", said Hrafn, "as you have become wounded".
Gunnlaugr var þá allæfr ok reiðr mjök ok kvað ekki reynt vera.	Gunnlaug was then enraged and angry much and said not tested was.	Gunnlaug was then enraged and very much angry, and said that the matter was not resolved.
Illugi, faðir hans, kvað þá eigi skyldu reyna meir at sinni.	Illugi, father his, said they not should attempt more than this.	His father Illugi said that they should not attempt any more than this.

The Saga of Gunnlaug Serpent-Tongue (Old Norse)

Old Norse	Literal	English
Gunnlaugr svarar: "Þat mynda ek vilja", segir hann, "at vit Hrafn mættimst svá öðru sinni, at þú værir fjarri, faðir, at skilja okkr".	Gunnlaug answered: "That should I will", said he, "that with Hrafn meet-we so other this, that you be away, father, that separate we".	Gunnlaug answered: "I should want", he said, "the next time Hrafn and I meet, that you be away, father that separate us".
Ok við þetta skilðu þeir at sinni, ok gengu menn heim til búða sinna.	And with this separated they that this, and went men home to booths theirs.	And with this, they then separated, and men went home to their booths.
Ok annan dag eftir í lögréttu var þat í lög sett, at af skyldi taka hólmgöngur allar þaðan í frá, ok var þat gert at ráði allra vitrustu manna, er við váru staddir, en þar váru allir þeir, er vitrastir váru á landinu.	And another day after in law-assembly was that in law set, that of should take duelling all from-there in from, and was that done that advised all wisest men, that with were present, and then were all they, the wisest were of the-land.	And another day after in the law assembly it was set in law, that all duelling should be all removed, and so it was done with the advice of all the wisest men who were present, and then they were all the wisest of the land.
Ok þessi hefir hólmganga síðast framið verit á Íslandi, er þeir Hrafn ok Gunnlaugr börðust.	And this had duelling last committed made of Iceland, as they Hrafn and Gunnlaug fought.	And this was the last duelling that had ever been committed in Iceland, as Hrafn and Gunnlaug fought.
Þat hefir it þriðja þing verit fjölmennast, annat eftir brennu Njáls, it þriðja eftir Heiðarvíg.	That had the third assembly been full-men-most, another after Brennu Njal's, the third after heath-slayings.	That was the third largest assembly, the other being Brennu Njal's, and the third after the heath slayings.
Ok einn morgin, er þeir bræðr, Hermundr ok Gunnlaugr, gengu til Öxarár at þvá sér, þá gengu öðru megin at ánni konur margar, ok var þar Helga in fagra í því liði.	And one morning, when they brothers, Hermund and Gunnlaug, went to Oxarar to wash themselves, then went other ways to river women many, and was there Helga the fair in before group.	And one morning, when the brothers Hermund and Gunnlaug went to Oxarar to wash themselves, several women were on the other bank of the river, and Helga the Fair was before the group.
Þá mælti Hermundr: "Sér þú Helgu, vinkonu þína, hér fyrir handan ána?"	Then spoke Hermund: "See you Helga, girlfriend yours, here before beyond river?"	Then Hermund spoke: "Do you see Helga, your girlfriend, here before the river beyond?"
Gunnlaugr svarar: "Sé ek hana víst".	Gunnlaug answered: "See I her certainly".	Gunnlaug answered: "I certainly see her".

The Saga of Gunnlaug Serpent-Tongue (Old Norse)

Old Norse	Literal	English
Ok þá kvað Gunnlaugr vísu þessa:	And then said Gunnlaug verse this:	And then Gunnlaug said this verse:
Alin vas rýgr at rógi, runnr olli því Gunnar, lág vask auðs at eiga óðgjarn, fira börnum. Nú eru svanmærrar síðan svört augu mér bauga lands til lýsi-Gunnar lítilþörf at títa.	Measured was woman to feud, Tree cause because-of warrior, Placed was wealth to own Sorely, burning children. Now were swan-mares since Black eyes to-me circle Lands to light-warrior-god Little-need that look.	Measured was woman to feud, Tree cause because of a warrior, Placed was wealth to own, Sorely, burning children. Now were swan mares since, Black eyes to me circle, Lands to light warrior god, Little need that look.
Síðan gengu þeir yfir ána, ok töluðu þau Helga ok Gunnlaugr um stund.	Since went they across river, and talked they Helga and Gunnlaug about while.	Afterwards they went across the river, and Helga and Gunnlaug talked for a while.
Ok er þeir gengu austr yfir ána, þá stóð Helga ok starði á Gunnlaug lengi eftir.	And as they went east across river, then stood Helga and stared at Gunnlaug long after.	And as they went west across the river, then Helga stood and stared at Gunnlaug long afterwards.
Gunnlaugr leit þá aftr yfir ána ok kvað vísu þessa:	Gunnlaug looked then returned across river and said verse this:	Gunnlaug then looked across the river and said this verse:
Brámáni skein brúna brims und ljósum himni Hristar hörvi glæstrar haukfránn á mik lauka, en sá geisli sýslir síðan gullmens Fríðar hvarma tungls ok hringa Hlínar óþurft mína.	Brightly shone brow Brim under lights heaven Shakes linen glistens Hawk-from of me leek, And saw beams work Since golden beautiful Eyelids moon and rings Hlínar un-needed mine.	Brightly shone the brow Brim under lights heaven Shakes linen glistens Hawk from of me leek, And saw beams work, Since golden beautiful, Eyelids moon and rings, Hlínar un-needed mine.
Ok eftir þetta um liðit riðu menn af þinginu, ok var Gunnlaugr heima at Gilsbakka.	And after this about group rode men of assembly, and was Gunnlaug home at Gilsbakka.	And after this happened the group of men of the assembly rode home, and Gunnlaug was home at Gilsbakka.
Ok einn morgin, er hann vaknaði, þá váru allir menn upp risnir, nema hann lá.	And one morning, as he awoke, then were all men up rising, except him lying.	And one morning, as he awoke, all men were up, except him laying.
Hann hvíldi í lokrekkju innar af seti.	He rested in bed-closet inside of set.	He rested in bed closet set inside the hall.

The Saga of Gunnlaug Serpent-Tongue (Old Norse)

Old Norse	Literal	English
Þá gengu í skálann tólf menn, allir alvápnaðir, ok var þar kominn Hrafn Önundarson.	They went in hut twelve men, all -weaponed, and were they come-in Hrafn son-of-Onund.	Then twelve men, all armed, came into the hall: Hrafn Onundarson.
Gunnlaugr spratt upp þegar ok gat fengit vápn sín.	Gunnlaug sprang up then and opening caught weapons his.	Gunnlaug sprang up then and managed to get his weapons.
Þá mælti Hrafn: "Við engu skal þér hætt vera", segir hann, "en þat er erendi mitt hingat, at þú skalt nú heyra.	Then spoke Hrafn: "With none shall to-you end be", said he, "but this is errand mine here, that you shall now hear.	Then Hrafn spoke: "You shall not be to your end", he said, "but this is my errand here, that you shall now hear.
Þú bautt mér hólmgöngu í sumar á alþingi, ok þótti þér sú ekki reynd verða.	You bid me duel in summer of assembly, and thought to-you that not resolved was.	You bid me duel in summer at the assembly, and you thought that it was not resolved.
Nú vil ek þér bjóða, at vit farim báðir á brott af Íslandi ok útan í sumar ok gangim á hólm í Nóregi.	Now wish I to-you bid, to with travel both to away of Iceland and out in summer and going to duel in Norway.	Now I wish to bid that we both travel away from Iceland in the summer and go to duel in Norway.
Þar munu eigi frændr okkrir fyrir standa".	There shall none kinsmen ours before stand".	None of our kinsmen shall stand there before us".
Gunnlaugr svarar: "Mæl drengja heilastr, ok þenna kost vil ek gjarna þiggja,	Gunnlaug answered: "Said fellow well, and then benefit wish I gladly receive,	Gunnlaug answered "Well said fellow, and the benefit I gladly wish to receive,
ok er hér at þiggja, Hrafn", segir hann, "þann greiða, sem þú vill".	and is here to receive, Hrafn", said he, "then assistance, as you will".	and here is yours to receive, Hrafn", he said, "such assistance as you will".
Hrafn svarar: "Þat er vel boðit, en ríða munum vér fyrst at sinni".	Hrafn answered: "That is well bid, but ride should we first to ours".	Hrafn answered: "That is well bid, but first we should ride our way".
Ok við þetta skilðu þeir.	And with that separated they.	And with that they separated.
Þetta þótti frændum hvárstveggja þeira stórum illa, en fengu þó ekki at gert fyrir ákafa þeira sjálfra, enda varð þat fram at koma, sem til dró.	That thought kinsmen either-side they great ill, and got though nothing to do for extremely they themselves, ended was that from that came, as to draw.	Both kinsmen of either side thought this was a great ill, and though they could do nothing, but what end from that came, which was drawn by fate.

The Saga of Gunnlaug Serpent-Tongue (Old Norse)

Old Norse	Literal	English
12	12	12
Nú er at segja frá Hrafni, at hann bjó skip sitt í Leiruvágum.	Now is to say from Hrafn, that he prepared ship his in Leiruvog.	Now it is to say of Hrafn, that he prepared his ship in Leiruvog.
Tveir menn eru þeir nefndir, er fóru með Hrafni, systursynir Önundar, föður hans.	Two men were they named, to travel with Hrafn, sister-sons Onund, father his.	Two men were named, to travel with Hrafn, they were the sons of Onund's father.
Hét annarr Grímr, en annarr Óláfr, ok váru báðir gildir menn.	Named another Grim, and another Olaf, and were both valid men.	One of them was named Grim, another Olaf, and they were both valid men.
Öllum frændum Hrafns þótti mikill svipr, er hann fór í brott.	All kinsmen Hrafn's thought much seemed, as he travelled to away.	All of Hrafn's kinsmen thought it a great blow, when he travelled away.
En hann sagði svá, kvaðst því Gunnlaug á hólm skorat hafa, at hann kvaðst engar nytjar hafa Helgu, ok kvað annan hvárn verða at hníga fyrir öðrum.	And he said so, said of Gunnlaug of duel challenged had, that he said none use have Helga, and said another each be to sink before other.	And he said of Gunnlaug that he had challenged him to a duel, because he had nothing with Helga, and said that one of them would have to fall before the other.
Síðan sigldi Hrafn í haf, er þeim gaf byr, ok kómu skipi sínu í Þrándheim, ok var þar of vetrinn ok frétti ekki til Gunnlaugs á þeim vetri, ok þar beið hann Gunnlaugs um sumarit.	Since sailed Hrafn to sea, as they given fair-wind, and came ships theirs in Trondheim, and were there about winter and heard nothing to Gunnlaug of them winter, and there waited he Gunnlaug about summer.	Afterwards Hrafn sailed to sea, as soon as they were given fair wind, and their ship came to Trondheim, and they were there during the winter, and heard nothing of Gunnlaug during the winter, and waited there for Gunnlaug during the summer.
Ok enn annan vetr var hann í Þrándheimi, þar sem heitir í Lifangri.	And still another winter was he in Trondheim, there which named of Levanger.	And he was still in Trondheim for another winter, in a place named Levanger.

The Saga of Gunnlaug Serpent-Tongue (Old Norse)

Old Norse	Literal	English
Gunnlaugr ormstunga réðst til skips með Hallfreði vandræðaskáldi norðr á Sléttu, ok urðu þeir síðbúnir mjök, ok sigldu þeir í haf, þegar byr gaf, ok kómu við Orkneyjar litlu fyrir vetr.	Gunnlaug Serpent-Tongue rode to ship with Hallfred troublesome-poet north to Slettu, and became they later-ready much, and sailed they to sea, then fair-wind given, and came to Orkney-Islands little before winter.	Gunnlaug Serpent-Tongue rode to ships with Hallfred the Troublesome Poet north to Slettu, and they became ready much later, and they sailed to sea, then they were given a fair wind, and came to the Orkney islands a little before winter.
Sigurðr jarl Hlöðvisson réð þá fyrir eyjunum, ok fór Gunnlaugr til hans ok var þar um vetrinn, ok virði jarl hann vel.	Sigurd earl son-of-Hlodvi ruled then for islands, and travelled Gunnlaug to him and was there about winter, and valued earl him well.	Earl Sigurd Hlodvisson ruled the islands then, and Gunnlaug travelled to him and was there during the winter, and the earl received him well.
Ok um várit bjóst jarl í hernað.	And about spring prepared earl in raiding.	And about spring the earl prepared for raiding.
Gunnlaugr bjóst til ferðar með honum, ok herjuðu um sumarit víða um Suðreyjar ok Skotlandsfjörðu ok áttu margar orrostur, ok reyndist Gunnlaugr inn hraustasti ok inn vaskasti drengr ok inn harðasti karlmaðr, hvar sem þeir kómu.	Gunnlaug prepared to travel with him, and raiding about summer widely about South-Islands and Scotland's-firths and had many battles, and turned-out Gunnlaug the strongest and then boldest fellow and then hardest many, where that they came.	Gunnlaug prepared to travel with him, and raided there during the summer widely about the South Islands and Scotland firths, and had many battles, and it turned out that Gunnlaug was the strongest and the boldest fellow, and the hardest wherever they came.
Sigurðr jarl snerist snemmendis sumars aftr, en Gunnlaugr sté þá á skip með kaupmönnum, þeim er sigldu til Nóregs, ok skilðu þeir Sigurðr jarl með mikilli vináttu.	Sigurd earl turned around summer back, and Gunnlaug stepped there to ship with trading-men, they then sailed to Norway, and separated they Sigurd earl with much friendliness.	Earl Sigurd turned back in the summer, and Gunnlaug took passage on a ship with trading men, they then sailed to Norway, and they separated from Earl Sigurd with much friendliness.
Gunnlaugr fór norðr til Þrándheims á Hlaðir á fund Eiríks jarls, ok var þar öndverðan vetr, ok tók jarl vel við honum ok bauð honum með sér at vera, ok þat þekkðist hann.	Gunnlaug travelled north to Trondheim of Lade to meet Erik earl, and was there early winter, and took earl well with him and invited him with himself to be, and that took he.	Gunnlaug travelled north of Trondheim to Lade to meet Earl Erik, and he was there early in winter, and the earl received him well and invited him to stay with him, and he accepted.

The Saga of Gunnlaug Serpent-Tongue (Old Norse)

Old Norse	Literal	English
Frétt hafði jarl áðr viðskipti þeira Hrafns, svá sem var, ok segir Gunnlaugi, at hann legði bann fyrir, at þeir berðist þar í hans ríki.	News had earl before exchanged they Hrafn's, so as was, and said Gunnlaug, that he had banned for, that they fight there in his kingdom.	The earl had already heard the news of his exchanges with Hrafn, such as it was, and said to Gunnlaug that he had banned them from fighting in his kingdom.
Gunnlaugr kvað hann slíku ráða mundu, ok var Gunnlaugr þar um vetrinn ok jafnan fálátr.	Gunnlaug said he such advised would-be, and was Gunnlaug there about winter and usually reserved.	Gunnlaug said that such was his to decide, and Gunnlaug was there during the winter and was usually reserved.
Ok um várit einn dag gekk Gunnlaugr úti ok Þorkell, frændi hans, með honum.	And about spring one day went Gunnlaug out and Thorkell, kinsman his, with him.	And one day in the spring, Gunnlaug went out, and his kinsman Thorkell went with him.
Þeir gengu í brott frá bænum.	They went in away from dwelling.	They went away from the town.
Ok á völlum fyrir þeim var mannhringr, ok í hringinum innan váru tveir menn með vápnum ok skylmðust.	And of fields before them was man-ring, and in ring inside were two men with weapons and shields.	And in the fields in front of them there was a ring of men, and inside the ring were two men with weapons and shields.
Var þar annarr nefndr Hrafn, en annarr Gunnlaugr.	Was there another named Hrafn, and another Gunnlaug.	One was named Hrafn, and another was named Gunnlaug.
Þeir mæltu, er hjá stóðu, at Íslendingar hyggi smátt ok væri seinir til at muna orð sín.	They spoke, as beside standing, that Icelander thought small and was later to that should words theirs.	Those who stood by said that the Icelanders thought a little and were late in remembering their words.
Gunnlaugr fann, at hér fylgði mikit háð ok hér var mikit spott at dregit, ok gekk Gunnlaugr í brott þegjandi.	Gunnlaug found, that here followed much mockery and here was much ridicule was drawn, and went Gunnlaug to away silently.	Gunnlaug found that there followed much mockery, and much ridicule was drawn, and Gunnlaug went away silently.
Ok litlu síðar eftir þetta segir hann jarli, at hann kveðst eigi lengr nenna at þola háð ok spott hirðmanna hans um mál þeira Hrafns, ok beiddi jarl fá sér leiðtoga inn í Lifangr.	And little since after this said he earl, that he said not longer bothered to endure mockery and ridicule followers his about matter theirs Hrafn's, and asked earl get himself guide then in Levanger.	And a little afterwards he said to the earl that he no longer bothered to endure mockery and ridicule from his followers about his matter with Hrafn, and he asked the earl to get him a guide then in Levanger.

The Saga of Gunnlaug Serpent-Tongue (Old Norse)

Old Norse	Literal	English
Jarli var sagt áðr, at Hrafn var í brottu ór Lifangri ok farinn austr til Svíþjóðar, ok því gaf hann Gunnlaugi orlof at fara ok fekk honum leiðtoga tvá til ferðarinnar.	Earl was told already, that Hrafn was to away from Levanger and travelling eastern to Sweden, and therefore gave he Gunnlaug leave to travel and got him guide two to travelling.	The earl was told already, that Hrafn had left Levanger and was travelling east to Sweden, and therefore gave Gunnlaug leave to travel and got him a couple of guides to travel with.
Nú ferr Gunnlaugr af Hlöðum við sjaunda mann inn í Lifangr, ok þann morgin hafði Hrafn farit þaðan með fimmta mann, er Gunnlaugr kom þar um kveldit.	Now went Gunnlaug of Lade with seven men then in Levanger, and then morning had Hrafn travelled from-there with five men, as Gunnlaug came there about evening.	Now Gunnlaug went from Lade with six other men and went to Levanger, and that morning Hrafn travelled from there with five men, as Gunnlaug arrived there that evening.
Þaðan fór Gunnlaugr í Veradal ok kom þar at kveldi jafnan, sem Hrafn hafði áðr verit um nóttina.	From-there travelled Gunnlaug in Veradal and came there at evening equally, as Hrafn had before been about night.	Gunnlaug travelled from there into Veradal and arrived there the same evening, as Hrafn has been before the previous evening.
Gunnlaugr ferr, til þess er'hann kom á efsta bæ í dalnum, er á Súlu hét, ok hafði Hrafn þaðan farit um morgininn.	Gunnlaug went, to this as-he came to upper dwelling in valleys, which of Sulu named, and had Hrafn from-there travelled about morning.	Gunnlaug went to this as he came to the upper dwelling in the valleys, which was named Sula, and Hrafn had travelled from there about morning.
Gunnlaugr dvalði þá ekki ferðina ok fór þegar um nóttina.	Gunnlaug dwelled then not travelling and fared then about night.	Gunnlaug did not delay his travelling and travelled during the night.
Ok um morgininn í sólarroð, þá sá hvárir aðra.	And about morning in sunrise, they saw each other.	And about morning during the sunrise, they saw each other.
Hrafn var þar kominn, sem váru vötn tvau, ok á meðal vatnanna váru vellir sléttir.	Hrafn was there coming, as were waters two, and of between waters were fields smooth.	Hrafn had come to a place in which there were two lakes, and between the waters were smooth fields.
Þat heita Gleipnisvellir.	That called Gleipnisvellir.	That was named Gleipnisvellir.
En fram í vatnit annat gekk nes lítit, er heitir Dinganes.	And from in lake another went headland little, was called Dingenes.	And from in the second lake went a little headland, which was named Dingenes.

The Saga of Gunnlaug Serpent-Tongue (Old Norse)

Old Norse	Literal	English
Þar námu þeir Hrafn við í nesinu ok váru fimm saman.	There took they Hrafn with in headland and were five together.	There Hrafn's group of five took up position on the headland, they were five together.
Þeir váru þar með Hrafni frændr hans, Grímr ok Óláfr.	They were there with Hrafn kinsmen his, Grim and Olaf.	Hrafn was there with his kinsmen Grim and Olaf.
Ok er þeir mættust, þá mælti Gunnlaugr: "Þat er nú vel, er vit höfum fundizt".	And as they met, then spoke Gunnlaug: "It is now well, that we have met".	And as they met, then Gunnlaug spoke: "It is now well, that we have met".
Hrafn kvaðst þat ekki lasta mundu, "ok er nú kostr, hvárr er þú vill", segir Hrafn, "at vér berimst allir eða vit tveir, ok sé jafnmargir hvárir".	Hrafn said that not blame should, "And is now choice, where as you wish", said Hrafn, "that we fight all or with two, and so equal-many each".	Hrafn said that he had no blame with it, "And now is your choice, where as you wish", said Hrafn, "that we will all fight, as two, but either side must be equal".
Gunnlaugi kveðst vel líka, hvárt at heldr er.	Gunnlaug said well liked, either as rather was.	Gunnlaug said he liked either.
Þá mæltu þeir frændr Hrafns, Grímr ok Óláfr, kváðust eigi vilja standa hjá, er þeir berðist.	Then spoke they kinsmen Hrafn's, Grim and Olaf, said not willed stand beside, as they fought.	Then Hrafn's kinsmen spoke, Grim and Olaf said they did not wish to stand beside as they fought.
Svá mælti ok Þorkell svarti, frændi Gunnlaugs.	So spoke and Thorkell the-Black, kinsman Gunnlaug's.	So spoke also Thorkell the Black and Gunnlaug's kinsmen.
Þá mælti Gunnlaugr við leiðtogana jarls: "Þit skuluð sitja hjá ok veita hvárigum ok vera til frásagnar um fund várn".	Then spoke Gunnlaug with guides earl's: "You should sitting beside and grant neither and be to from-saying about meeting ours".	Then Gunnlaug spoke with the earl's guides: "You should sit beside and grant neither side, and be there to say about our meeting".
Ok svá gerðu þeir.	And so did they.	And so they did.
Síðan gengust þeir at, börðust frækniga allir.	Since went they to, fought bravely all.	Afterwards they went to, and all fought bravely.
Þeir Grímr ok Óláfr gengu báðir í mót Gunnlaugi einum, ok lauk svá þeira viðskipti, at hann drap þá báða, en hann varð ekki sárr.	They Grim and Olaf went both to meet Gunnlaug one, and ended so they exchanged, that he killed them both, and he became not wounded.	Grim and Olaf both went to meet Gunnlaug as one, and their exchange ended so that he killed them both, and he did not become wounded.

The Saga of Gunnlaug Serpent-Tongue (Old Norse)

Old Norse	Literal	English
Þetta sannar Þórðr Kolbeinsson í kvæði því, er hann orti um Gunnlaug ormstungu:	This true Thord son-of-Kolbein in poem because, that he wrote about Gunnlaug Serpent-Tongue's:	Thord Kolbeinsson confirms this in the poem that he wrote about Gunnlaug Serpent-Tongue:
Hlóð, áðr Hrafni næði, hugreifum Óleifi, Göndlar þeys ok Grími Gunnlaugr hjörvi þunnum. Hann varð hvatra manna, hugmóðr, drifinn blóði, Ullr réð ýta falli unnviggs, bani þriggja.	Destroyed, before Hrafn neared, Courageous Olaf, Cock dashing, and Grim, Gunnlaug struck heavily. He quickly became a man, Spirit mother, driven by blood, Ullr ruled pushed fall Down, bane three.	Destroyed, before Hrafn neared, Courageous Olaf, Cock dashing, and Grim, Gunnlaug struck heavily. He quickly became a man, Spirit mother, driven by blood, Ullr ruled pushed fall Down, bane three.
Þeir Hrafn sóttust meðan ok Þorkell svarti, frændi Gunnlaugs, ok fell Þorkell fyrir Hrafni ok lét líf sitt, ok allir fellu förunautar þeira at lyktum.	They Hrafn fought meanwhile and Thorkell the-Black, kinsman Gunnlaug, and fell Thorkell for Hrafn and lay life his, and all fell companions theirs in the end.	Meanwhile, Hrafn and Thorkell the Black, Gunnlaug's kinsman, were fighting, and Thorkell fell before Hrafn and laid his life, and all of their companions fell in the end.
Ok þá börðust þeir tveir með stórum höggum ok öruggum atgangi, er hvárr veitti öðrum, ok sóttust einart í ákafa.	And then fought they two with great blows and fearlessly to-running, as were given other, and attended resolute in extremely.	Then the two of them fought with great blows, and running fearlessly, and each gave the other, and fought alone fiercely.
Gunnlaugr hafði þá sverðit Aðalráðsnaut, ok var þat it bazta vápn.	Gunnlaug had then sword Æthelred-gift, and was it the best weapon.	Gunnlaug then had the sword that Æthelred had given him, and it was the best weapon.
Gunnlaugr hjó þá um síðir til Hrafns mikit högg með sverðinu ok undan Hrafni fótinn.	Gunnlaug struck then about eventually to Hrafn's much striking with sword and under Hrafn leg.	Gunnlaug then eventually struck at Hrafn, striking with his sword under Hrafn's leg.
Hrafn fell þó eigi at heldr ok hnekkði þá at stofni einum ok studdi þar á stúfinum.	Hrafn fell though not that held and over-turned then to strain one and stood there of stump.	Hrafn fell but did not overturn, and dropped back on to a tree stump, and stood there.
Þá mælti Gunnlaugr: "Nú ertu óvígr", segir hann, "ok vil ek eigi lengr berjast við þik, örkumlaðan mann".	Then spoke Gunnlaug: "Now are-you not-fighting", said he, "and wish I not longer fight with you, crippled man".	Then Gunnlaug spoke: "Now you are not fighting", he said, "and I no longer wish to fight with a crippled man".

The Saga of Gunnlaug Serpent-Tongue (Old Norse)

Old Norse	Literal	English
Hrafn svaraði: "Svá er þat", segir hann, "at mjök hefir á leikizt minn hluta, en þó myndi mér enn vel duga, ef ek fenga at drekka nökkut".	Hrafn answered: "So it is", said he, "that much had of played mine lot, and though should me still well help, if I get to drink something".	Hrafn answered: "So it is", he said, "that much has my lot played out, and though I should still be well, if I could get something to drink".
Gunnlaugr svarar: "Svík mik þá eigi", segir hann, "ef ek færi þér vatn í hjálmi mínum".	Gunnlaug answered: "Betray me then not", said he, "if I journey to-you water in helmet mine".	Gunnlaug answered: "Do not betray me then", he said, "if I journey to bring you water in my helmet".
Hrafn svarar: "Eigi mun ek svíkja þik", segir hann.	Hrafn answered: "Not should I betray you", said he.	Hrafn answered: "I should betray you", he said.
Síðan gekk Gunnlaugr til lækjar eins ok sótti í hjálminum ok færði Hrafni, en hann seildist í mót inni vinstri hendinni, en hjó í höfuð Gunnlaugi með sverðinu inni hægri hendi, ok varð þat allmikit sár.	Then went Gunnlaug to stream likewise and attended in helmet and took Hrafn, and he stretched to meet the left hand, and struck to hand Gunnlaug's with sword the right hand, and became that all-much wounded.	Then Gunnlaug went to a stream, and got water in his helmet and took it to Hrafn, and as he stretched out to meet his left hand, he struck at Gunnlaug with the sword in his right hand, and there he became very much wounded.
Þá mælti Gunnlaugr: "Illa sveiktu mik nú, ok ódrengiliga fór þér, þar sem ek trúða þér".	Then spoke Gunnlaug: "Badly tricked me now, and un-fellow-like fared you, there as I trusted you".	Then Gunnlaug spoke: "You have tricked me badly now, and in an unmanly way, there as I trusted you".
Hrafn svarar: "Satt er þat", segir hann, "en þat gekk mér til þess, at ek ann þér eigi faðmlagsins Helgu innar fögru".	Hrafn answered: "True is that", said he, "and that goes me to this, that I love you not embrace Helga the Fair".	Hrafn answered: "That is true", he said, "and I did this so that you will not love the embrace of Helga the Fair".
Ok þá börðust þeir enn í ákafa.	And then fought they still in extremely.	And then they fought in the extreme.
En svá lauk at lykðum, at Gunnlaugr bar af Hrafni, ok lét Hrafn þar líf sitt.	And so ended to completion, that Gunnlaug bore of Hrafn, and lay Hrafn there life his.	And so in the end it was finished, that Gunnlaug overpowered Hrafn, and there Hrafn lay down his life.
Þá gengu fram leiðtogar jarlsins ok bundu höfuðsárit Gunnlaugs.	They went from guides earl's and bound head-wound Gunnlaug's.	Then the earl's guides went and bound Gunnlaug's head wound.

The Saga of Gunnlaug Serpent-Tongue (Old Norse)

Old Norse	Literal	English
Hann sat þá meðan ok kvað þá vísu þessa:	He sat then meanwhile and said then verse this:	Meanwhile he sat and said this verse:
Oss gekk mætr á móti mótrunnr í dyn spjóta, hríðgervandi hjörva, Hrafn framliga jafnan. Hér varð mörg í morgin malmflaug of Gunnlaugi, hergerðandi, á Hörða, hringþollr, nesi Dinga.	Us went measure of meet Against-running in storm spear, Aggravating sword, Hrafn from-like equal. Here was many to morning Metal-missile about Gunnlaug, Ranks, of hard, Ring-endurance, headland Dinge.	We went to measure in meeting, Against running storm spear, Aggravating sword, Hrafn from like equal, Here were many this morning, Metal missile about Gunnlaug, Ranks, of hard, Ring endurance, headland Dinge.
Síðan bjuggu þeir um dauða menn ok færðu Gunnlaug á hest sinn eftir þat ok kómust með hann allt ofan í Lifangr.	Since settled they about death men and went Gunnlaug of Horse his after that and came with he all over to Levanger.	Afterwards they saw to the dead men, and Gunnlaug travelled on his horse after that, and the men came with him to Levanger.
Ok þar lá hann þrjár nætr ok fekk alla þjónustu af presti ok andaðist síðan ok var þar jarðaðr at kirkju.	And there laid he three nights and got all service of priest and ended after and was there earthed at church.	And there he lay for three nights, and got a service from the priest, and died, afterwards he was buried there at the church.
Öllum þótti mikill skaði at um hvárntveggja þeira, Gunnlaug ok Hrafn, með þeim atburðum, sem varð um líflát þeira.	All thought great harm that about either-side theirs, Gunnlaug and Hrafn, with them events, as became about loss theirs.	Everyone thought it was a great harm on either side, Gunnlaug and Hrafn, with the events, that became their loss.
13	13	13
Ok um sumarit, áðr þessi tíðendi spurðust út hingat til Íslands, þá dreymði Illuga svarta, ok var hann þá heima á Gilsbakka.	And about summer, before these tidings learned back-from there to Iceland, then dreamed Illugi the-Black, and was he then home of Gilsbakka.	That summer, before this news was learned back in Iceland, then Illugi the Black dreamed that he was at home in Gilsbakka.
Honum þótti Gunnlaugr at sér koma í svefninum ok var blóðugr mjök ok kvað vísu þessa fyrir honum í svefninum.	He thought Gunnlaug that himself came in sleep and was bloodied much and said verse this for him in sleep.	He thought that Gunnlaug himself came in his sleep, and was much bloodied, and said this verse for him in his sleep.

The Saga of Gunnlaug Serpent-Tongue (Old Norse)

Old Norse	Literal	English
Illugi munði vísuna, er hann vaknaði, ok kvað síðan fyrir öðrum:	Illugi remembered verse, as he awoke, and said since before others:	Illugi remembered this verse, as he awoke, and said afterwards before others:
Vissak Hrafn, en Hrafni hvöss kom egg í leggi, hjaltugguðum höggva hrynfiski mik brynju, þás hræskæri hlýra hlaut fen ari benja. Klauf gunnsproti Gunnar Gunnlaugs höfuð runna.	Know Hrafn, and Hrafn Sharp came ridge in leg, Hilt-chewed strike Caved-fish me armour, Then corpse-scorer warm Got fens eagle wound. Cleaved war-twig Gunnar Gunnlaug hand round.	I know Hrafn, and Hrafn Sharp came ridge in leg, Hilt chewed strike, Caved fish me armour, Then corpse scorer warm, Got fens eagle wound, Cleaved war twig Gunnar, Gunnlaug hand round.
Sá atburðr varð suðr at Mosfelli ina sömu nátt, at Önund dreymði, at Hrafn kæmi at honum ok var allr alblóðugr.	So event was south at Mosfell the same night, that Onund dreamed, that Hrafn came to him and was all -bloodied.	So it became that south at Mosfell that same night, that Onund dreamed that Hrafn came to him and was all bloodied.
Hann kvað vísu þessa:	He said verse this:	He said this verse:
Roðit vas sverð, en sverða sverð-Rögnir mik gerði. Váru reynd í röndum randgölkn fyr ver handan. Blóðug hykk í blóði blóðgögl of skör stóðu. Sárfíkinn hlaut sára sárgammr enn á þramma.	Reddened was sword, and sword sword-reddened me made. Were resolved in shield Giants for were beyond. Bloodied mind to blood Blood-goslings about fragile standing. Wound-eager got wound Wound-vulture still of trample.	Reddened was sword, and sword Sword reddened me made. Were resolved in shield Giants for were beyond. Bloodied mind to blood Blood goslings about fragile standing. Wound eager got wound Wound vulture still of trample.
Ok um sumarit annat eftir á alþingi mælti Illugi svarti til Önundar at Lögbergi: "Hverju villtu bæta mér son minn", sagði hann, "er Hrafn, sonr þinn, sveik hann í tryggðum?"	And about summer next after of assembly spoke Illugi the-Black to Onund at Law-Rock: "How will-you compensate me son mine", said he, "as Hrafn, son yours, betrayed him in loyalty?"	And about next summer after the assembly, Illugi the Black spoke to Onund at the Law Rock: "How will you compensate me for my son", he said, "as Hrafn your son betrayed him in loyalty?"
Önundr svarar: "Fjarkominn þykkist ek til þess", sagði hann, "at bæta hann, svá sárt sem ek helt á þeira fundi.	Onund answered: "Far-away think I to this", said he, "that compensate he, so wounded as I held of their meeting.	Onund answered: "I think far away of this", he said, "to compensate him, so wounded as I am because of their meeting.

The Saga of Gunnlaug Serpent-Tongue (Old Norse)

Old Norse	Literal	English
Mun ek ok engra bóta beiða þik fyrir minn son."	Should I and none compensation bid you for my son".	I shall not ask for compensation from you for my son".
Illugi svarar: "Kenna skal þá nökkurr at skauti þinn frændi eða þinna ættmanna."	Illugi answered: "Know shall then anyone that fringes yours kinsman or your relatives".	Illugi answered: "Know then that anyone on the fringes of your kinsmen or your relatives shall".
Ok eftir þingit um sumarit var Illugi jafnan dapr mjök.	And remaining assembly about summer was Illugi equally depressed much.	And for the rest of the assembly and during the summer, Illugi was very much depressed.
Þat er sagt, um haustit, at Illugi reið heiman af Gilsbakka með þrjátigu manna ok kom til Mosfells snemma morguns.	That is said, about autumn, that Illugi rode home of Gilsbakka with thirty men and came to Mosfell early morning.	It is said, about autumn, that Illugi rode home from Gilsbakka with thirty men and came to Mosfell early in the morning.
Önundr komst í kirkju ok synir hans, en Illugi tók frændr hans tvá.	Onund came in church and sons his, and Illugi took kinsmen his two.	Onund and his sons came into the church, but Illugi captured two of his kinsmen.
Hét annarr Björn, en annarr Þorgrímr.	Named another Bjorn, and another Thorgrim.	One was named Bjorn, and another Thorgrim.
Hann lét drepa Björn, en fóthöggva Þorgrím.	He had kill Bjorn, and foot-striking Thorgrim.	He had Bjorn killed, and Thorgrim's foot cut off.
Reið Illugi heim eftir þat, ok varð þessa engi rétting af Önundi.	Rode Illugi home after that, and was this none righting of Onund.	Illugi rode home after that, and Onund did not seek reprisal.
Hermundr Illugason unði lítt eftir Gunnlaug, bróður sinn, ok þótti ekki hans hefnt at heldr, þótt þetta væri at gert.	Hermund son-of-Illugi satisfied little after Gunnlaug, brother his, and thought not he had that rather, though this was as done.	Hermund Illugason was very upset with Gunnlaug, about his brother, and thought that even though this had been done, he had not been avenged.
Maðr hét Hrafn ok var bróðursonr Önundar at Mosfelli.	Man named Hrafn and was brother's-son Onund at Mosfell.	There was a man named Hrafn and was Onund's brother's son at Mosfell.
Hann var farmaðr mikill ok átti skip, er uppi stóð í Hrútafirði.	He was travelling-man great and had ship, was up stood in Hrutafjord.	He was a great travelling man and had a ship, which was stood in Hrutafjord.

The Saga of Gunnlaug Serpent-Tongue (Old Norse)

Old Norse	Literal	English
Ok um várit reið Hermundr Illugason heiman einn samt ok norðr Holtavörðuheiði ok svá til Hrútafjarðar ok út á Borðeyri til skips kaupmannanna.	And about spring rode Hermund son-of-Illugi home one together and north Holtavarda-Heath and so to Hrutafjord and out-of of Bordeyri to ships trading-men's.	And about spring Hermund Illugason rode out from home on his own, and north to Holtvarda Heath, and then to Hrutafjord and out of Bordeyri to trading men's ships.
Kaupmenn váru þá búnir mjök.	Trading-men were they readying much.	The trading men had much to prepare.
Hrafn stýrimaðr var á landi ok margt manna hjá honum.	Hrafn steersman was of land and many men beside him.	Hrafn the captain was ashore and there were many men beside him.
Hermundr reið at honum ok lagði í gegnum hann spjótinu ok reið þegar í brott, en þeim varð öllum bilt, félögum Hrafns, við Hermund.	Hermund rode to him and laid to through him spear and rode then to away, and they became all startled, company Hrafn's, with Hermund.	Hermund rode to him and laid a spear through him, and then rode away, and Hrafn's company all became startled about Hermund.
Engar kómu bætr fyrir víg þetta.	None came compensation for killing this.	No compensation came for this killing.
Ok með þessu skilr skipti þeira Illuga svarta ok Önundar at Mosfelli.	And with this separated exchanges theirs Illugi the-Black and Onund at Mosfell.	And with this separated the exchanges between Illugi the Black and Onund at Mosfell.
Þorsteinn Egilsson gifti Helgu, dóttur sína, er stundir liðu fram, þeim manni, er Þorkell hét ok var Hallkelsson.	Thorstein son-of-Egil gave Helga, daughter his, when awhile passed from, that man, was Thorkell named and was son-of-Hallkel.	After a while had passed, Thorstein Egilsson gave his daughter Helga to a man that was named Thorkell, and he was the son of Hallkel.
Hann bjó út í Hraunsdal, ok fór Helga til bús með honum ok varð honum lítt unnandi, því at hon verðr aldri afhuga Gunnlaugi, þótt hann væri dauðr.	He lived out in Hraunsdal, and fared Helga to house with him and became him little loved, because that she became never out-of-mind Gunnlaug, though he was dead.	He lived out in Hraunsdal, and Helga travelled home with him, and he became little loved, because she never got Gunnlaug out of her mind, though he was dead.
En Þorkell var þó vaskr maðr at sér ok auðigr at fé ok skáld gott.	But Thorkell was thought bold man as himself and rich in wealth and poet good.	But Thorkell was thought a bold man, as he himself was rich in wealth and a good poet.

The Saga of Gunnlaug Serpent-Tongue (Old Norse)

Old Norse	Literal	English
Þau áttu börn saman eigi allfá.	They had children together not few.	They had children together, not few.
Þórarinn hét sonr þeira ok Þorsteinn, ok enn fleiri börn áttu þau.	Thorarin named son theirs and Thorstein, and still more children had They.	Their sons were named Thorarin and Thorstein, and they still had more children.
Þat var helzt gaman Helgu, at hon rekði skikkjuna Gunnlaugsnaut ok horfði þar á löngum.	That was rather enjoyed Helga, that she unfolded cloak Gunnlaug's-gift and looked there of long.	It was Helga's greatest pleasure to unfold the cloak that Gunnlaug had given her, and she looked long at it.
Ok eitt sinn kom þar sótt mikil á bæ þeira Þorkels ok Helgu, ok krömðust margir lengi.	And once then came there sickness much of dwelling there Thorkell and Helga, and chronic-illness many long.	And one time there came a great sickness in the home of Thorkell and Helga, and many people suffered long with it.
Helga tók þá ok þyngð ok lá þó eigi.	Helga took then and heavy and laying though not.	Helga then took and heavily, but did not lay with it.
Ok einn laugaraftan sat Helga í eldaskála ok hneigði höfuð í kné Þorkatli, bónda sínum, ok lét senda eftir skikkjunni Gunnlaugsnaut.	And one Saturday-afternoon sat Helga in cooking-hut and inclined head in knee Thorkell, husband hers, and let send after cloak Gunnlaug's-gift.	And one Saturday afternoon, Helga sat in the cooking hut, resting her head in her husband Thorkell's lap, and had sent for Gunnlaug's cloak gift.
Ok er skikkjan kom til hennar, þá settist hon upp ok rakði skikkjuna fyrir sér ok horfði á um stund.	And as cloak came to her, then sat she up and unfolded cloak for herself and looked of about awhile.	And as the cloak came to her, then she sat up and unfolded the cloak for herself and look at it for a while.
Ok síðan hné hon aftr í fang bónda sínum ok var þá örend.	And then sank her back in arms husband hers and was then dead.	And then she fell back into her husband's arms, and then was dead.
Þorkell kvað þá vísu þessa:	Thorkell said then verse this:	Thorkell said this verse:
Lagðak orms at armi arms góða mér tróðu, goð brá Lofnar lífi líns, andaða mína. þó 's beiðöndum bíða bliks þungara miklu.	Laid serpent to arms Arms good to-me trod, God drew praised live Linen, ended mine. Thought was waited-end bid Gleam heavy much.	Laid serpent to arms, Arms good to me trod, God drew praised life Linen, ended mine. Thought was waited end bid, Gleam heavy much.

The Saga of Gunnlaug Serpent-Tongue (Old Norse)

Old Norse	Literal	English
Helga var til kirkju færð, en Þorkell bjó þar eftir ok þótti allmikit fráfall Helgu, sem ván var at.	Helga was to church carried, and Thorkell lived there after and thought all-much death Helga, which looked was to.	Helga was carried to church, and Thorkell lived there after and thought much about the death of Helga, which was expected.
Ok lýkr þar nú sögunni.	And ends there now the-saga.	And now there ends the saga.

The Saga of Gunnlaug Serpent-Tongue (Old Icelandic)

Old Icelandic	Literal	English
1	1	1
Þorsteinn hét maður.	Thorstein was-named a-man.	There was a man named Thorstein
Hann var Egilsson, Skalla-Grímssonar, Kveld-Úlfssonar hersis úr Noregi en Ásgerður hét móðir Þorsteins og var Bjarnardóttir.	He was son-of-Egil, son-of-Skalla-Grim, son-of-Kveld-Ulf local-leader from Norway and Asgerd named mother Thorstein's and was daughter-of-Bjorn.	He was the son of Egil, the son of Skalla Grim, son of Kveld Ulf the local leader from Norway, and Thorstein's mother was named Asgerd, the daughter of Bjorn.
Þorsteinn bjó að Borg í Borgarfirði.	Thorstein lived at Borg in Borgafjord.	Thorstein lived at Borg in Borgafjord.
Hann var auðigur að fé og höfðingi mikill, vitur maður og hógvær og hófsmaður um alla hluti.	He was rich of wealth and leader great, wise man and moderate and modest about all things.	He was rich in wealth and a great leader, a wise man and humble and moderate in all things.
Engi var hann afreksmaður um vöxt eða afl sem Egill faðir hans því að svo er sagt af fróðum mönnum að Egill hafi mestur kappi verið á Íslandi og hólmgöngumaður og mest ætlað af bóndasonum, fræðimaður var hann og mikill og manna vitrastur.	None was he accomplished about growth or strength as Egil father his because as so is said of learned people that Egil had greatest warrior been of Iceland and duelling-man and most intended of farmer's-sons, scholar was he and great and man wisest.	He was not as accomplished in size or strength as his father Egil because it is said by learned people that Egil had been the greatest warrior and duelling man of Iceland, and the most promising man of farmer's sons, as well as a great scholar and the wisest of men.
Þorsteinn var og hið mesta afarmenni og vinsæll af allri alþýðu.	Thorstein was also the most outstanding-man and popular of all people.	Thorstein was also the most outstanding and popular man of all people.
Þorsteinn var vænn maður, hvítur á hár og eygur manna best.	Thorstein was handsome man, white of hair and eyes man's best.	Thorstein was a handsome man, with white hair, and the best eyes of men.
Svo segja fróðir menn að margir í ætt Mýramanna, þeir sem frá Egli eru komnir, hafi verið menn vænstir en það sé þó mjög sundurgreinilegt því að sumir í þeirri ætt er kallað að ljótastir menn hafi verið.	So say wise men that many of descendents Myrar, they who from Egil were came, had been people expected but that so thought many asunder-mixed because that some of their descendents were called the ugliest people had been.	Wise men say that the Myrar folk, the family descended from Egil, were men of expectation, but people thought differently that they were mixed because some of their descendants were called the ugliest people.

The Saga of Gunnlaug Serpent-Tongue (Old Icelandic)

Old Icelandic	Literal	English
Í þeirri ætt hafa og verið margir atgervismenn um marga hluti sem var Kjartan Ólafsson pá og Víga-Barði og Skúli Þorsteinsson.	Among their descendents have also been many talented-people about many things that were Kjartan son-of-Olaf Peacock and Viga-Bardi and Skuli son-of-Thorstein.	Among their descendents have also been many people talented in many things, such as Kjartan, the son of Olaf Peacock and Viga-Bardi, and Skuli, the son of Thorstein.
Sumir voru og skáldmenn miklir í þeirri ætt, Björn Hítdælakappi, Einar prestur Skúlason, Snorri Sturluson og margir aðrir.	Some were also poets great among their descendents, Bjorn Hitardal-champion, Einar priest Skulason, Snorri Sturluson and many others.	There were also some poets among their descendents, Bjorn the champion of the Hitardal people, the priest Einar Skulason, Snorri Sturluson and many others.
Þorsteinn átti Jófríði Gunnarsdóttur Hlífarsonar.	Thorstein married Jofrid daughter-of-Gunnar son-of-Hlifar.	Thorstein married Jofrid, the daughter of Gunnar, the son of Hlifar.
Gunnar hefir best vígur verið og mestur fimleikamaður verið á Íslandi af búandmönnum, annar Gunnar að Hlíðarenda, þriðji Steinþór á Eyri.	Gunnar had best spear-man been and greatest athletic-man had-been in Iceland of settling-people, another Gunnar of Hlidarendi, third Steinthor of Eyri.	Gunnar had been the best warrior and the greatest athlete in Iceland among the settlers, the second was Gunnar at Hlíðarendur, and the third was Steinþór at Eyri.
Jófríður var átján vetra er Þorsteinn fékk hennar.	Jofrid was eighteen winters when Thorstein married her.	Jofrid was eighteen winters old when Thorstein married her.
Hún var ekkja.	She was widow.	She was a widow.
Hana hafði átt fyrr Þóroddur son Tungu-Odds og var þeirra dóttir Húngerður er þar fæddist upp að Borg með Þorsteini.	She had married before Thorodd son Tunga-Odd's and was their daughter Hungerd was there fostered up at Borg with Thorstein.	She had previously married Thorodd, the son of Tunga-Odd, and their daughter Hungerd was fostered with Thorstein at Borg.
Jófríður var skörungur mikill.	Jofrid was noble great.	Jofrid was very much noble.
Þau Þorsteinn áttu mart barna en þó koma fá við þessa sögu.	Then Thorstein had many children and though came few with this saga.	Then Thorstein had many children, but few of them came into this saga.
Skúli var elstur sona þeirra, annar Kollsveinn, þriðji Egill.	Skuli was oldest son theirs, another Kollsveinn, third Egil.	Skuli was their oldest son, the second was Kollsveinn, the third was Egil.

The Saga of Gunnlaug Serpent-Tongue (Old Icelandic)

Old Icelandic	Literal	English
Eitt sumar er það sagt að skip kom af hafi í Gufárós.	One summer was it said that ship came of sea in Gufua.	One summer it was said that a ship came ashore in Gufua.
Bergfinnur er nefndur stýrimaður fyrir skipinu, norrænn að ætt, auðigur að fé og heldur við aldur.	Bergfinn was named steersman for ship, Norwegian of ancestry, rich of wealth and advanced with age.	The captain of the ship was named Bergfinn, a Norwegian by ancestry, rich in wealth and old aged.
Hann var vitur maður.	He was wise man.	He was a wise man.
Þorsteinn bóndi reið til skips og réð jafnan mestu hver kaupstefna var og svo var enn.	Thorstein farmer rode to ships and decided usually most whose trading-posts were and so was still.	Thorstein the farmer rode to the ships and usually decided most of where trading posts were, and it was the same this time.
Austmenn vistuðust en Þorsteinn tók við stýrimanninum fyrir því að hann beiddist þangað.	Easterners found-a-place but Thorstein took with steersman for because that he invited there.	The easterners found themselves lodgings, and Thorstein took in the captain, because he had invited him there.
Bergfinnur var fátalaður of veturinn en Þorsteinn veitti honum vel.	Bergfinn was quiet about winter but Thorstein provided-for him well.	Bergfinn was quiet during the winter, and Thorstein provided for him well.
Austmaðurinn henti mikið gaman að draumum.	Eastern-man gave much enjoyment to dreams.	The easterner was very interested in dreams.
Um vorið einn dag ræddi Þorsteinn um við Bergfinn ef hann vildi ríða með honum upp undir Valfell.	About spring one day discussed-with Thorstein about with Bergfinn if he wished ride with him up to Valfell.	One day in the spring, Thorstein discussed with Bergfinn, if he would like to ride with him up to Valfell.
Þar var þá þingstöð þeirra Borgfirðinga en Þorsteini var sagt að fallnir væru búðarveggir hans.	There was then assembly-post theirs Borgafjord-people but Thorstein was told that fallen were booth-walls his.	There was an assembly of the Borgafjord people. Then Thorstein said that the walls of his booth had fallen in.
Austmaðurinn kveðst það víst vilja og riðu þeir heiman of daginn þrír saman og húskarl Þorsteins þar til er þeir koma upp undir Valfell til bæjar þess er að Grenjum heitir.	Eastern-man said that certain willed and rode they home about days three together and servant Thorstein's there to that they came up to Valfell to farm this was to Grenjar called.	The easterner said that he certainly would like to, and they rode from his home for about three days, together with Thorstein's servant, so that they came to Valfell, where there was a farm named Grenjar.
Þar bjó einn maður félítill er Atli hét.	There lived a man poor was Atli called.	There lived a poor man who was named Atli.

The Saga of Gunnlaug Serpent-Tongue (Old Icelandic)

Old Icelandic	Literal	English
Hann var landseti Þorsteins og beiddi Þorsteinn Atla að hann færi til starfs með þeim og hefði pál og reku.	He was tenant Thorstein's and asked Thorstein Atli that he journey to work with them and have hoe and shovel.	He was a tenant of Thorstein's, and Thorstein asked Atli, that he journey to work with them and bring a hoe and a shovel.
Hann gerði svo.	He did so.	He did so.
Og er þeir koma til búðartóftanna þá tóku þeir til starfs allir og færðu út veggina.	And when they came to booth-ruins then took they to work all and went out-of walls.	And when they came up to Valfell to the booth ruins, then they took to work digging out the walls.
Veðrið var heitt af sólu.	Weather was hot of sun.	The weather was hot with the sun.
Og er þeir höfðu út fært veggina þá settist Þorsteinn niður og Austmaður í búðartóftina og sofnaði Þorsteinn og lét illa í svefni.	And as they had out-of gone walls there sat Thorstein down and Eastern-man in booth and slept Thorstein and lay badly in sleep.	And when they had finished digging out the booths, Thorstein and the easterner sat down in the booth, and Thorstein slept, but his sleep was uneasy.
Austmaður sat hjá honum og lét hann njóta draums síns.	Eastern-man sat beside him and let him enjoy dreams his.	The easterner sat beside him and let him enjoy his dreams.
Og er hann vaknaði var honum erfitt orðið.	And when he awoke was he difficult of-words.	And when he awoke, he found it hard to speak.
Austmaður spurði hvað hann hefði dreymt er hann lét svo illa í svefni.	Eastern-man asked what he had dreamt that he laid so badly in sleep.	The easterner asked what he had dreamt, since he lay so badly in his sleep.
Þorsteinn svaraði: "Ekki er mark að draumum".	Thorstein answered: "Nothing is proof of dreams".	Thorstein answered: "Dreams don't mean anything".
Og er þeir riðu heim um kveldið þá spyr Austmaður hvað Þorstein hefði dreymt.	And as they riding home about evening then asked Eastern-man what Thorstein had dreamt.	And as they rode home that evening, then the easterner asked what Thorstein had dreamt.
Þorsteinn svarar: "Ef eg segi þér drauminn þá skaltu ráða hann sem hann er til".	Thorstein answered: "If I say to-you dream then shall-you advise it as it is to".	Thorstein said: "If I say to you what I dreamt, you must advise what it really means".
Austmaður kveðst á það hætta mundu.	Eastern-man said to that risk would.	The easterner said he would risk it.

The Saga of Gunnlaug Serpent-Tongue (Old Icelandic)

Old Icelandic	Literal	English
Þorsteinn mælti þá: "Það dreymdi mig að eg þóttist heima vera að Borg og úti fyrir karldyrum og sá eg upp á húsin og á mæninum álft eina væna og fagra og þóttist eg eiga og þótti mér allgóð.	Thorstein spoke then: "The dream mine that I thought home was at Borg and out before man-door and looked I above the house and at roof-ridge swan one kind and fair and thought I owned and thought me all-good.	Thorstein then spoke: "I dreamt that I thought I was home at Borg, standing by the main door, and I looked up at the house, and I saw a fine, beautiful swan up on the roof ridge, and I thought that I owned her, and I was very pleased with her.
Þá sá eg fljúga ofan frá fjöllunum örn mikinn.	Then saw I flying over from the-mountains eagle great.	Then I saw a great eagle flying over from the mountains.
Hann fló hingað og settist hjá álftinni og klakaði við hana blíðlega og hún þótti mér það vel þekkjast.	He flew here and sat beside the-swan and chattered with her gently and she seemed to-me that well familiar.	He flew here and sat beside the swan and chatted with her happily, and she seemed to be pleased with that.
Þá sá eg að örninn var svarteygur og járnklær voru á honum.	Then saw I that eagle was black-eyed and iron-claws were of him.	Then I looked at the eagle, and it had black eyes and iron claws.
Vasklegur sýndist mér hann.	Bold seemed to-me him.	He seemed to me to be very bold.
Því næst sá eg fljúga annan fugl af suðurátt.	Then next saw I flying another bird from the-south.	Because next I saw another bird flying from the south.
Sá fló hingað til Borgar og settist á húsin hjá álftinni og vildi þýðast hana.	So flew here to Borg and sat on the-house beside the-swan and wished join her.	I saw it fly here to Borg, and sit on the house beside the swan, and it wanted to join her.
Það var og örn mikill.	That was and eagle great.	It was a great eagle.
Brátt þótti mér sá örninn er fyrir var ýfast mjög er hinn kom til og þeir börðust snarplega og lengi og það sá eg að hvorumtveggja blæddi.	Soon thought I so the-eagle that before was ruffled much that he came to and they fought sharply and long and this saw I that both bled.	It soon looked to me like the eagle that came before was very much ruffled, and came towards him, and they fought viciously for a long time, and they were both bleeding.
Og svo lauk þeirra leik að sinn veg hné hvor þeirra af húsmæninum og voru þá báðir dauðir en álftin sat eftir hnipin mjög og dapurleg.	And so ended their sport that they fell sank where they of house-roof-ridge and there they both died but the-swan sat remaining dejected much and sad.	And so ended their sport, that they both fell from the roof of the house, and then they were both dead, and the swan remained sitting, dejected and very sad.
Og þá sá eg fljúga fugl úr vestri.	And then saw I flying bird from the-west.	And then I saw a bird flying from the west.

The Saga of Gunnlaug Serpent-Tongue (Old Icelandic)

Old Icelandic	Literal	English
Það var valur.	It was falcon.	That was a falcon.
Hann settist hjá álftinni og lét blítt við hana og síðan flugu þau í brott bæði samt í sömu átt og þá vaknaði eg.	He sat beside the-swan and lay gently with her and since flew they to away both together in same direction and then awoke I.	He sat beside the swan and he was gentle towards her, and afterwards they both flew away together in the same direction, and then I woke up.
Og er draumur þessi ómerkilegur", segir hann, "og mun vera fyrir veðrum að þau mætast í lofti úr þeim áttum er mér þóttu fuglarnir fljúga".	And was dream this un-marked-like", said he, "and should be therefore winds that they meet in the-sky from those directions that I thought the-birds flew".	And this dream was unremarkable", he said, "and must be to do with the winds, which meet in the sky from different directions, that the birds were flying from".
Austmaður segir: "Ekki er það mín ætlan", segir hann, "að svo sé".	Eastern-man said: "Not is that my supposing", said he, "that so say".	The easterner said: "I don't think that's what it's about", he said, "as I see it".
Þorsteinn mælti: "Ger af drauminum slíkt er þér sýnist líklegast og lát mig heyra".	Thorstein spoke: "Make of the-dream such as you seem likely and let me hear".	Thorstein then spoke: "Make of the dream what you think is likely, and let me hear".
Austmaður mælti: "Fuglar þeir munu vera stórra manna fylgjur en húsfreyja þín er eigi heil og mun hún fæða meybarn frítt og fagurt og munt þú unna því mikið.	Eastern-man spoke: "Birds they shall be great men followers and housewife yours is not well and will she give-birth baby-girl free and beautiful and shall you love therefore much.	The easterner spoke: "The birds must be the followers of important men". When your housewife is with child, she will give birth to a baby girl, free and fair, and you will love her very much".
En göfgir menn munu biðja dóttur þinnar úr þeim áttum sem þér þóttu ernirnir fljúga að og leggja á hana ofurást og berjast of hana og látast báðir af því efni.	Then noble men shall propose-to daughter yours from those directions, as to-you thought the-eagles flew from, and lay to her love and fight about her and die both of therefore prospects.	Then noble men shall propose to your daughter from those directions, that you thought the eagles flew from, and propose to her, and fight over her, and both of them shall die".
Og því næst mun hinn þriðji maður biðja hennar úr þeirri átt er valurinn fló að og þeim mun hún gift vera.	And therefore next should then third man propose to-her from there direction, that falcon flew from, and then should she married become.	And then next a third man will propose to her from the direction that the falcon flew from, and then shall she become married.
Nú hefi eg þýddan draum þinn.	Now have I translated dream yours.	Now I have translated your dream.
Eg hygg eftir mun ganga".	I think along shall go".	And I think that is how it will go".

The Saga of Gunnlaug Serpent-Tongue (Old Icelandic)

Old Icelandic	Literal	English
Þorsteinn svarar: "Illa er draumur ráðinn og óvingjarnlega", sagði hann, "og munt þú ekki drauma ráða kunna".	Thorstein answered: "Wicked is dream determined and unfriendly", said he, "and should you not dreams advise to-know".	Thorstein answered: "Your interpretation of the dream is bad and unfriendly", he said, "and you cannot know to advise".
Austmaður svarar: "Þú munt að raun um komast hversu eftir gengur".	Eastern-man answered: "you shall that see about comes how-so after it-goes".	The easterner answered: "You shall see how it comes about, with what goes after".
Þorsteinn lagði fæð á Austmanninn og fór hann á brott um sumarið og er hann nú úr sögunni.	Thorstein took-to sadness of Eastern-man, and fared he of away about summer, and is he now out-of the-saga.	Thorstein began to dislike the easterner, and he travelled away in the summer, and he is now out of the saga.
3	3	3
Um sumarið bjóst Þorsteinn til þings og mælti til Jófríðar húsfreyju áður hann fór heiman: "Svo er háttað", segir hann, "að þú ert með barni og skal það barn út bera ef þú fæðir meybarn en upp fæða ef sveinn er".	About summer prepared Thorstein to the-assembly and spoke to Jofrid housewife, before he travelled-from home: "So is the-way", said he, "that you are with child, and shall that child out born, if you give-birth-to baby-girl, then up give-birth, if boy is".	About summertime, Thorstein prepared to go to the assembly, and spoke to his wife Jofrid, before he travelled from home: "So it will be", said he, "that you are with child, and if the child born is a baby girl, then it must be given up to die, but if it is a boy, it will be brought up".
Og það var þá siðvandi nokkur er land var allt alheiðið að þeir menn er félitlir voru en stóð ómegð mjög til handa létu út bera börn sín og þótti þó illa gert ávallt.	And that was then custom something-of, when land was all -heathen, that the people, who poor were, and stood without much to hand, laid out born children theirs, and thought though badly done always.	And that was the custom, when the land was all heathen, that people who were poor without much to hand, laid outside their born children, though it was always thought a bad thing to do.
Og er Þorsteinn hafði þetta mælt þá svarar Jófríður: "Þetta er óþínslega mælt", segir hún, "slíkur maður sem þú ert og mun þér eigi sýnast þetta að láta gera svo auðigur maður sem þú ert".	And when Thorstein had this said, then answered Jofrid: "This is unhealthily spoken", said she, "such man as you are, and should you not appear this to let be-done, so wealthy man as you are".	And when Thorstein had said this, then Jofrid answered: "This is most unworthily said", she said, "that a man such as you, should appear to allow this to be done, wealthy man that you are".
Þorsteinn svarar: "Veist þú skaplyndi mitt", segir hann, "að eigi mun hlýðisamt verða ef af er brugðið".	Thorstein answered: "Know you temper mine", said he, "that not should obedient be, if out-of is brought".	Thorstein answered: "You know my temper", he said, "if obedience is brought out".

The Saga of Gunnlaug Serpent-Tongue (Old Icelandic)

Old Icelandic	Literal	English
Síðan reið hann til þings en Jófríður fæddi meðan meybarn ákafa fagurt.	Afterwards rode he to assembly, and Jofrid bore meanwhile baby-girl extremely beautiful.	Afterwards he rode to the assembly, and meanwhile Jofrid gave birth to an extremely beautiful baby girl.
Konur vildu það bera að henni en hún kvað þess litla þörf og lét þangað kalla smalamann sinn er Þorvarður hét og mælti hún: "Hest minn skaltu taka og leggja söðul á og færa barn þetta vestur í Hjarðarholt Þorgerði Egilsdóttur og bið hana upp fæða með leynd svo að Þorsteinn verði ei var við.	Women wanted to carry to her but she said this little need and let from-there call shepherd he was Thorvard called and spoke she: "Horse mine shall-you take and lay saddle to and take child this west to Hjardarholt Thorgerd daughter-of-Egil and ask her up feed with secrecy so that Thorstein will-be not where known.	The women wanted to carry the child to Jofrid, but she said there was little need, and had her shepherd whose name was Thorvard, brought to her, and she spoke: "You shall take my horse and saddle it, and take this child west to Hjardarholt, to Thorgerd, daughter of Egil, and ask her to foster her in secrecy, so that Thorstein will not be not be aware of it.
Og þeim ástaraugum renni eg til barns þessa að víst eigi nenni eg að það sé út borið.	And those lovely-eyes run I to child this that know not care I to that see out carried.	And my loving eyes look over the child, such that I care not to carry it out to die.
En hér eru þrjár merkur silfurs er þú skalt hafa að verkkaupi.	Then here are three marks silver which you shall have to spend.	Now here are three marks of silver for you to spend.
En Þorgerður skal fá þér fari vestur þar og vist um haf".	But Thorgerd shall get you-to go west there and provisions for the-sea".	And Thorgerd shall help you travel west and provide for your voyage by sea".
Þorvarður gerði sem hún mælti.	Thorvard did as she spoke.	Thorvard did as she spoke.
Síðan reið hann vestur í Hjarðarholt með barnið og fékk Þorgerði í hendur en hún lét upp fæða landseta sína er bjuggu inn á Leysingjastöðum í Hvammsfirði.	Afterwards rode he west to Hjardarholt with child and got Thorgerd to hand, and she had up foster tenants hers, as lived then of Leysingastadir in Hvammsfjord.	Afterwards he rode west to Hjardarholt with the child and gave it to Thorgerd, she had it brought up by her tenants, that lived in Leysingastadir in Hvammsfjord.
En hún tók Þorvarði fari norður í Steingrímsfirði í Skeljavík og vist of haf og fór hann þar utan og er hann nú úr sögunni.	Then she took Thorvard going north in Steingrimsfjord in Skeljavik and provisions about the-sea, and fared he there out-of, and is he now out-of the-saga.	She also took Thorvard going north in Steingrimsfjord in Skeljavik, and provisions for the sea, and he travelled abroad from there, and he is now out of the saga.

The Saga of Gunnlaug Serpent-Tongue (Old Icelandic)

Old Icelandic	Literal	English
Og er Þorsteinn kom heim af þingi þá segir Jófríður honum að barnið er út borið sem hann hafði fyrir mælt en smalamaður var í brott hlaupinn og stolið í brott hesti hennar.	And when Thorstein came home of assembly, then said Jofrid to-him, that child was out carried, as he had before said, and shepherd was to away run and stole to away horse hers.	And when Thorstein came home from the assembly, Jofrid said to him that the child had been carried out, as he had said before, and the shepherd stole the horse and ran away.
Þorsteinn kvað hana hafa vel gert og fékk sér smalamann annan.	Thorstein said she had well done and got himself shepherd another.	Thorstein said she had done well, and he got himself another shepherd.
Nú liðu svo sex vetur að þetta varð ekki víst.	Now passed so six winters that this became not known.	Now six winters passed, without this becoming known.
Og þá reið Þorsteinn til heimboðs vestur í Hjarðarholt til Ólafs pá mags síns Höskuldssonar er þá þótti vera með mestri virðingu allra höfðingja vestur þar.	And then rode Thorstein to home-invitation west in Hjardarholt to Olaf Peacock's, brother-in-law his, son-of-Hoskuld, were they thought to-be with most worthy all chieftains west there.	And then Thorstein rode to a home invitation west in Hjardarholt to Olaf Peacock, his brother in law, son of Hoskuld, and they were thought to be the most worthy of all chieftains there.
Þorsteini var þar vel fagnað sem líklegt var.	Thorstein was there well welcomed, as likely was.	Thorstein was well welcomed there, as was expected.
Og á einnhvern dag að veislunni er það sagt að Þorgerður sat á tali við Þorstein bróður sinn í öndvegi en Ólafur átti tal við aðra menn.	And one day at feast, was it said, that Thorgerd sat of talking with Thorstein, brother hers, in foremost, while Olaf had talked with other men.	And one day at the feast, it was said, that Thorgerd sat talking with her brother Thorstein, on the front benches, while Olaf had talked with other men.
En yfir gegnt þeim á bekkinum sátu meyjar þrjár.	Then across opposite them a group sitting girls three.	There was a group of three girls sitting opposite.
Þá mælti Þorgerður: "Hversu líst þér bróðir á meyjarnar þessar er hér sitja gegnt okkur?"	Then spoke Thorgerd: "How-so like you brother of girls these which here sitting opposite us?"	Then Thorgerd spoke: "Brother, how do you these girls seem to you, who are sitting opposite us?"
Hann svarar: "Allvel", segir hann, "og er þó ein fegurst miklu og hefir hún vænleik Ólafs en hvíti og yfirbragð vort Mýramanna".	He answered: "All-well", said he, "and is though one beautiful much and has she likeness Olaf's and white and complexion our Myrar-folk".	He answered: "Very well", he said, "And though one of them is very fair, with the likeness of Olaf, and white in complexion like our Myrar folk".

The Saga of Gunnlaug Serpent-Tongue (Old Icelandic)

Old Icelandic	Literal	English
Þorgerður svarar: "Víst er það satt er þú segir bróðir að hún hefir hvíti og yfirbragð vort Mýramanna en ei vænleik Ólafs þá því að hún er eigi hans dóttir".	Thorgerd answered: "Wise is that true what you say brother that she has white and complexion our Myrar-folk but not likeness Olaf Peacock's because that she is not his daughter".	Thorgerd answered: "It is certainly try as you say, brother, that she has a white complexion of our Myrar folk, but not a likeness of Olaf Peacock, because she is not his daughter".
"Hversu má það vera", segir Þorsteinn, "en þó sé hún þín dóttir?"	"How-so may this be", answered Thorstein, "but though so she your daughter?"	"How can that be?", said Thorstein, "since she is your daughter?"
Hún svarar: "Með sannindum að segja þér frændi", kvað hún, "þá er þessi þín dóttir en eigi mín, hin fagra mær" og segir honum síðan allt sem farið hafði og biður hann fyrirgefa sér og konu sinni þessi afbrigði.	She answered: "With truth to say to-you, kinsman", said she, "then is this your daughter, and not mine, the fair girl", and said she since all, as went had, and asked he forgive her and wife his this deviation.	She answered: "To say truthfully to you, kinsman", she said, "then this the fair girl is your daughter, and not mine", and afterwards she said all of what had happened, and asked him to forgive her and his wife for this deviation.
Þorsteinn mælti: "Ekki kann eg ykkur að ásaka um þetta og veltur þangað sem vera vill um flesta hluti og hafið þið vel yfir slétt vanhyggju mína.	Thorstein spoke: "Nothing can I you to forsake about this, and depend there, so be will, about most things, and have you well across smoothed carelessness mine.	Thorstein spoke: "I cannot blame you for any of this, and as it often is, what will be will be, and you have smoothed across my carelessness well".
Líst mér svo á mey þessa að mér þykir mikil gifta í að eiga jafnfagurt barn.	Appears to-me so of girl this, that to-me consider much gift to that have equally-beautiful child.	It appears to me that it is a great gift to have such a beautiful child.
Eða hvað heitir hún?"	But what named is-she?"	But what is her name?"
"Helga heitir hún", segir Þorgerður.	"Helga named she-is", said Thorgerd.	"Her name is Helga", said Thorgerd.
"Helga hin fagra", segir Þorsteinn.	"Helga the fair", said Thorstein.	"Helga the Fair", said Thorstein.
"Nú skalt þú búa ferð hennar heim með mér".	"Now shall you prepare journey her home with me".	"Now you shall prepare her to journey home with me".
Hún gerði svo.	She did so.	She did so.

The Saga of Gunnlaug Serpent-Tongue (Old Icelandic)

Old Icelandic	Literal	English
Þorsteinn var þaðan út leiddur með góðum gjöfum og reið Helga heim með honum og fæddist þar upp með mikilli virðing og ást af föður og móður og öllum frændum.	Thorstein was from-there back led with good gifts, and rode Helga home with him and fostered there up with much honour and love of father and mother and all kinsmen.	Thorstein was given splendid gifts there, and Helga rode home with him and was brought up there with much honour and the love of her father and mother and all kinsmen.
4	4	4
Þenna tíma bjó uppi á Hvítársíðu á Gilsbakka Illugi svarti Hallkelsson Hrosskelssonar.	In those times lived up of Hvitarsida of Gilsbakka Illugi the-Black son-of-Hallkel, son-of-Hrosskel.	In those times, Illugi the Black, son of Hallkel, son of Hrosskel, lived in Hvitarsida in Gilsbakka.
Móðir Illuga var Þuríður dylla dóttir Gunnlaugs ormstungu.	Mother Illugi's was Thurid Dylla, daughter Gunnlaug Serpent-Tongue's.	Illugi's mother was Thurid Dylla, the daughter of Gunnlaug Serpent-Tongue.
Illugi var annar mestur höfðingi í Borgarfirði en Þorsteinn Egilsson.	Illugi was second greatest leader in Borgafjord but-for Thorstein son-of-Egil.	Illugi was the second greatest leader in Borgafjord, after Thorstein Egilsson.
Illugi svarti var stóreignamaður og harðlyndur mjög og hélt vel vini sína.	Illugi the-Black was large-property-man and hardy much and held well friends his.	Illugi the Black was a big property owner, and very much hardy, and stood by his friends.
Hann átti Ingibjörgu dóttur Ásbjarnar Harðarsonar úr Örnólfsdal.	He married Ingibjorg, daughter Asbjarnar son-of-Hardar's from Ornolfsdal.	He married Ingibjorg, daughter of Asbjarnar, son of Hardar from Ornolfsdal.
Móðir Ingibjargar var Þorgerður dóttir Miðfjarðar-Skeggja.	Mother Ingibjorg's was Thorgerd, daughter Midfjorder-Skeggi's.	Ingibjorg's mother was Thorgerd, daughter of Midfjorder Skeggi.
Börn Ingibjargar og Illuga voru mörg en fá koma við þessa sögu.	Children Ingibjorg's and Illugi's were many, and few coming with this saga.	Ingibjorg and Illugi had many children, but few of them come into this saga.
Hermundur hét son þeirra en annar Gunnlaugur.	Hermund named son theirs, and another Gunnlaug.	Their son was named Hermund, the second was Gunnlaug.
Báðir voru þeir efnilegir menn og þá frumvaxta.	Both were they promising men and they prime-grown.	Both were promising men, and they were grown in their prime.

The Saga of Gunnlaug Serpent-Tongue (Old Icelandic)

Old Icelandic	Literal	English
Svo er sagt frá Gunnlaugi að hann var snemmendis bráðger, mikill og sterkur, ljósjarpur á hár og fór allvel, svarteygur og nokkuð nefljótur og skapfelligur í andliti, miðmjór og herðimikill, kominn á sig manna best, hávaðamaður mikill í öllu skaplyndi og framgjarn snemmendis og við allt óvæginn og harður og skáld mikið og heldur níðskár og kallaður Gunnlaugur ormstunga.	So is said from Gunnlaug, that he was precocious quick, great and strong, light of hair, and fared all-well, black-eyes and some-what ugly-nose and pleasant in face, medium-narrow and hardy-much, becoming of himself man best, a-loud-man much in all temper and ambitious precocious and with all ruthless and hard and poet great and rather abusive and called Gunnlaug Serpent-Tongue.	So it is said of Gunnlaug, that he was precocious, great and strong, with light hair, well travelled, with black eyes, and a somewhat ugly nose, with a pleasant face, medium narrow and very much hardy, becoming the best man he could, a loud man of mood, stubborn and ruthless and hard in his ambition, he was a gifted poet, but sometimes an abusive one, and he was called Gunnlaug Serpent-Tongue.
Hermundur var þeirra vinsælli og hafði höfðingjabragð á sér.	Hermund was of-them more-popular and had chieftaincy about him.	Hermund was the more popular of them, and had an air of chieftaincy about him.
Og er Gunnlaugur var tólf vetra gamall bað hann föður sinn fararefna og kvaðst hann vilja fara utan og sjá sið annarra manna.	And when Gunnlaug was twelve winters old asked he father his travel-goods and said he wished travelling out and see traditions other people.	And when Gunnlaug was twelve winters old, he asked his father for some travel goods, and said that he wanted to travel abroad and see the traditions of other people.
Illugi bóndi tók því seinlega, kvað hann eigi mundu þykja góðan í öðrum löndum er hann þóttist trautt mega semja við hann þar heima sem hann vildi.	Illugi farmer took therefore reluctance, saying he not would be-valued good in other-lands, for he thought scarcely able-to negotiate with him there home, as he wished.	Illugi the farmer took reluctance to this, saying that he would not be appreciated in other lands, because he thought that he was scarcely able to negotiate with him at home as he wished.
Og einnhvern morgun var það alllitlu síðar að Illugi bóndi gekk út snemma og sá að útibúr hans var opið og voru lagðir út vörusekkar nokkurir á hlaðið sex og þar lénur með.	And one morning was it very-little afterwards, that Illugi farmer went out early and saw, that out-house his was opened, and were laying out sacks some of farmyard six and there laying along.	Soon after this, Illugi went out early one morning, and saw that his outhouse was open, and there were six sacks laying outside the farmyard.
Hann undraðist þetta mjög.	He was-surprised at-this much.	He was very surprised at this.
Þar gekk þá að maður og leiddi fjögur hross og var þar Gunnlaugur son hans og mælti: "Ég hefi sekkana út lagið", segir hann.	There went then by man and led four horses, and was there Gunnlaug, son his, and spoke: "I have sacks out laid", said he.	Then went a man also leading four horses, and it was his son Gunnlaug, and he spoke: "I have laid out the sacks", he said.

The Saga of Gunnlaug Serpent-Tongue (Old Icelandic)

Old Icelandic	Literal	English
Illugi spyr hví hann gerði svo.	Illugi asked, why he did so.	Illugi asked why he had done so.
Hann segir að það skyldi vera fararefni hans.	He said, that it should be travel-goods his.	He said that it should be his travel goods.
Illugi mælti: "Engi ráð skalt þú taka af mér og fara hvergi fyrr en eg vil" og kippti inn aftur vörusekkunum.	Illugi spoke; "None authority shall you take of me and travelling neither, before that I wish", and dragged then back ware-sacks.	Illugi spoke: "You shall not take away from my authority, or travel either, before I say so", and dragged the sacks of wares back.
Gunnlaugur reið þá í brott þaðan og kom um kveldið ofan til Borgar og bauð Þorsteinn bóndi honum þar að vera og það þiggur hann.	Gunnlaug rode then to away from-there and came about evening over to Borg, and invited Thorstein farmer him there to be, and that accepted he.	Gunnlaug then rode away from there and arrived at Borg in the evening, and Thorstein the Farmer invited him to stay there, and he accepted.
Gunnlaugur segir Þorsteini hversu farið hafði með þeim feðgum.	Gunnlaug said Thorstein, how-so gone had with them father-and-son.	Gunnlaug said to Thorstein how it had gone between them, father and son.
Þorsteinn bað hann þar vera þeim stundum sem hann vildi og þar var hann þau misseri og nam lögspeki að Þorsteini og virðist öllum mönnum þar vel til hans.	Thorstein invited him there to-be them awhile, as he wished, and there was he then a-season and took lawspeaking by Thorstein, and worthied all people there well to him.	Thorstein invited him to stay there for a while, as long as he wished, and he was there for a season, and took to learning lawspeaking from Thorstein, and all the people there thought well of him.
Jafnan skemmtu þau Helga sér að tafli og Gunnlaugur.	Equally entertained then Helga privately at board-games and Gunnlaug.	Gunnlaug and Helga entertained each other privately by playing board games.
Lagði hvort þeirra góðan þokka til annars bráðlega sem raunir bar á síðan.	Took either-way they good charm to each-other soon, as experience bore out since.	They took to charming each other as events later bore out.
Þau voru mjög jafnaldrar.	They were much equal-aged.	There were very much the same age.
Helga var svo fögur að það er sögn fróðra manna að hún hafi fegurst kona verið á Íslandi.	Helga was so fair, as that was said wise men, that she had fairest woman been of Iceland.	Helga was so fair, so say wise men, that she had been the fairest woman of all Iceland.

The Saga of Gunnlaug Serpent-Tongue (Old Icelandic)

Old Icelandic	Literal	English
Hár hennar var svo mikið að það mátti hylja hana alla og svo fagurt sem gull barið og engi kostur þótti þá þvílíkur sem Helga hin fagra í öllum Borgarfirði og víðara annars staðar.	Hair hers was so great, as that may cover her all, and so fair as gold beaten, and none credited thought they like as Helga in fairness in all Borgafjord and wider other places.	Her hair was so great, that it covered all of her, and was as fair as beaten gold, and no one thought there was anyone like Helga in fairness, in Borgafjord and in places further afield.
Og einhvern dag er menn sátu í stofu að Borg þá mælti Gunnlaugur til Þorsteins: "Einn er sá hlutur í lögum, er þú hefir eigi kennt mér, að fastna mér konu".	And one day, were men sitting in main-room at Borg, then spoke Gunnlaug to Thorstein: "One is seen part of law, that you have not taught me, to propose myself wife".	Now one day, men were sitting around the main room at Borg, then Gunnlaug spoke to Thorstein: "There is one part of the law, that you have not taught me, how to propose to a wife".
Þorsteinn segir: "Það er lítið mál" og kenndi honum atferli.	Thorstein said: "That is little matter", and taught him procedure.	Thorstein said: "That is a small matter", and taught him the procedure.
Þá mælti Gunnlaugur: "Nú skalt þú vita hvort mér hafi skilist og mun eg nú taka í hönd þér og láta sem eg festi mér Helgu dóttur þína".	Then spoke Gunnlaug: "Now shall you know, whether to-me have understood, and should I now take in hand to-you and have as I to-propose me Helga, daughter yours".	Then Gunnlaug spoke: "Now to know, whether I have understood, I should now take your hand, and act as thought I am proposing to Helga, your daughter".
Þorsteinn segir: "Þarfleysi ætla eg það vera", segir hann.	Thorstein said: "Needless intend I that to-be", said he.	Thorstein said: "I don't see any need for that", he said.
Gunnlaugur þreifaði þá þegar í hönd honum og mælti: "Veit mér nú þetta", segir hann.	Gunnlaug felt then there in hand him and spoke: "Know me now this", said he.	Gunnlaug then felt for his hand and spoke: "Now know this of me", he said.
"Ger sem þú vilt", segir Þorsteinn, "en það skulu þeir vita er hjá eru staddir að þetta skal vera sem ómælt og þessu skulu engi undirmál fylgja".	"Do as you like", said Thorstein, "and that should they know, that beside are standing, that this shall be as not-spoken and this should none under-speech follow".	"Do as you like", said Thorstein, "and they should know, those who are standing here, that this shall not be as spoken, and this should have no hidden meaning".
Síðan nefndi Gunnlaugur sér votta og fastnaði sér Helgu og spurði síðan hvort þá nætti svo nýta.	Then named Gunnlaug himself witnesses and betrothed himself Helga and asked then, whether they may so use.	Then Gunnlaug named his witnesses and betrothed himself to Helga, and he asked them whether they may use.
Hann kvað svo vera mega og varð mönnum mikið gaman að þessu, þeim er við voru staddir.	He said so be able-to, and became people much enjoyment at this, them as with were standing.	He said it may be, and people were much joyed at this, those who were standing there.

The Saga of Gunnlaug Serpent-Tongue (Old Icelandic)

Old Icelandic	Literal	English
5	5	5
Önundur hét maður er bjó suður að Mosfelli.	Onund was-called a-man who lived south at Mosfell.	There was a man named Onund, that lived in the south at Mosfell.
Hann var auðmaður hinn mesti og hafði goðorð suður þar um nesin.	He was rich-man the most and held godord south there about the-headland.	He was the richest man and held the position of godord in the south around the headland.
Hann var kvongaður maður og hét Geirný kona hans, Gnúpsdóttir, Molda-Gnúpssonar er nam suður Grindavík.	He was married man, and named Geirny wife his daughter-of-Gnup, son-of-Molda-Gnup, that took-land south Grindavik.	He was a married man, and his wife was named Geirny, daughter of Gnup, son of Molda Gnup, that took land south Grindavik.
Þeirra synir voru þeir Hrafn og Þórarinn og Eindriði..	Their sons were they Hrafn and Thorarin and Eindridi.	Their sons were Hrafn and Thorarin and Eindridi.
Allir vooru þeir efnilegir menn en þó var Hrafn fyrir þeim í hvívetna.	All were they promising men, and thought was Hrafn before them in everything.	They were all promising men, and it was thought that Hrafn was the best of them at everything.
Hann var mikill maður og sterkur, manna sjálegastur og skáld gott og er hann var mjög roskanður þá fór hann landa á milli og virðist hvervetna vel þar sem hann kom.	He was great man and strong, man most-visible and poet good and when he was much mature then travelled he lands in between and seemed everywhere well there where he went.	He was a great and strong man, worth looking at, and a good poet, and when he had matured, he travelled between lands and was will thought of wherever he went.
Þá bjó suður á Hjalla í Ölfusi þeir Þóroddur hinn spaki Eyvindarson og Skafti son hans er þá var lögsögumaður á Íslandi.	They lived south of Hjalli in Olfus they Thorod the Wise son-of-Eyvind and Skafti, son his, that then was lawspeaker of Iceland.	Thorodd Eyvindarson the Wise, and his son Skafti lived at Hjalli in Olfus in those days, then Skafti was lawspeaker in Iceland.
Móðir Skafta var Rannveig dóttir Gnúps Molda-Gnúpssonar og voru þeir systrasynir Skafti og Önundarsynir.	Mother Skafti's was Rannveig, daughter-of Gnup son-of-Molda-Gnup, and were they cousins Skafti and Onund's-sons.	Skafti's mother was Rannveig, daughter of Gnup, son of Molda Gnup, and so Skafti and Onund's sons were cousins.
Var þar vinátta mikil með frændsemi.	Was there friendship much with kinship.	There was much friendship and kinship.

The Saga of Gunnlaug Serpent-Tongue (Old Icelandic)

Old Icelandic	Literal	English
Þá bjó út að Rauðamel Þorfinnur Sel-Þórisson og átti sjö sonu og voru allir efnilegir menn.	They lived out at Raudamel Thorfinn son-of-Sel-Thori and had seven sons, and were all promising men.	Thorfinn Seal-Thorisson then lived at Raudamel, and he had seven sons, and all were promising men.
Þeir hétu svo: Þorgils, Eyjólfur og Þórir, og voru þeir mestir menn út þangað.	They-were named so: Thorgils, Eyolf and Thorir, and were they best men out there.	They were named: Thorgils, Eyolf, and Thorir, and they were the best men out there.
Og þessir menn er nú eru nefndir voru allir uppi á einn tíma.	And these men which now are mentioned were all about at one time.	All these men that are mentioned were living at this time.
Og þessu nær urðu þau tíðindi er best hafa orðið hér á Íslandi að landið varð allt kristið og allt fólk hafnaði fornum átrúnaði.	And this near became then news, the best having word here of Iceland, that land became all Christian, and all people rejected ancient religion.	And it was about this time, the best thing ever to have happened here in Iceland, that all the land became Christian, and all the people rejected ancient religion.
Gunnlaugur ormstunga, er áður var frá sagt, var nú ýmist að Borg með Þorsteini eða Illuga föður sínum á Gilsbakka sex vetur og var hann þá átján vetra og samdist þá mikið með þeim feðgum.	Gunnlaug Serpent-Tongue, as before was from said, was now either to Borg with Thorstein or Illugi father his in Gilsbakka six winters and was he then eighteen winters and agreed they much with them father-and-son.	Gunnlaug Serpent-Tongue, as was mentioned before, was now either at Borg with Thorstein or his father Illugi's, at Gilsbakka, for six winters, and he was then eighteen winters old, and father and son agreed with each other very much.
Maður hét Þorkell svarti.	Man was-named Thorkell the-Black.	There was a man named Thorkell the Black.
Hann var heimamaður Illuga og náfrændi og hafði þar upp vaxið.	He was house-man Illugi's and near-kin and had there up grown.	He was a houseman of Illugi's and a kinsman, and he had grown up there.
Honum tæmdist arfur norður í Vatnsdal í Ási og beiddi hann Gunnlaug fara með sér.	He came-into inheritance north in Vatnsdal in As and asked he Gunnlaug to-travel with him.	He came into inheritance at As in Vatnsdal in the north, and asked Gunnlaug to go with him, and he did so.
Og hann gerði svo og riðu norður tveir saman í Ás og fengu féið, og greiddu þeir féið af höndum er varðveitt höfðu með atgöngu Gunnlaugs.	And he did so and rode north two together to As and got wealth, and paid they wealth of hands as preserved had with to-going Gunnlaug.	And the two rode north together to As, and collected the wealth, and they paid the wealth from the hands of those who had preserved, going to Gunnlaug.

The Saga of Gunnlaug Serpent-Tongue (Old Icelandic)

Old Icelandic	Literal	English
Og er þeir riðu norðan gistu þeir í Grímstungum að auðigs bónda er þar bjó.	And as they rode from-north, guested they in Grimstungur at wealthy farmer, who there lived.	As they rode from the north, they were guests of Grimstungur, a wealthy farmer who lived there.
Og um morguninn tók smalamaður hest Gunnlaugs og var þá sveittur mjög er þeir fengu.	And about morning took shepherd horse Gunnlaug's, and was then sweat much, when they got.	And about morning, a shepherd took Gunnlaug's horse, which was then very sweaty, when they got it back.
Gunnlaugur laust smalamanninn í óvit.	Gunnlaug loosed the-shepherd to senseless.	Gunnlaug struck the shepherd senseless.
Bóndi vildi eigi svo búið hafa og beiddi bóta fyrir.	Farmer wished not so to-settle have and asked compensation for.	The farmer did not want to settle, and asked for compensation for this.
Gunnlaugur bauð að gjalda bónda mörk.	Gunnlaug offered to pay farmer a-mark.	Gunnlaug offered to pay the farmer a mark.
Bónda þótti það of lítið.	Farmer thought that about little.	The farmer thought little of this.
Gunnlaugur kvað þá vísu:	Gunnlaug said then verse:	Gunnlaug then said a verse:
Mörk bauð eg mundangs sterkum mannni, tyggja ranna. Grásíma skaltu góma glóðspýtis það nýta. Iðrast muntu ef yðrum allráðr flóða úr sjóði lætr eyðanda líða linns samlagar kindar.	Mark invited middle strong, man, chew lodgings. Grey-wire shall-your gums, fire that use. sea-serpent should, if your all-ruling flood from funds has destroyed passing serpents same-lying sheep.	A mark offered the middle strong, Man, chewing lodgings, Grey-wire shall your gums, Fire that, use, Sea-serpent should, if your All-ruling flood from funds, Has destroyed passing, Serpents lying together with sheep.
Þessi varð sætt þeirra sem Gunnlaugur bauð og riðu þeir suður heim við svo búið.	This became settlement theirs, which Gunnlaug offered, and rode they south home with such settled.	Thus became their settlement, which Gunnlaug had offered, and when it was settled they rode home south.
Og litlu síðar beiddi Gunnlaugur föður sinn fararefna í annað sinn.	And little afterwards asked Gunnlaug father his travel-goods a second-time his.	And a little while later, Gunnlaug asked his father for travel goods a second time.
Illugi segir: "Nú skal vera sem þú vilt", segir hann.	Illugi said: "Now shall be as you will", said he.	Illugi said: "Now it shall be as you wish", he said.

The Saga of Gunnlaug Serpent-Tongue (Old Icelandic)

Old Icelandic	Literal	English
"Hefir þú nú heldur samið þig úr því sem var".	"Have you now held agreement you of before, than was".	"Now that you are more agreeable than you were before".
Reið Illugi þá heiman skjótt og keypti skip hálft til handa Gunnlaugi, er uppi stóð í Gufuárósi, að Auðuni festargram.	Rode Illugi then home quickly and bought ship half to hand Gunnlaug, was up stood in Gufua, at Audun's Festargram.	Illugi then rode from home quickly and bought a half share of a ship to give to Gunnlaug, that was stood in Gufua, at Audun's Festargram.
Þessi Auðun vildi eigi utan flytja sonu Ósvífs hins spaka eftir víg Kjartans Ólafssonar sem segir í Laxdæla sögu og varð það þó síðar en þetta.	This Audun willed not to-out carry sons Osvif's the Wise after killing Kjartan son-of-Olaf, as said in Laxdardal saga, and became that though later than this.	This was the same Audun who would not take the sons of Osvif the Wise abroad after the killing of Kjartan Olafsson, as said in Laxardal saga, which happened later though than this.
Og er Illugi kom heim þá þakkaði Gunnlaugur honum vel.	And as Illugi came home, then thanked Gunnlaug him well.	And as Illugi came home, he then thanked Gunnlaug well.
Þorkell svarti réðst til ferðar með Gunnlaugi og var fluttur varnaður þeirra til skips en Gunnlaugur var að Borg meðan þeir bjuggust og þótti glaðara að tala við Helgu en vera í starfi með kaupmönnum.	Thorkell the-Black rode to travel with Gunnlaug, and were transferred wares theirs to ship, and Gunnlaug was at Borg, while they prepared ship, and thought gladder to talk with Helga than be in work with trading-men.	Thorkell the Black travelled with Gunnlaug, and their wares were transferred to their ship, when Gunnlaug was at Borg, while they prepared the ship, and he was happier to talk with Helga than be at work with trading men.
Einnhvern dag spurði Þorsteinn Gunnlaug ef hann vildi ríða til hrossa með honum upp í Langavatnsdal.	One day asked Thorstein Gunnlaug, if he wished ride to horses with him up in Langvatnsdal.	One day Thorstein asked Gunnlaug, if he would like ride up to his horses with him up to Langvatnsdal.
Gunnlaugur kvaðst það vilja.	Gunnlaug said that willed.	Gunnlaug said that he would like to.
Nú ríða þeir tveir saman þar til er þeir koma til selja Þorsteins er heita á Þorgilsstöðum og voru þar stóðhross er Þorsteinn átti fjögur saman og voru rauð að lit.	Now rode they two together, there towards as they came to shelter Thorsteins, was called of Thorglisstadir, and were there stud-horses, that Thorstein had, four together and were red in colour.	Now the two rode together, until there they came to Thorstein's shelters, where Thorstein's horses were, and they were a stud of four red horses.
Hestur var allvænlegur og lítt reyndur.	Horse was promising and little experienced.	The horse was a promising creature, but little experienced.

The Saga of Gunnlaug Serpent-Tongue (Old Icelandic)

Old Icelandic	Literal	English
Þorsteinn bauð að gefa Gunnlaugi hrossin en hann kvaðst eigi hrossa þurfa er hann ætlaði af landi.	Thorstein offered to give Gunnlaug horses, and he said not horses needed, that he intended out-of land.	Thorstein offered to give Gunnlaug his horses, but he said he did not need horses, but he intended to travel abroad.
Og þá riðu þeir til annarra stóðhrossa.	And then rode they to other stud-horses.	And then they rode to another stud of horses.
Var þar hestur grár með fjórum merum og var sá bestur í Borgarfirði og bauð Þorsteinn að gefa þann Gunnlaugi.	Was there horse grey with four mares, and was seen best in Borgafjord, and invited Thorstein to give then Gunnlaug.	There was a grey horse with four mares, and he was the best horse in Borgafjord, and Thorstein offered to give him to Gunnlaug.
Hann svarar: "Eigi vil eg þessi heldur en hin.	He answered: "Not will I this rather as others, but why invite you me not that, which I wish receive?"	He answered: "I do not want this horse any more than the others.
Eða hví býður þú mér eigi það er eg vil þiggja?"	But why offer you me not that which I will receive?"	But why don't you offer me something I will accept?"
"Hvað er það?" segir Þorsteinn.	"What is that?" said Thorstein.	"What is that?" said Thorstein.
Gunnlaugur mælti: "Helga hin fagra dóttir þín".	Gunnlaug spoke: "Helga the fair daughter yours".	Gunnlaug spoke: "Your daughter, Helga the Fair".
Þorsteinn svarar: "Ei mun svo skjótt ráðast", segir hann og tók annað mál og riðu heimleiðis ofan með Langá.	Thorstein answered: "Not should that so quickly arranged", said he and took another matter, and rode homeway over with Langa.	Thorstein answered: "That will not be so quickly arranged", he said, and changed the subject, and they rode home over the Langa river.
Þá mælti Gunnlaugur: "Vita vil eg", segir hann, "hverju þú vilt svara mér um bónorðið".	Then spoke Gunnlaug: "Know wish I", said he, "how you will answer me about marriage-proposal".	Then Gunnlaug spoke: "I wish to know", he said, "how you will answer my marriage proposal".
Þorsteinn svarar: "Ekki sinni eg hégóma þínum", segir hann.	Thorstein answered: "No mind I vanity yours", said he.	Thorstein answered: "I will give no mind to your vanity", he said.
Gunnlaugur mælti: "Þetta er alhugi minn en eigi hégómi".	Gunnlaug spoke: "This is all-mind mine, and not vanity".	Gunnlaug: "This is all my mind and no vanity".
Þorsteinn svarar: "Vita skyldir þú fyrst hvað þú vildir.	Thorstein answered: "Know should you first, what you will.	Thorstein answered: "You should know first, what you want.

The Saga of Gunnlaug Serpent-Tongue (Old Icelandic)

Old Icelandic	Literal	English
Ertu ei ráðinn til utanferðar og lætur þó sem þú skulir kvongast? Er það ekki jafnræði með ykkur Helgu meðan þú ert svo óráðinn og mun því ekki verða á litið".	Are-you not determined to out-travel and have thought that you seek marriage? Is that not equally with you Helga, meanwhile you are so undecided, and should therefore not be of considering".	Are you not determined to go abroad and you have thoughts about getting married? It is not suitable for you and Helga, while you are so undecided, and therefore I shall not consider it".
Gunnlaugur mælti: "Hvar til ætlar þú um gjaforð dóttur þinnar ef þú vilt eigi gifta syni Illuga svarta, eða hvar eru þeir í Borgarfirði er meira háttar séu en hann?"	Gunnlaug spoke: "Where to intend you about give daughter yours, if you will not gift son-of Illugi the-Black, and where are they in Borgafjord, are more such so than he?"	Gunnlaug spoke: "Where do you intend to find a match for your daughter, if you will not give her to the son of Illugi the Black, and where are there in Borgafjord, people as important as him?"
Þorsteinn svarar: "Ekki fer eg í mannjöfnuð", segir hann, "en værir þú slíkur maður sem hann þá mundi þér ei frá vísað".	Thorstein answered: "Nothing go I in men-comparing", said he, "and be you such man as he, then would to-you not from turn".	Thorstein answered: "I do not go in for comparing men", he said, "and if you were such a man as him, then you would not be turned away".
Gunnlaugur mælti: "Hverjum viltu heldur gifta dóttur þína en mér?"	Gunnlaug spoke: "Who will you rather gift daughter yours than to-me?"	Gunnlaug spoke: "Who would you rather give your daughter to than me?"
Þorsteinn svarar: "Mart er hér gott mannval.	Thorstein answered: "Many are here good men-choice.	Thorstein answered: "There are many good men to choose from.
Þorfinnur að Rauðamel á sjö sonu og alla vel mannaða".	Thorfinn at Raudamel of seven sons and all well manly".	Thorfinn at Raudamel has seven sons, and they are all very manly".
Gunnlaugur svarar: "Hvorgi þeirra Önundar né Þorfinns er jafnmenni föður míns því að þig skortir sýnt við hann.	Gunnlaug answered: "Neither they Onund nor Thorfinn are equal-man father mine as that you short showed with he.	Gunnlaug answered: "Neither Onund nor Thorfinn are equal to my father, even you fall short of him.
Eða hvað hefir þú í móti því er hann deildi kappi við Þorgrím goða Kallaksson á Þórnessþingi og við sonu hans og hafði einn það er við lá?"	And what have you to meet therefore as he dealt champion with Thorgrim the-Good son-of-Kallak at Thorsnes-Assembly and with sons his and had one that was with had?"	And what have you therefore to match him, as he dealt with the warrior Thorgrim Kjallakson the godi and his sons at the Thorsnes Assembly by himself and came away with everything that was to be had?"

The Saga of Gunnlaug Serpent-Tongue (Old Icelandic)

Old Icelandic	Literal	English
Þorsteinn svarar: "Eg stökkti í brott Steinari syni Önundar sjóna og þótti það heldur mikilræði".	Thorstein answered: "I drove to away Steinar, son-of Onund Sjoni, and thought that rather great-issue".	Thorstein answered: "I drove away Steinar, the son of Onund Sjoni, and that was thought of as a great achievement".
Gunnlaugur svarar: "Egils naustu að því, föður þíns, enda mun þar fám bóndum vel endast að synja mér mægðar".	Gunnlaug answered: "Egil next-to that since, father yours, an-end should that get farmer well ended that refuses me marriage".	Gunnlaug answered: "You had your father Egil to help you then, and such an end a farmer would get if they refused me marriage".
Þorsteinn svarar: "Hafðu í frammi kúgan við þá uppi við fjöllin en það kemur þér fyrir ekki hér út á Mýrunum".	Thorstein answered: "Have-you to from bullying with those up within hills, and that comes to-you for nothing here out of the-moors".	Thorstein answered: "Have your bullying with the people in the hills, and nothing will come of that for you here in the moorlands".
Um kveldið koma þeir heim.	About evening came they home.	About evening came they home.
Og um morguninn ríður Gunnlaugur upp á Gilsbakka og bað föður sinn ríða til kvonbæna með sér út til Borgar.	And about morning rode Gunnlaug up of Gilsbakka and asked father his ride to marriage-proposal with himself out to Borg.	And about morning, Gunnlaug rode up to Gilsbakka and asked his father to ride back to Borg with him to make a marriage proposal.
Illugi svarar: "Þú ert óráðinn maður þar sem þú ert ráðinn til utanferðar en lætur nú sem þú skulir starfa í kvonbænum og veit eg að slíkt er ekki við skaplyndi Þorsteins".	Illugi answered: "You are undecided man, there as you are determined to out-travel, and have now that you should work to marriage-proposal, and know I, that such is nothing with temper Thorsteins".	Illugi answered: "You are an unsettled man, there as you are determined to go abroad, and now you have you should strive for a marriage proposal, and I know that this does nothing for Thorstein's temper".
Gunnlaugur svarar: "Eg ætla þó utan allt eins og líkar mér ekki utan þú fylgir þessu".	Gunnlaug answered: "I intend though out-of all one and like I nothing, out-of you following this".	Gunnlaug answered: "I intend though abroad, and I like nothing outside of you following me in this".
Síðan reið Illugi heiman með tólfta mann ofan til Borgar og tók Þorsteinn vel við honum.	Since rode Illugi home with twelve men over to Borg, and took Thorstein well with him.	Then Illugi rode to Borg with twelve men, and Thorstein received him well.
Um morguninn snemma ræddi Illugi til Þorsteins: "Eg vil tala við þig".	About morning early decided Illugi to Thorsteins: "I wish speak with you".	Early in the morning, Illugi said to Thorstein: "I would like to speak with you".
Þorsteinn svarar: "Göngum upp á borgina og tölum þar".	Thorstein answered: "Go-we up to Borg and talk there".	Thorstein answered: "Let's go up to Borg and talk there".

The Saga of Gunnlaug Serpent-Tongue (Old Icelandic)

Old Icelandic	Literal	English
Og svo gerðu þeir.	And so did they.	And so they did.
Gunnlaugur gekk með þeim.	Gunnlaug went with them.	Gunnlaug went with them.
Þá mælti Illugi: "Gunnlaugur frændi minn kveðst hafa vakið bónorð við þig fyrir sína hönd að biðja Helgu dóttur þinnar.	There spoke Illugi: "Gunnlaug kinsman mine said has awoken proposal with you for her hand to bid Helga daughter yours.	Then Illugi spoke: "My kinsman Gunnlaug said he has brought up a marriage proposal with you for the hand of your daughter Helga.
En nú vil eg vita hvern stað eiga skal málið.	But now will I know how stand marriage shall matter.	And now I wish to know how the matter stands".
Er þér kunnig ætt hans og fjáreign vor.	Is to-you known descendents his and wealth being.	His descendants and wealth are known to you.
Skal hvorki til spara af vorri hendi staðfestu né mannaforráð ef þá er nær en áður".	Shall neither to save of provisions to-hand established nor looked-after, if then is nearer than before".	It shall neither be sparing of provisions to hand, nor overlooked, if this brings it nearer than before".
Þorsteinn svarar: "Það eitt finn eg Gunnlagi að mér þykir hann vera óráðinn", segir hann, "en ef hann væri þér líkur í skaplyndi þá mundi eg lítt seinka".	Thorstein answered: "That one find I Gunnlaug, that to-me think he was undecided", said he, "but if he was to-you like in temper, then would I little delay".	Thorstein answered: "The one finding I have with Gunnlaug, is that he seems unsettled to me", he said, "but if he was more like you in temperament, then I would little delay".
Illugi svarar: "Þetta mun okkur verða að vinslitum ef þú synjar okkur feðgum jafnræðis".	Illugi answered: "This should our be it friendship, if you refuse we father-and-son equally".	Illugi answered: "This would be our friendship, if you refuse us father and son equally".
Þorsteinn svarar: "Fyrir þín orð", segir hann, "og okkra vingan þá skal Helga vera heitkona Gunnlaugs en eigi festarkona og bíða þrjá vetur.	Thorstein answered: "For your words", said he, "and our friendship then shall Helga be promised-woman Gunnlaug but not engaged-woman and wait three winters.	Thorstein answered: "For your words", he said, "and our friendship, Helga will be promised to Gunnlaug, but not betrothed, and shall wait three winters.
En Gunnlaugur skal fara utan og skapa sig eftir góðra manna siðum en eg skal laus allra mála ef hann kemur ei svo út eða mér virðist eigi skapferði hans".	Then Gunnlaug shall travelling out-of and create himself after good man customs, and I shall lose all matter, if he comes not so back-from or me seems not temperament his".	Then Gunnlaug shall travel abroad and make himself after the customs of good men, and I shall loose any obligation, if he does not come back so, or if to me his temperament is not worthy".
Og við þetta skilja þeir.	And with that separated they.	And with this they separated.

The Saga of Gunnlaug Serpent-Tongue (Old Icelandic)

Old Icelandic	Literal	English
Ríður Illugi heim en Gunnlaugur til skips.	Rode Illugi home and Gunnlaug to ships.	Illugi rode home, and Gunnlaug to his ships.
Og er þeim gaf byr létu þeir í haf og komu skipi sínu norður við Noreg og sigldu inn eftir Þrándheimi til Niðaróss og lágu þar í lægi og skipuðu upp.	And were they given fair-wind, left they in sea and came ships theirs north with Norway and sailed then past Trondheim to Nidaros and low there in lay and ships up.	And when they were given a fair wind, they headed to sea, and their ships came north to Norway, and they sailed past Trondheim to Nidaros, there they had the ship laid up.

6

Þenna tíma réð fyrir Noregi Eiríkur jarl Hákonarson og Sveinn bróðir hans.	In those times ruled along Norway Erik earl son-of-Hakon and Svein, brother his.	In those times Erik Hakonarson and his brother Svein ruled Norway.
Eiríkur jarl hafði þá aðsetu inn á Hlöðum að föðurleifð sinni og var ríkur höfðingi.	Erik earl had then to-seat then of Lade at estate his and was kingdom leader.	Earl Erik had an estate in Lade, and was a powerful leader.
Skúli Þorsteinsson var þá með jarli og var hirðmaður hans og vel metinn.	Skuli son-of-Thorstein was then with earl and was court-man his and well appreciated.	Skuli Thorsteinsson was there with him, and was one of his court men, and he was well appreciated.
Það er frá sagt að þeir Gunnlaugur og Auðun Festargramur gengu tólf menn saman inn á Hlaðir.	That is from said, that they Gunnlaug and Audun Festargram went twelve men together then of Lade.	It is said from this, that Gunnlaug and Audun Festargram went with ten other men went to Lade.
Gunnlaugur var svo búinn að hann var í grám kyrtli og í hvítum leistbrókum.	Gunnlaug was son-of-Thorstein prepared that he was among grey tunic and in white breeches.	Gunnlaug Thorsteinsson was dressed in a grey tunic and white breeches.
Sull hafði hann á fæti niðri á ristinni.	Boil had he on foot down at instep.	He had a boil in the instep of his foot.
Freyddi úr upp blóð og vogur er hann gekk við.	Rose out-of up blood and opened when he walked with.	Blood rose up from it and it opened as he walked.
Og með þeim búningi gekk hann fyrir jarlinn og þeir Auðun og kvöddu hann vel.	And with these clothes went he before earl and they Audun and greeted him well.	And with those clothes, he went before the earl with Audun, and greeted him well.
Jarl kenndi Auðun og spyr hann tíðinda af Íslandi en Auðun sagði slík sem voru.	Earl knew Audun and asked him news of Iceland, and Audun said such, as was.	The earl knew Audun and asked him for news from Iceland, and Audun said as such there was.

The Saga of Gunnlaug Serpent-Tongue (Old Icelandic)

Old Icelandic	Literal	English
Jarl spyr Gunnlaug hver hann væri en hann sagði honum nafn sitt og ætt.	Earl asked Gunnlaug, who he was, and he said to-him name his and descendents.	The earl asked Gunnlaug who he was, and he said to him his name and descendants.
Jarl mælti: "Skúli Þorsteinsson", segir hann, "hvað manna er þessi á Íslandi?"	Earl spoke: "Skuli son-of-Thorstein", said he, "what man is this of Iceland?"	The earl spoke: "Skuli Thorsteinsson", he said, "what man is this of Iceland?"
"Herra", segir hann, "takið honum vel.	"Lord", said he, "take him well.	"Lord", he said, "take him well.
Hann er hins besta manns son á Íslandi, Illuga svarta af Gilsbakka, og fóstbróðir minn".	He is the best man's son of Iceland, Illugi Black of Gilsbakka, and foster-brother mine".	He is the best man's son of Iceland, Illugi the Black of Gilsbakka, and my foster brother".
Jarl mælti: "Hvað er fæti þínum Íslendingur?"	Earl spoke: "What with feet yours Icelander?"	The earl spoke: "What is with your foot, Icelander?"
"Sullur er á herra", sagði hann.	"Boil is it lord", said he.	"Boil is it lord", said he.
"Og gekkst þú þó ekki haltur?"	"And walked you though not limping?"	"And though you walked limping?"
Gunnlaugur svarar: "Eigi skal haltur ganga meðan báðir fætur eru jafnlangir".	Gunnlaug answered: "Not shall limp walk while both feet are equally-long".	Gunnlaug answered: "One shall not walk with a limp, while both feet are equally long".
Þá mælti hirðmaður jarls er Þórir hér: "Þessi rembist mikið, Íslendingurinn, og væri vel að vér freistuðum hans nokkuð".	Then spoke court-man earl's, was Thorir named: "This haughty much, Icelander, and would-be well, that we test him somewhat".	Then one of the earl's court men who was named Thorir spoke: "This Icelander is rather haughty, and we should test him somewhat".
Gunnlaugur leit við honum og mælti:	Gunnlaug looked to him and spoke:	Gunnlaug looked at him and spoke:
Hirðmaðr er einn, *sá er einkar meinn* *Trúið honum vart,* *hann er illr og svartr.*	"Court-man which one, So was especially painful. Believe him hardly, He was ill and black".	"A certain court man, So especially horrible, Believe him hardly, He's evil and black".
Þá vildi Þórir grípa til exar.	Then willed Thorir gripped to axe.	Then Thorir wanted to grip his axe.
Jarl mælti: "Lát vera kyrrt", segir hann, "ekki skulu menn gefa að slíku gaum.	Earl spoke: "Let be still", said he, "nothing should men give to such heed,	The earl spoke: "Let's be calm", he said, "it's nothing for men to give such heed to,

The Saga of Gunnlaug Serpent-Tongue (Old Icelandic)

Old Icelandic	Literal	English
Eða hve gamall maður ertu Íslendingur?"	but how old man are-you, Icelander?"	but how old are you, Icelander?"
Gunnlaugur svarar: "Eg em nú átján vetra", segir hann.	Gunnlaug answered: "I am now eighteen winters", said he.	Gunnlaug answered: "I am now eighteen winters", he said.
"Það læt eg um mælt", segir jarl, "að þú verðir ei annarra átján".	"That have I about say", said earl, "that you will-be not another eighteen".	"About that I have to say", said the earl, "that you will not be another eighteen".
Gunnlaugur mælti og heldur lágt: "Bið mér öngra forbæna", segir hann, "en bið þér heldur".	Gunnlaug spoke and rather low: "Bid me none afflictions", said he, "but bid to-you honour".	Gunnlaug spoke rather low: "Bid me no afflictions", he said, "but bid to your honour".
Jarl mælti: "Hvað sagðir þú nú Íslendingur?"	Earl spoke: "What said you now, Icelander?"	The earl spoke: "What did you saw just now, Icelander?"
Gunnlaugur svarar: "Svo sem mér þótti vera eiga að þú bæðir mér öngra forbæna en bæðir sjálfum þér hallkvæmri bæna".	Gunnlaug answered: "So, as to-me thought was owned, that you bid me none afflictions, and bid yourself to-you more-effective prayer".	Gunnlaug answered: "So as I deemed fit, that you should not bid me afflictions, and bid for yourself more effective prayer".
"Hverra þá?" segir jarl.	"What then?" said the-earl.	"What then?" said the earl.
"Að þú fengir ei þvílíkan dauðdaga sem Hákon jarl faðir þinn".	"That you get not what deathday as Hakon Earl, father yours".	"That you do not meet your death as your father Earl Hakon did".
Jarl setti svo rauðan sem blóð og bað taka fól þetta skjótt.	Earl put so red as blood and asked take fool this quickly.	The earl went as red as blood and asked for this fool to be taken away quickly.
Þá gekk Skúli fyrir jarl og mælti: "Gerið fyrir mín orð herra og gefið manninum grið og fari hann á brott sem skjótast".	Then went Skuli before earl and spoke: "Do for my words, lord, and give this-man mercy, and go him to away as quickest".	Then Skuli went before the earl and spoke: "Lord, please do as I ask, and give this man mercy, and let him go away as quickly as possible".
Jarl mælti: "Verði hann á brottu sem skjótast ef hann vill griðin hafa og komi aldrei í mitt ríki síðan".	Earl spoke: "Will-be he of away as quickest, if he will mercy have, and come never in mine kingdom since".	The earl spoke: "Let him be away as quickly as possible, if he will have mercy, and never come to my kingdom after".
Þá gekk Skúli út með Gunnlaugi og ofan á bryggjur.	Then went Skuli out-of with Gunnlaug and over of quay.	Then Skuli went out with Gunnlaug outside and down to the quay.

The Saga of Gunnlaug Serpent-Tongue (Old Icelandic)

Old Icelandic	Literal	English
Þar var Englandsfar albúið til útláts.	There was England-voyage prepared to out-let,	There was an England voyage prepared to head out,
Og þá tók Skúli Gunnlaugi far og Þorkatli frænda hans.	and then took Skuli Gunnlaug travel and Thorkell, kinsman his.	And then Skuli took Gunnlaug to travel, and his kinsman Thorkell.
En Gunnlaugur fékk Auðuni skip sitt til varðveislu og fé sitt það er hann hafði ei með sér.	Then Gunnlaug got Audun's ship his to custody and wealth his, that as he had not with himself.	Then Gunnlaug gave custody of his ship to Audun, and all that which he did not have with him.
Nú sigla þeir Gunnlaugur í Englandshaf og komu um haustið suður við Lundúnabryggjur og réðu þar til hlunns skipi sínu.	Now sailed they Gunnlaug in England's-sea and came about autumn south with London-town and rode there to point ships theirs.	Now Gunnlaug sailed to the English sea and came at about autumn to London town and drew their ship up there.
7	7	7
Þá réð fyrir Englandi Aðalráður konungur Játgeirsson og var góður höfðingi.	Then ruled along England Æthelred king son-of-Edgar and was good leader.	Then England was ruled by King Æthelred, son of Edgar, and he was a good leader.
Hann sat þenna vetur í Lúndúnaborg.	He sat that winter in London-town.	He sat that winter in London town.
Ein var þá tunga á Englandi sem í Noregi og í Danmörku.	One was then tongue of England as in Norway and in Denmark.	Then the language of England was one with that in Norway and in Denmark.
En þá skiptust tungur í Englandi er Vilhjálmur bastarður vann England.	Then they exchanged tongue in England, when William Bastard won England.	Then they changed language in England, when William the Bastard conquered England.
Gekk þaðan af í Englandi valska er hann var þaðan ættaður.	Went from-there of in England French, as he was from-there descended.	French went from then on in England, as he was from there descended.
Gunnlaugur gekk bráðlega fyrir konung og kvaddi hann vel og virðulega.	Gunnlaug went soon before king and greeted him well and worthily.	Gunnlaug soon went before the king and greeted him well and worthily.
Konungur spyr hvaðan af löndum hann væri.	King asked, where of lands he was.	The king asked which land he was from.

The Saga of Gunnlaug Serpent-Tongue (Old Icelandic)

Old Icelandic	Literal	English
Gunnlaugur segir sem var "en því hefi eg sótt á yðvarn fund herra að eg hefi kvæði ort um yður og vildi eg að þér hlýdduð kvæðinu".	Gunnlaug said as was, "Then because have I sought of yours meeting, lord, that I have poem worded about you, and will I, that to-you listen poem".	Gunnlaug said as it was, "Then because I have sought to meet you, lord, that I have worded a poem about you, and I would like you to listen to the poem".
Konungur kvað svo vera skyldu.	King said so be should.	
Gunnlaugur flutti fram kvæðið vel og skörulega en þetta er stefið í:	Gunnlaug brought from poem well and boldly, and this is staved in:	Gunnlaug performed the poem well and boldly, and it has this stave.
Her sést allr við örva *Englands sem guðs engil.* *Ætt lýtr grams og gumna* *gunnbráðs Aðalráði.*	"Army see all still excitement England's as good angel. descendents bow warrior and men war-swift Æthelred".	"All the army are still in awe, At England's good angel, Descendents bow warrior men, war-swift Æthelred".
Konungur þakkaði honum kvæðið og gaf honum að bragarlaunum skarlatsskikkju skinndregna hinum bestum skinnum og hlaðbúna í skaut niður og gerði hann hirðmann sinn.	King thanked him poem and gave him as character-reward scarlet-cloak skinned in best skins and loaded in hem down and made he court-man his,	The king thanked him for the poem and gave him to reward his character a scarlet cloak, skinned in the best skins, and with an embroidered band down to the hem, and he made him his court man.
Og var Gunnlaugur með konungi um veturinn og virðist vel.	and was Gunnlaug with king about winter and seemed well.	And Gunnlaug was with the king all winter, and was well thought of.
Og einn dag um morguninn snemnma þá mætti Gunnlaugur þremur mönnum á stræti einu og nefndist sá Þórormur er fyrir þeim var.	And one day about morning early then met Gunnlaug three people on street one, and named that Thororm, was before them was.	And early one morning Gunnlaug met three men in the street, and the one before them was named Thororm.
Hann var mikill og sterkur og furðu torveldlegur.	He was great and strong and surprisingly difficult.	He was big and strong, and surprisingly difficult.
Hann mælti: "Norðmaður", segir hann, "sel mér fé nokkuð að láni".	He spoke: "Northman", said he, "sell me money some of loan".	He spoke: "Northman", he said, "lend me some money".
Gunnlaugur svarar: "Ekki mun það ráðlegt að selja fé sitt ókunnum mönnum".	Gunnlaug answered: "Not should that advised to sell wealth one's unknown people".	Gunnlaug answered: "It's not well advised to lend one's wealth to unknown people".
Hann svarar: "Eg skal gjalda þér að nefndum degi".	He answered: "I shall pay to-you that named day".	He answered: "I shall pay you on the named day".

The Saga of Gunnlaug Serpent-Tongue (Old Icelandic)

Old Icelandic	Literal	English
"Þá skal á það hætta", segir Gunnlaugur.	"Then shall of that risk", said Gunnlaug.	"Then I shall take that risk", said Gunnlaug.
Síðan seldi hann honum féið.	Afterwards sold he him wealth.	Afterwards he lent him wealth.
Og litlu síðar fann Gunnlaugur konunginn og segir honum fjárlánið.	And little afterwards found Gunnlaug king and said to-him of fee-loan.	A little while afterwards, Gunnlaug met the king and told him about the loan.
Konungur svarar: "Nú hefir lítt til tekist.	King answered: "Now have little to take.	The king answered: "Now have things less taken.
Þessi er hinn mesti ránsmaður og víkingur og eig ekki við hann en eg skal fá þér jafnmikið fé".	This is the most robber-man and viking, and own not with him, and I shall get to-you equal wealth".	This is the most notorious robber and viking, have nothing to do with him, and I shall get you the same money".
Gunnlaugur svarar: "Illa er oss þá farið", segir hann, "hirðmönnum yðrum, göngum upp á saklausa menn en láta slíka sitja yfir voru og skal það aldrei verða".	Gunnlaug answered: "Badly are us then going", said he, "court-men yours, go-we up of sake-less men, and let such sitting over wares, and shall that never be".	Gunnlaug answered: "We are going badly", he said, "your court men, we go above helpless men, and let such a man sit over our heads, and that shall never be.
Og litlu síðar hitti hann Þórorm og heimti féið að honum en hann kvaðst eigi gjalda mundu.	And little afterwards met he Thororm and claimed wealth of him, and he said not pay would.	And little afterwards he met Thororm and claimed back the money, but he said he would not pay.
Gunnlaugur kvað þá vísu þessa:	Gunnlaug said then verse this:	Gunnlaug then said this verse:
Meðalráð er þér Móði	Among-advice which to-you, Móði	"You are ill advised, Modi,
málma galdrs að halda,	metals spell, to keep,	It is bad for wealth, to keep,
att hafið þér við prettum	to have that with trick	That you have with deceived,
oddrjóð, fyrir mér hoddum.	point-reddener, before me hoard.	Point reddener, before me hoarding.
Vita máttu hitt að eg heiti,	know might other, that named,	Know may also, that promised,
hér sé eg á því færi,	here see of because opportunity,	Here to see is opportunity,
það fékkst nafn af nökkvi,	that received name of given-name,	That received name of something,
naðrstunga, mér ungum.	venomous-sting, me young.	Venomous sting, from my youth.

The Saga of Gunnlaug Serpent-Tongue (Old Icelandic)

Old Icelandic	Literal	English
"Nú vil eg bjóða þér lög", segir Gunnlaugur, "að þú gjalt mér fé mitt eða gakk á hólm við mig ella á þriggja nátta fresti".	"Now will I offer to-you law", said Gunnlaug, "that you expenses to-me wealth mine or go of duel with me otherwise of three nights from-now".	"Now I will offer to you the law", said Gunnlaug, "that you pay me my money, or otherwise go to a duel with me three nights from now".
Þá hló víkingurinn og mælti: "Til þess hefir engi orðið fyrri en þú að skora mér á hólm svo skarðan hlut sem margur hefir fyrir mér borið og em eg þessa albúinn".	Then laughed viking and spoke: "to this had none become before as you that challenged me of duel, so wronged lot as many have before me carried, and am I this all-ready".	Then the viking laughed and spoke: "No one has challenged me to a duel before, so many have suffered at my hands, and I am ready for this".
Og við það skildu þeir Gunnlaugur að sinni.	And with that separated they Gunnlaug to them.	And with that Gunnlaug parted.
Gunnlaugur segir konungi svo búið.	Gunnlaug said king so settled.	Gunnlaug told the king how it was settled.
Hann svarar: "Nú er komið í allóvænt efni.	He answered: "Now has come in all-not-expected prospects.	He answered: "Now have come unexpected prospects.
Þessi maður deyfir hvert vopn.	This man blunts any weapon.	This man blunts any weapon.
Nú skaltu mínum ráðum fram fara og er hér sverð er eg vil gefa þér og með þessu skaltu vega en sýn honum annað".	Now shall-you my advice from going, and is here sword, that I wish give to-you, and with this shall-you fight, and show him another".	Now shall you go from my advice, here is a sword that I wish to give you, and you shall fight with this, but show him another".
Gunnlaugur þakkaði konungi vel.	Gunnlaug thanked king well.	Gunnlaug thanked the king well.
Og er þeir voru til hólms búnir þá spyr Þórormur hverninn sverð það væri er hann hafði.	And when they were to duel ready, then asked Thororm, which sword that is, that he had.	And when they were ready to duel, then Thororm asked what sword it was that he had.
Gunnlaugur sýnir honum og bregður en hafði lykkju á meðalkafla á konungsnaut og dregur á hönd sér.	Gunnlaug showed him and drew, and had loop about average-head of king's-gift and drew of hand himself.	Gunnlaug showed him and drew, but had a loop about the middle section of the king's gift, and dragged it over his hand.
Berserkurinn mælti er hann sá sverðið: "Ekki hræðist eg það sverð", segir hann og hjó til Gunnlaugs með sverði og af honum mjög svo skjöldinn allan.	Berserker spoke, as he looked sword: "Nothing afraid I that sword", said he and struck to Gunnlaug with sword and of him much so shield all.	The berserker spoke as he looked at the sword: "No fear do I have at that sword", he said and struck towards Gunnlaug with his sword, and much of his shield was off.

The Saga of Gunnlaug Serpent-Tongue (Old Icelandic)

Old Icelandic	Literal	English
Gunnlaugur hjó þegar í mót með konungsnaut en berserkurinn stóð hlífarlaus fyrir og hugði að hann hefði hið sama vopn og hann sýndi en Gunnlaugur hjó hann þegar banahögg.	Gunnlaug struck then to meet with king's-gift, and the-berserker stood helpless before and thought, that he had the same weapon and he showed, then Gunnlaug struck him then death-blow.	Gunnlaug struck to meet him with the king's gift, and the berserker stood helpless before him and thought that he had the same weapon that he showed him, then Gunnlaug struck him his death blow.
Konungur þakkaði honum verkið og af þessu fékk hann mikla frægð í Englandi og víða annars staðar.	King thanked him the-work, and of this got he much fame in England and widely other places.	The king thanked him for the work, and of this he got much fame in England and widely among other places.
Um vorið er skip gengu milli landa þá bað Gunnlaugur Aðalráð konung orlofs að sigla nokkuð.	About spring, were ships going between lands, then asked Gunnlaug Æthelred king leave to sail some.	About spring, there were ships travelling between lands, and then Gunnlaug asked Æthelred for leave to go sailing.
Konungur spyr hvað hann vildi þá.	King asked, what he wished then.	The king asked him what he wanted to do.
Gunnlaugur svarar: "Eg vildi efna það sem eg hefi heitið" og kvað vísu þessa:	Gunnlaug answered: "I will carry-out that, as I have promised", and said verse this:	Gunnlaug answered: "I would like to carry out a promise I have made", and said this verse:
Koma skal eg víst að vitja vígsdöglinga þriggja, því hef eg hlutvöndum heitið, hjarls og tveggja jarla. hverfka eg aftr áðr arfi, auðveitir gefr rauðan ormabeð fyrir ermar, odd-Gefnar mér stefni.	Come shall surely visit slayers of-the-dead three, because have bond called earldoms and two earls. Districts return, before inheritance, wealth-provides give red serpent bed for sleeves, point-given me summoned.	I shall come to surely visit, Three slayers of the dead, As promised worthy men, And two earls of lands. Districts return, before inheritance, Wealth provides giving red, Serpent bed for sleeves, Point given me summoned.
"Svo skal og vera skáld", segir konungur og gaf honum gullhring er stóð sex aura "en því skaltu heita mér", segir konungur, "að koma aftur til mín að öðru hausti fyrir því að eg vil ei láta þig fyrir sakir íþróttar þinnar".	"So shall and be, poet", said king and gave him gold-ring, which stood six ounces, "and because shall-you call me", said king, "to come back to me to another autumn, for because that I wish not leave you for sake as-vigorous yours".	"So shall it will be, poet", said the king and gave him a gold ring, which stood at six ounces, "and therefore you shall call me", said the king, "to come back another autumn, because I do not wish to lose as vigorous a man as you".

The Saga of Gunnlaug Serpent-Tongue (Old Icelandic)

Old Icelandic	Literal	English
Síðan siglir Gunnlaugur af Englandi með kaupmönnum norður til Dyflinnar.	Then sailed Gunnlaug of England with trading-men north to Dublin.	Then Gunnlaug sailed north with trading men to Dublin.
Þá réð fyrir Írlandi Sigtryggur konungur silkiskegg, son Ólafs kvarans og Kormlaðar drottningar.	Then ruled along Ireland Sigtrygg king Silk-Beard, son Olaf's Kvarans and Kormlod queen.	Then Ireland was ruled by King Sigtrygg Silk-Beard, the son of Olaf Kvaran and Queen Kormlod.
Hann hafði þá skamma stund ráðið ríkinu.	He had then short while ruling kingdom.	He had only been ruling for a short while then.
Gunnlaugur gekk þá fyrir konung og kvaddi hann vel og virðulega.	Gunnlaug went before king and called him well and worthily.	Gunnlaug went before the king and greeted him worthily.
Konungur tók honum sæmilega.	King took him same-like.	The king received him in the same way.
Gunnlaugur mælti: "Kvæði hefi eg ort um yður og vildi eg hljóð fá".	Gunnlaug spoke: "Poem have I worded about you, and will I listen have".	Gunnlaug spoke: "I have worded a poem about you, and I would like it to have a hearing".
Konungur svarar: "Ekki hafa menn til þess orðið fyrri að færa mér kvæði og skal víst hlýða".	King answered: "Nothing have men to this word before that bring me poem, and shall certain listen".	The king answered: "I have not had men wording me a poem before, and I shall certainly listen".
Gunnlaugur kvað þá drápuna og er þetta stefið í:	Gunnlaug said then drapa, and is this staved in:	Gunnlaug then said a drapa, and it has this stave in it:
Elr sváru skæ Sigtryggr við hræ.	Nourishes swears askew Sigtrygg with corpses.	Nourishes the sorceress's wolf, Sigtrygg with corpses.
Og þetta er þar:	And this is there:	And this is also there:
Kann eg máls of skil hvern eg mæra vil konungmanna kon, hann er Kvarans son. Muna gramr við mig, venr hann gjöfli sig, þess mun grepp vara, gullhring spara. Segi siklingr mér ef hann heyri sér dýrlegra brag,	Can I speak about understand, Each I praise wish King-descendents man, He was Kvaran's son. Should warrior with me, Custom he gifts him, This should poet wares, Gold-ring save. Say war-king to-me, If he heard himself Glorious poetry,	I know how to speak of, Who I wish to praise, Descendants of kings, He was Kvaran's son. Should the king with me, His custom give gifts, This should poet wares, Gold ring save, Say war king to me, If he heard himself, Glorious poetry,

The Saga of Gunnlaug Serpent-Tongue (Old Icelandic)

Old Icelandic	Literal	English
Það er drápu lag.	That which drapa-layer.	That is a drapa layer.
Konungur þakkaði honum kvæðið og kallaði til sín féhirði sinn og mælti svo: "Hverju skal launa kvæðið?"	King thanked him poem and called to his fee-servant theirs and spoke so: "How shall repay poem?"	The king thanked him for the poem and called to his fee servant, and spoke so: "How shall I repay the poem?"
Hann svarar: "Hverju viljið þér herra?" segir hann.	He answered: "How will to-you, lord?" said he.	He answered: "How would you like to, lord?" he said.
"Hversu er launað", segir konungur, "ef eg gef honum knörru tvo?"	"How is repaid", said he, "if I give him knorrs two?"	"How is he repaid", he said, "if I give him two knorrs?"
Féhirslumaður svarar: "Of mikið er það herra", segir hann.	Fee-servant answered: "About much is that, lord", said he.	The fee servant answered: "That would be of too much, lord", he said.
"Aðrir konungar gefa að bragarlaunum gripi góða, sverð góð eða gullhringa góða".	"Other kings give as character-reward treasure good, sword good or gold-ring good".	"Other kings give as character reward good treasure, a good sword, or a good gold ring".
Konungur gaf honum klæði sín af nýju skarlati, kyrtil hlaðbúinn og skikkju með ágætum skinnum og gullhring er stóð mörk.	King gave him clothing his of new scarlet, tunic laden and cloak with wonderful skins and gold-ring which stood mark.	The king have him his clothing of scarlet, laden with tunic, and a cloak with wonderful skins, and a gold ring, which weighed a mark.
Gunnlaugur þakkaði honum vel og dvaldist þar skamma stund og fór þaðan til Orkneyja.	Gunnlaug thanked him well and dwelled there short while and travelled from-there to Orkney.	Gunnlaug thanked him well and stayed there a short while, and travelled from there to Orkney.
Þá réð fyrir Orkneyjum Sigurður jarl Hlöðvisson.	Then ruled along Orkneys Sigurd earl son-of-Hlodvi.	Then Sigurd Hlodvisson ruled along the Orkneys.
Hann var vel til íslenskra manna.	He was well towards Icelander people.	He thought well of Icelander men.
Gunnlaugur kvaddi jarl vel og kveðst hafa að færa honum kvæði.	Gunnlaug greeted earl well and said he had of brought him poem.	Gunnlaug greeted the earl well and said that he had brought him a poem.
Jarl kvaðst hlýða vilja kvæði hans, svo stórra manna sem hann var á Íslandi.	Earl said listen willed poem his, so great man as he was of Iceland.	The earl said he wanted to hear his poem, as he was a great man of Iceland.
Gunnlaugur flutti kvæðið og var það flokkur og vel ortur.	Gunnlaug performed poem, and was that flokk and well worded.	Gunnlaug performed the poem, and it was a flokk that was well worded.

The Saga of Gunnlaug Serpent-Tongue (Old Icelandic)

Old Icelandic	Literal	English
Jarl gaf honum breiðöxi, sifurrekna alla þar er bæta þótti, að kvæðislaunum og bauð honum með sér að vera.	Earl gave him broad-axe, silver-inlay all, as poem's-reward and invited he with him to be.	The earl gave him a broad axe, with silver inlay, as a poem's reward, and he invited him to stay with him.
Gunnlaugur þakkaði honum gjöfina og svo boð hið sama en kveðst verða að fara austur til Svíþjóðar og gekk síðan á skip með kaupmönnum þeim er sigldu til Noregs og komu um haustið austur við Konungahellu.	Gunnlaug thanked him gift and bid to same, and said be that travelling east to Sweden and went since of ship with trading-men, they were sailed to Norway, and came about autumn east with Kungalf.	Gunnlaug thanked him for the gift and for the invitation, and said that he was travelling east to Sweden, then he went to ship with trading men, and they sailed to Norway, and they arrived at Kungalf in the east.
Þorkell frændi hans fylgdi honum jafnan.	Thorkell, kinsman his, followed him equally.	His kinsman Thorkell followed him as usual.
Úr Konungahellu fengu þeir sér leiðtoga upp í Gautland hið vestra og komu fram í kaupstað þeim er í Skörum heitir.	Out-of Kungalf got they guide up in Geatland the West, and came from in trading-station they, as in Skarar named.	Out of Kungalf they got a guide in West Geatland, and came to a market town that was named Skarar.
Þar réð fyrir jarl sá er Sigurður hét og var við aldur.	There ruled along earl so, was Sigurd named and was with age.	There ruled there an earl named Sigurd, who was with age.
Gunnlaugur gekk fyrir hann og kvaddi hann vel og kvaðst kvæði hafa ort um hann.	Gunnlaug went before him and greeted him well and said poem had worded about him.	Gunnlaug went before him and greeted him well, and said a poem that he had worded about him.
Jarl gaf gott hljóð til.	Earl gave good hearing to.	The earl gave good hearing to.
Gunnlaugur kvað kvæðið og var það flokkur.	Gunnlaug said poem and was that flokk.	Gunnlaug said the poem, and it was a flokk.
Jarl þakkaði honum og launaði honum vel og bauð honum með sér að vera um veturinn.	Earl thanked him and rewarded him well and invited him with him to be about winter.	The earl thanked him and rewarded him well and invited him to stay about winter.
Sigurður jarl hafði jólaboð mikið um veturinn.	Sigurd earl had Yule-invitation much about winter.	Earl Sigurd held a great Yule feast about the winter.
Og affangadag jóla koma þar sendimenn Eiríks jarls norðan af Noregi tólf saman.	And eve-day Yule came there sending-men Erik's earl north of Norway, twelve together.	And on the eve of Yule, messengers of Earl Erik arrived, from Norway in the north, there were twelve of them together.

The Saga of Gunnlaug Serpent-Tongue (Old Icelandic)

Old Icelandic	Literal	English
Þeir fóru með gjöfum til Sigurðar jarls.	They travelled with gifts to Sigurd earl's.	They travelled to Earl Sigurd with gifts.
Jarlinn fagnaði þeim vel og skipaði þeim um jólin hjá Gunnlaugi.	Earl celebrated them well and directed them about Yule beside Gunnlaug.	The earl received them well and directed them to the Yule festival beside Gunnlaug.
Þar voru ólæti mikil.	There was unrest much.	There was much unrest.
Gautar ræddu um að engi jarl væri meiri og frægri en Sigurður.	Geatlanders discussed about, that none earl was better and more-famous than Sigurd.	The Geatlanders discussed about, that no earl was better and more famous than Sigurd.
Noregsmönnum þótti Eiríkur jarl miklu framar og um þetta þrættu þeir og tóku Gunnlaug til úrskurðarmanns hvorirtveggju um þetta mál.	Norwegian-men thought Erik earl much above and about this quarrelled they and took Gunnlaug to ruling-person either-side about this matter.	The Norwegian men thought Earl Erik was high above. And they quarrelled about this, and took to Gunnlaug as the deciding person either way about this matter.
Gunnlaugur kvað þá vísu þessa:	Gunnlaug said then verse this:	Gunnlaug then said this verse:
Segið ér frá jarli, oddfeimu stafir, þeima, hann hefir litnar hávar, hár karl er sá, bárur. Sigreynir hefir sénar sjálfr í miklu gjálfri austur fyrir unnar hesti Eiríkr bláar fleiri.	Saying that from earl, Spear-sister stave, them, He had colours high, Has man who saw, waves. Triumphs has seen Himself in much gifts Eastern for won horse Erik blue more.	You speak of the earl, Staves of the spear sisters, He had colours high, Has the man seen, waves, Triumphs has seen, Himself in much gifts, Eastern for won horse, Erik blue more.
Hvorirtveggju undu vel við úrskurðinn en betur Noregsmenn.	Either-side won well with decision, and better Norwegian-men.	Either side were pleased with the decision, especially the Norwegians.
Sendimenn fóru þaðan eftir jólin með fégjöfum er Sigurður jarl sendi Eiríki jarli.	Sending-men travelled from-there after Yule with fee-gifts, that Sigurd earl sent Erik earl.	Messengers travelled from there after Yule with gifts of wealth, that Sigurd had sent Earl Erik.
Sögðu þeir nú Eiríki jarli úrskurðinn Gunnlaugs.	Said they now Erik earl ruling Gunnlaug's.	They said to Earl Erik about Gunnlaug's summary.

The Saga of Gunnlaug Serpent-Tongue (Old Icelandic)

Old Icelandic	Literal	English
Jarli þótti Gunnlaugur hafa sýnt við sig einurð og vináttu og lét þau orð um fara að Gunnlaugur skyldi þar friðland hafa í hans ríki.	Earl thought Gunnlaug had showed with him fairness and friendliness and lay then words about travelling, that Gunnlaug should there peace-land have in his kingdom.	The earl thought Gunnlaug had showed fairness and friendliness with him, and had word travel, that Gunnlaug should have peace there in his kingdom.
Það frétti Gunnlaugur síðan hvað jarl hafði um mælt.	That heard Gunnlaug since, what earl had about said.	Gunnlaug heard of this afterwards, what the earl had said about it.
Sigurður jarl fékk Gunnlaugi leiðtoga austur í Tíundaland í Svíþjóð sem hann beiddi.	Sigurd earl got Gunnlaug guide eastern in Tiundaland in Sweden, as he asked.	Earl Sigurd got Gunnlaug a guide to take him east into Tiundaland in Sweden, as he had asked.
9	9	9
Þenna tíma réð fyrir Svíþjóð Ólafur konungur sænski son Eiríks konungs sigursæla og Sigríðar hinnar stórráðu dóttur Sköglar-Tósta.	In those times ruled along Sweden Olaf king Swede, son Erik's king victorious and Sigrid the ambitious, daughter Forest-Tostig.	In those times King Olaf the Swede ruled Sweden, son of King Erik the Victorious, and Sigrid the Ambitious, daughter of Forest Tostig.
Hann var ríkur konungur og ágætur, metnaðarmaður mikill.	He was powerful king and fine, ambitious-man great.	He was a powerful king and fine king, and a man of great ambition.
Gunnlaugur kom til Uppsala nær þingi þeirra Svía um vorið og er hann náði konungs fundi kvaddi hann konunginn.	Gunnlaug came to Uppsala near assembly theirs Sweden about spring, and as he caught king meeting, called he king.	Gunnlaug came to Uppsala near to the time of their assembly about springtime, and when he caught the king's attention, he greeted the king.
Hann tók honum vel og spyr hver hann væri.	He took him well and asked, who he was.	He received him well and asked who he was.
Hann kvaðst vera Íslandsmaður.	He said was Icelander man.	He said he was an Icelander man.
Þar var þá með Ólafi konungi Hrafn Önundarson.	Then were they with Olaf king Hrafn son-of-Onund.	Then Hrafn Onundarson was with the king.
Konungur mælti: "Hrafn", segir hann, "hvað manna er hann á Íslandi?"	King spoke: "Hrafn", said he, "what man is he of Iceland?"	The king spoke: "Hrafn", he said, "what kind of man of Iceland is he?"

The Saga of Gunnlaug Serpent-Tongue (Old Icelandic)

Old Icelandic	Literal	English
Maður stóð upp af hinum óæðra bekk, mikill og vasklegur, gekk fyrir konung og mælti: "Herra", segir hann, "hann er hinnar bestu ættar og sjálfur hinn vaskasti maður".	Man stood up of in lower bench, great and bold, went before king and spoke: "Lord", said he, "he is the best noble and himself the boldest man".	A large and bold man stood up from the lower bench, went before the king and spoke: "Lord", he said, "he is the best noble and the boldest man".
"Fari hann þá og sitji hjá þér", sagði konungur.	"Go he then and sit beside to-you", said king.	"Let him go and sit next to you", said the king.
Gunnlaugur mælti: "Kvæði hefi eg að færa yður", sagði hann, "og vildi eg að þér hlýdduð og gæfuð hljóð til".	Gunnlaug spoke: "Poem have I that brought you", said he, "and will I, that to-you listen and give hearing to".	Gunnlaug spoke: "I have brought you a poem", he said, "and I would like that you listen and give hearing to".
"Gangið fyrst og sitjið", sagði konungur.	"Go first and sit", said king,	"Go first and sit", said the king,
"Ekki er nú tóm til yfir kvæðum að sitja".	"not is now time to across poem to sitting".	"now is not the time to sit over poems".
Þeir gerðu svo.	They did so.	They did so.
Tóku þeir þá tal með sér Gunnlaugur og Hrafn.	Took they then talking with themselves, Gunnlaug and Hrafn.	Gunnlaug and Hrafn then took to talking among themselves.
Sagði hvor öðrum frá ferðum sínum.	Said where others from voyage theirs.	They said to each other about their travels.
Hrafn kvaðst farið hafa áður um sumarið af Íslandi til Noregs og öndverðan vetur austur til Svíþjóðar.	Hrafn said travel had back about summer of Iceland to Norway and before winter eastern to Sweden.	Hrafn said that he had left Iceland for Norway the summer before, and before winter east to Sweden.
Þar gerist brátt vel með þeim.	There was soon well with them.	They soon became friends.
Og einn dag er liðið var þingið voru þeir báðir fyrir konungi Gunnlaugur og Hrafn.	And one day, when ended was assembly, were they both before king, Gunnlaug and Hrafn.	And one day, when the assembly had ended, Gunnlaug and Hrafn were both before the king.
Þá mælti Gunnlaugur: "Nú vildi eg herra", segir hann, "að þér heyrðuð kvæðið".	Then spoke Gunnlaug: "Now will I, lord", said he, "that you hear poem".	Then Gunnlaug spoke: "Now I would like, lord", he said, "for you to hear the poem".
"Það má nú", segir hann.	"That may now", said king.	"That may be now", said the king.

The Saga of Gunnlaug Serpent-Tongue (Old Icelandic)

Old Icelandic	Literal	English
"Nú vil eg flytja kvæði mitt herra", segir Hrafn.	"Now wish I carry poem mine, lord", said Hrafn.	"Now I would like to perform my poem, lord", said Hrafn.
"Það má vel", segir hann.	"That may well", said he.	"That may well be", he said.
Þá vil eg flytja fyrr kvæði mitt herra", segir Gunnlaugur, "ef þér viljið svo".	"Then will I carry before poem mine, lord", said Gunnlaug, "if you will so".	"Then I would like to perform my poem first, lord", he said, "if you will it so".
"Eg á fyrr að flytja herra", segir Hrafn, "er eg kom fyrr til yðvar".	"I to before that carry, lord", said Hrafn, "as I came before to you".	"I should go before, lord", said Hrafn, "as I came before to you first".
Gunnlaugur mælti: "Hvar komu feður okkrir þess", segir hann, "að minn faðir væri eftirbátur þíns föður, hvar nema alls hvergi? Skal og svo með okkur vera".	Gunnlaug spoke: "Where came father yours this", said he, "that father mine was aftermath father yours, where taken all either? Shall and so with us be".	Gunnlaug spoke: "Where did our fathers come from," he said, "that my father was your father's follower, where but nowhere at all? So it shall be with us".
Hrafn svarar: "Gerum þá kurteisi", segir hann, "að vér færum þetta ei í kappmæli og látum konung ráða".	Hrafn answered: "Let-us-be then courteous", said he, "that we able this not in contest, and let king decide".	Hrafn answered: "Let us then be courteous", he said, "that we do not contest this, and let the king decide".
Konungur mælti: "Gunnlaugur skal fyrri flytja því að honum eirir illa ef hann hefir ei sitt mál".	King said: "Gunnlaug shall before carry because that he spares badly if he has not his matter".	The king spoke: "Gunnlaug shall perform before, because he has it badly, if he does not have his own way".
Þá kvað Gunnlaugur drápuna er hann hafði orta um Ólaf konung.	Then said Gunnlaug drapa, that he had worded about Olaf king,	Then Gunnlaug performed the drapa that he had worded about King Olaf,
Og er lokið var drápunni þá mælti konungur:	And when ended was drapa, then spoke king:	And when the drapa was ended, then the king spoke:
"Hrafn", sagði hann, "hversu er kvæðið ort?"	"Hrafn", said he, "how is poem worded?"	"Hrafn", he said, "how is the poem worded?"
"Vel herra", sagði hann.	"Well, lord", said he,	"Well, lord", he said,
"Það er stórort kvæði og ófagurt og nakkvað stirðkveðið sem Gunnlaugur er sjálfur í skaplyndi".	"It is large poem and ugly and somewhat stiff-spoken, as Gunnlaug is himself in temper".	"It is a large poem, and ugly, and somewhat stiff spoken, as Gunnlaug is himself in temper".
"Nú skaltu flyta þitt kvæði Hrafn", segir konungur.	"Now shall carry your poem Hrafn", said king.	"Now you shall perform your poem, Hrafn", said the king.

The Saga of Gunnlaug Serpent-Tongue (Old Icelandic)

Old Icelandic	Literal	English
Hann gerir svo.	He did so.	He did so.
Og er lokið var þá mælti konungur:	And when ended was, then spoke king:	And when it was finished, then the king spoke:
"Gunnlaugur", segir hann, "hversu er kvæði þetta ort?"	"Gunnlaug", said he, "how is poem this worded?"	"Gunnlaug", he said, "How is this poem worded?"
Gunnlaugur svarar: "Vel herra", segir hann.	Gunnlaug answered: "Well, lord", said he,	Gunnlaug answered: "Well lord", he said,
"Þetta er fagurt kvæði sem Hrafn er sjálfur að sjá og yfirbragðslítið.	"This is beautiful poem, as Hrafn is himself to see, and little-appearance.	"This is a beautiful poem, as Hrafn is himself to look at, and of little appearance.
Eða hví ortir þú flokk um konunginn", segir hann, "eða þótti þér hann ei drápunnar verður?"	But why worded you flokk about king", said he, "or thought you he not drapa worth?"	"But why did you compose a flokk about the king", he said, "but did you not think he was worth a drapa?"
Hrafn svarar: "Tölum þetta ei lengur.	Hrafn answered: "Talk this not longer,	Hrafn answered: "Let us not talk about this longer,
Til mun verða tekið þótt síðar sé", segir hann og skildu nú við svo búið.	To should be taken, though afterwards so", said he, and separated now with so settled.	It should be taken up afterwards", he said, and with that they separated.
Litlu síðar gerðist Hrafn hirðmaður Ólafs konungs og bað hann orlofs til brottferðar.	Little afterwards became Hrafn court-man Olaf's king and asked he leave to away-travel.	A little afterwards, Hrafn was made one of King Olaf's court men, and he asked for leave to travel.
Konungur veitti honum það.	The king supported his request.	The king supported his request.
Og er Hrafn var til brottferðar búinn þá mælti hann til Gunnlaugs: "Lokið skal nú okkarri vináttu fyrir því að þú vildir hræpa mig hér fyrir höfðingjum.	And as Hrafn was to away-travel prepared, spoke he to Gunnlaug: "Ended shall now our friendliness, for because that you willed down me here before chiefs.	And as Hrafn was preparing to travel away, he spoke to Gunnlaug: "Our friendship is now ended, because you wanted to do me down before the court.
Nú skal eg einhverju sinni eigi þig minnur vanvirða en þú vildir mig hér".	Now shall I any this not you less disrespect as you willed me here".	Now I shall give you no less disrespect than you willed me here".

The Saga of Gunnlaug Serpent-Tongue (Old Icelandic)

Old Icelandic	Literal	English
Gunnlaugur svarar: "Ekki hryggja mig hót þín", segir hann, "og hvergi munum við þess koma að eg sé minna virður en þú".	Gunnlaug answered: "Nothing back me threat yours", said he, "and neither should with this come, that I so less worth than you".	Gunnlaug answered: "Nothing of your threats holds me back", he said, "and neither will become of this that I am thought of as a lesser man than you".
Ólafur konungur gaf Hrafni góðar gjafir að skilnaði og fór hann í brott síðan.	Olaf king gave Hrafn good gifts to separate, and travelled he to away since.	King Olaf gave Hrafn good gifts when they separated, and after that he travelled away.
Hrafn fór austan um vorið og kom til Þrándheims og bjó skip sitt og sigldi til Íslands um sumarið og kom skipi sínu í Leiruvog fyrir neðan Heiði og urðu honum fegnir frændur og vinir og var hann heima þann vetur með föður sínum.	Hrafn travelled east about spring and came to Trondheim and prepared ship his and sailed to Iceland about summer and came ship theirs in Leiruvog before below Heath, and became he celebrated kinsmen and friends, and was he home then winter with father his.	Hrafn travelled east in the spring and came to Trondheim, and prepared his ship, and sailed to Iceland in the summer, and his ship came to Leiruvog, below the heath, and he became celebrated with his kinsmen and friends, and he was them home in the winter with his father.
Og um sumarið á alþingi fundust þeir frændur, Skafti lögmaður og Skáld-Hrafn.	And about summer of assembly found they kinsmen, Skafti lawman and Poet-Hrafn.	And at the assembly in the summer Hrafn the Poet met his kinsman Skafti the Lawspeaker.
Þá mælti Hrafn: "Þitt fullting vildi eg hafa til kvonbænar við Þorstein Egilsson að biðja Helgu dóttur hans".	Then spoke Hrafn: "Your help will I have to propose with Thorstein son-of-Egil, to propose Helga, daughter his".	Then Hrafn spoke: "I would like to have your help to propose with Thorstein Egilsson, a proposal to his daughter Helga".
Skafti svarar: "Er hún eigi áður heitkona Gunnlaugs ormstungu?"	Skafti answered: "Is she not before promised-woman Gunnlaug Serpent-Tongue's?"	Skafti answered: "Hasn't she already been promised to Gunnlaug Serpent-Tongue?"
Hrafn svarar: "Er ei liðin sú stefna nú", segir hann, "sem mælt var með þeim? Enda er miklu meiri hans ofsi er hann muni nú þess gá eða geyma".	Hrafn answered: "Is not passed that agreement now", said he, "as said was with them? Ended is much better his vehemence than he should now this give or retain".	Hrafn answered: "Hasn't that agreement passed now", he said", as was said with them? In the end, his is so proud these days, he won't now care about this".
Skafti svarar: "Gerum sem þér líkar".	Skafti answered: "Let-us-be as to-you like".	Skafti answered: "Let it be as you like".
Síðan gengu þeir fjölmennir til búðar Þorsteins Egilssonar.	Since went they crowded to booth Thorsteins son-of-Egil.	Afterwards they crowded to the booth of Thorstein Egilsson.
Hann fagnaði þeim vel.	He received them well.	He received them well.

The Saga of Gunnlaug Serpent-Tongue (Old Icelandic)

Old Icelandic	Literal	English
Skafti mælti: "Hrafn frændi minn vill biðja Helgu dóttur þinnar og er þér kunnig ætt hans og auður fjár og menning góð, frænda afli mikill og vina".	Skafti spoke: "Hrafn, kinsman mine, will propose Helga, daughter yours, and as you know descendents his and rich wealth and culture good, kinsmen great and friends".	Skafti spoke: "Hrafn, my kinsman, wishes to propose to your daughter Helga, and as you know his descendants and wealth and good culture, great kinsmen and friends".
Þorsteinn svarar: "Hún er áður heitkona Gunnlaugs og vil ég halda öll mál við hann, þau sem mælt voru".	Thorstein answered: "She is before promised-woman Gunnlaug, and wish I keep all matter with he, then as said was".	Thorstein answered: "She is already a promised woman to Gunnlaug, and I wish to keep this matter with him, as was said".
Skafti mælti: "Eru nú eigi liðnir þrír vetur er til voru nefndir með yður?"	Skafti spoke: "Were now not passed three winters, as to were mentioned with you?"	Skafti spoke: "Haven't those three winters now already passed, as were promised with you?"
"Já", sagði Þorsteinn, "en ei er sumarið liðið og má hann enn til koma í sumar".	"Yes", said Thorstein, "but not is summer passed, and may he still to come in summer".	"Yes", said Thorstein, "but this summer is not yet passed, and he may still come home this summer".
Skafti svarar: "En ef hann kemur eigi til sumarlangt hverja von skum vér þá eiga þessa máls?"	Skafti answered: "And if he comes not to summer-long, what hope shall we then own this matter?"	Skafti answered: "And if he does not come back in the summer, what hope shall we then have in this matter?"
Þorsteinn svarar: "Hér munum vér koma annað sumar og má þá sjá hvað ráðlegast þykir en ekki tjár nú þetta að tala lengur að sinni".	Thorstein answered: "Here should we come next summer, and may then see, what advice-lies seems, and not force now this that speak longer to this".	Thorstein answered: "We shall come here next summer, and we may then see, what decision seems best, and not force it now by talking about it any longer".
Og við það skildu þeir og riðu menn heim af þingi.	And with that separated they, and rode men home of assembly.	And with that they separated, and men rode home from the assembly.
Ekki fór þetta tal leynt að Hrafn bað Helgu.	Nothing went this talked secret, that Hrafn asked Helga.	Nothing about this was talked about as a secret, that Hrafn asked Helga.
Ei kom Gunnlaugur út að sumri.	Not came Gunnlaug out of before summer.	Gunnlaug did not come back that summer.

The Saga of Gunnlaug Serpent-Tongue (Old Icelandic)

Old Icelandic	Literal	English
Og annað sumar á alþingi fluttu þeir Skafti bónorðið ákaflega, kváðu þá Þorstein lausan allra mála við Gunnlaug.	And next summer of assembly moved they Skafti marriage-proposal extremely, saying then Thorstein lost all matter with Gunnlaug.	And next summer at the assembly, Skafti petitioned for the marriage proposal vociferously, saying then that Thorstein had lost the agreement with Gunnlaug.
Þorsteinn svarar: "Eg á fár dætur fyrir að sjá og vildi eg gjarna að öngum manni yrðu þær að rógi.	Thorstein answered: "I of few daughters therefore that see, and will I gladly, that no men should therefore then slander.	Thorstein answered: "I have few daughters to see for, and I wish that no men should slander before them".
Nú vil eg finna fyrst Illuga svarta".	Now will I find first Illugi the-Black".	Now I wish first to find Illugi the Black".
Og svo gerði hann.	And so did he.	And so he did.
Og er þeir fundust þá mælti Þorsteinn: "Þykir þér eg laus allra mála við Gunnlaug son þinn?"	And as they met, they spoke Thorstein: "Seems to-you I not lost all matter with Gunnlaug, son yours?"	And as they met, then Thorstein spoke: "Does it seem to you that I have lost all agreement with your son Gunnlaug?"
Illugi mælti: "Svo er víst", segir hann, "ef þú vilt.	Illugi spoke: "So is certain", said he, "if you will.	Illugi spoke: "So it is certain", he said, "If you wish.
Kann eg hér nú fátt til að leggja er eg veit eigi gjörla efni sonar mín Gunnlaugs".	Can I here now few to that have, as I know not completely prospects son mine, Gunnlaug".	I can add little to that here, as I don't completely know my son Gunnlaug's prospects".
Þorsteinn gekk þá til Skafta og keyptu þeir svo að brúðlaup skyldi vera að veturnáttum að Borg ef Gunnlaugur kæmi eigi út á því sumri en Þorsteinn laus allra mála við Hrafn ef Gunnlaugur kæmi til og vitjaði ráðsins.	Thorstein went then to Skafti's, and kept they so, to wedding should be at winter-nights at Borg, if Gunnlaug came not out-of of before summer, then Thorstein lost all matter with Hrafn, if Gunnlaug came to and visited council.	Then Thorstein went back to Skafti, and they settled matters so that, if Gunnlaug did not come back that summer, Hrafn and Helga's marriage should take place at Borg at the Winter Nights, but that Thorstein would be without any obligation to Hrafn if Gunnlaug were to come back and go through with the wedding.
Eftir það riðu menn heim af þinginu og frestaðist tilkoma Gunnlaugs en Helga hugði illt til ráða.	After that rode men home of assembly, and postponed till-came Gunnlaug, and Helga thought ill to decision.	After the men rode home from the assembly, and Gunnlaug's return was still delayed, and Helga thought badly of the decision.

The Saga of Gunnlaug Serpent-Tongue (Old Icelandic)

Old Icelandic	Literal	English
Nú er að segja frá Gunnlaugi að hann fór af Svíþjóðu það sumar til Englands er Hrafn fór til Íslands og þá góðar gjafir af Ólafi konungi að skilnaði þeirra.	Now is to say from Gunnlaug that he travelled out-of Sweden that summer to England as Hrafn travelled to Iceland and there good gifts of Olaf king as separated they.	Now it is to say of Gunnlaug that he travelled from Sweden to England that summer, when Hrafn travelled to Iceland, and was given good gifts from King Olaf as they separated.
Aðalráður konungur tók við Gunnlaugi allvel og var hann með honum um veturinn með góðri sæmd.	Æthelred king took with Gunnlaug all-well and was he with him about winter with good honour.	King Æthelred received Gunnlaug well, and he was with him over the winter with good honour.
Í þenna tíma réð fyrir Danmörku Knútur hinn ríki Sveinsson og hafði nýtekið við föðurleifð sinni og heitaðist jafnan að herja til Englands fyrir því að Sveinn konungur faðir hans hafði unnið mikið ríki á Englandi áður hann andaðist vestur þar.	In Those times ruled along Denmark Canute then kingdom son-of-Svein and had newly-taken with estate his and was-called equally that army to England's, for because that Svein king, father his, had won much kingdom of England, before he died west there.	In those times the ruler of Denmark was Canute the Great, son of Svein, and he had newly taken with his estate and was always promising to invade England, because King Svein his father had conquered much of England, before he died there in the west.
Og í þann tíma var mikill her danskra manna vestur þar og var sá höfðingi fyrir er Hemingur hét, son Strút-Haralds jarls og bróðir Sigvalda jarls, og hélt hann það ríki undir Knút konung er Sveinn konungur hafði áður unnið.	And in those times was great band Danish men west there, and was seen leader for, was Heming named, son-of Strut-Harald earl and brother-of Sigvalda earl, and held he that kingdom to Canute king, which Svein king had before won.	And in those times there was a great band of Danish men, whose leader was Heming, the son of Earl Strut-Harald and the brother of Earl Sigvalda, and he held the kingdom under Canute that Svein had conquered before.
Um vorið bað Gunnlaugur konunginn sér orlofs til brottferðar.	About spring asked Gunnlaug king himself leave to away-travel.	During the spring, Gunnlaug asked the king for leave to travel away.
Hann svarar: "Ei samir þér nú að fara frá mér til slíks ófriðar sem nú horfir hér í Englandi þar sem þú ert minn hirðmaður".	He answered: "Not so to-you now to travel from me, to such un-peace as now looks here in England, there as you are my court-man".	He answered: "It is not so now for you to travel from me, while such war looks likely here in England, as you are my court man".
Gunnlaugur svarar: "Þér skuluð ráða minn herra og gef mér orlof að sumri til brottferðar ef Danir koma eigi".	Gunnlaug answered: "You should advise, mine lord, and give me leave at summer to away-travel, if Danish come not".	Gunnlaug answered: "You shall decide, my lord, and give me leave in the summer if the Danes don't come".
Konungur svarar: "Sjáum við þá".	King answered: "We-see with then".	The king answered: "We'll see then".

The Saga of Gunnlaug Serpent-Tongue (Old Icelandic)

Old Icelandic	*Literal*	*English*
Nú leið það sumar og veturinn eftir og komu Danir eigi.	Now passed that summer and winter remaining, and came Danish not.	Now passed the summer and the following winter, and the Danes did not come.
Og eftir mitt sumar fékk Gunnlaugur orlof til brottferðar af konungi og fór Gunnlaugur þaðan austur til Noregs og fann Eirík jarl í Þrándheimi á Hlöðum og tók jarl honum þá vel og bauð honum þá með sér að vera.	And after mid summer got Gunnlaug leave to away-travel of king, and fared Gunnlaug from-there eastern to Norway and found Erik earl in Trondheim of Lade, and took earl him then well and invited him then with himself to be.	After mid summer Gunnlaug was given leave to travel away from the kind, and Gunnlaug travelled east from there to Norway, and found Earl Erik at Lade in Trondheim, and the earl received him well and invited him to stay there with him.
Gunnlaugur þakkar honum boðið og kveðst þó vilja fara fyrst út til Íslands á vit festarmeyjar sinnar.	Gunnlaug thanked his offer and said though willed travelling first out to Iceland of with intended-maiden his.	Gunnlaug thanked him for his kind offer, and said that first he wanted to travel out to Iceland to his promised maiden.
Jarl mælti: "Nú eru öll skip í brottu, þau er til Íslands bjuggust".	Earl spoke: "Now are all ships away, they are to Iceland prepared".	The earl spoke: "Now all the ships that were prepared to go to Iceland have gone".
Þá mælti hirðmaður einn: "Hér lá Hallfreður vandræðaskáld í gær út undir Agðanesi".	Then spoke court-man one: "Here lying Hallfred Troublesome-Poet in yesterday out-of to Agdanes".	Then one of the court men spoke: "Hallfred the Troublesome Poet was lying out in Agdanes yesterday".
Jarl svarar: "Svo má vera", segir hann.	Earl answered: "So may be", said he.	The earl answered: "So may it be then", he said.
"Hann sigldi héðan fyrir fimm náttum".	"He sailed hence before five nights".	"He sailed from there five nights ago".
Eiríkur jarl lét þá flytja Gunnlaug út til Hallfreðar.	Erik earl let then carry Gunnlaug out to Hallfred.	Earl Erik then had Gunnlaug taken out to Hallfred
Hallfreður tók við honum með fagnaði og gaf þegar byr undan landi og voru vel kátir.	Hallfred took with him well received and gave then fair-wind under land and were well merry.	And he received him and celebrated him well, and then they were given fair wind offshore, and they were very merry.
Það var síð sumars.	That was later summer.	That was later summer.
Hallfreður mælti til Gunnlaugs: "Hefir þú frétt bónorðið Hrafns Önundarsonar við Helgu hina fögru?"	Hallfred spoke to Gunnlaug: "Had you news marriage-proposal Hrafn's son-of-Onund with Helga the Fair?"	Hallfred spoke to Gunnlaug: "Have you heard the news about Hrafn Onundarson's marriage proposal with Helga the Fair?"

The Saga of Gunnlaug Serpent-Tongue (Old Icelandic)

Old Icelandic	Literal	English
Gunnlaugur kveðst frétt hafa og þó ógjörla.	Gunnlaug said news had and thought insignificant.	Gunnlaug said that he had not heard the news, and that he thought it was insignificant.
Hallfreður segir honum slíkt sem hann vissi af og það með að margir menn mæltu það að Hrafn væri ei óröskari en Gunnlaugur.	Hallfred said him such, as he knew of, and that with, that many men spoke that, to Hrafn was not less-brave than Gunnlaug.	Hallfred told him as much as he knew about it, and with that many men spoke that Hrafn was no less brave than Gunnlaug.
Gunnlaugur kvað þá vísu:	Gunnlaug said then verse:	Gunnlaug then said a verse:
Ræki eg lítt þó leiki, létt veðr er nú, þéttan austanvindr að öndri andness viku þessa.	Care little, though toyed, Light weather as now, dense East-wind that second Against-headland week this.	With little care, though toyed, Light weather as now, dense, East wind, that second, Against the headland, this week.
Meir sjáumk hitt, en hæru	More see other, and grey-hair	More seeing other, and grey hair,
hoddstríðandi bíðit, orð að eg eigi verði jafnröskr taliðr Hrafni.	Hoard-warrior bid, Words, that not worth Equally spoke-of Hrafn.	Hoard warrior bid, Words, that not worth, Equally spoke of Hrafn".
Hallfreður mælti þá: "Þess þyrfti félagi að þér veitti betur málin við Hrafn en mér.	Hallfred spoke then: "This need, companion, that to-you provided-for better than me matters with Hrafn.	Hallfred then spoke: "Companion, you will need to have better matters than me, that I had with Hrafn".
Eg kom skipi mínu í Leiruvog fyrir neðan Heiði fyrir fám vetrum og átti eg að gjalda hálfa mörk silfurs húskarli Hrafns og hélt eg því fyrir honum.	I came ships mine in Leiruvog for below Heath for few winters, and had I to pay half mark silver housekeeper Hrafn's, and held I because before him.	I came with my ship to Leiruvog below Heath a few winters ago, and I had to pay half a mark of silver to Hrafn's housekeeper, and I held it for him.
En Hrafn reið til vor með sextigu manna og hjó strengina og rak skipið upp á leirur og búið við skipbroti.	Then Hrafn rode to spring with sixty men and struck strings, and drove ship up of clays and settled with shipwreck.	Then in the spring Hrafn rode with sixty men and cut the ropes, and the ship drove up on the clays and settled shipwrecked.
Varð eg þá að selja Hrafni sjálfdæmi og galt eg mörk og eru slíkar mínar að segja frá honum.	Became I then to shelter Hrafn self-judgement, and paid I mark, and was silver mine to say from him".	It became that I granted Hrafn self-judgement, and I paid him a mark of silver, and that is all I have to say about him".

The Saga of Gunnlaug Serpent-Tongue (Old Icelandic)

Old Icelandic	Literal	English
Og þá varð þeim eintalað um Helgu og lofaði Hallfreður mjög vænleik hennar.	And then were they only-spoken about Helga, and praised Hallfred much kindness hers.	And then they were only talking about Helga, and Hallfred praised her kindness very much".
Gunnlaugur kvað þá:	Gunnlaug said then:	Gunnlaug then said:
Munat háðvörum hyrjar hríðmundaðar Þundi hafna hörvi drifna hlýða jörð að þýðast því að lautsíkjar lékum lyngs, er vorum yngri, alnar gims á ýmsum andnesjum því landi.	Should-not slander fire While-formed thunder Wary linen drive Listen earth to attach, To drape-oneself played Headlands, which we younger, Measured noble of various Headlands therefore land.	The slander fire should not, While formed the thunder, Weary linen driven, Listen to the earth court, To drape oneself played, Headlands, which we younger, Measured of various noble, Headlands therefore the land.
"Þetta er vel ort", segir Hallfreður.	"This is well worded", said Hallfred.	"That is well worded", said Hallfred.
Þeir tóku land norður á Melrakkasléttu í Hraunhöfn hálfum mánuði fyrir vetur og skipuðu þar upp.	They took land north of Melrakkasletta in Hraunhofn half month before winter and ships there up.	They took land north of Melrakkasletta in Hraunhofn half a month before winter, and unloaded the ship.
Þórður hét maður.	Thord was-named a-man.	There was a man named Thord.
Hann var bóndason þar á Sléttunni.	He was farmer's-son there of the-plains.	He was a farmer's son there on the plains.
Hann gekk í glímur við þá kaupmennina og gekk þeim illa við hann.	He went in wrestling with then trading-men, and went they badly with him.	He went wrestling with the trading men, and they fared badly with him.
Þá varð komið saman fangi með þeim Gunnlaugi.	Then were come together received with them Gunnlaug.	Then they came together with Gunnlaug.
Og um nóttina áður hét Þórður á Þór til sigurs sér.	And about night before called Thord of Thor to victory himself,	And during the night before Thor called upon Thor to gain victory,
Og um daginn er þeir fundust tóku þeir til glímu.	and about day, were they found, took they to wrestling.	and in the day, they met, and took to wrestling.

The Saga of Gunnlaug Serpent-Tongue (Old Icelandic)

Old Icelandic	Literal	English
Þá laust Gunnlaugur báða fæturna undan Þórði og felldi hann mikið fall en fóturinn Gunnlaugs stökk úr liði, sá er hann stóð á, og féll Gunnlaugur þá með Þórði.	Then swept Gunnlaug both feet under Thord and fell he greatly falling, and foot Gunnlaug jumped from body, so as he stood to, and fell Gunnlaug then with Thord.	Then Gunnlaug swept both feet away from under Thord, and he fell a great fall, but Gunnlaug's foot jumped out of his body, the one he was standing on, and Gunnlaug then fell with Thord.
Þá mælti Þórður: "Vera má", segir hann, "að þér vegni eigi annað betur".	Then spoke Thord: "Be-it may", said he, "that to-you going not else better".	Then Thord spoke: "Maybe", he said, "that there is nothing going better for you".
"Hvað þá?" segir Gunnlaugur.	"What then?" said Gunnlaug.	"What do you mean?" said Gunnlaug.
"Málin við Hrafn ef hann fær Helgu hinnar vænu að veturnóttum og var eg hjá í sumar á alþingi er það réðst".	"Matters with Hrafn, if he can Helga inside kind at winter-nights, and was I beside in summer of assembly, as that decided".	"The matter with Hrafn, if he gets Helgi in good spirits on winter nights, and I was with him this summer at the Assembly, when it was decided."
Gunnlaugur svarar öngu.	Gunnlaug answered nothing.	Gunnlaug gave no answer.
Þá var vafiður fóturinn og í liðinn færður og þrútnaði allmjög.	Then was wrapped foot and in passed brought and swollen all-very.	Then his foot was wrapped and joint reset and it was very swollen.
Þeir Hallfreður riðu tólf menn saman og komu suður á Gilsbakka í Borgarfirði það laugarkveld er þeir sátu að brúðlaupinu að Borg.	There Hallfred rode twelve men together and came south of Gilsbakka in Borgafjord that Saturday-night, were they sitting at wedding-feast at Borg.	Hallfred and Gunnlaug rode south with ten other men and came south of Gilsbakka in Borgarfjord that Saturday night, they were sitting at the wedding feast at Borg.
Illugi varð feginn Gunnlaugi syni sínum og hans förunautum.	Illugi became relieved Gunnlaug, son his, and his companions.	Illugi became relieved to see his son Gunnlaug and his companions.
Gunnlaugur kvaðst þá þegar vilja ofan ríða til Borgar.	Gunnlaug said then straight-away willed over ride to Borg.	Gunnlaug said that he wanted to ride over to Borg there and then.
Illugi kvað það ekki ráð og svo sýndist öllum nema Gunnlaugi en Gunnlaugur var þó ófær fyrir fótarins sakir þótt hann léti ekki á sjást og varð því ekki af ferðinni.	Illugi said that nothing advice, and so seemed all taken Gunnlaug. But Gunnlaug was thought incapable for foot's sake, though he let not of see, and became because not of travelling.	Illugi said that was not advisable, and so thought all except Gunnlaug. But Gunnlaug was thought incapable for the sake of his foot, though he did not let it show, and it became that he did not travel.

The Saga of Gunnlaug Serpent-Tongue (Old Icelandic)

Old Icelandic	Literal	English
Hallfreður reið heim um morguninn til Hreðuvatns í Norðurárdal.	Hallfred rode home about morning to Hreduvatn in Norduradal.	Hallfred rode home about morning to Hreduvatn in Norduradal.
Þar réð fyrir eignum þeirra Galti bróðir hans og var vaskur maður.	There managed before owned their Galti, brother his, and was bold man.	There his brother Galti managed his brother's property there, and was a bold man.
11	11	11
Nú er að segja frá Hrafni að hann sat að brúðlaupi sínu að Borg og er það flestra manna sögn að brúðurin væri heldur döpur, og er það satt sem mælt er að lengi man það er ungum getur og var henni nú og svo.	Now is to say from Hrafn that he sat to wedding his at Borg and was that most many said that bride was rather sad, and was that true since spoke that to long remembered that which young can and was she now and so.	Now it is to say of Hrafn, that he sat at their wedding feast at Borg, and it was said by most people, that the bride was rather sad, and that was true as it was said, that things learned young last longest, and that was certainly the case with her then.
Það varð til nýlundu þar að veislunni að sá maður bað Húngerðar Þóroddsdóttur og Jófríðar er Svertingur hét og var Hafur-Bjarnarson Molda-Gnúpssonar og skyldu þau ráð takast um veturinn eftir jól uppi að Skáney.	So became to newcomer there at feast, that saw man asked Hungerd daughter-of-Thorodd and Jofrid, was Sverting named and was son-of-Hafur-Bjarni, son-of-Molda-Gnup, and should they advice take about winter after Yule up at Skaney.	It so happened that a newcomer there at the feast, a man named Sverting, the son of Goat Bjorn, the son of Molda Gnup, asked for the hand of Hungerd, daughter of Thorod and Jofrid, and the wedding was to take place about winter after Yule up at Skaney.
Þar bjó Þorkell frændi Húngerðar, son Torfa Valbrandssonar.	There lived Thorkell, kinsman Hundergar's, son Torfi son-of-Valbrand.	There lived Thorkell, a kinsman of Hungerd, the son of Torfi Valbrandsson.
Móðir Torfa var Þórodda systir Tungu-Odds.	Mother Torfi was Thorodd, sister Tunga-Odd's.	Torfi's mother was Thorodd, sister of Tunga Odd.
Hrafn fór heim til Mosfells með Helgu konu sína.	Hrafn fared home to Mosfell with Helga, wife his.	Hrafn travelled home to Mosfell with Helga, his wife.
Og er þau höfðu þar skamma stund verið þá var það einn morgun áður þau risu upp að Helga vakir en Hrafn svaf og lét hann illa í svefni.	And as then had there short while been, then was it one morning, before they rose up, that Helga woke, and Hrafn slept, and lay he badly in sleep.	And when they had been there a short while, then one morning before they rose up, Helga woke, and Hrafn slept, and he lay badly in his sleep.
Og er hann vaknaði spyr Helga hvað hann hefði dreymt.	And as he awoke, asked Helga, what he had dreamt.	And as he awoke, Helga asked what he had dreamt.

The Saga of Gunnlaug Serpent-Tongue (Old Icelandic)

Old Icelandic	Literal	English
Hrafn kvað þá vísu:	Hrafn said then verse:	Hrafn then said a verse:
Hugðumst orms á armi *ý döggvar þér höggvinn,* *væri, brúðr, í blóði* *beðr þinn roðinn mínu,*	Though serpent of arms By dew to-you cut-down, Was, brother, in blood Bedding yours reddened mine,	As though of serpents on arms, By dew yours, cut down, Was, brother, in blood, Bedding yours, was reddened by mine,
knættit endr um undir *ölstafns Njörun Hrafni,* *líka getr það lauka* *lind, höggþyrnis binda.*	Bowl end about to Ale-staff Njörun Hrafn, Like can it leek Linden, shock-thorn bind.	Bowl end about to, Ale-staff Njörun Hrafn, Like can that leek, Linden, shock thorn bind.
Helga mælti: "Það mun eg aldrei gráta", segir hún.	Helga spoke: "That would I never weep", said she.	Helga spoke: "I shall never weep over that", she said.
"Hafið þér illa svikið mig.	"Have you badly tricked me.	"You have badly tricked me.
Mun Gunnlaugur út kominn" og grét Helga þá mjög.	Must Gunnlaug back have-come" and wept Helga then much.	And Gunnlaug must come back", and then Helga wept much.
Og litlu síðar fluttist útkoma Gunnlaugs.	And little afterwards returned out-coming Gunnlaug.	And little afterwards came the news of Gunnlaug's return.
Helga gerðist þá svo stirð við Hrafn að hann fékk eigi haldið henni heima þar og fóru þau þá heim aftur til Borgar og nýtti Hrafn lítið af samvistum við hana.	Helga became then so stiff with Hrafn, that he got not stayed her home there, and travelled they then home returning to Borg, and use Hrafn little of together-staying with her.	Helga then became so stiff with Hrafn, that he could not keep her at home, and so they want back to Borg, and Hrafn had little of staying together with her.
Nú búast menn til boðs um veturinn.	Now prepared men to settle about winter.	Now men prepared to settle for the winter.
Þorkell frá Skáney bauð Illuga svarta og sonum hans.	Thorkell from Skaney invited Illugi the-Black and sons his.	Thorkell from Skaney invited Illugi the Black and his sons.
Og er Illugi bóndi bjóst þá sat Gunnlaugur í stofu og bjóst ekki.	And was Illugi farm prepared, then sat Gunnlaug in main-room and readied not.	And as Illugi's farm was prepared, then Gunnlaug sat in the main room and did not get ready.
Illugi gekk til hans og mælti: "Hví býst þú ekki frændi?"	Illugi went to him and spoke: "Why prepared you not kinsman?"	Illugi went to him and spoke: "Why are you not prepared, kinsman?"
Gunnlaugur svarar: "Eg ætla eigi að fara".	Gunnlaug answered: "I intend not at travel".	Gunnlaug answered: "I do not intend to travel".

The Saga of Gunnlaug Serpent-Tongue (Old Icelandic)

Old Icelandic	Literal	English
Illugi mælti: "Fara skaltu víst frændi", segir hann, "og slá ekki slíku á þig að þrá eftir einni konu og lát sem þú vitir eigi og mun þig aldrei konur skorta".	Illugi spoke: "Travelling shall-you certain, kinsman", said he, "and strike not such of you, that desire after one wife, and let as you know not, and should you never women shortage".	Illugi spoke: You shall certainly travel, kinsman", he said, "and don't strike so much of you to desire one wife, behave as though you don't know, and you should never be short of women".
Gunnlaugur gerði sem faðir hans mælti og komu þeir til boðsins og var þeim Illuga og sonum hans skipað í öndvegi en þeim Þorsteini Egilssyni og Hrafni mági hans og sveitinni brúðguma í annað öndvegi gegnt Illuga.	Gunnlaug did as father his spoke, and came they to invitation, and were they Illugi and sons his directed in foremost, and they Thorstein son-of-Egil and Hrafn, son-in-law his, and party bridegroom's in other foremost opposite Illugi.	Gunnlaug did as his father had spoken, and they came to the feast, and Illugi and his sons were given one high seat at the front, and Thorstein Egilsson, his son in law Hrafn and the bridegroom's group in the other front opposite Illugi.
Konur sátu á palli og sat Helga hin fagra næst brúðinni og renndi oft augum til Gunnlaugs, og kemur þar að því sem mælt er að eigi leyna augu ef ann kona manni.	Women sitting of platform, and sat Helga the Fair next bride and ran often eyes to Gunnlaug, and came there that because, as said is, that not hiding eyes, if love a-woman man.	The women were sitting at a cross bench, and Helga the Fair sat next to the bride, and often ran her eyes to Gunnlaug, and so it came, as it is said, that if a woman loves a man, her eyes won't hide it.
Gunnlaugur var þá vel búinn og hafði þá klæðin þau hin góðu er Sigtryggur konungur gaf honum og þótti hann þá mikið afbragð annarra manna fyrir margs sakir, bæði afls og vænleiks og vaxtar.	Gunnlaug was then well prepared and had then clothes there in good, as Sigtrygg king gave him, and thought he then much outstanding other men for many's sake, both strength and good-looks and build.	Gunnlaug was then well prepared with good clothes, that King Sigtrygg gave him, and he seemed very much outstanding compared to other men, in both strength, good looks, and build.
Lítil var gleði manna að boðinu.	Little were glad people at invitation.	There was little gladness at the feast.
Og þann dag er menn voru í brottbúningi þá brugðu konur göngu sinni og bjuggust til heimferðar.	And that day, when men were in leaving-prepared, then brought women going theirs and prepared to home-travel.	And that day, when men were preparing to leave, then the woman prepared to travel home.
Gunnlaugur gekk þá til tals við Helgu og töluðu lengi.	Gunnlaug went then to talk with Helga and talked long.	Gunnlaug then went to talk with Helga, and they talked for a long time.
Og þá kvað Gunnlaugur vísu:	And then said Gunnlaug verse:	And then Gunnlaug said a verse:
Ormstungu varð engi	Serpent-Tongue's were none	For Serpent-Tongue were none

The Saga of Gunnlaug Serpent-Tongue (Old Icelandic)

Old Icelandic	Literal	English
allr dagr und sal fjalla hægr síð er Helga hin fagra Hrafns kvonar réð nafni.	All day under hall mountain Right, since Helga but fair Hrafn's wife decided name.	All days under the hall mountain Right, since Helga but Fair Hrafn's wife decided took the name.
Lítt sá höldr hinn hvíti, hjörþeys, faðir meyjar, gefin var Eir til aura ung, við minni tungu.	Little saw handled still white Faced father girl's, Given was Eir to ounces Young, with less tongue.	Little saw handled still white Faced father girl's, Given was Eir to ounces Young, with less tongue.
Og enn kvað hann:	And still said he:	And still he said:
Væn á eg verst að launa, vín-Gefn, föður þínum, fold nemr flaum af skaldi flóðhyrs, og svo móður, því að gerðu Bil borða bæði senn und klæðum, herr hafi hölds og svarra hagvirki, svo fagra.	Fair, that worst to repay, Wine-given, father yours, Ground taken flame of poet Flood-deer, and so mother, Because to make space bore Both they under clothed, Band had flesh and answer Advantage, so fair.	Fair, the worst to repay, Wine-given, father yours, Ground taken flame of poet, Flood-deer, and so mother, Because to make space bore Both they under clothed, Band had flesh and answer Advantage so fair.
Og þá gaf Gunnlaugur Helgu skikkjuna Aðalráðsnaut og var það gersemi sem mest.	And then gave Gunnlaug Helga cloak Æthelred-gift, and was that treasured as most.	And then Gunnlaug gave Helga the cloak that Æthelred had given him, and that was treasured most.
Hún þakkaði honum vel gjöfina.	She thanked him well the-gift.	She thanked him well for the gift.
Síðan gekk Gunnlaugur út og voru þá komin hross og hestar söðlaðir og margir allvænlegir og bundnir heima á hlaðinu.	Afterwards went Gunnlaug out, and were then coming horses and stallions saddled and many all-promising and bound home of farmyard.	Afterwards Gunnlaug went outside, and there were horses and stallions saddled, many of them promising, and bound home at the farmyard.
Gunnlaugur hljóp á bak einhverjum hesti og reið á skeið eftir túninu og að þangað er Hrafn stóð fyrir og varð Hrafn að opa undan.	Gunnlaug jumped of back somebody's horse and rode of sheathed-sword after the-field and that there, as Hrafn stood before, and was Hrafn to avoid under.	Gunnlaug jumped on the back of somebody's horse and rode with sheathed sword to the field where Hrafn was standing, Hrafn had to avoid him.
Gunnlaugur mælti: "Ekki er að opa undan Hrafn", segir hann, "fyrir því að önga ógn býð eg þér að sinni en þú veist til hvers þú hefir unnið".	Gunnlaug spoke: "Nothing is that avoid under, Hrafn", said he, "for because that none threat offer I to-you at once, and you know, to what you had deserved".	Gunnlaug spoke: "Nothing is that to avoid, Hrafn", he said, "because I offer you no threat at once, but you know, to what you deserve".

The Saga of Gunnlaug Serpent-Tongue (Old Icelandic)

Old Icelandic	*Literal*	*English*
Hrafn svarar og kvað vísu:	Hrafn answered and said verse:	Hrafn answered and said a verse:
Samira okkr um eina, *Ullr beinflugu, Fullu,* *frægir fólka Ságu,* *fangs í brigð að ganga.* *Mjök eru margar slíkar,* *morðrunnr, fyrir haf sunnan,* *ýti eg sævar Sóta,* *sannfróðr, konur góðar.*	Same we about one, Ullr bone-flying, full, Famous folk saw, Embrace in trickery to go. Much were many silver, Murder-running, for the-sea south, out seas sought, true-knowledge, women good.	We are one and the same, Ullr bone flying, full, Famous folk saw, Embrace in trickery to go, Much were many silver, Murder running, for the south sea, Out seas sought, True knowledge, good women.
Gunnlaugur svarar: "Vera má", segir hann, "að margar séu en eigi þykir mér svo".	Gunnlaug answered: "be-it may", said he, "that many so, but not seemed me so".	Gunnlaug answered: "It may be", he said, "that there are many, but it does not seem to me".
Þá hlupu þeir Illugi að og Þorsteinn og vildu ekki að þeir ættust við.	Then ran they Illugi to and Thorstein, and willed not, that they come-together with.	Then Illugi and Thorstein ran over to them, and did not wan them to come together.
Þá kvað Gunnlaugur vísu:	Then said Gunnlaug verse:	Then Gunnlaug said this verse:
Gefin var Eir til aura *ormdags hin litfagra,* *þann kveða menn né minna* *minn jafnoka, Hrafni,* *allra nýstr meðan austan* *Aðalráðr farar dvaldi,* *því er menrýris minni* *málgráðr, í gný stála.*	Given was Eir to ounces Serpent-days and fair-colour, Then greeted men not less Mine equal, Hrafn, All new meanwhile east Æthelred travel dwelled, Because was men-equal less Degree, in rage steel.	Given was Eir to ounces, Serpent days and fair colour, Then greeted men not less My equal, Hrafn, All new meanwhile east, Æthelred travel dwelled, Because were men less equal, Degree, in rage steel.
Og eftir þetta riðu menn heim hvorirtveggju og var allt kyrrt og tíðindalaust um veturinn.	And after this rode men home either-side, and was all still and news-less about winter.	After this men rode home each way, and all was still and without news over the winter.
Nýtti Hrafn ekki síðan af samvistum við Helgu þá er þau Gunnlaugur höfðu fundist.	Use Hrafn not since of together-staying with Helga, then as then Gunnlaug had found.	Hrafn had no use to stay together with Helga, once Gunnlaug had found her.

The Saga of Gunnlaug Serpent-Tongue (Old Icelandic)

Old Icelandic	Literal	English
Og um sumarið riðu menn fjölmennir til þings, Illugi svarti og synir hans með honum Gunnlaugur og Hermundur, Þorsteinn Egilsson og Kollsveinn son hans, Önundur frá Mosfelli og synir hans allir, Svertingur Hafur-Bjarnarson.	And about summer rode men crowded to the-assembly, Illugi the-Black and sons his with him, Gunnlaug and Hermund, Thorstein Egilsson and Kollsveinn, son his, Onund from Mosfell and sons his all, Sverting son-of-Hafur-Bjarni.	And about summer men rode and crowded to the assembly, Illugi the Black with his sons, Gunnlaug and Hermund, Thorstein Egilsson and his son Kollsveinn, Onund from Mosfell and all his sons, and Sverting son of Hafur Bjarni.
Skafti hafði þá enn lögsögn.	Skafti had then still lawspeaker.	Skafti still had the job of lawspeaker.
Og einn dag á þinginu er menn gengu fjölmennir til Lögbergs og er þar var lykt að mæla lögskilum þá kvaddi Gunnlaugur sér hljóðs og mælti: "Er Hrafn hér Önundarson?"	And one day of assembly, as men went crowded to Law-Rock and as there was smell of business legal-settlement, they called Gunnlaug himself be-heard and spoke: "Is Hrafn here son-of-Onund?"	And one day at the assembly, as men crowded to the Law-Rock, and as there was the smell of the business of legal settlement, they called that Gunnlaug himself be heard, and he spoke: "Is Hrafn Onundarson here?"
Hann kveðst þar vera.	He said there was.	He said that he was there.
Gunnlaugur ormstunga mælti þá: "Það veist þú að þú hefir fengið heitkonu minnar og dregst til fjandskapar við mig nú fyrir það.	Gunnlaug Serpent-Tongue spoke then: "That know you, as you had caught wife mine and drawn to hostility with me.	Gunnlaug Serpent-Tongue then spoke: "You know as you caught my intended wife, that you have drawn hostility from me.
Vil eg bjóða þér hólmgöngu hér á þinginu á þrigga nátta fresti í Öxarárhólmi".	Now for that will I bid to-you duel here of assembly of three nights from-now in Oxararholm".	Now for that I will bid you to duel here at the assembly three nights from now in Oxararholm".
Hrafn svarar: "Þetta er vel boðið sem von var að þér", segir hann, "og em eg þessa albúinn þegar þú vilt".	Hrafn answered: "This is well bid, as looked was that to-you", said he, "and am I this all-ready, when you will".	Hrafn answered: "This is well bid, as is expected from you", he said, "and I am all ready for this, when you will".
Þetta þótti illt frændum hvorstveggja þeirra en þó voru það lög í þann tíma að bjóða hólmgöngu sá er vanhluta þóttist verða fyrir öðrum.	This thought ill kinsmen either-side they, and though was that law in that time that bid duel, looked that party thought becoming before other.	This the kinsmen on either side thought was bad, but though it was the law in that time, that a duel could be bid, if it seemed that one party had been wronged by another.

The Saga of Gunnlaug Serpent-Tongue (Old Icelandic)

Old Icelandic	Literal	English
Og er þrjár nætur voru liðnar bjuggust þeir til hólmgöngu og fylgdi Illugi svarti syni sínum til hólmsins með miklu fjölmenni.	And when three nights were passed prepared they to duel and followed Illugi the-Black sons his to duel-his with many followers.	And when the three nights were passed, they prepared to duel, and Illugi the Black went to the island with his son, with many followers,
En Skafti lögmaður fylgdi Hrafni og faðir hans og aðrir frændur hans.	Then Skafti law-man followed Hrafn and father his and other kinsmen his.	And Skafti the Lawspeaker followed Hrafn, his father, and other kinsmen.
Og áður Gunnlaugur gengi út í hólminn þá kvað hann vísu þessa:	And before Gunnlaug went out in duel, then said he verse this:	And before Gunnlaug went out into the duel, then he said this verse:
Nú em eg út á eyri alvangs búinn ganga, happs unni guð greppi, gert, með tognum hjörvi. Hnakk skal Helgu lokka, haus vinn eg frá bol lausan loks með ljósum mæki ljúfsvelgs, í tvö kljúfa.	Now am-I out-of of island Field prepared go, Luck love good grasp Be, with extended sword. Saddle shall Helga lure, House win from trunk lost Finally with lights sword Sweet-swallower, in two cleave.	Now I am out on an island, Field prepared to go, Luck love good grasp, Be, with extended sword. Saddle shall Helga lure, House win from trunk lost Finally with lights sword Sweet swallower, in two cleave.
Hrafn svarar og kvað þetta:	Hrafn answered and said this:	Hrafn answered and said this:
Veitat greppr hvor greppa gagnsælli hlýtr fagna. Hér er bensigðum brugðið.	Provided grasp, where grasp Benefit-happier get welcomes. Here was wound-sickles brought-out,	Provided grasp, where grasp Benefit happier gift welcomes. Here was the sickle's wound brought out,
Búin er egg í leggi. Það mun ein og ekkja ung mær, þó að við særumst, þorna spöng af þingi þegns hugrekki fregna.	Done which ridge in leg. That should one and widow Young girl, though we wound, Thorn arch of assembly Citizen courage news.	Done which ridge in leg. That should one and widow Young girl, though we wound, Thorn arch of assembly Citizen courage news.
Hermundur hélt skildi fyrir Gunnlaug bróður sinn en Svertingur Hafur-Bjarnarson fyrir Hrafn.	Hermund held shield for Gunnlaug, brother his, and Sverting son-of-Hafur-Bjarni for Hrafn.	Gunnlaug's brother Hermund held his shield, and Sverting son of Hafur Bjarni did for Hrafn.
Þrem mörkum silfurs skyldi sá leysa sig af hólminum er sár yrði.	Three marks silver should so resolve him of duel, as wound should.	Three marks of silver should resolve he who was wounded in the duel.

The Saga of Gunnlaug Serpent-Tongue (Old Icelandic)

Old Icelandic	Literal	English
Hrafn átti fyrr að höggva er á hann var skorað og hjó hann í skjöld Gunnlaugs ofanverðan og brast sverðið þegar sundur undir hjöltunum er til var hoggið af miklu afli.	Hrafn had before to strike, as that he was challenged, and struck he in shield Gunnlaug above, and burst sword then asunder to hilt, as to was struck of much strength.	Hrafn was to strike first, as it was him that had been challenged, and he struck at Gunnlaug's shield, and the blow was so mighty that the sword broke to the hilt.
Blóðrefillinn hraut upp af skildinum og kom á kinn Gunnlaugi og skeindist hann heldur en eigi.	Point-of-sword jumped up of shield and came in cheek Gunnlaug and scratched him rather but not.	The point of the sword jumped from the shield and struck Gunnlaug's cheek, scratching him slightly.
Þá hlupu feður þeirra þegar á millum og margir aðrir menn.	Then ran father theirs then in between and many other men.	Then their fathers ran between them, along with many other men.
Þá mælti Gunnlaugur: "Nú kalla eg að Hrafn sé sigraður er hann er slyppur".	Then spoke Gunnlaug: "Now call I, that Hrafn so defeated, as he that escapes".	Then Gunnlaug spoke: "Now I declare that Hrafn is defeated, as he has escaped".
"En eg kalla að þú sért sigraður", segir Hrafn, "er þú ert sár orðinn".	"And I call, that you yourself defeated", said Hrafn, "as you are wounded have-become".	"And I declare that you yourself are defeated", said Hrafn, "as you have become wounded".
Gunnlaugur var þá allæfur og reiður mjög og kvað ekki reynt vera.	Gunnlaug was then enraged and angry much and said not tested was.	Gunnlaug was then enraged and very much angry, and said that the matter was not resolved.
Illugi faðir hans kvað þá eigi skyldu reyna meir að sinni.	Illugi, father his, said they not should attempt more than this.	His father Illugi said that they should not attempt any more than this.
Gunnlaugur svarar: "Það mundi eg vilja", segir hann, "að við Hrafn mættumst svo öðru sinni að þú værir fjarri faðir að skilja okkur".	Gunnlaug answered: "That should I will", said he, "that with Hrafn meet-we so other this, that you be away, father, that separate we".	Gunnlaug answered: "I should want", he said, "the next time Hrafn and I meet, that you be away, father that separate us".
Og við þetta skildu þeir að sinni og gengu menn heim til búða sinna.	And with this separated they that this, and went men home to booths theirs.	And with this, they then separated, and men went home to their booths.

The Saga of Gunnlaug Serpent-Tongue (Old Icelandic)

Old Icelandic	Literal	English
Og annan dag eftir í lögréttu var það í lög sett að af skyldi taka hólmgöngur allar þaðan í frá og var það gert að ráði allra vitrustu manna er við voru staddir en þar voru allir þeir er vitrastir voru á landinu.	And another day after in law-assembly was that in law set, that of should take duelling all from-there in from, and was that done that advised all wisest men, that with were present, and then were all they, the wisest were of the-land.	And another day after in the law assembly it was set in law, that all duelling should be all removed, and so it was done with the advice of all the wisest men who were present, and then they were all the wisest of the land.
Og þessi hefir hólmganga síðast framin verið á Íslandi er þeir Hrafn og Gunnlaugur börðust.	And this had duelling last committed made of Iceland, as they Hrafn and Gunnlaug fought.	And this was the last duelling that had ever been committed in Iceland, as Hrafn and Gunnlaug fought.
Það hefir hið þriðja þing verið fjölmennast, annað eftir brennu Njáls, hið þriðja eftir Heiðarvíg.	That had the third assembly been full-men-most, another after Brennu Njal's, the third after heath-slayings.	That was the third largest assembly, the other being Brennu Njal's, and the third after the heath slayings.
Og einn morgun er þeir bræður Hermundur og Gunnlaugur gengu til Öxarár að þvo sér þá gengu öðrumegin að ánni konur margar og var þar Helga hin fagra í því liði.	And one morning, when they brothers, Hermund and Gunnlaug, went to Oxarar to wash themselves, then went other ways to river women many, and was there Helga the fair in before group.	And one morning, when the brothers Hermund and Gunnlaug went to Oxarar to wash themselves, several women were on the other bank of the river, and Helga the Fair was before the group.
Þá mælti Hermundur: "Sérð þú Helgu vinkonu þína hér fyrir handan ána?"	Then spoke Hermund: "See you Helga, girlfriend yours, here before beyond river?"	Then Hermund spoke: "Do you see Helga, your girlfriend, here before the river beyond?"
Gunnlaugur svarar: "Sé eg hana víst".	Gunnlaug answered: "See I her certainly".	Gunnlaug answered: "I certainly see her".
Og þá kvað Gunnlaugur vísu þessa:	And then said Gunnlaug verse this:	And then Gunnlaug said this verse:
Alin var rýgr að rógi, runnr olli því Gunnar,	Measured was woman to feud, Tree cause because-of warrior,	Measured was woman to feud, Tree cause because of a warrior,
lág var eg auðs að eiga óðgjarn, fira börnum. Nú eru svanmærrar síðan svört augu mér bauga lands til lýsi-Gunnar lítilþörf að líta.	Placed was wealth to own Sorely, burning children. Now were swan-mares since Black eyes to-me circle Lands to light-warrior-god Little-need that look.	Placed was wealth to own, Sorely, burning children. Now were swan mares since, Black eyes to me circle, Lands to light warrior god, Little need that look.

The Saga of Gunnlaug Serpent-Tongue (Old Icelandic)

Old Icelandic	Literal	English
Síðan gengu þeir yfir ána og töluðu þau Helga og Gunnlaugur um stund.	Since went they across river, and talked they Helga and Gunnlaug about while.	Afterwards they went across the river, and Helga and Gunnlaug talked for a while.
Og er þeir gengu austur yfir ána þá stóð Helga og starði á Gunnlaug lengi eftir.	And as they went east across river, then stood Helga and stared at Gunnlaug long after.	And as they went west across the river, then Helga stood and stared at Gunnlaug long afterwards.
Gunnlaugur leit þá aftur yfir ána og kvað vísu þessa:	Gunnlaug looked then back over river and spoke verse this:	Gunnlaug then looked across the river and said this verse:
Brámáni skein brúna brims af ljósum himni Hristar hörvi glæstrar haukfránn á mig lauka. En sá geisli sýslar síðan gullmens Fríðar hvarma tungls og hringa Hlínar óþurft mína.	Brightly shone brow Brim under lights heaven Shakes linen glistens Hawk-from of me leek, And saw beams work Since golden beautiful Eyelids moon and rings Hlínar un-needed mine.	Brightly shone the brow Brim under lights heaven Shakes linen glistens Hawk from of me leek, And saw beams work, Since golden beautiful, Eyelids moon and rings, Hlínar un-needed mine.
Og eftir þetta um liðið riðu menn heim af þinginu og var Gunnlaugur heima á Gilsbakka.	And after this about group rode men of assembly, and was Gunnlaug home at Gilsbakka.	And after this happened the group of men of the assembly rode home, and Gunnlaug was home at Gilsbakka.
Og einn morgun er hann vaknaði þá voru allir menn upp risnir nema hann lá.	And one morning, as he awoke, then were all men up rising, except him lying.	And one morning, as he awoke, all men were up, except him laying.
Hann hvíldi í lokrekkju innar af seti.	He rested in bed-closet inside of set.	He rested in bed closet set inside the hall.
Þá gengu í skálann tólf menn, allir alvopnaðir, og var þar kominn Hrafn Önundarson.	They went in hut twelve men, all -weaponed, and were they come-in Hrafn son-of-Onund.	Then twelve men, all armed, came into the hall: Hrafn Onundarson.
Gunnlaugur spratt upp þegar og gat fengið vopn sín.	Gunnlaug sprang up then and opening caught weapons his.	Gunnlaug sprang up then and managed to get his weapons.
Þá mælti Hrafn: "Við öngu skal þér hætt vera", segir hann, "en það er erindi mitt hingað að þú skalt nú heyra.	Then spoke Hrafn: "With none shall to-you end be", said he, "but this is errand mine here, that you shall now hear.	Then Hrafn spoke: "You shall not be to your end", he said, "but this is my errand here, that you shall now hear.
Þú bauðst mér hómgöngu í sumar á alþingi og þótti þér sú ekki reynd verða.	You bid me duel in summer of assembly, and thought to-you that not resolved was.	You bid me duel in summer at the assembly, and you thought that it was not resolved.

The Saga of Gunnlaug Serpent-Tongue (Old Icelandic)

Old Icelandic	Literal	English
Nú vil eg þér bjóða að við förum báðir á brott af Íslandi og utan í sumar og göngum á hólm í Noregi.	Now wish I to-you bid, to with travel both to away of Iceland and out in summer and going to duel in Norway.	Now I wish to bid that we both travel away from Iceland in the summer and go to duel in Norway.
Þar munu eigi frændur okkrir fyrir standa".	There shall none kinsmen ours before stand".	None of our kinsmen shall stand there before us".
Gunnlaugur svarar: "Mæl drengja heilastur og þenna kost vil eg gjarna þiggja.	Gunnlaug answered: "Said fellow well and then benefit will I gladly receive.	Gunnlaug answered "Well said fellow, and the benefit I gladly wish to receive,
Og er hér að þiggja Hrafn", segir hann, "þann greiða sem þú vilt".	And is here to receive Hrafn", said he, "then assistance as you will".	and here is yours to receive, Hrafn", he said, "such assistance as you will".
Hrafn svarar: "Það er vel boðið en ríða munum vér fyrst að sinni".	Hrafn answered: "That is well bid, but ride should we first to ours".	Hrafn answered: "That is well bid, but first we should ride our way".
Og við þetta skildu þeir.	And with that separated they.	And with that they separated.
Þetta þótti frændum hvorstveggja þeirra stórum illa en fengu þó ekki að gert fyrir ákafa þeirra sjálfra enda varð það fram að koma sem til dró.	That thought kinsmen either-side they great ill, and got though nothing to do for extremely they themselves, ended was that from that came, as to draw.	Both kinsmen of either side thought this was a great ill, and though they could do nothing, but what end from that came, which was drawn by fate.
12	12	12
Nú er að segja frá Hrafni að hann bjó skip sitt í Leiruvogum.	Now is to say from Hrafn, that he prepared ship his in Leiruvog.	Now it is to say of Hrafn, that he prepared his ship in Leiruvog.
Tveir menn eru þeir nefndir er fóru með Hrafni, systursynir Önundar föður hans.	Two men were they named, to travel with Hrafn, sister-sons Onund, father his.	Two men were named, to travel with Hrafn, they were the sons of Onund's father.
Hét annar Grímur en annar Ólafur og voru báðir gildir menn.	Named another Grim, and another Olaf, and were both valid men.	One of them was named Grim, another Olaf, and they were both valid men.
Öllum frændum Hrafns þótti mikill svipur er hann fór í brott	All kinsmen Hrafn's thought much seemed, as he travelled to away.	All of Hrafn's kinsmen thought it a great blow, when he travelled away.

The Saga of Gunnlaug Serpent-Tongue (Old Icelandic)

Old Icelandic	Literal	English
en hann sagði svo, kvaðst því Gunnlaug á hólm skorað hafa að hann kvaðst öngvar nytjar hafa Helgu og kvað annan hvorn verða að hníga fyrir öðrum.	And he said so, said of Gunnlaug of duel challenged had, that he said none use have Helga, and said another each be to sink before other.	And he said of Gunnlaug that he had challenged him to a duel, because he had nothing with Helga, and said that one of them would have to fall before the other.
Síðan sigldi Hrafn í haf er þeim gaf byr og komu skipi sínu í Þrándheim og var þar of veturinn og frétti ekki til Gunnlaugs á þeim vetri og þar beið hann Gunnlaugs um sumarið.	Since sailed Hrafn to sea, as they given fair-wind, and came ships theirs in Trondheim, and were there about winter and heard nothing to Gunnlaug of them winter, and there waited he Gunnlaug about summer.	Afterwards Hrafn sailed to sea, as soon as they were given fair wind, and their ship came to Trondheim, and they were there during the winter, and heard nothing of Gunnlaug during the winter, and waited there for Gunnlaug during the summer.
Og enn annan vetur var hann í Þrándheimi þar sem heitir í Lifangri.	And still another winter was he in Trondheim, there which named of Levanger.	And he was still in Trondheim for another winter, in a place named Levanger.
Gunnlaugur ormstunga réðst til skips með Hallfreði vandræðaskáldi norður á Sléttu og urðu þeir síðbúnir mjög og sigldu þeir í haf þegar byr gaf og komu við Orkneyjar litlu fyrir vetur.	Gunnlaug Serpent-Tongue rode to ship with Hallfred troublesome-poet north to Slettu, and became they later-ready much, and sailed they to sea, then fair-wind given, and came to Orkney-Islands little before winter.	Gunnlaug Serpent-Tongue rode to ships with Hallfred the Troublesome Poet north to Slettu, and they became ready much later, and they sailed to sea, then they were given a fair wind, and came to the Orkney islands a little before winter.
Sigurður jarl Hlöðvisson réð þá fyrir eyjunum og fór Gunnlaugur til hans og var þar um veturinn og virti jarl hann vel.	Sigurd earl son-of-Hlodvi ruled then for islands, and travelled Gunnlaug to him and was there about winter, and valued earl him well.	Earl Sigurd Hlodvisson ruled the islands then, and Gunnlaug travelled to him and was there during the winter, and the earl received him well.
Og um vorið bjóst jarl í hernað.	And about spring prepared earl in raiding.	And about spring the earl prepared for raiding.
Gunnlaugur bjóst til ferðar með honum og herjuðu um sumarið víða um Suðureyjar og Skotlandsfjörðu og áttu margar orustur og reyndist Gunnlaugur hinn hraustasti og hinn vaskasti drengur og hinn harðasti karlmaður hvar sem þeir komu.	Gunnlaug prepared to travel with him, and raiding about summer widely about South-Islands and Scotland's-firths and had many battles, and turned-out Gunnlaug the strongest and then boldest fellow and then hardest many, where that they came.	Gunnlaug prepared to travel with him, and raided there during the summer widely about the South Islands and Scotland firths, and had many battles, and it turned out that Gunnlaug was the strongest and the boldest fellow, and the hardest wherever they came.

The Saga of Gunnlaug Serpent-Tongue (Old Icelandic)

Old Icelandic	Literal	English
Sigurður jarl snerist snemmendis sumars aftur en Gunnlaugur sté þá á skip með kaupmönnum þeim er sigldu til Noregs og skildu þeir Sigurður jarl með mikilli vináttu.	Sigurd earl turned around summer back, and Gunnlaug stepped there to ship with trading-men, they then sailed to Norway, and separated they Sigurd earl with much friendliness.	Earl Sigurd turned back in the summer, and Gunnlaug took passage on a ship with trading men, they then sailed to Norway, and they separated from Earl Sigurd with much friendliness.
Gunnlaugur fór norður til Þrándheims á Hlaðir á fund Eiríks jarls og var þar öndverðan vetur og tók jarl vel við honum og bauð honum með sér að vera og það þekktist hann.	Gunnlaug travelled north to Trondheim of Lade to meet Erik earl, and was there early winter, and took earl well with him and invited him with himself to be, and that took he.	Gunnlaug travelled north of Trondheim to Lade to meet Earl Erik, and he was there early in winter, and the earl received him well and invited him to stay with him, and he accepted.
Frétt hafði jarl áður viðskipti þeirra Hrafns svo sem var og segir Gunnlaugi að hann lagði bann fyrir að þeir berðust þar í hans ríki.	News had earl before exchanged they Hrafn's, so as was, and said Gunnlaug, that he had banned for, that they fight there in his kingdom.	The earl had already heard the news of his exchanges with Hrafn, such as it was, and said to Gunnlaug that he had banned them from fighting in his kingdom.
Gunnlaugur kvað hann slíku ráða mundu og var Gunnlaugur þar um veturinn og jafnan fálátur.	Gunnlaug said he such advised would-be, and was Gunnlaug there about winter and usually reserved.	Gunnlaug said that such was his to decide, and Gunnlaug was there during the winter and was usually reserved.
Og um vorið einn dag gekk Gunnlaugur úti og Þorkell frændi hans með honum.	And about spring one day went Gunnlaug out and Thorkell, kinsman his, with him.	And one day in the spring, Gunnlaug went out, and his kinsman Thorkell went with him.
Þeir gengu í brott frá bænum og á völlum fyrir þeim var mannhringur.	They went to away from dwelling and to fields before them was man-ring.	They went away from the town, and to the fields in front of them, where there was a ring of men.
Og í hringinum innan voru tveir menn með vopnum og skylmdust.	And in ring inside were two men with weapons and shields.	And inside the ring were two men with weapons and shields.
Var þar annar nefndur Hrafn en annar Gunnlaugur.	Was there another named Hrafn, and another Gunnlaug.	One was named Hrafn, and another was named Gunnlaug.
Þeir mæltu er hjá stóðu að Íslendingar hyggi smátt og væru seinir til að muna orð sín.	They spoke, as beside standing, that Icelander thought small and was later to that should words theirs.	Those who stood by said that the Icelanders thought a little and were late in remembering their words.

The Saga of Gunnlaug Serpent-Tongue (Old Icelandic)

Old Icelandic	Literal	English
Gunnlaugur fann að hér fylgdi mikið háð og hér var mikið spott að dregið og gekk Gunnlaugur í brott þegjandi.	Gunnlaug found, that here followed much mockery and here was much ridicule was drawn, and went Gunnlaug to away silently.	Gunnlaug found that there followed much mockery, and much ridicule was drawn, and Gunnlaug went away silently.
Og litlu síðar eftir þetta segir hann jarli að hann kveðst eigi lengur nenna að þola háð og spott hirðmanna hans um mál þeirra Hrafns og beiddi jarl fá sér leiðtoga inn í Lifangur.	And little since after this said he earl, that he said not longer bothered to endure mockery and ridicule followers his about matter theirs Hrafn's, and asked earl get himself guide then in Levanger.	And a little afterwards he said to the earl that he no longer bothered to endure mockery and ridicule from his followers about his matter with Hrafn, and he asked the earl to get him a guide then in Levanger.
Jarli var sagt áður að Hrafn var í brottu úr Lifangri og farinn austur til Svíþjóðar og því gaf hann Gunnlaugi orlof að fara og fékk honum leiðtoga tvo til ferðarinnar.	Earl was told already, that Hrafn was to away from Levanger and travelling eastern to Sweden, and therefore gave he Gunnlaug leave to travel and got him guide two to travelling.	The earl was told already, that Hrafn had left Levanger and was travelling east to Sweden, and therefore gave Gunnlaug leave to travel and got him a couple of guides to travel with.
Nú fer Gunnlaugur af Hlöðum við sjöunda mann inn í Lifangur og þann mogun hafði Hrafn farið þaðan með fimmta mann er Gunnlaugur kom þar um kveldið.	Now went Gunnlaug of Lade with seven men then in Levanger, and then morning had Hrafn travelled from-there with five men, as Gunnlaug came there about evening.	Now Gunnlaug went from Lade with six other men and went to Levanger, and that morning Hrafn travelled from there with five men, as Gunnlaug arrived there that evening.
Þaðan fór Gunnlaugur í Veradal og kom þar að kveldi jafnan sem Hrafn hafði áður verið um nóttina.	From-there travelled Gunnlaug in Veradal and came there at evening equally, as Hrafn had before been about night.	Gunnlaug travelled from there into Veradal and arrived there the same evening, as Hrafn has been before the previous evening.
Gunnlaugur fer til þess er hann kom á efsta bæ í dalnum er á Súlu hét og hafði Hrafn þaðan farið um moguninn.	Gunnlaug went, to this as-he came to upper dwelling in valleys, which of Sulu named, and had Hrafn from-there travelled about morning.	Gunnlaug went to this as he came to the upper dwelling in the valleys, which was named Sula, and Hrafn had travelled from there about morning.
Gunnlaugur dvaldi þá ekki ferðina og fór þegar um nóttina.	Gunnlaug dwelled then not travelling and fared then about night.	Gunnlaug did not delay his travelling and travelled during the night.
Og um morguninn í sólarroð þá sáu hvorir aðra.	And about morning in sunrise, they saw each other.	And about morning during the sunrise, they saw each other.

The Saga of Gunnlaug Serpent-Tongue (Old Icelandic)

Old Icelandic	Literal	English
Hrafn var þar kominn sem voru vötn tvö og á meðal vatnanna voru vellir sléttir.	Hrafn was there coming, as were waters two, and of between waters were fields smooth.	Hrafn had come to a place in which there were two lakes, and between the waters were smooth fields.
Það heita Gleipnisvellir.	That called Gleipnisvellir.	That was named Gleipnisvellir.
En fram í vatnið annað gekk nes lítið er heitir Dinganes.	And from in lake another went headland little, was called Dingenes.	And from in the second lake went a little headland, which was named Dinganes.
Þar námu þeir Hrafn við í nesinu og voru fimm saman.	There took they Hrafn with in headland and were five together.	There Hrafn's group of five took up position on the headland, they were five together.
Þeir voru þar með Hrafni frændur hans, Grímur og Ólafur.	They were there with Hrafn kinsmen his, Grim and Olaf.	Hrafn was there with his kinsmen Grim and Olaf.
Og er þeir mættust þá mælti Gunnlaugur: "Það er nú vel er við höfum fundist".	And as they met, then spoke Gunnlaug: "It is now well, that we have met".	And as they met, then Gunnlaug spoke: "It is now well, that we have met".
Hrafn kvaðst það ekki lasta mundu "og er nú kostur hvor er þú vilt", segir Hrafn, "að vér berjumst allir eða við tveir og séu jafnmargir hvorir".	Hrafn said that not blame should, "And is now choice, where as you wish", said Hrafn, "that we fight all or with two, and so equal-many each".	Hrafn said that he had no blame with it, "And now is your choice, where as you wish", said Hrafn, "that we will all fight, as two, but either side must be equal".
Gunnlaugi kveðst vel líka hvort að heldur er.	Gunnlaug said well liked, either as rather was.	Gunnlaug said he liked either.
Þá mæltu þeir frændur Hrafns, Grímur og Ólafur, kváðust eigi vilja standa hjá er þeir berðust.	Then spoke they kinsmen Hrafn's, Grim and Olaf, said not willed stand beside, as they fought.	Then Hrafn's kinsmen spoke, Grim and Olaf said they did not wish to stand beside as they fought.
Svo mælti og Þorkell svarti frændi Gunnlaugs.	So spoke and Thorkell the-Black, kinsman Gunnlaug's.	So spoke also Thorkell the Black and Gunnlaug's kinsmen.
Þá mælti Gunnlaugur við leiðtogana jarls: "Þið skuluð sitja hjá og veita hvorigum og vera til frásagnar um fund vorn".	Then spoke Gunnlaug with guides earl's: "You should sitting beside and grant neither and be to from-saying about meeting ours".	Then Gunnlaug spoke with the earl's guides: "You should sit beside and grant neither side, and be there to say about our meeting".
Og svo gerðu þeir.	And so did they.	And so they did.

The Saga of Gunnlaug Serpent-Tongue (Old Icelandic)

Old Icelandic	Literal	English
Síðan gengust þeir að, börðust fræknlega allir.	Since went they to, fought bravely all.	Afterwards they went to, and all fought bravely.
Þeir Grímur og Ólafur gengu báðir í mót Gunnlaugi einum og lauk svo þeirra viðskipti að hann drap þá báða en hann varð ekki sár.	They Grim and Olaf went both to meet Gunnlaug one, and ended so they exchanged, that he killed them both, and he became not wounded.	Grim and Olaf both went to meet Gunnlaug as one, and their exchange ended so that he killed them both, and he did not become wounded.
Þetta sannar Þórður Kolbeinsson í kvæði því er hann orti um Gunnlaug ormstungu:	This true Thord son-of-Kolbein in poem because, that he wrote about Gunnlaug Serpent-Tongue's:	Thord Kolbeinsson confirms this in the poem that he wrote about Gunnlaug Serpent-Tongue:
Hlóð, áðr Hrafni næði, hugreifum Óleifi Göndlar þeys og Grími Gunnlaugr með hjör þungum. Hann varð hvatra manna hugmóðr drifinn blóði, Ullr réð ýta falli unnviggs, bani þriggja.	Destroyed, before Hrafn neared, Courageous Olaf, Cock dashing, and Grim, Gunnlaug struck heavily. He quickly became a man, Spirit mother, driven by blood, Ullr ruled pushed fall Down, bane three.	Destroyed, before Hrafn neared, Courageous Olaf, Cock dashing, and Grim, Gunnlaug struck heavily. He quickly became a man, Spirit mother, driven by blood, Ullr ruled pushed fall Down, bane three.
Þeir Hrafn sóttust meðan og Þorkell svarti frændi Gunnlaugs og féll Þorkell fyrir Hrafni og lét líf sitt.	They Hrafn attended while and Thorkell the-Black kinsman Gunnlaug's and fell Thorkell before Hrafn and laid life his.	Meanwhile, Hrafn and Thorkell the Black, Gunnlaug's kinsman, were fighting, and Thorkell fell before Hrafn and laid his life,
Og allir féllu förunautar þeirra að lyktum.	And all fell companions theirs that in the end.	And all of their companions fell in the end.
Og þá börðust þeir tveir með stórum höggum og öruggum atgangi er hvor veitti öðrum og sóttust einart í ákafa.	And then fought they two with great blows and fearlessly to-running, as were given other, and attended resolute in extremely.	Then the two of them fought with great blows, and running fearlessly, and each gave the other, and fought alone fiercely.
Gunnlaugur hafði þá sverðið Aðalráðsnaut og var það hið besta vopn.	Gunnlaug had then sword Æthelred-gift, and was it the best weapon.	Gunnlaug then had the sword that Æthelred had given him, and it was the best weapon.
Gunnlaugur hjó þá um síðir til Hrafns mikið högg með sverðinu og undan Hrafni fótinn.	Gunnlaug struck then about eventually to Hrafn's much striking with sword and under Hrafn leg.	Gunnlaug then eventually struck at Hrafn, striking with his sword under Hrafn's leg.

The Saga of Gunnlaug Serpent-Tongue (Old Icelandic)

Old Icelandic	Literal	English
Hrafn féll þó eigi að heldur og hnekkti þá að stofni einum og studdi þar á stúfinum.	Hrafn fell though not that held and over-turned then to strain one and stood there of stump.	Hrafn fell but did not overturn, and dropped back on to a tree stump, and stood there.
Þá mælti Gunnlaugur: "Nú ertu óvígur", segir hann, "og vil eg eigi lengur berjast við þig örkumlaðan mann".	Then spoke Gunnlaug: "Now are-you not-fighting", said he, "and wish I not longer fight with you, crippled man".	Then Gunnlaug spoke: "Now you are not fighting", he said, "and I no longer wish to fight with a crippled man".
Hrafn svaraði: "Svo er það", segir hann, "að mjög hefir á leikist minn hluta en þó mundi mér enn vel duga ef eg fengi að drekka nokkuð".	Hrafn answered: "So it is", said he, "that much had of played mine lot, and though should me still well help, if I get to drink something".	Hrafn answered: "So it is", he said, "that much has my lot played out, and though I should still be well, if I could get something to drink".
Gunnlaugur svarar: "Svík mig þá ei", segir hann, "ef eg færi þér vatn í hjálmi mínum".	Gunnlaug answered: "Betray me then not", said he, "if I journey to-you water in helmet mine".	Gunnlaug answered: "Do not betray me then", he said, "if I journey to bring you water in my helmet".
Hrafn svarar: "Ei mun eg svíkja þig", segir hann.	Hrafn answered: "Not should I betray you", said he.	Hrafn answered: "I should betray you", he said.
Síðan gekk Gunnlaugur til lækjar eins og sótti í hjálminum og færði Hrafni.	Then got Gunnlaug to stream one and attended in helmet and took Hrafn.	Then Gunnlaug went to a stream, and got water in his helmet and took it to Hrafn,
En hann seildist í mót hinni vinstri hendinni en hjó í höfuð Gunnlaugi með sverðinu hinni hægri hendi og varð það allmikið sár.	Then he stretched to meet the left hand then struck to hand Gunnlaug's with sword his right hand and was that all-much wound.	And as he stretched out to meet his left hand, he struck at Gunnlaug with the sword in his right hand, and there he became very much wounded.
Þá mælti Gunnlaugur: "Illa sveikstu mig nú og ódrengilega fór þér þar sem eg trúði þér".	Then spoke Gunnlaug: "Ill tricked me now and un-fellow-like do you there as I trusted you".	Then Gunnlaug spoke: "You have tricked me badly now, and in an unmanly way, there as I trusted you".
Hrafn svarar: "Satt er það", segir hann, "en það gekk mér til þess að eg ann þér eigi faðmlagsins Helgu hinnar fögru".	Hrafn answered: "True is that", said he, "and that goes me to this, that I love you not embrace Helga the Fair".	Hrafn answered: "That is true", he said, "and I did this so that you will not love the embrace of Helga the Fair.
Og þá börðust þeir enn í ákafa en svo lauk að lyktum að Gunnlaugur bar af Hrafni og lét Hrafn þar líf sitt.	And then fought they still to eagerly but so ended to completion that Gunnlaug bore of Hrafn and laid Hrafn there life his.	And then they fought in the extreme. And so in the end it was finished, that Gunnlaug overpowered Hrafn, and there Hrafn lay down his life.

The Saga of Gunnlaug Serpent-Tongue (Old Icelandic)

Old Icelandic	Literal	English
Þá gengu fram leiðtogar jarls og bundu höfuðsárið Gunnlaugs.	They went from guides earl's and bound head-wound Gunnlaug's.	Then the earl's guides went and bound Gunnlaug's head wound.
Hann sat þá meðan og kvað þá vísu þessa:	He sat then meanwhile and said then verse this:	Meanwhile he sat and said this verse:
Oss gekk mætr á móti mótrunnr í dyn spjóta hríðgjörvandi hjörva Hrafn framlega jafnan. Hér varð mörg í morgun málmflaug um Gunnlaugi, hergerðandi á Hörða hringþollr, nesi Dinga.	Us went measure of meet Against-running in storm spear, Aggravating sword, Hrafn from-like equal. Here was many to morning Metal-missile about Gunnlaug, Ranks, of hard, Ring-endurance, headland Dinge.	We went to measure in meeting, Against running storm spear, Aggravating sword, Hrafn from like equal, Here were many this morning, Metal missile about Gunnlaug, Ranks, of hard, Ring endurance, headland Dinge.
Síðan bjuggu þeir um dauða menn og færðu Gunnlaug á hest sinn eftir það og komust með hann allt ofan í Lifangur.	Since settled they about death men and went Gunnlaug of Horse his after that and came with he all over to Levanger.	Afterwards they saw to the dead men, and Gunnlaug travelled on his horse after that, and the men came with him to Levanger.
Og þar lá hann þrjár nætur og fékk alla þjónustu af presti og andaðist síðan og var þar jarðaður að kirkju.	And there laid he three nights and got all service of priest and ended after and was there earthed at church.	And there he lay for three nights, and got a service from the priest, and died, afterwards he was buried there at the church.
Öllum þótti mikill skaði að um hvorntveggja þeirra, Gunnlaug og Hrafn, með þeim atburðum sem varð um líflát þeirra.	All thought much harm that about either-way they, Gunnlaug and Hrafn, with them events which were about loss theirs.	Everyone thought it was a great harm on either side, Gunnlaug and Hrafn, with the events, that became their loss.
13	13	13
Og um sumarið áður þessi tíðindi spurðust út hingað til Íslands þá dreymdi Illuga svarta og var hann þá heima á Gilsbakka.	And about summer, before these tidings learned back-from there to Iceland, then dreamed Illugi the-Black, and was he then home of Gilsbakka.	That summer, before this news was learned back in Iceland, then Illugi the Black dreamed that he was at home in Gilsbakka.
Honum þótti Gunnlaugur að sér koma í svefninum og var blóðugur mjög og kvað vísu þessa fyrir honum í svefninum.	He thought Gunnlaug that himself came in sleep and was bloodied much and said verse this for him in sleep.	He thought that Gunnlaug himself came in his sleep, and was much bloodied, and said this verse for him in his sleep.

The Saga of Gunnlaug Serpent-Tongue (Old Icelandic)

Old Icelandic	Literal	English
Illugi mundi vísuna er hann vaknaði og kvað síðan fyrir öðrum:	Illugi remembered verse, as he awoke, and said since before others:	Illugi remembered this verse, as he awoke, and said afterwards before others:
Vissi eg Hrafn, en Hrafni hvöss kom egg í leggi, hjaltugguðum höggva hrynfiski mig brynju, þá er hræskærri hlýrra hlaut fen ari benja. Klauf gunnsproti Gunnar Gunnlaugs höfuð runna.	Know Hrafn, and Hrafn Sharp came ridge in leg, Hilt-chewed strike Caved-fish me armour, Then corpse-scorer warm Got fens eagle wound. Cleaved war-twig Gunnar Gunnlaug hand round.	I know Hrafn, and Hrafn Sharp came ridge in leg, Hilt chewed strike, Caved fish me armour, Then corpse scorer warm, Got fens eagle wound, Cleaved war twig Gunnar, Gunnlaug hand round.
Sá atburður varð suður að Mosfelli hina sömu nátt að Önund dreymdi að Hrafn kæmi að honum og var allur alblóðugur.	So event was south at Mosfell the same night, that Onund dreamed, that Hrafn came to him and was all -bloodied.	So it became that south at Mosfell that same night, that Onund dreamed that Hrafn came to him and was all bloodied.
Hann kvað vísu þessa:	He said verse this:	He said this verse:
Roðið sverð en sverða sverð-Rögnir mig gerði. Voru reynd í röndum randgálkn fyrir ver handan. Blóðug hygg eg í blóði blóðgögl of skör stóðu. Sárfíkinn hlaut sára sárgammr enn á þramma.	Reddened was sword, and sword sword-reddened me made. Were resolved in shield Giants for were beyond. Bloodied mind to blood Blood-goslings about fragile standing. Wound-eager got wound Wound-vulture still of trample.	Reddened was sword, and sword Sword reddened me made. Were resolved in shield Giants for were beyond. Bloodied mind to blood Blood goslings about fragile standing. Wound eager got wound Wound vulture still of trample.
Og um sumarið annað eftir á alþingi mælti Illugi svarti til Önundar að Lögbergi: "Hverju viltu bæta mér son minn", sagði hann, "er Hrafn son þinn sveik hann í tryggðum?"	And about summer next after of assembly spoke Illugi the-Black to Onund at Law-Rock: "How will-you compensate me son mine", said he, "as Hrafn, son yours, betrayed him in loyalty?"	And about next summer after the assembly, Illugi the Black spoke to Onund at the Law Rock: "How will you compensate me for my son", he said, "as Hrafn your son betrayed him in loyalty?"
Önundur svarar: "Fjarkominn þykist eg til þess", sagði hann, "að bæta hann svo sárt sem eg hélt á þeirra fundi.	Onund answered: "Far-away think I to this", said he, "that compensate he, so wounded as I held of their meeting.	Onund answered: "I think far away of this", he said, "to compensate him, so wounded as I am because of their meeting.

The Saga of Gunnlaug Serpent-Tongue (Old Icelandic)

Old Icelandic	Literal	English
Mun eg og öngra bóta beiða þig fyrir minn son".	Should I and none compensation bid you for my son".	I shall not ask for compensation from you for my son".
Illugi svarar: "Kenna skal þá nakkvar að skauti, þinn frændi eða þinna ættmanna".	Illugi answered: "Know shall then anyone that fringes yours kinsman or your relatives".	Illugi answered: "Know then that anyone on the fringes of your kinsmen or your relatives shall".
Og eftir þingið um sumarið var Illugi jafnan dapur mjög.	And remaining assembly about summer was Illugi equally depressed much.	And for the rest of the assembly and during the summer, Illugi was very much depressed.
Það var sagt um haustið að Illugi reið heiman af Gilsbakka með þrjátigu manna og kom til Mosfells snemma morguns.	That is said, about autumn, that Illugi rode home of Gilsbakka with thirty men and came to Mosfell early morning.	It is said, about autumn, that Illugi rode home from Gilsbakka with thirty men and came to Mosfell early in the morning.
Önundur komst í kirkju og synir hans en Illugi tók frændur hans tvo.	Onund came in church and sons his, and Illugi took kinsmen his two.	Onund and his sons came into the church, but Illugi captured two of his kinsmen.
Hét annar Björn en annar Þorgrímur.	Named another Bjorn, and another Thorgrim.	One was named Bjorn, and another Thorgrim.
Hann lét drepa Björn en fóthöggva Þorgrím.	He had kill Bjorn, and foot-striking Thorgrim.	He had Bjorn killed, and Thorgrim's foot cut off.
Reið Illugi heim eftir það og varð þessa engi rétting af Önundi.	Rode Illugi home after that, and was this none righting of Onund.	Illugi rode home after that, and Onund did not seek reprisal.
Hermundur Illugason undi lítt eftir Gunnlaug bróður sinn og þótti ekki hans hefnt að heldur þótt þetta væri að gert.	Hermund son-of-Illugi satisfied little after Gunnlaug, brother his, and thought not he had that rather, though this was as done.	Hermund Illugason was very upset with Gunnlaug, about his brother, and thought that even though this had been done, he had not been avenged.
Maður hét Hrafn og var bróðurson Önundar að Mosfelli.	Man named Hrafn and was brother's-son Onund at Mosfell.	There was a man named Hrafn and was Onund's brother's son at Mosfell.
Hann var farmaður mikill og átti skip er uppi stóð í Hrútafirði.	He was travelling-man great and had ship, was up stood in Hrutafjord.	He was a great travelling man and had a ship, which was stood in Hrutafjord.

The Saga of Gunnlaug Serpent-Tongue (Old Icelandic)

Old Icelandic	Literal	English
Og um vorið reið Hermundur Illugason heiman einn samt og norður Holtavörðuheiði og svo til Hrútafjarðar og út á Borðeyri til skips kaupmannanna.	And about spring rode Hermund son-of-Illugi home one together and north Holtavarda-Heath and so to Hrutafjord and out-of Bordeyri to ships trading-men's.	And about spring Hermund Illugason rode out from home on his own, and north to Holtvarda Heath, and then to Hrutafjord and out of Bordeyri to trading men's ships.
Kaupmenn voru þá búnir mjög.	Trading-men were they readying much.	The trading men had much to prepare.
Hrafn stýrimaður var á landi og mart manna hjá honum.	Hrafn steersman was of land and many men beside him.	Hrafn the captain was ashore and there were many men beside him.
Hermundur reið að honum og lagði í gegnum hann spjótinu og reið þegar í brott.	Hermund rode to him and lay to through him spear and rode then to away.	Hermund rode to him and laid a spear through him, and then rode away,
En þeim varð öllum bilt félögum Hrafns við Hermund.	Then they were all startled company Hrafn's with Hermund.	And Hrafn's company all became startled about Hermund.
Öngar komu bætur fyri víg þetta og með þessu skilur skipti þeirra Illuga svarta og Önundar að Mosfelli.	None came compensation for killing this and with this separated exchanges theirs Illugi the-Black and Onund at Mosfell.	No compensation came for this killing. And with this separated the exchanges between Illugi the Black and Onund at Mosfell.
Þorsteinn Egilsson gifti Helgu dóttur sína er stundir liðu fram þeim manni er Þorkell hét og var Hallkelsson.	Thorstein son-of-Egil gave Helga, daughter his, when awhile passed from, that man, was Thorkell named and was son-of-Hallkel.	After a while had passed, Thorstein Egilsson gave his daughter Helga to a man that was named Thorkell, and he was the son of Hallkel.
Hann bjó út í Hraunsdal og fór Helga til bús með honum og varð honum lítt unnandi því að hún verður aldrei afhuga Gunnlaugi þótt hann væri dauður.	He lived out in Hraunsdal, and fared Helga to house with him and became him little loved, because that she became never out-of-mind Gunnlaug, though he was dead.	He lived out in Hraunsdal, and Helga travelled home with him, and he became little loved, because she never got Gunnlaug out of her mind, though he was dead.
En Þorkell var þó vaskur maður að sér og auðigur að fé og skáld gott.	But Thorkell was thought bold man as himself and rich in wealth and poet good.	But Thorkell was thought a bold man, as he himself was rich in wealth and a good poet.
Þau áttu börn saman eigi allfá.	They had children together not few.	They had children together, not few.

The Saga of Gunnlaug Serpent-Tongue (Old Icelandic)

Old Icelandic	Literal	English
Þórarinn hét son þeirra og Þorsteinn og enn fleiri börn áttu þau.	Thorarin named son theirs and Thorstein, and still more children had They.	Their sons were named Thorarin and Thorstein, and they still had more children.
Það var helst gaman Helgu að hún rekti skikkjuna Gunnlaugsnaut og horfði þar á löngum.	That was rather enjoyed Helga, that she unfolded cloak Gunnlaug's-gift and looked there of long.	It was Helga's greatest pleasure to unfold the cloak that Gunnlaug had given her, and she looked long at it.
Og eitt sinn kom þar sótt mikil á bæ þeirra Þorkels og Helgu og krömdust margir lengi.	And once then came there sickness much of dwelling there Thorkell and Helga, and chronic-illness many long.	And one time there came a great sickness in the home of Thorkell and Helga, and many people suffered long with it.
Helga tók þá og þyngd og lá þó eigi.	Helga took then and heavy and laying though not.	Helga then took and heavily, but did not lay with it.
Og einn laugaraftan sat Helga í eldaskála og hneigði höfuð í kné Þorkatli bónda sínum og lét senda eftir skikkjunni Gunnlaugsnaut.	And one Saturday-afternoon sat Helga in cooking-hut and inclined head in knee Thorkell, husband hers, and let send after cloak Gunnlaug's-gift.	And one Saturday afternoon, Helga sat in the cooking hut, resting her head in her husband Thorkell's lap, and had sent for Gunnlaug's cloak gift.
Og er skikkjan kom til hennar þá settist hún upp og rakti skikkjuna fyrir sér og horfði á um stund.	And as cloak came to her, then sat she up and unfolded cloak for herself and looked of about awhile.	And as the cloak came to her, then she sat up and unfolded the cloak for herself and look at it for a while.
Og síðan hné hún aftur í fang bónda sínum og var þá örend.	And then sank her back in arms husband hers and was then dead.	And then she fell back into her husband's arms, and then was dead.
Þorkell kvað þá vísu þessa:	Thorkell said then verse this:	Thorkell said this verse:
Lagði eg orms að armi armgóða mér tróðu, guðbrá Lofnar lífi líns, andaða mína. Þó er beiðendum bíða bliks þungara miklu.	Laid serpent to arms Arms good to-me trod, God drew praised live Linen, ended mine. Thought was waited-end bid Gleam heavy much.	Laid serpent to arms, Arms good to me trod, God drew praised life Linen, ended mine. Thought was waited end bid, Gleam heavy much.
Helga var til kirkju færð en Þorkell bjó þar eftir og þótti allmikið fráfall Helgu sem von var að.	Helga was to church carried, and Thorkell lived there after and thought all-much death Helga, which looked was to.	Helga was carried to church, and Thorkell lived there after and thought much about the death of Helga, which was expected.
Og lýkur þar nú sögunni.	And ends there now the-saga.	And now there ends the saga.

Word List *(Norse to English)*

OI = Old Icelandic   ON = Old Norse

Norse	English
' '	
's	was ON

A, a

Norse	English
að	as OI, at OI, by OI, in OI, of OI, than OI, that OI, the OI, this OI, to OI, was OI
aðalráð	Ethelred (name) OI, Ethelred (name) ON
aðalráði	Ethelred (name) OI, Ethelred (name) ON
aðalráðr	Ethelred (name) OI, Ethelred (name) ON
aðalráðsnaut	Ethelred-Gift (name) OI, Ethelred-Gift (name) ON, Ethelred-given (name) OI
aðalráður	Ethelred (name) OI
aðra	other OI, other ON
aðrir	other OI, other ON, others OI, others ON
aðsetu	seat OI
af	from OI, from OI, of OI, of OI, of ON, of ON, out-of OI, out-of OI, out-of ON, out-of ON, that OI, to OI
afarmenni	outstanding-man OI, outstanding-man ON
afbragð	outstanding OI, outstanding ON
afbrigði	deviation OI, deviation ON
affangadag	celebration-day OI
afhuga	out-of-mind OI, out-of-mind ON
afl	strength OI, strength ON
afli	strength OI, strength ON
afls	strength OI, strength ON
afreksmaðr	accomplished ON
afreksmaður	accomplished OI
aftr	back ON, return OI, return ON, returned ON, returning ON
aftur	back OI, returned OI
agðanesi	Adganes (place) OI, Adganes (place) ON
alblóðugr	all-bloodied ON
alblóðugur	bloodied OI
albúið	all-prepared OI
albúinn	all-ready OI, all-ready ON, all-ready ON, prepared OI
albúit	prepared ON
aldr	age ON, age ON
aldrei	never OI
aldri	never ON
aldur	age OI, age OI
alheiðið	all-heathen OI
alheiðit	all-heathen ON
alhugi	all-mind OI, all-mind ON
alin	measured OI, measured ON
alla	all OI, all ON, all ON
allæfr	enraged ON
allæfur	enraged OI
allan	all OI, all ON
allar	all OI, all ON
allfá	few OI, few ON
allgóð	all-good OI, all-good ON
allir	all OI, all ON
alllitlu	very-little OI, very-little ON
allmikið	all-much OI
allmikit	all-much ON
allmjög	all-greatly OI
allmjök	all-very ON
allóvænt	all-not-expected OI, all-not-expected ON

Word List (Norse to English)

Norse	English
allr	all OI, all ON
allra	all OI, all ON, everyone's OI
allráðr	all-ruling OI, all-ruling ON
allri	all OI, all ON
alls	all OI, all ON
allt	all OI, all ON, altogether OI
allur	all OI
allvænlegir	all-promising OI
allvænlegur	promising OI
allvænligir	all-promising ON
allvænligr	promising ON
allvel	all-well OI, all-well ON, well OI
alnar	measured OI, measured ON
alþingi	assembly OI, assembly ON
alþýðu	people OI, people ON
alvangs	field OI, field ON
alvápnaðir	all-weaponed ON
alvopnaðir	all-weaponed OI
andaða	ended OI, ended ON
andaðist	died ON, ended OI, ended ON
andliti	face OI, face ON
andnesjum	headlands OI, headlands ON
andness	against-headland OI, against-headland ON
ann	love OI, love ON
annað	another OI, next OI, second-time OI
annan	another OI, another ON
annar	another OI, one OI, second OI
annarr	another ON, second ON
annarra	another OI, another ON, other OI, other ON
annars	each-other OI, each-other ON, other OI, other ON
annat	another ON, next ON, other ON, second-time ON
arfi	inheritance OI, inheritance ON
arfr	inheritance ON
arfur	inheritance OI
ari	eagle OI, eagle ON
armgóða	arm-good OI
armi	arms OI, arms ON
arms	arms ON
at	as ON, at ON, but ON, by ON, from ON, in ON, it ON, of ON, than ON, that ON, then ON, to ON, was ON
atburðr	event ON
atburðum	events OI, events ON
atburður	event OI
atfangadag	celebration-day ON
atferli	procedure OI, procedure ON
atgangi	to-running OI, to-running ON
atgervismenn	talented-people OI
atgöngu	to-going OI, to-going ON
atla	Atli (name) OI, Atli (name) ON
atli	Atli (name) OI, Atli (name) ON
atsetu	to-seat ON
att	that OI, to ON
auðigr	rich ON, wealthy ON
auðigs	wealthy OI, wealthy ON
auðigur	rich OI
auðmaðr	rich-man ON
auðmaður	rich-man OI
auðr	rich ON
auðs	wealth OI, wealth ON
auðun	Audun (name) OI, Audun (name) ON
auðuni	Audun (name) OI, Audun's (name) OI, Audun's (name) ON
auðunn	Audun (name) ON
auður	fortune OI
auðveitir	wealth-provides OI, wealth-provides ON
augu	eyes OI, eyes ON
augum	eyes OI, eyes ON
aura	money OI, ounces OI, ounces ON

Word List (Norse to English)

Norse	English
austan	east OI, east ON
austanvindr	east-wind OI, east-wind ON
austmaðr	easterner ON
austmaðrinn	eastern-man ON
austmaður	eastern-man OI
austmaðurinn	eastern-man OI
austmanni	eastern-man ON
austmanninn	eastern-man OI, eastern-man ON
austmenn	easterners OI, easterners ON
austr	east ON, eastern ON
austur	east OI

Á, á

Norse	English
á	a OI, a ON, about OI, about ON, am OI, at OI, at ON, by OI, in OI, it OI, of OI, of ON, on OI, on ON, out OI, out ON, that OI, that ON, the OI, then OI, to OI, to ON
áðr	after OI, after ON, back OI, back ON, before ON
áður	around OI, back OI, before OI, returned OI
ágætr	fine ON
ágætum	wonderful OI, wonderful ON
ágætur	fine OI
ák	that ON
ákafa	anger OI, eagerly OI, eagerness OI, extremely OI, extremely ON
ákaflega	extremely OI
ákafliga	extremely ON
álft	swan OI, swan ON
álftin	swan ON, the-swan OI
álftinni	the-swan OI, the-swan ON
ána	river OI, river ON
ánni	river OI, river ON
ás	as OI, as ON
ásaka	forsake OI, forsake ON
ásbjarnar	Asbjarnar (name) OI, Asbjarnar (name) ON
ásgerðr	Asgerd (place) ON
ásgerður	Asgerd (place) OI
ási	as OI, as ON
ást	love OI, love ON
ástaraugum	lovely-eyes OI, lovely-eyes ON
átján	eighteen OI, eighteen ON
átrúnaði	religion OI, religion ON
átt	direction OI, married OI, married ON
átti	had OI, had ON, married OI, married ON
áttu	had OI, had ON
áttum	directions OI
ávallt	always OI, always ON

Æ, æ

Norse	English
ætla	intend OI, intend ON
ætlað	intended OI
ætlaði	intended OI, intended ON
ætlan	supposing OI, supposing ON
ætlar	intend OI, intend ON
ætt	ancestry OI, descendents OI, descendents ON, direction ON, family OI, generations OI
ættaðr	descended ON
ættaður	descended OI
ættar	noble OI, noble ON
ættist	come-together ON
ættmanna	relatives OI, relatives ON
ættum	directions ON
ættust	come-together OI

B, b

Norse	English
bað	asked OI, asked ON, bid OI, invited OI, proposed-to OI

Word List (Norse to English)

Norse	English
báða	both OI, both ON
báðir	both OI, both ON
bæ	dwelling OI, dwelling ON, farm OI
bæði	both OI, both ON
bæðir	bid OI, bid ON, pray OI
bæjar	farm OI, farm ON
bæna	prayer OI, prayer ON
bænum	dwelling OI, dwelling ON
bæta	compensate OI, compensate ON, compensation OI
bætr	compensation ON
bætur	compensation OI
bak	back OI, back ON
banahögg	death-blow OI, death-blow ON
bani	bane OI, bane ON
bann	ban OI, ban ON
bar	bore OI, bore ON
barið	beaten OI
barit	beaten ON
barn	child OI, child ON
barna	children OI, children ON
barni	child OI, child ON
barnið	child OI
barnit	child ON
barns	child OI, child ON
bárur	waves OI, waves ON
bastarðr	bastard ON
bastarður	bastard OI
bauð	bid OI, bid ON, invited OI, invited ON, offered OI
bauðk	invited ON
bauðst	bid OI
bauga	circle OI, circle ON
bautt	bid ON
bazta	best ON
baztr	best ON
beð	bed ON
beðr	bedding OI, bedding ON
beið	waited OI, waited ON
beiða	bid OI, bid ON
beiddi	asked OI, asked ON, bid OI
beiddist	invited OI, invited ON
beiðendum	waited-end OI
beiðöndum	waited-end ON
beinflugu	bone-flying OI
bekk	bench OI, bench ON
bekkinum	group OI, group ON
benja	wound OI, wound ON
benloga	bone-flying ON
bensigðum	wound-sickles OI, wound-sickles ON
bera	bore OI, born OI, born ON, carry OI, carry ON
berðist	fight ON, fought ON
berðust	fight OI
bergfinn	Bergfinn (name) OI, Bergfinn (name) ON
bergfinnr	Bergfinn (name) ON
bergfinnur	Bergfinn (name) OI
berimst	fight ON
berjast	fight OI, fight ON
berjumst	fight OI
berserkrinn	berserker ON, the-berserker ON
berserkurinn	the-berserker OI
best	best OI, the-best OI
besta	best OI
bestu	best OI
bestum	best OI
bestur	best OI
betr	better ON
betur	better OI
bezt	best ON
bezta	best ON
beztu	best ON
beztum	best ON
bið	ask OI, ask ON, bid OI, bid ON
bíða	bid OI, bid ON, wait OI, wait ON
bíðit	bid OI, bid ON
biðja	bid OI, propose OI, propose ON, propose-to ON
biðr	asked ON
biður	asked OI

Word List (Norse to English)

Norse	English
bil	space OI, space ON
bilt	startled OI, startled ON
binda	bind OI, bind ON
bjarnardóttir	daughter-of-Bjorn (name) OI, daughter-of-Bjorn (name) ON
bjó	lived OI, lived ON, prepared OI, prepared ON
bjóða	bid OI, bid ON
björn	Bjorn (name) OI, Bjorn (name) ON
bjóst	prepared OI, prepared ON, readied OI, readied ON
bjuggu	lived OI, lived ON, prepared OI, prepared ON, settled ON
bjuggust	prepared OI, prepared ON
bláar	blue OI, blue ON
blæddi	bled OI, bled ON
blíðlega	gently OI
blíðliga	happily ON
bliks	gleam OI, gleam ON
blítt	gently OI, gently ON
blóð	blood OI, blood ON
blóðgögl	blood-goslings OI, blood-goslings ON
blóði	blood OI, blood ON, bloodied OI
blóðrefillinn	point-of-sword OI, point-of-sword ON
blóðug	bloodied OI, bloodied ON
blóðugr	bloodied ON
blóðugur	bloodied OI
boð	bid ON, invitation OI
boðið	bid OI, invitation OI, invited OI
boðinu	invitation OI, invitation ON
boðit	bid ON, offer ON
boðs	settle OI, settle ON
boðsins	invitation OI, invitation ON
bol	trunk OI, trunk ON
bónda	farmer OI, farmer ON, husband OI, husband ON, the-farmer OI
bóndason	farmer's-son OI, farmer's-son ON
bóndasonum	farmer's-sons OI
bóndi	farm ON, farmer OI, farmer ON
bóndum	farmer ON, farmers OI
bónorð	proposal OI, proposal ON
bónorðið	marriage-proposal OI, proposal OI
bónorðit	marriage-proposal ON
borða	bore OI, bore ON
borðeyri	Bordeyri (place) OI, Bordeyri (place) ON
börðust	battled OI, fought OI, fought ON
borg	Borg (place) OI, Borg (place) ON
borgar	Borg (place) OI, Borg (place) ON
borgarfirði	Borgafjord (place) OI, Borgafjord (place) ON
borgfirðinga	Borgafjord-people (name) OI, Borgafjord-people (name) ON
borgina	borg OI, Borg (place) ON
borið	bore OI, carried OI
borit	carried ON
börn	children OI, children ON
börnum	children OI, children ON
bóta	compensation OI, compensation ON
brá	drew ON
bráðger	quick OI
bráðgerr	quick ON
bráðlega	quickly OI, soon OI
bráðliga	soon ON
bræðr	brothers ON
bræður	brothers OI
brag	poetry OI, poetry ON
bragarlaunum	character-reward OI, character-reward ON, poem-repay OI
brámáni	brightly OI, brightly ON
brast	burst OI, burst ON
brátt	soon OI, soon ON
bregðr	tricked ON

Word List (Norse to English)

Norse	English
bregður	tricked OI
breiðöxi	broad-axe OI, broad-axe ON
brennu	brennu OI, brennu ON
brigð	trick OI, trick ON
brims	brim OI, brim ON
bróðir	brother OI, brother ON, brother-of ON
bróður	brother OI, brother ON
bróðurson	brother's-son OI
bróðursonr	brother's-son ON
brott	away OI, away ON
brottbúningi	leaving-prepared OI, leaving-prepared ON
brottferðar	away-travel OI, away-travel ON, travel-away OI
brottu	away OI, away ON
brúðguma	bridegroom's OI, bridegroom's ON
brúðinni	bride OI, bride ON
brúðlaup	wedding OI, wedding ON
brúðlaupi	wedding OI, wedding ON
brúðlaupinu	wedding-feast OI, wedding-feast ON
brúðr	brother OI, brother ON
brúðrin	bride ON
brúðurin	bride OI
brugðið	brought-out OI, drawn OI
brugðit	brought ON, brought-out ON
brugðu	brought OI, brought ON
brúna	brow OI, brow ON
bryggjur	quay OI, quay ON
brynju	armour OI, armour ON
búa	prepare OI, prepare ON
búandmönnum	settling-people OI
búast	prepared OI, prepared ON
búða	booths OI, booths ON
búðar	booth OI, booth ON
búðartóftanna	booth-ruins OI, booth-ruins ON
búðartóftina	booth OI, booth ON
búðarveggir	booth-walls OI, booth-walls ON
búið	prepared OI, settled OI, to-settle OI
búin	done ON, prepared OI
búinn	prepared OI, prepared ON
búit	settled ON, to-settle ON
bundnir	bound OI, bound ON
bundu	bound OI, bound ON
búningi	clothes OI, clothes ON
búnir	preparing OI, ready OI, ready ON, readying ON
bús	house ON, live OI
býð	offer OI, offer ON
býðr	invite ON
býður	offer OI
byr	fair-wind OI, fair-wind ON
býst	prepared OI, prepared ON

D, d

Norse	English
dætr	daughters ON
dætur	daughters OI
dag	day OI, day ON
daginn	day OI, day ON, days OI, days ON
dagr	day OI, day ON
dalnum	valleys OI, valleys ON
danir	Danish OI, Danish ON
danmörku	Denmark (place) OI, Denmark (place) ON
danskra	danish OI, danish ON
dapr	depressed ON
daprlig	sad ON
dapur	depressed OI
dapurleg	sad OI
dauða	death OI, death ON
dauðdaga	death-day OI, death-day ON
dauðir	dead ON, died OI
dauðr	dead ON
dauður	dead OI
degi	day OI, day ON
deildi	dealt OI, dealt ON
deyfir	blunts OI, blunts ON

Word List (Norse to English)

Norse	English	Norse	English
dinga	Dinge (place) OI, Dinge (place) ON	dvaldi	delayed OI, dwelled OI
dinganes	Dingenes (place) OI, Dingenes (place) ON	dvalði	dwelled ON
		dvaldist	dwelled OI
döggvar	dew OI, dew ON	dvalðist	dwelled ON
döglinga	of-the-dead ON	dyflinnar	Dublin (place) OI, Dublin (place) ON
döpr	sad ON		
döpur	sad OI	dylla	dylla OI, dylla ON
dóttir	daughter OI, daughter ON, daughter-of OI, daughter-of ON	dyn	storm OI, storm ON
		dýrlegra	glorious OI
		dýrligra	glorious ON
dóttur	daughter OI, daughter ON		
drap	killed OI, killed ON		

E, e

Norse	English
drápu	drapa OI
drápulag	drapa-layer ON
drápuna	drapa OI, drapa ON
drápunnar	drapa OI, drapa ON
drápunni	drapa OI, drapa ON
draum	dream OI, dream ON
drauma	dreams OI, dreams ON
drauminn	dream OI, dream ON
drauminum	the-dream OI, the-dream ON
draumr	dream ON
draums	dreams OI, dreams ON
draumum	dreams OI, dreams ON
draumur	dream OI
dregið	drawn OI
dregit	drawn ON
dregr	drew ON
dregst	drawn OI, drawn ON
dregur	drew OI
drekka	drink OI, drink ON
drengja	fellow OI, fellow ON
drengr	fellow ON
drengur	fellow OI
drepa	kill OI, kill ON
dreymdi	dream OI, dreamed OI
dreymði	dreamed ON
dreymt	dreamt OI, dreamt ON
drifinn	driven OI, driven ON
drifna	drive OI, drive ON
dró	draw OI, draw ON
drottningar	queen OI
dróttningar	queen ON
duga	help OI, help ON

Norse	English
eða	but OI, but ON, or OI, or ON
ef	if OI, if ON, maybe OI, of OI
efna	carry-out OI, carry-out ON
efni	prospects OI, prospects ON
efnilegir	promising OI
efniligir	promising ON
efsta	upper OI, upper ON
eftir	after OI, after ON, along OI, behind OI, remaining OI, remaining ON
eftirbátr	aftermath ON
eftirbátur	aftermath OI
eg	am OI, going OI, i OI
egg	edge OI, ridge OI, ridge ON
egill	Egil (name) OI, Egil (name) ON
egils	Egil (name) OI, Egil (name) ON
egilsdóttur	daughter-of-Egil (name) OI, daughter-of-Egil (name) ON
egilsson	son-of-Egil (name) OI, son-of-Egil (name) ON
egilssonar	son-of-Egil (name) OI, son-of-Egil (name) ON
egilssyni	son-of-Egil (name) OI, son-of-Egil (name) ON
egli	Egil (name) OI
ei	not OI

Word List (Norse to English)

Norse	English
eig	own OI, own ON
eiga	have OI, have ON, marriage OI, own OI, own ON, owned OI, owned ON
eigi	none OI, none ON, not OI, not ON
eignum	owned OI, owned ON
ein	one OI, one ON
eina	one OI, one ON
einar	Einar (name) OI
einart	resolute OI, resolute ON
eindriði	Eindridi (name) OI, Eindridi (name) ON
einhverju	any OI, any ON
einhverjum	somebody's OI, somebody's ON
einhvern	one OI
einkar	especially OI, especially ON
einn	a OI, one OI, one ON
einnhvern	one OI, one ON
einni	one OI, one ON
eins	likewise OI, likewise ON, one OI, one ON
eintalað	only-spoken OI
eintalat	only-spoken ON
einu	one OI, one ON
einum	one OI, one ON
einurð	determination OI, determination ON
eir	Eir (name) OI, Eir (name) ON
eirík	Erik (name) OI, Erik (name) ON
eiríki	Erik (name) OI, Erik (name) ON
eiríkr	Erik (name) OI, Erik (name) ON
eiríks	Erik (name) OI, Erik (name) ON, Erik's (name) OI, Erik's (name) ON
eiríkur	Erik (name) OI
eirir	spares OI, spares ON
eitt	once OI, once ON, one OI, one ON
ek	i ON
ekki	no ON, not OI, not ON, nothing OI, nothing ON
ekkja	widow OI, widow ON
eldaskála	cooking-hut OI, cooking-hut ON
ella	otherwise OI, otherwise ON
ellstr	oldest ON
elr	nourishes OI, nourishes ON
elstur	oldest OI
em	am OI, am ON
emk	am-i ON
en	and OI, and ON, as OI, as ON, before OI, but OI, but ON, but-for OI, but-for ON, than OI, than ON, that OI, that ON, then OI, then ON, when ON, while OI
enda	an-end ON, end OI, ended ON, ending OI, in-the-end OI
endast	ended OI, ended ON
endr	end OI, end ON
enga	none ON
engar	none ON
engi	no OI, none OI, none ON, not OI
engil	angel OI
england	England (place) OI, England (place) ON
englandi	England (place) OI, England (place) ON
englands	England (place) OI, England (place) ON, England's (place) OI, England's (place) ON
englandsfar	England-voyage OI, England-voyage ON
englandshaf	Englands-Sea (place) OI, Englands-Sea (place) ON
engra	none ON
engu	none ON, nothing ON
engum	no ON
enn	but OI, still OI, still ON, then ON, yet OI

Word List (Norse to English)

Norse	English
er	are OI, are ON, as OI, as ON, for OI, for ON, has OI, has ON, is OI, is ON, that OI, that ON, the OI, the ON, then OI, then ON, to OI, to ON, was OI, was ON, were OI, were ON, what OI, when OI, when ON, where OI, which OI, which ON, while OI, who OI, who ON, with OI
erendi	errand ON
erfitt	difficult OI, difficult ON
er'hann	as-he ON
erindi	errand OI
ermar	sleeves OI, sleeves ON
ernirnir	the-eagles OI, the-eagles ON
ert	are OI, are ON
ertu	are-you OI, are-you ON
eru	are OI, are ON, are-we OI, was ON, we-are OI, were OI, were ON
es	as ON, was ON, which ON, who ON
exar	axe OI
eyðanda	destroyer OI, destroyer ON
eygr	eyes ON
eygur	eyes OI
eyjólfr	Eyolf (name) ON
eyjólfur	Eyolf (name) OI
eyjunum	islands OI, islands ON
eyri	Eyri (place) OI, island OI, island ON
eyvindarson	son-of-Eyvind (name) OI, son-of-Eyvind (name) ON

É, é

Norse	English
én	and ON
ér	that OI, that ON

F, f

Norse	English
fá	few OI, few ON, get OI, get ON, have OI, have ON, pay OI
faðir	father OI, father ON, fathers OI
faðmlagsins	embrace OI, embrace ON
fæð	sadness OI, sadness ON
fæða	brought OI, feed OI, foster ON, give) OI, give-birth OI, give-birth ON, give-birth) ON
fæddi	bore OI, bore ON
fæddist	brought OI, fostered OI, fostered ON
fæðir	give-birth-to OI, give-birth-to ON
fær	can OI, can ON
færa	bring OI, bring ON, brought OI, brought ON, take OI, take ON
færð	carried OI, carried ON
færði	took OI, took ON
færðr	brought ON
færðu	went OI, went ON
færður	brought OI
færi	bring OI, journey OI, journey ON, opportunity OI, opportunity ON
færim	able ON
fært	gone OI, gone ON
færum	able OI
fæti	feet OI, foot OI, foot ON
fætr	feet ON
fætrna	feet ON
fætur	feet OI
fæturna	feet OI
fagna	welcome OI, welcome ON
fagnað	celebrated OI
fagnaði	celebrated OI, celebrated ON, received OI
fagnat	welcomed ON
fagra	fair OI, fair ON, fairness ON
fagrt	beautiful ON, fair ON

152

Word List (Norse to English)

Norse	English
fagurt	beautiful OI
fálátr	reserved ON
fálátur	reserved OI
fall	falling OI, falling ON
falli	fall OI, fall ON
fallnir	fallen OI, fallen ON
fám	few OI, few ON, get OI, get ON
fang	arms OI, arms ON
fangi	received OI, received ON
fangs	embrace OI, embrace ON
fann	found OI, found ON
far	travel OI, travel ON
fár	have OI, have ON
fara	go OI, going ON, to-travel OI, travel OI, travel ON, traveling OI, traveling ON, travelling ON
farar	travel OI, travel ON
fararefna	travel-goods OI, travel-goods ON
fararefni	travel-goods OI, travel-goods ON
fari	fare ON, go OI, go ON, going ON, passage OI, take OI
farið	going OI, travel OI, travelled OI, went OI
farim	travel ON
farinn	travelling OI, travelling ON
farit	going ON, gone ON, travel ON, travelled ON, went ON
farmaðr	travelling-man ON
farmaður	travelling-man OI
fastna	propose OI, propose ON
fastnaði	betrothed OI, betrothed ON
fátalaðr	quiet ON
fátalaður	quiet OI
fátt	few OI, few ON
fé	money OI, pay OI, wealth OI, wealth ON
feðgum	father-and-son OI, father-and-son ON
feðr	father ON
feður	fathers OI
feginn	relieved OI, relieved ON
fégjöfum	fee-gifts OI, fee-gifts ON
fegnir	celebrated OI, celebrated ON
fegrst	fair ON, fairest ON
fegurst	beautiful OI, most-beauty OI
féhirði	fee-servant OI, fee-servant ON
féhirðir	fee-servant ON
féhirslumaður	fee-servant OI
féið	fee OI, wealth OI
féit	wealth ON
fekk	got ON
fékk	gave OI, get OI, got OI, married OI, went OI
fekksk	received ON
fékkst	received OI
félagi	companion OI, companion ON
félítill	poor OI, poor ON
félitlir	poor OI, poor ON
fell	fell ON
féll	fell OI
felldi	fell OI, fell ON
fellu	fell ON
féllu	fell OI
félögum	company OI, company ON
fen	fens OI, fens ON
fenga	get ON
fengi	get OI
fengið	caught OI, found OI
fengir	get OI, get ON
fengit	caught ON
fengu	caught ON, got OI, got ON
fer	go OI, go ON, travelled OI, went OI
ferð	journey OI, journey ON
ferðar	travel OI, travel ON
ferðarinnar	travelling OI, travelling ON
ferðina	travelling OI, travelling ON

Word List (Norse to English)

Norse	English	Norse	English
ferðinni	travelling OI, travelling ON	flóða	flood OI, flood ON
ferðum	voyage OI, voyage ON	flóðhyrs	flood-deer OI, flood-deer ON
ferr	went ON	flokk	flokk OI, flokk ON
festa	to-propose ON	flokkr	flokk ON
festargram	festargram OI, festargram ON	flokkur	flokk OI
festargramr	festagramr ON	flugu	flew OI, flew ON
festargramur	Festargramur (place) OI	flutti	brought OI, brought ON
festarkona	engaged-woman OI, engaged-woman ON	fluttist	moved OI, returned ON
festarmeyjar	intended-maiden OI, intended-maiden ON	fluttr	transferred ON
festi	to-propose OI	fluttu	moved OI, moved ON
fimleikamaður	athletic-man OI	fluttur	transferred OI
fimm	five OI, five ON	flyta	carry OI
fimmta	five OI, five ON	flytja	carry OI, carry ON
finn	find OI, find ON	föður	father OI, father ON
finna	find OI, find ON	föðurleifð	estate OI, estate ON, inheritance OI
fira	burning OI, burning ON	fögr	fair ON
fjalla	mountain OI, mountain ON	fögru	fair OI, fair ON
fjandskapar	hostility OI, hostility ON	fögur	beautiful OI
fjár	wealth OI, wealth ON	fól	fool OI, fool ON
fjáreign	wealth OI, wealth ON	fold	ground OI, ground ON
fjarkominn	far-away OI, far-away ON	fólk	people OI, people ON
fjárlánið	fee-loan OI	folka	folk ON
fjárlánit	fee-loan ON	fólka	folk OI
fjarri	away OI, away ON	fór	do OI, fared OI, fared ON, journeyed OI, travelled OI, travelled ON, went OI, went ON
fjögur	four OI, four ON	forbæna	afflictions OI, afflictions ON
fjöllin	hills OI, hills ON	fornum	ancient OI, ancient ON
fjöllunum	the-mountains OI, the-mountains ON	fóru	travel OI, travel ON, travelled OI, travelled ON, went OI
fjölmennast	full-men-most OI, full-men-most ON	förum	travel OI
fjölmenni	followers OI, followers ON	förunautar	companions OI, companions ON
fjölmennir	crowded OI, crowded ON	förunautum	companions OI, companions ON
fjórum	four OI, four ON	fóstbróðir	foster-brother OI, foster-brother ON
flaum	flame OI, flame ON	fótarins	foot's OI, foot's ON
fleiri	more OI, more ON	fóthöggva	foot-striking OI, foot-striking ON
flesta	most OI, most ON	fótinn	leg OI, leg ON
flestra	best ON, most OI	fótrinn	feet ON, foot ON
fljúga	flew OI, flew ON, flying OI, flying ON	fóturinn	feet OI
fló	flew OI, flew ON, flying ON		

154

Word List (Norse to English)

Norse	English
frá	away-from OI, from OI, from ON, from-there OI, of OI
fræðimaður	scholar OI
frægð	fame OI, fame ON
frægir	famous OI, famous ON
frægri	more-famous OI, more-famous ON
fræknlega	bravely OI
fræknliga	bravely ON
frænda	kinsman OI, kinsman ON, kinsmen OI
frændaafli	kinsmen ON
frændi	kinsman OI, kinsman ON, kinsmen OI
frændr	kinsmen ON
frændsemi	kinship OI, kinship ON
frændum	kinsmen OI, kinsmen OI, kinsmen ON
frændur	kinsmen OI, kinsmen OI
fráfall	death OI, death ON
fram	from OI, from ON
framar	above OI, above ON
framgjarn	ambitious OI, ambitious ON
framið	committed ON
framin	committed OI
framlega	from-like OI
framliga	from-like ON
frammi	from OI, from ON
frásagnar	from-saying OI, from-saying ON
fregna	news OI, news ON
freistaðim	test ON
freistuðum	test OI
frestaðist	postponed OI, postponed ON
fresti	from-now OI, from-now ON, later OI
frétt	news OI, news ON
frétti	heard OI, heard ON
freyddi	rose OI, rose ON
fríðar	beautiful OI, beautiful ON
friðland	peace-land OI, peace-land ON
frítt	free OI, free ON
fróðir	wise OI
fróðra	wise OI, wise ON
fróðum	learned OI
frumvaxta	prime-grown OI, prime-grown ON
fugl	bird OI, bird ON
fuglar	birds OI, birds ON
fuglarnir	the-birds OI, the-birds ON
fullting	help OI, help ON
fullu	full OI, full ON
fund	find OI, meet OI, meet ON, meeting OI, meeting ON
fundi	meet OI, meeting OI, meeting ON
fundist	found OI, met OI
fundizt	found ON
fundust	found OI, found ON, met OI
furðu	surprisingly OI, surprisingly ON
fylgdi	followed OI
fylgði	followed ON
fylgir	following OI, following ON
fylgja	follow OI, follow ON
fylgjur	followers OI, followers ON
fyr	before ON, for ON
fyri	for OI
fyrir	along OI, along ON, because OI, before OI, before ON, for OI, for ON, present OI, therefore OI, therefore ON
fyrirgefa	forgive OI, forgive ON
fyrr	before OI, before ON, until OI
fyrri	before OI, before ON
fyrst	first OI, first ON

G, g

Norse	English
gá	give OI, give ON
gæfið	give ON
gæfuð	give OI

Word List (Norse to English)

Norse	English
gær	yesterday OI, yesterday ON
gaf	gave OI, gave ON, given OI, given ON
gagnsæli	benefit-happier ON
gagnsælli	benefit-happier OI
gakk	go OI, go ON
galdrs	spell OI, spell ON
galt	paid OI, paid ON
galti	Galti (name) OI, Galti (name) ON
gamall	old OI, old ON
gaman	enjoyed OI, enjoyed ON, enjoyment OI, enjoyment ON, joyed OI
ganga	go OI, go ON, going OI, walk OI, walk ON
gangið	go OI, go ON
gangim	going ON
gat	opening OI, opening ON
gaum	heed OI, heed ON
gautar	Geatlanders OI, Geatlanders ON
gautland	Geatland (place) OI, Geatland (place) ON
gef	give OI, give ON
gefa	gift OI, give OI, give ON
gefið	give OI, give ON
gefin	given OI, given ON
gefr	give OI, give ON
gegnt	opposite OI, opposite ON
gegnum	through OI, through ON
geirný	Geirny (name) OI, Geirny (name) ON
geisli	beams OI, beams ON
gekk	go OI, goes ON, got OI, walked OI, walked ON, went OI, went ON
gekkst	walked OI
gengi	going OI, went ON
gengr	goes ON
gengu	going OI, going ON, went OI, went ON
gengur	it-goes OI
gengust	went OI, went ON
ger	do OI, make OI, make ON
gera	be-done ON, done OI
gerði	did OI, did ON, made OI, made ON
gerðist	became OI, became ON
gerðu	did OI, did ON, make OI, make ON
gerið	do OI, do ON
gerir	did OI, did ON
gerist	was OI, was ON
gerla	completely ON
gersemi	treasured OI
gersimi	treasured ON
gert	be OI, do OI, do ON, done OI, done ON
gerum	be OI, let-us-be OI, let-us-be ON
getr	can OI, can ON
getur	can OI
geyma	retain OI, retain ON
gift	married OI, married ON
gifta	gift OI, gift ON, give OI
gifti	gave OI, gave ON
gildir	valid OI, valid ON
gilsbakka	Gilsbakka (place) OI, Gilsbakka (place) ON, Gilsbakki (place) OI
gims	noble OI, noble ON
gistu	guested OI, guested ON
gjafar	gifts ON
gjafir	gifts OI
gjaforð	give OI, give ON
gjalda	expenses OI, pay OI, pay ON
gjalfri	gifts ON
gjálfri	gifts OI
gjalt	expenses OI, expenses ON
gjarna	gladly OI, gladly ON
gjöfina	gift OI, gift ON, the-gift OI
gjöfli	gifts OI, gifts ON
gjöfum	gifts OI, gifts ON
gjörla	completely OI
glaðara	gladder OI, gladder ON
glæstrar	glistens OI, glistens ON

156

Word List (Norse to English)

Norse	English	Norse	English
gleði	glad OI, glad ON	grenjum	Grenjar (place) OI, Grenjar (place) ON
gleipnisvellir	Gleipnisvellir (place) OI, Gleipnisvellir (place) ON	grepp	grip OI, treasure ON
		greppa	grip OI, grip ON
glímu	wrestling OI, wrestling ON	greppi	grip OI, grip ON
glímur	wrestling OI, wrestling ON	greppr	grip OI, grip ON
		grét	wept OI, wept ON
glóðspýtis	embers OI, embers ON	grið	mercy OI, mercy ON
gnúps	Gnup (name) ON, Gnup's (name) OI	griðin	mercy OI, mercy ON
gnúpsdóttir	daughter-of-Gnup (name) OI, daughter-of-Gnup (name) ON	grími	Grim (name) OI, Grim (name) ON
		grímr	Grim (name) ON
		grímstungum	Grimstungur (place) OI, Grimstungur (place) ON
gný	rage OI, rage ON		
goð	god ON, good ON		
góð	good OI, good ON	grímur	Grim (name) OI
goða	the-good OI, the-good ON	grindavík	Grindavik (place) OI, Grindavik (place) ON
góða	good OI, good ON	grípa	gripped OI, gripped ON
góðan	good OI, good ON	gripi	treasure OI, treasure ON
góðar	good OI, good ON		
goðorð	godord OI, godord ON	guð	god OI
góðr	good ON	guðbrá	god-drew OI
góðra	good OI, good ON	guðs	god's OI
góðri	good OI, good ON	gufárós	Gufua (place) OI
góðu	good OI, good ON	gufuárósi	Gufua (place) OI, Gufua (place) ON
góðum	good OI, good ON		
góður	good OI	gull	gold OI, gold ON
göfgir	noble OI, noble ON	gullhring	gold-ring OI, gold-ring ON
gollhring	gold-ring ON	gullhringa	gold-ring OI, gold-ring ON
góma	gums OI, gums ON		
göndlar	cock OI, cock ON	gullmens	golden OI, golden ON
göngu	going OI, going ON	gumna	men OI, men ON
göngum	going OI, go-we OI, go-we ON	gunnar	Gunnar (name) OI, Gunnar (name) ON, warrior OI, warrior ON
gört	be ON		
gott	good OI, good ON	gunnarsdóttur	daughter-of-Gunnar (name) OI, daughter-of-Gunnar (name) ON
grám	grey OI, grey ON		
gramr	warrior OI, warrior ON		
grams	warrior OI, warrior ON	gunnbráðs	war-swift OI, war-swift ON
grár	grey OI, grey ON	gunniaugr	Gunnlaug (name) ON
grásíma	grey-call OI, grey-call ON	gunnlagi	Gunnlaug (name) OI
		gunnlaug	Gunnlaug (name) OI, Gunnlaug (name) ON
gráta	weep OI, weep ON		
greiða	assistance OI, assistance ON	gunnlaugi	Gunnlaug (name) OI, Gunnlaug (name) ON, Gunnlaug's (name) OI, Gunnlaug's (name) ON
greiddu	paid OI, paid ON		

Word List (Norse to English)

Norse	English
gunnlaugr	Gunnlaug (name) OI, Gunnlaug (name) ON
gunnlaugs	Gunnlaug (name) OI, Gunnlaug (name) ON, Gunnlaug's (name) OI, Gunnlaug's (name) ON
gunnlaugsnaut	Gunnlaug's-gift (name) OI, Gunnlaug's-gift (name) ON
gunnlaugur	Gunnlaug (name) OI
gunnsproti	war-twig OI, war-twig ON

H, h

Norse	English
háð	mockery OI, mockery ON
háðvörum	slander OI, slander ON
hægr	right OI, right ON
hægri	right OI, right ON
hæru	grey-hair OI, grey-hair ON
hætt	end OI, end ON
hætta	risk OI, risk ON
haf	sea OI, sea ON, the-sea OI, the-sea ON
hafa	had OI, had ON, has OI, has ON, have OI, have ON, having ON
hafði	had OI, had ON, had-been OI, held OI
hafðu	have OI, have-you ON
hafi	had OI, had ON, have OI, have ON, sea OI, sea ON
hafið	have OI, have ON
hafna	wary OI
hafnaði	rejected OI, rejected ON
hafnar	wary ON
hafr-bjarnarson	son-of-Hafur-Bjarni (name) ON
hafur-bjarnarson	son-of-Hafur-Bjarni (name) OI
hagvirki	advantage OI, advantage ON
hákon	Hakon (name) OI, Hakon (name) ON
hákonarson	son-of-Hakon (name) OI, son-of-Hakon (name) ON
halda	hold OI, keep OI, keep ON
haldið	staying OI
haldit	stayed ON
hálfa	half OI, half ON
hálft	half OI, half ON
hálfum	half OI, half ON
hallfreðar	Hallfred (name) OI, Hallfred (name) ON
hallfreði	Hallfred (name) OI, Hallfred (name) ON
hallfreðr	Hallfred (name) ON
hallfreður	Hallfred (name) OI
hallkelsson	son-of-Hallkel (name) OI, son-of-Hallkel (name) ON
hallkvæmri	more-effective OI, more-effective ON
haltr	limp ON, limping ON
haltur	limp OI, limping OI
hana	her OI, her ON, she OI, she ON, to-her OI
handa	hand OI, hand ON
handan	beyond OI, beyond ON, hands OI
hann	he OI, he ON, held OI, here OI, him OI, him ON, it OI, it ON
hans	he OI, he ON, him OI, him ON, his OI, his ON
hánum	him ON
happs	luck OI, luck ON
hár	hair OI, hair ON, has OI
harðarsonar	son-of-Hardar's (name) OI, son-of-Hardar's (name) ON
harðasti	hardest OI, hardest ON
harðlyndr	hardy ON
harðlyndur	hardy OI
harðr	hard ON
harður	hard OI
hárr	has ON
háttað	the-way OI
háttar	such OI, such ON
háttat	the-way ON

Word List (Norse to English)

Norse	English
haukfránn	hawk-from OI, hawk-from ON
haus	house OI, house ON
hausti	autumn OI, autumn ON
haustið	autumn OI
haustit	autumn ON
hávaðamaðr	a-loud-man ON
hávaðamaður	a-loud-man OI
hávar	high OI, high ON
heðan	hence ON
héðan	from-here OI
hef	have OI
hefði	had OI, had ON, have OI, have ON
hefi	have OI, have ON
hefir	had OI, had ON, has OI, has ON, have OI, have ON
hefk	have ON
hefnt	had OI, had ON
hégóma	vanity OI, vanity ON
hégómi	vanity OI, vanity ON
heiðarvíg	heath-slayings OI, heath-slayings ON
heiði	heath OI, heath ON
heidr	honour ON
heil	well OI, well ON
heilastr	well ON
heilastur	well OI
heim	home OI, home ON
heima	at-home OI, home OI, home ON
heimamaðr	house-man ON
heimamaður	house-man OI
heiman	home OI, home ON
heimboðs	home-invitation OI, home-invitation ON
heimferðar	home-travel OI, home-travel ON
heimleiðis	home-way OI, home-way ON
heimti	claimed OI, claimed ON
heita	call OI, call ON, called OI, called ON
heitaðist	was-called OI, was-called ON
heiti	named OI
heitið	pledged OI
heitik	named ON
heitir	called OI, called ON, named OI, named ON
heitit	called ON
heitit-	called ON
heitkona	intended-woman OI, promised-woman OI, promised-woman ON
heitkonu	wife OI, wife ON
heitt	hot OI, hot ON
heldr	held ON, rather ON
heldur	advanced OI, held OI, hold OI, rather OI
helga	Helga (name) OI, Helga (name) ON
helgu	Helga (name) OI, Helga (name) ON
helst	rather OI
helt	held ON
hélt	held OI
helzt	rather ON
hemingr	Heming (name) ON
hemingur	Heming (name) OI
hendi	hand OI, hand ON, to-hand OI, to-hand ON
hendinni	hand OI, hand ON
hendr	hand ON
hendur	hands OI
hennar	for-her OI, her OI, her ON, hers OI, hers ON, to-her OI, to-her ON
henni	her OI, her ON, she OI
henti	gave OI
her	army OI, war OI
hér	here OI, here ON
herðimikill	hardy-much OI, hardy-much ON
hergerðandi	ranks OI, ranks ON
herja	army OI, army ON
herjuðu	raiding OI, raiding ON
hermund	Hermund (name) OI, Hermund (name) ON
hermundr	Hermund (name) ON
hermundur	Hermund (name) OI
hernað	raiding OI, raiding ON
herr	army ON, band OI, band ON
herra	lord OI, lord ON

Word List (Norse to English)

Norse	English
hersis	local-leader OI, local-leader ON
hest	horse OI, horse ON
hestar	stallions OI, stallions ON
hesti	horse OI, horse ON
hestr	horse ON
hestur	horse OI
hét	called OI, called ON, named OI, named ON, was-called OI, was-named OI, was-named ON
hétu	called OI, called ON
heyra	hear OI, hear ON
heyrði	heard ON
heyrðið	hear ON
heyrðuð	hear OI
heyri	hears OI
hið	the OI
hildingr	hero ON
himni	heaven OI, heaven ON
hin	others OI, others ON, the OI
hina	the OI
hingað	here OI
hingat	here ON, there ON
hinn	he OI, he ON, the OI, then OI
hinnar	other OI, the OI
hinni	his OI, the OI
hins	the OI
hinum	the OI
hirðmaðr	court-man OI, court-man ON
hirðmaður	court-man OI
hirðmann	court-man OI, court-man ON
hirðmanna	followers OI, followers ON
hirðmönnum	court-men OI, court-men ON
hítdælakappi	Hitdardal-champion (name) OI
hitt	other OI, other ON
hitti	met OI, met ON
hjá	beside OI, beside ON, heard OI, near OI
hjalla	Hjalli (name) OI, Hjalli (name) ON
hjálmi	helmet OI, helmet ON
hjálminum	helmet OI, helmet ON
hjaltugguðum	hilt-chewed OI, hilt-chewed ON
hjarðarholt	Hjardarholt (place) OI, Hjardarholt (place) ON
hjarls	earldoms OI, earldoms ON
hjó	struck OI, struck ON
hjöltunum	hilt OI, hilt ON
hjör	striking OI
hjörþeys	faced OI, faced ON
hjörva	sword OI, sword ON
hjörvi	sword OI, sword ON
hlaðbúinn	laden OI, laden ON
hlaðbúna	loaded OI, loaded ON
hlaðið	farmyard OI
hlaðinu	farmyard OI, farmyard ON
hlaðir	Lade (place) OI, Lade (place) ON
hlaðit	farmyard ON
hlaupinn	run OI, run ON
hlaut	got OI, got ON
hlíðarenda	Hlidarendi (place) OI
hlífarlaus	helpless OI
hlífarlauss	helpless ON
hlífarsonar	son-of-Hlífar (name) OI, son-of-Hlífar (name) ON
hlínar	Hlínar (place) OI, Hlínar (place) ON
hljóð	listen OI, listen ON, sound OI, sound ON
hljóðs	be-heard OI, be-heard ON
hljóp	ran OI, ran ON
hljópu	ran ON
hló	laughed OI, laughed ON
hlóð	composition OI, composition ON
hlöðum	Lade (place) OI, Lade (place) ON
hlöðvisson	son-of-Hlodvi (name) OI, son-of-Hlodvi (name) ON, son-of-Hlodvi (name) ON

Word List (Norse to English)

Norse	English
hlunns	point OI, point ON
hlupu	ran OI
hlut	lot OI, lot ON
hluta	lot OI, lot ON
hluti	things OI, things ON
hlutr	part ON
hlutur	part OI
hlutvöndum	bond OI, bond ON
hlýða	listen OI, listen ON, obey OI
hlýddið	listen ON
hlýdduð	listen OI
hlýðisamt	obedient OI, obedient ON
hlýra	warm ON
hlýrra	warm OI
hlýtr	get OI, get ON
hnakk	saddle OI, saddle ON
hné	knelt OI, sank OI, sank ON
hneigði	inclined OI, inclined ON
hnekkði	over-turned ON
hnekkti	over-turned OI
hníga	sink OI, sink ON
hnipin	dejected OI, dejected ON
hoddstríðandi	hoard-warrior OI, hoard-warrior ON
hoddum	hoard OI, hoard ON
höfðingi	chief OI, leader OI, leader ON
höfðingja	chieftans OI, chieftans ON
höfðingjabragð	chieftancy OI, chieftancy ON
höfðingjum	chiefs OI, chiefs ON
höfðu	had OI, had ON
hófsmaðr	moderate-man ON
hófsmaður	modest OI
höfuð	hand OI, hand ON, head OI, head ON
höfuðsárið	head-wound OI
höfuðsárit	head-wound ON
höfum	have OI, have ON
högg	striking OI, striking ON
hoggið	struck OI
höggþyrnis	shock-thorn OI, shock-thorn ON
höggum	blows OI, blows ON
höggva	strike OI, strike ON, striking OI
höggvinn	cut-down OI, cut-down ON
höggvit	struck ON
hógvær	moderate OI
hógværr	humble ON
höldr	handled OI
hölðr	handled ON
hölds	flesh OI
hölðs	flesh ON
hólm	duel OI, duel ON
hólmganga	duelling OI, duelling ON
hólmgöngu	duel OI, duel ON
hólmgöngumaður	duelling-man OI
hólmgöngur	duelling OI, duelling ON
hólminn	duel OI, duel ON
hólminum	duel OI, duel ON
hólms	duel OI, duel ON
hólmsins	duel-his OI, duel-his ON
holtavörðuheiði	Holtavarda-Heath (place) OI, Holtavarda-Heath (place) ON
hómgöngu	duel OI
hon	her ON, she ON
hönd	hand OI, hand ON
höndum	hands OI, hands ON
honum	he OI, he ON, him OI, him ON, his OI, his ON, she ON, to-him OI, to-him ON, to-him-of ON
hopa	avoid ON
hörða	hard OI, hard ON
horfði	looked OI, looked ON
horfir	looks OI, looks ON
hörvi	linen OI, linen ON
höskuldssonar	son-of-Hoskuld (name) OI, son-of-Hoskuld (name) ON
hót	threat OI, threat ON
hræ	corpses OI, corpses ON
hræðist	afraid OI
hræðumst	afraid ON
hræpa	down OI, down ON
hræskæri	corpse-scorer ON

Word List (Norse to English)

Norse	English	Norse	English
hræskærri	corpse-scorer OI	hún	is-she OI, she OI, she-is OI
hrafn	he OI, Hrafn (name) OI, Hrafn (name) ON	húngerðar	hundergar's OI, Hungerd (place) OI, Hungerd (place) ON
hrafni	Hrafn (name) OI, Hrafn (name) ON, Hrafn's (name) OI	húngerðr	Hungerd (place) ON
hrafns	Hrafn (name) OI, Hrafn's (name) OI, Hrafn's (name) ON	húngerður	Hungerd (place) OI
		húngersar	hundergar's ON
hraunhöfn	Hraunhofn (place) OI, Hraunhofn (place) ON	húsfreyja	housewife OI, housewife ON
hraunsdal	Hraunsdal (place) OI, Hraunsdal (place) ON	húsfreyju	housewife OI, housewife ON
hraustasti	strongest OI, strongest ON	húsin	house OI, house ON, the-house OI
hraut	jumped OI, jumped ON	húskarl	servant OI, servant ON
hreðuvatns	Hreduvatn (place) OI, Hreduvatn (place) ON	húskarli	housekeeper OI, housekeeper ON
hríðgervandi	aggravating ON	húsmæninum	house-roof-ridge OI, house-roof-ridge ON
hríðgjörvandi	aggravating OI	hvað	what OI
hríðmundaðar	while-formed OI, while-formed ON	hvaðan	where OI, where ON
hringa	rings OI, rings ON	hvammsfirði	Hvammsfjord (place) OI, Hvammsfjord (place) ON
hringinum	ring OI, ring ON		
hringbollr	ring-endurance OI, ring-endurance ON	hvar	where OI, where ON
		hvárigum	neither ON
hristar	shakes OI, shakes ON	hvárir	each ON
hross	horses OI, horses ON	hvárirtveggju	either-side ON
hrossa	horses OI, horses ON	hvárki	neither ON
hrossin	horses OI, horses ON	hvarma	eyelids OI, eyelids ON
hrosskelssonar	son-of-Hrosskel (name) OI, son-of-Hrosskel (name) ON	hvárn	each ON
		hvárntveggja	either-side ON
hrútafirði	Hrutafjord (place) OI, Hrutafjord (place) ON	hvárr	where ON
		hvárrgi	neither ON
hrútafjarðar	Hrutafjord (place) OI, Hrutafjord (place) ON	hvárstveggja	either-side ON, either-side ON
hryggja	back OI, back ON	hvárt	either ON, whether ON
hrynfiski	caved-fish OI, caved-fish ON	hvárumtveggja	either-side ON
		hvat	what ON
hugði	thought OI, thought ON	hvatra	quickly OI, quickly ON
hugðumk	thought ON	hve	how OI
hugðumst	thought OI	hvé	how ON
hugmóðr	spirit-mother OI, spirit-mother ON	hver	who OI, whose OI, whose ON
hugreifum	striking-down OI, striking-down ON	hverfka	districts OI
		hverfkak	districts ON
hugrekki	courage OI, courage ON	hvergi	either ON, neither OI, neither ON

162

Word List (Norse to English)

Norse	English
hverja	what OI, what ON
hverju	how OI, how ON
hverjum	who OI, who ON
hvern	each ON, how OI, how ON, which OI
hvernig	which ON
hverninn	what OI
hverr	who ON
hverra	what OI, what ON
hvers	which OI, which ON
hversu	how OI, how ON, how-so OI, how-so ON
hvert	any OI, any ON
hvervetna	everywhere OI, everywhere ON
hví	why OI, why ON
hvíldi	rested OI, rested ON
hvítársíðu	Hvitarsida (place) OI, Hvitarsida (place) ON
hvíti	white OI, white ON
hvítr	white ON
hvítum	white OI, white ON
hvítur	white OI
hvívetna	everything OI, everything ON
hvor	each OI, where OI, which OI
hvorgi	neither OI
hvorigum	neither OI
hvorir	each OI
hvorirtveggju	either-side OI
hvorki	neither OI
hvorn	each OI
hvorntveggja	either-way OI
hvorstveggja	either-side OI, either-way OI
hvort	either OI, whether OI
hvorumtveggja	both OI
hvöss	sharp OI, sharp ON
hygg	mind OI, think OI, think ON
hyggi	thought OI, thought ON
hykk	mind ON
hylja	cover OI, cover ON
hyrjar	fire OI, fire ON

I, i

Norse	English
iðrask	serpent ON
iðrast	repent OI
illa	bad OI, badly OI, badly ON, ill OI, ill ON, wicked OI
illr	ill OI, ill ON
illt	ill OI, ill ON
illuga	Illuga (name) ON, Illuga's (name) ON, Illugi (name) OI, Illugi's (name) OI, Illugi's (name) OI, Illugi's (name) ON, Ilugi (name) ON
illugason	son-of-Illugi (name) OI, son-of-Illugi (name) ON
illugi	Illugi (name) OI, Ilugi (name) ON
in	in ON, the ON
ina	the ON
ingibjargar	Ingibjorg (name) OI, Ingibjorg's (name) OI, Ingibjorg's (name) ON
ingibjörgu	Ingibjorg (name) OI, Ingibjorg (name) ON
inn	in OI, the ON, then OI, then ON
innan	inside OI, inside ON
innar	inside OI, inside ON, the ON
inni	the ON
ins	the ON
inum	in ON
it	the ON, to ON

Í, í

Norse	English
í	a OI, a ON, about OI, among OI, at OI, in OI, in ON, into OI, into ON, is OI, of OI, of ON, one OI, out OI, the OI, this OI, to OI, to ON
írlandi	ireland OI, ireland ON

Word List (Norse to English)

Norse	English	Norse	English
íslandi	Iceland (place) OI, Iceland (place) ON, Icelander OI	*jarls*	earl OI, earl ON, earl's OI, earl's ON
íslands	Iceland (place) OI, Iceland (place) ON	*jarlsins*	earl's ON
íslandsmaður	Icelander OI	*járnklær*	iron-claws OI, iron-claws ON
íslendingar	Icelander OI, Icelander ON	*játgeirsson*	son-of-Edgar (name) OI, son-of-Edgar (name) ON
íslendingr	icelander ON	*jófríðar*	Jofrid (name) OI, Jofrid (name) ON
íslendingrinn	icelander ON	*jófríði*	Jofrid (name) OI, Jofrid (name) ON
íslendingur	Icelander OI		
íslendingurinn	Icelander OI	*jófríðr*	Jofrid (name) ON
íslenskra	icelander OI	*jófríður*	Jofrid (name) OI
íslenzkr	icelander ON	*jól*	yule OI, yule ON
íslenzkra	icelander ON	*jóla*	jule OI, yule ON
íþróttar	as-vigourous OI, as-vigourous ON	*jólaboð*	yule-invitation OI, yule-invitation ON
		jólin	jule OI, yule OI, yule ON
		jörð	earth OI, earth ON

J, j

já	yes OI, yes ON		

K, k

Norse	English
jafnaldrar	equal-aged OI, equalaged ON
jafnan	equal OI, equal ON, equally OI, equally ON, usually OI, usually ON
jafnfagrt	equally-beautiful ON
jafnfagurt	equally-beautiful OI
jafnlangir	equally-long OI, equally-long ON
jafnmargir	equal-many OI, equal-many ON
jafnmenni	equal-man OI, equal-man ON
jafnmikið	equal-much OI
jafnmikit	equal ON
jafnoka	equal OI, equal ON
jafnræði	equally OI, equally ON
jafnræðis	equally OI, equally ON
jafnröskr	equally OI, equally ON
jarðaðr	earthed ON
jarðaður	earthed OI
jari	Earl ON
jarl	earl OI, earl ON
jarla	earls OI, earls ON
jarli	earl OI, earl ON
jarlinn	earl OI, earl ON
kæmi	came OI, came ON
kalla	call OI, call ON
kallað	called OI
kallaði	called OI, called ON
kallaðr	called ON
kallaður	called OI
kallaksson	son-of-Kallak (name) OI
kann	can OI, can ON, known OI
kappi	champion OI, warrior OI, warrior ON
kappmæli	contest OI, contest ON
karl	man OI, man ON
karldurum	man-door ON
karldyrum	man-door OI
karlmaðr	many ON
karlmaður	man OI
kátir	merry OI, merry ON
kaupmannanna	trading-men's OI, trading-men's ON
kaupmenn	trading-men OI, trading-men ON
kaupmennina	trading-men OI, trading-men ON

Word List (Norse to English)

Norse	English	Norse	English
kaupmönnum	trading-men OI, trading-men ON	koma	came OI, came ON, come OI, come ON, coming OI, coming ON
kaupstað	trading-station OI, trading-station ON	komast	comes OI, comes ON
kaupstefna	trading-posts OI, trading-posts ON	komi	come OI, come ON
kemr	came ON, comes ON	komið	come OI, coming OI
kemur	came OI, comes OI	komin	coming OI, coming ON
kenna	know OI, know ON	kominn	becoming OI, becoming ON, came OI, come OI, come-in ON, coming ON, have-come OI
kenndi	knew OI, knew ON, taught OI, taught ON		
kennt	taught OI, taught ON		
keypti	bought OI, bought ON	komit	come ON
keyptu	kept OI, kept ON	komnir	came OI
kindar	kindar OI, sheep ON	komst	came OI, came ON
kinn	cheek OI, cheek ON	komu	came OI
kippði	dragged ON	kómu	came ON
kippti	dragged OI	komust	came OI
kirkju	church OI, church ON	kómust	came ON
kjallaksson	son-of-Kallak (name) ON	kon	man OI, man ON
kjartan	Kjartan (name) OI	kona	a-woman OI, a-woman ON, wife OI, wife ON, woman OI, woman ON
kjartans	Kjartan (name) OI, Kjartan (name) ON		
klæði	clothing OI, clothing ON	kontmgs	king ON
klæðin	clothes OI, clothes ON	konu	a-woman OI, wife OI, wife ON, woman OI
klæðum	clothed OI, clothed ON	konung	king OI, king ON
klakaði	chattered OI, chattered ON	konungahellu	Kungalf (name) OI, Kungalf (name) ON
klauf	cleaved OI, cleaved ON	konungar	kings OI, kings ON
kljúfa	cleave OI, cleave ON	konungi	king OI, king ON, to-the-king OI
knættit	bowl OI, bowl ON		
kné	knee OI, knee ON	konunginn	king OI, king ON
knörru	knorrs OI, knorrs ON	konungmanna	king-descendents OI, king-descendents ON
knút	Canute (name) OI, Canute (name) ON	konungr	king ON
knútr	Canute (name) ON	konungs	king OI, king ON, king's OI
knútur	Canute (name) OI		
kolbeinsson	son-of-Kolbein (name) OI, son-of-Kolbein (name) ON	konungsnaut	king's-gift OI, king's-gift ON
		konungur	king OI
kollsveinn	Kollsvein (name) OI, Kollsveinn (name) OI, Kollsveinn (name) ON	konur	woman OI, women OI, women ON
		kormlaðar	Kormlod (name) OI, Kormlod (name) ON
kom	came OI, came ON, went OI	kost	benefit OI, benefit ON
		kostr	choice ON
		kostur	choice OI, other OI

Word List (Norse to English)

Norse	English
kristið	christian OI
kristit	christian ON
krömdust	chronic-illness OI
krömðust	chronic-illness ON
kúgan	bullying OI, bullying ON
kunna	to-know OI, to-know ON
kunnig	know OI, know ON, known ON
kurteisi	courteous OI, courteous ON
kvað	said OI, said ON, saying OI, saying ON, spoke OI
kvaddi	called OI, called ON
kvaðst	said OI, said ON, spoke OI, spoke ON
kváðu	saying OI, saying ON
kváðust	said OI, said ON
kvæði	poem OI, poem ON, said OI
kvæðið	poem OI
kvæðinu	poem OI, poem ON
kvæðislaunum	poem's-reward OI, poem's-reward ON
kvæðit	poem ON
kvæðum	poem OI, poem ON
kvánar	wife ON
kvánbæna	marriage-proposal ON
kvánbænar	propose ON
kvánbænum	marriage-proposal ON
kvángaðr	married ON
kvángast	marriage ON
kvarans	kvaran OI, Kvaran's (name) OI
kvárans	Kvaran's (name) ON, kvarans ON
kveða	greeted OI, greeted ON
kveðst	said OI, said ON
kveldi	evening OI, evening ON
kveldið	evening OI
kveldit	evening ON
kveld-úlfssonar	son-of-Kveld-Ulf (name) OI, son-of-Kveld-Ulf (name) ON
kvöddu	greeted OI, greeted ON
kvonar	wife OI
kvonbæna	marriage-proposal OI
kvonbænar	propose OI
kvonbænum	marriage-proposal OI
kvongaður	married OI
kvongast	marry OI
kyrrt	still OI, still ON
kyrtil	tunic OI, tunic ON
kyrtli	tunic OI, tunic ON

L, l

Norse	English
lá	laid ON, lay OI, laying OI, laying ON, lying ON
lægi	lay OI, lay ON
lækjar	stream OI, stream ON
læt	lay OI, lay ON
lætr	lay ON, lets OI, lets ON
lætur	behave OI, let OI
lag	layer OI
lág	placed OI, placed ON
lagðak	laid ON
lagði	became OI, laid OI, laid ON, lay OI, took-to OI, took-to ON
lagðir	laying OI, laying ON
lagið	laid OI
lagit	laid ON
lágt	low OI, low ON
lágu	low OI, low ON
land	land OI, land OI, land ON, land ON
landa	lands OI, lands ON
landi	land OI, land ON
landið	land OI
landinu	the-land OI, the-land ON
landit	land ON
lands	lands OI, lands ON
landseta	tenants OI, tenants ON
landseti	tenant OI, tenant ON
langá	Langa (place) OI, Langa (place) ON
langavatnsdal	Langvatnsdal (place) OI, Langvatnsdal (place) ON
láni	loan OI, loan ON

Word List (Norse to English)

Norse	English	Norse	English
lasta	blame OI, blamed OI	leiruvogum	Leiruvog (place) OI
lát	let OI, let ON	leistbrókum	breeches OI, breeches ON
láta	lay-out OI, leave OI, leave ON, let OI, let ON, letting OI	leit	looked OI, looked ON
		lékum	played OI, played ON
látast	die OI, die ON	lengi	along OI, long OI, long ON
látum	let OI, let ON	lengr	longer ON
laugaraftan	saturday-afternoon OI, saturday-afternoon ON	lengur	longer OI
		lénur	laying OI, laying ON
laugarkveld	saturday-night OI, saturday-night ON	lét	allowed OI, laid OI, lay OI, lay ON, let OI, let ON
lauk	ended OI, ended ON, ended ON	léti	let OI, let ON
		létt	light OI, light ON
lauka	leek OI, leek ON	létu	allowed OI, laid ON, left OI, left ON
launa	repay OI, repay ON, repay ON, reward OI	leyna	hiding OI, hiding ON
launað	repaid OI	leynd	secrecy OI, secrecy ON
launaði	rewarded OI, rewarded ON	leynt	secret OI, secret ON
		leysa	solve OI, solve ON
launat	repaid ON	leysingjastöðum	Leysingastadir (place) OI, Leysingastadir (place) ON
laus	less OI, loose OI, lost OI		
lausan	loose OI, lost OI, lost ON	líða	pass OI, pass ON
		liði	group OI, group ON
lauss	lose ON, lost ON	liðið	group OI, passed OI
laust	loosed OI, loosed ON, lost OI, lost ON	liðin	passed OI, passed ON
		liðinn	company OI, passed ON
lautsíkjar	drape-oneself OI, drape-oneself ON	liðit	company ON, group ON, passed ON
laxdæla	Laxdardal (place) OI, Laxdardal (place) ON		
		liðnar	passed OI, passed ON
legði	lay ON	liðnir	passed OI, passed ON
leggi	lay OI, leg OI, leg ON	liðu	passed OI, passed ON
leggja	lay OI, lay ON	líf	life OI, life ON
leið	passed OI, passed ON	lifangr	Levanger (place) ON
leiddi	led OI, led ON	lifangri	Levanger (place) OI, Levanger (place) ON
leiddr	laid ON		
leiddur	led OI	lifangur	Levanger (place) OI
leiðtoga	guide OI, guide ON, guides OI	lífi	live OI, live ON
		líflát	loss OI, loss ON
leiðtogana	guides OI, guides ON	líka	like OI, like ON, liked OI, liked ON
leiðtogar	guides OI, guides ON		
leik	sport OI, sport ON	líkar	like OI, like ON
leiki	toyed OI, toyed ON	líklegast	likely OI
leikist	played OI	líklegt	likely OI
leikizt	played ON	líkligast	likely ON
leirur	clays OI, clays ON	líkligt	likely ON
leiruvág	Leiruvog (place) ON		
leiruvog	Leiruvog (place) OI		

167

Word List (Norse to English)

Norse	English
líkr	like ON
líkur	like OI
lind	linden OI, linden ON
linns	linns OI, linns ON
líns	linen OI, linen ON
líst	behold OI, like OI
lit	colour OI, colour ON
líta	look OI
litfagra	fair-colour OI, fair-colour ON
litið	consider OI
lítið	little OI, small OI
lítil	little OI, little ON
lítilþörf	little-need OI, little-need ON
litit	considering ON
lítit	little ON
litla	little OI, little ON
litlu	little OI, little ON
litnar	colours OI, colours ON
lítt	little OI, little ON
lízt	appears ON
ljósjarpr	light ON
ljósjarpur	light OI
ljósum	light OI, lights OI, lights ON
ljótastir	ugliest OI
ljúfsvelgs	sweet-swallower OI, sweet-swallower ON
lofaði	praised OI, praised ON
lofnar	praised OI, praised ON
lofti	the-sky OI, the-sky ON
lög	law OI, law ON
lögbergi	law-rock OI, law-rock ON
lögbergs	law-rock OI, law-rock ON
lögmaðr	law-man ON
lögmaður	law-man OI
lögréttu	law-assembly OI, law-assembly ON
lögskilum	legal-settlement OI, legal-settlement ON
lögsögn	lawspeaker OI
lögsögu	lawspeaker ON
lögsögumaðr	lawspeaker ON, law-speaker-man ON
lögsögumaður	lawspeaker OI
lögspeki	lawspeaking OI, lawspeaking ON
lögum	law OI, law ON
lokið	ended OI
lokit	ended ON
lokka	lure OI, lure ON
lokrekkju	bed-closet OI, bed-closet ON
loks	finally OI, finally ON
löndum	lands OI, lands ON
löngum	long OI, long ON
lundúnaborg	London-town (place) ON
lúndúnaborg	London-town (place) OI
lundúnabryggjur	London-town (place) OI, London-town (place) ON
lykðum	completion ON
lykkju	loop OI, loop ON
lýkr	ends ON
lykt	smell OI, smell ON
lyktum	completion OI
lýkur	ends OI
lyngs	heather-lands OI, heather-lands ON
lýsi-gunnar	light-warrior-god OI, light-warrior-god ON
lýtr	bow OI, bow ON

M, m

Norse	English
má	may OI, may ON
maðr	a-man ON, man ON, men ON
maður	a-man OI, man OI
mægðar	marriage OI, marriage ON
mæki	sword OI, sword ON
mæl	said OI, said ON
mæla	business OI, business ON
mælt	said OI, said ON, say OI, say ON, spoke OI, spoken OI, spoken ON
mælti	said OI, spoke OI, spoke ON
mæltu	speaking OI, spoke OI, spoke ON

Word List (Norse to English)

Norse	English
mæninum	roof-ridge OI, roof-ridge ON
mær	girl OI, girl ON, maiden OI
mæra	praise OI, praise ON
mætast	meet OI, meet ON
mætr	measure OI, measure ON
mætti	may ON, met OI, met ON
mættimst	meet-we ON
mættumst	meet-we OI
mættust	met OI, met ON
mági	son-in-law OI, son-in-law ON
mags	brother-in-law OI
mágs	brother-in-law ON
mál	matter OI, matter ON, matters OI, subject OI
mála	matter OI, matter ON
málgráðr	degree OI, degree ON
málið	matter OI
málin	matters OI, matters ON
málit	matter ON
malma	metals ON
málma	metals OI
malmflaug	metal-missile ON
málmflaug	metal-missile OI
máls	matter OI, matter ON, speak OI, speak ON
man	remembered OI, remembered ON
mánaði	month ON
mann	man OI, man ON, men OI, men ON
manna	man OI, man ON, man's ON, man's OI, many OI, men OI, men ON, of-men OI, people OI, people ON
mannaða	manly OI, manly ON
mannaforráð	looked-after OI, looked-after ON
mannhringr	man-ring ON
mannhringur	man-ring OI
manni	man OI, man ON, men OI, men ON
manninum	this-man OI, this-man ON
mannjöfnuð	men-comparing OI, men-comparing ON
mannni	man OI
manns	man's OI, man's ON
mannval	men-choice ON, men-choices OI
mánuði	month OI
marga	many OI
margar	many OI, many ON
margir	many OI, many ON
margr	many ON
margs	many OI, many's ON
margt	many ON
margur	many OI
mark	proof OI, proof ON
mart	many OI
mátt	might ON
mátti	may OI, may ON
máttu	might OI
með	along OI, among OI, well OI, while OI, with OI, with ON
meðal	between OI, between ON
meðalkafla	average-head OI, average-head ON
meðalráð	among-advice OI, among-advice ON
meðan	meanwhile OI, meanwhile ON, while OI, while ON
mega	able-to OI, able-to ON, may OI
megin	ways ON
meinn	painful OI, painful ON
meir	more OI, more ON
meira	more OI, more ON
meiri	better OI, better ON, more OI
melrakkaslettu	Melrakkasletta (place) OI, Melrakkasletta (place) ON
menn	many OI, men OI, men ON, people OI, people ON
menning	culture OI, culture ON
menrýris	men-equal OI, men-equal ON

Word List (Norse to English)

Norse	English
mér	i OI, i ON, me OI, me ON, mine OI, myself ON, myself-to OI, to-me OI, to-me ON
merkr	marks ON
merkur	marks OI
merum	mares OI, mares ON
mest	most OI, most ON
mesta	most OI, most ON
mesti	most OI, most ON
mestir	best ON, most OI
mestr	greatest ON
mestri	most OI, most ON
mestu	most OI, most ON
mestur	greatest OI
metinn	appreciated OI, appreciated ON
metnaðarmaðr	ambitious-man ON
metnaðarmaður	ambitious-man OI
mey	girl OI, girl ON
meybarn	baby-girl OI, baby-girl ON
meyjar	girls OI, girls ON, maiden OI
meyjarnar	girls OI
miðfjarðar-skeggja	Midfjorder-Skeggi's (name) OI, Midfjorder-Skeggi's (name) ON
miðmjór	medium-narrow OI, medium-narrow ON
mig	me OI, mine OI, my OI
mik	me ON
mikið	great OI, greatly OI, much OI
mikil	great OI, much OI, much ON
mikill	great OI, great ON, much OI, much ON
mikilli	much OI, much ON
mikilræði	great-issue OI, great-issue ON
mikinn	great OI, great ON
mikit	great ON, greatly ON, much ON
mikla	much OI, much ON
miklir	great OI
miklu	great OI, many OI, much OI, much ON
milli	between OI, between ON
millim	between ON
millum	between OI
mín	me OI, me ON, mine OI, mine ON, my OI, my ON
mína	mine OI, mine ON
mínar	mine OI, mine ON
minn	mine OI, mine ON, my OI, my ON
minna	less OI, less ON
minnar	mine OI, mine ON
minni	less OI, less ON
minnr	less ON
minnur	less OI
míns	mine OI, mine ON
mínu	mine OI, mine ON
mínum	mine OI, mine ON, my OI, my ON
missari	a-season ON
misseri	a-season OI
mitt	mid OI, mid ON, mine OI, mine ON, my OI
mjög	many OI, much OI
mjök	much OI, much ON
móði	Móði (name) OI, Móði (name) ON
móðir	mother OI, mother ON
móður	mother OI, mother ON
mogun	morning OI
moguninn	morning OI
molda-gnúpssonar	son-of-Molda-Gnup (name) OI, son-of-Molda-Gnup (name) ON
mönnum	men OI, people OI, people ON
morðrunnr	murder-running OI, murder-running ON
mörg	many OI, many ON
morgin	morning ON
morgininn	morning ON
morgun	morning OI
morguninn	morning OI
morguns	morning OI, morning ON
mörk	a-mark ON, mark OI, mark ON
mörkum	marks OI, marks ON

Word List (Norse to English)

Norse	English
mosfelli	Mosfell (place) OI, Mosfell (place) ON
mosfells	Mosfell (place) OI, Mosfell (place) ON
mót	meet OI, meet ON
móti	meet OI, meet ON, met OI
mótrunnr	against OI, against-running ON
mun	could OI, must OI, shall OI, should OI, should ON, will OI, would OI
muna	should OI, should ON
munat	remembered OI, remembered ON
mundangs	middle OI, middle ON
mundi	remembered OI, should OI, would OI
munði	remembered ON
mundu	should OI, should ON, would OI, would ON, would-be ON
muni	should OI, should ON
munt	shall OI, shall ON, should OI, should ON
muntu	should OI
munu	shall OI, shall ON, would ON
munum	should OI, should ON
mynda	should ON
myndi	should ON, would ON
mýramanna	Myrar (place) OI, Myrar-folk (name) OI, Myrar-folk (name) ON
mýrunum	the-moors OI, the-moors ON

N, n

Norse	English
náði	caught ON, got OI
naðrstunga	venomous-sting OI, venomous-sting ON
næði	neared OI, neared ON
nær	brought OI, close-to OI, near OI, near ON, nearer ON
næst	next OI, next ON, next-to OI
nætr	nights ON
nætti	night OI
nætur	nights OI
nafn	name OI, name ON, named OI
nafni	namesake OI, namesake ON
náfrændi	near-kin OI, near-kin ON
nakkvað	somewhat OI
nakkvar	some OI
nam	took OI, took ON, took-land OI, took-land ON
námu	took OI, took ON
nátt	night OI, night ON
nátta	nights OI, nights ON
náttum	nights OI, nights ON
naustu	next OI
nauztu	next-to ON
né	nor OI, nor ON, not OI, not ON
neðan	below OI, below ON
nefljótr	ugly-nose ON
nefljótur	ugly-nose OI
nefndi	mentioned OI, named ON
nefndir	mentioned OI, mentioned ON, named OI, named ON
nefndist	named OI, named ON
nefndr	named ON
nefndum	named OI, named ON
nefndur	named OI
nema	except OI, taken OI, taken ON, taking OI, taking ON
nemr	taken OI, taken ON
nenna	bothered OI, bothered ON
nenni	care OI, care ON
nes	headland OI, headland ON
nesi	headland OI, headland ON
nesin	the-headland OI, the-headland ON
nesinu	headland OI, headland ON
niðaróss	Nidaros (place) OI, Nidaros (place) ON

Word List (Norse to English)

Norse	English	Norse	English
niðr	down ON	nýtekið	newly-taken OI
niðri	down OI	nýtekit	newly-taken ON
níðskár	abusive OI, abusive ON	nytjar	use OI, use ON
niður	down OI	nýtti	use OI, use ON, used OI
njáls	Njal's (name) OI, Njal's (name) ON	nýztr	new ON
njörun	Njörun (name) OI, Njörun (name) ON		
njóta	enjoy OI, enjoy ON		

O, o

Norse	English
nokkuð	some OI, something OI, some-what OI
nokkur	somewhat OI
nokkurir	some OI
nökkurir	some ON
nökkurr	anyone ON, something-of ON
nökkut	some ON, something ON, somewhat ON, some-what ON
nökkvi	given-name OI, given-name ON
norðan	north OI, north ON
norðmaðr	Northman ON
norðmaður	Northman OI
norðr	north ON
norðrárdal	Norduradal (place) ON
norður	north OI
norðurárdal	Norduradal (place) OI
noreg	Norway (place) OI
nóreg	Norway (place) ON
noregi	Norway (place) OI
nóregi	Norway (place) ON
noregs	Norway (place) OI
nóregs	Norway (place) ON
noregsmenn	Norwegian-men OI
nóregsmenn	Norwegian-men ON
noregsmönnum	Norwegian-men OI
nóregsmönnum	Norwegian-men ON
norrænn	norwegian OI, norwegian ON
nóttina	night OI, night ON
nú	not OI, now OI, now ON
nýju	new OI, new ON
nýlundu	newcomer OI, newcomer ON
nýstr	new OI
nýta	use OI, use ON

Norse	English
oddfeimu	spear-sister OI, spear-sister ON
odd-gefnar	point-given OI, point-given ON
oddrjóð	point-reddener OI, point-reddener ON
of	about OI, about ON, of OI
ofan	down OI, over OI, over ON
ofanverðan	above OI, above ON
ofrást	love ON
ofsi	vehemence OI, vehemence ON
oft	often OI, often ON
ofurást	love OI
og	also OI, and OI, but OI, of OI
ok	and ON
okkarri	our OI, our ON
okkr	our ON, us ON, we OI, we ON
okkra	our OI, our ON
okkrir	ours OI, ours ON, yours OI, yours ON
okkur	ours OI, us OI
olli	cause OI, cause ON
opa	avoid OI
opið	open OI
opit	opened ON
orð	word OI, words OI, words ON
orðið	become OI, of-words OI, word OI, worded OI
orðinn	have-become OI, have-become ON
orðit	of-words ON, word ON
orkneyja	Orkney (place) OI, Orkney (place) ON

Word List (Norse to English)

Norse	English	Norse	English
orkneyjar	Orkney-islands (place) OI, Orkney-islands (place) ON	*ókunnum*	unknown OI, unknown ON
orkneyjum	Orkneys (place) OI, Orkneys (place) ON	*ólæti*	unrest OI
orlof	leave OI, vacation OI, vacation ON	*ólaf*	Olaf (name) OI
		óláf	Olaf (name) ON
orlofs	vacation OI, vacation ON	*ólafi*	Olaf (name) OI
		óláfi	Olaf (name) ON
orma	serpent ON	*óláfr*	Olaf (name) ON
ormabeð	serpent's-bed OI	*ólafs*	Olaf (name) OI, Olaf's (name) OI
ormdags	serpent-days OI, serpent-days ON	*óláfs*	Olaf (name) ON, Olaf's (name) ON
orms	serpent OI, serpent ON	*ólafsson*	son-of-Olaf (name) OI
ormstunga	serpent-tongue OI, serpent-tongue ON	*ólafssonar*	son-of-Olaf (name) OI
		óláfssonar	son-of-Olaf (name) ON
ormstungu	serpent-tongue OI, Serpent-Tongue's (name) ON, serpent-tongue's OI, serpent-tongue's ON	*ólafur*	Olaf (name) OI
		óleifi	Olaf (name) OI, Olaf (name) ON
		ómælt	not-spoken OI, not-spoken ON
oröit	become ON	*ómegð*	without OI, without ON
orrostur	battles ON	*ómerkilegur*	un-marked-like OI
ort	worded OI, worded ON	*ómerkiligr*	un-marked-like ON
orta	worded OI, worded ON	*ór*	from ON, of ON, out-of ON
orti	wrote OI, wrote ON	*óráðinn*	undecided OI, undecided ON, un-settled OI, unwise OI
ortir	worded OI, worded ON		
ortr	worded ON	*óröskari*	less-brave OI
ortur	worded OI	*óröskvari*	less-brave ON
orustur	battles OI	*órskurðarmanns*	ruling-person ON
oss	us OI, us ON	*órskurðinn*	ruling ON
		ósvífrs	Osvif's (name) ON
		ósvífs	Osvif's (name) OI

Ó, ó

Norse	English	Norse	English
		óþínslega	unhealthily OI
óæðra	lower OI, lower ON	*óþínsliga*	unhealthily ON
óðgjarn	sorely OI, sorely ON	*óþurft*	un-needed OI, un-needed ON
ódrengilega	un-fellow-like OI		
ódrengiliga	un-fellow-like ON	*óvæginn*	ruthless OI, ruthless ON
ófær	incapable OI		
ófærr	incapable ON	*óvígr*	not-fighting ON
ófagrt	ugly ON	*óvígur*	not-fighting OI
ófagurt	ugly OI	*óvingjarnlega*	unfriendly OI
ófriðar	un-peace OI, un-peace ON	*óvingjarnliga*	unfriendly ON
ógerla	indecent ON	*óvit*	unknown OI, unknown ON
ógjörla	indecent OI		
ógn	threat OI, threat ON		

Ö, ö

173

Word List (Norse to English)

Norse	English
öðru	another OI, another ON, other ON, otherwise OI
öðrum	other OI, other ON, others OI, others ON
öðrumegin	other-side OI
ök	and ON
ölfusi	Olfus (name) OI, Olfus (name) ON
öll	all OI, all ON
öllu	all OI, all ON
öllum	all OI, all ON
ölstafns	ale-staff OI, ale-staff ON
ölteiti	unrest ON
öndri	second OI, second ON
öndvegi	foremost OI, foremost ON
öndverðan	before OI, before ON, early OI, early ON
önga	not OI
öngar	none OI
öngra	none OI
öngu	none OI
öngum	none OI
öngvar	none OI
önund	Onund (name) OI, Onund (name) ON
önundar	Onund (name) OI, Onund (name) ON, Onund's (name) OI
önundarson	son-of-Onund (name) OI, son-of-Onund (name) ON
önundarsonar	son-of-Onund (name) OI
önundarsynir	Onund's-sons (name) OI, Onund's-sons (name) ON
önundi	Onund (name) OI, Onund (name) ON
önundr	Onund (name) ON
önundur	Onund (name) OI
örend	dead OI, dead ON
örkumlaðan	crippled OI, crippled ON
örn	eagle OI, eagle ON
örninn	eagle OI, eagle ON, the-eagle OI
örnólfsdal	Ornolfsdal (place) OI, Ornolfsdal (place) ON
öruggum	fearlessly OI, fearlessly ON
örva	excitement OI, excitement ON
öxar	axe ON
öxarár	Oxarar (place) OI, Oxarar (place) ON
öxarárhólmi	Oxararholm (place) OI, Oxararholm (place) ON

P, p

Norse	English
pá	peacock OI, peacock's ON, peacock's OI
pál	hoe OI, hoe ON
palli	platform OI, platform ON
presti	priest OI, priest ON
prestur	priest OI
prettum	trick OI, trick ON

R, r

Norse	English
ráð	advice ON, authority ON, counsel OI, propose OI, ride OI
ráða	advice OI, advice ON, advise OI, advise ON, advised ON, decide OI, decision OI
ráðast	arrange OI, arranged ON
ráði	advised OI, advised ON
ráðið	ruling OI
ráðinn	decided OI, determined OI, determined ON
ráðit	ruling ON
ráðlegast	advice-lies OI
ráðlegt	advised OI
ráðligast	advice-lies ON
ráðligt	advised ON
ráðsins	council OI, council ON
ráðum	advice OI, advice ON

Word List (Norse to English)

Norse	English
ræddi	decided ON, discussed ON, discussed-with OI, talked OI
ræddu	decided ON, discussed OI
ræki	care OI
rækik	care ON
rak	drove OI, drove ON
rakði	unfolded ON
rakti	spread OI
randgálkn	giants OI
randgölkn	giants ON
ranna	lodgings OI, lodgings ON
rannveig	Rannveig (name) OI, Rannveig (name) ON
ránsmaðr	robber-man ON
ránsmaður	robber-man OI
rauð	red OI, red ON
rauðamel	Raudamel (name) OI, Raudamel (name) ON
rauðan	red OI, red ON
raun	see OI, see ON
raunir	experience OI, experience ON
réð	decided OI, decided ON, dominated OI, engaged OI, rode OI, rode ON, ruled OI, ruled ON
réðst	decided OI, decided ON, rode OI, rode ON
réðu	rode OI, rode ON
reið	rode OI, rode ON
reiðr	angry ON
reiður	angry OI
rekði	unfolded ON
rekti	unfolded OI
reku	shovel OI, shovel ON
rembist	haughty OI
remb-ist	haughty ON
renndi	ran OI, ran ON
renni	run OI, run ON
rétting	righting OI, righting ON
reyna	attempt OI, attempt ON
reynd	resolved OI, resolved ON, tried OI
reyndist	turned-out OI, turned-out ON
reyndr	experienced ON
reyndur	experienced OI
reynt	tested OI, tested ON
ríða	ride OI, ride ON, rode OI, rode ON
ríðr	rode ON
riðu	riding OI, rode OI, rode ON
ríður	rode OI
ríki	kingdom OI, kingdom ON
ríkinu	kingdom OI, kingdom ON
ríkr	kingdom ON
ríkur	kingdom OI
risnir	rising OI, rising ON
ristinni	instep OI, instep ON
risu	rose OI, rose ON
roðið	reddened OI
roðinn	reddened OI, reddened ON
roðit	reddened ON
rógi	feud OI, feud ON, slander OI, slander ON
röndum	shield OI, shield ON
rosknaðr	mature ON
rosknaður	mature OI
runna	round OI, round ON
runnr	tree OI, tree ON
rýgr	woman OI, woman ON

S, s

Norse	English
sá	looked OI, looked ON, saw OI, saw ON, seen ON, so OI, so ON, that ON
sæmd	honour OI
sæmð	honour ON
sæmilega	same-like OI
sæmiliga	same-like ON
sænski	swede OI, swede ON
særimsk	wound ON
særumst	wound OI
sætt	settlement OI, settlement ON

Word List (Norse to English)

Norse	English
sævar	seas OI, seas ON
sagði	said OI, said OI, said ON
sagðir	said OI, said ON
sagt	said OI, said ON, told OI
ságu	saw OI, saw ON
sakar	sake ON
sak-ar	sake ON
sakir	sake OI
saklausa	sake-less OI, sake-less ON
sal	hall OI, hall ON
sama	same OI, same OI, same ON, same ON
saman	together OI, together ON
samdist	agreed OI
samðist	agreed ON
samið	agreement OI
samir	so OI, so ON
samira	same OI, same ON
samit	agreement ON
samlagar	same-lying OI, same-lying ON
samt	together OI, together ON
samvistum	cohabiting OI, together-staying OI, together-staying ON
sannar	true OI, true ON
sannendum	truth ON
sannfróðr	true-knowledge OI, true-knowledge ON
sannindum	truth OI
sár	wound OI, wounded OI, wounded ON, wounds OI
sára	wound OI, wound ON
sárfíkinn	wound-eager OI, wound-eager ON
sárgammr	wound-vulture OI, wound-vulture ON
sárr	wound ON, wounded ON
sárt	hurt OI, wounded ON
sat	sat OI, sat OI, sat ON, sat ON
satt	true OI, true ON
sátu	sat OI, sitting OI, sitting ON
sáu	saw OI
sé	saw ON, say OI, see OI, see ON, so OI, so ON
segi	say OI, say ON
segið	saying OI, saying ON
segir	answered OI, said OI, said ON, say OI, told OI
segja	say OI, say ON
seildist	stretched OI, stretched ON
seinir	later OI, later ON
seinka	delay OI, delay ON
seinlega	reluctance OI
seinliga	reluctance ON
sék	see ON
sekkana	sacks OI, sacks ON
sel	sell OI, sell ON
seldi	sold OI, sold ON
selja	repay OI, sell OI, sell ON, shelter OI, shelter ON
sel-þórisson	son-of-Sel-Thori (name) OI, son-of-Sel-Thori (name) ON
sem	as OI, as ON, since OI, so OI, so ON, than ON, that OI, that ON, the OI, where OI, which OI, which ON, who OI
semja	negotiate OI, negotiate ON
sénar	seen OI, seen ON
senda	send OI, send ON
sendi	sent OI, sent ON
sendimenn	messengers OI, sending-men OI, sending-men ON
senn	they OI, they ON
sér	he OI, her OI, her ON, herself ON, him OI, him ON, himself OI, himself ON, himself-to OI, his OI, privately ON, see OI, see ON, seeing OI, themselves OI, themselves ON, yourself ON
sérð	see OI
sért	are OI

176

Word List (Norse to English)

Norse	English
sésk	see ON
sést	see OI
seti	set OI, set ON
sett	set OI, set ON
setti	put OI, put ON
settist	sat OI, sat ON
séu	are OI
séumk	see ON
sex	six OI, six ON
sextigu	sixty OI, sixty ON
sið	traditions OI, traditions ON
síð	late OI, later OI, later ON
síðan	after OI, after ON, afterwards OI, afterwards ON, since OI, since ON, then OI, then ON, thereafter OI
síðar	afterwards OI, afterwards ON, later OI, later ON, since OI, since ON
síðast	last OI, last ON
síðbúnir	later-ready OI, later-ready ON
síðir	eventually OI, eventually ON
siðum	customs OI, customs ON
siðvandi	custom OI
siðvanði	custom ON
sifurrekna	silver-inlay OI
sig	him OI, himself OI, this OI
sigla	sail OI, sail ON, sailed OI, sailed ON
sigldi	sailed OI, sailed ON, sails OI, sails ON
sigldu	sailed OI, sailed ON
siglir	sailed OI, sailed ON
sigraðr	defeated ON
sigraður	defeated OI
sigreynir	triumphs OI, triumphs ON
sigríðar	Sigrid (name) OI, Sigrid (name) ON
sigrs	victory ON
sigrsæla	victorious ON
sigtryggr	Sigtrygg (name) OI, Sigtrygg (name) ON
sigtryggur	Sigtrygg (name) OI
sigurðar	Sigurd (name) OI, Sigurd (name) ON
sigurðr	Sigurd (name) ON
sigurður	Sigurd (name) OI
sigurs	victory OI
sigursæla	victorious OI
sigvalda	Sigvalda (name) OI, Sigvalda (name) ON
sik	he ON, him ON, himself ON
siklingr	king OI
silfrrekna	silver-inlay ON
silfrs	silver ON
silfurs	silver OI
silkiskegg	silk-beard OI, silk-beard ON
sín	his OI, his ON, theirs OI, theirs ON
sína	her OI, her ON, hers OI, hers ON, his OI, his ON
sinn	he OI, hers OI, his OI, his ON, theirs ON, then OI, then ON, they OI, they ON
sinna	theirs OI, theirs ON
sinnar	his OI, his ON
sinni	his OI, his ON, mind ON, once OI, once ON, ours OI, ours ON, theirs OI, theirs ON, them OI, them ON, this OI, this ON
síns	his OI, his ON
sínu	his OI, theirs OI, theirs ON
sínum	hers OI, hers ON, his OI, his ON, theirs OI, theirs ON
siti	sit ON
sitið	sit ON
sitja	sit OI, sitting OI, sitting ON
sitji	sit OI
sitjið	sit OI
sitt	his OI, his ON, one's ON, this OI
síz	late ON

Word List (Norse to English)

Norse	English	Norse	English
sjá	see OI, see ON	skapfelligr	temperamental ON
sjálegastur	most-visible OI	skapfelligur	temperamental OI
sjálfdæmi	self-example OI, self-example ON	skapferði	temperament OI, temperament ON
sjalfr	himself ON	skaplyndi	mind-mood OI, mood OI, temper OI, temper ON, temperament OI
sjálfr	himself OI, himself ON		
sjálfra	themselves OI, themselves ON	skarðan	wronged OI, wronged ON
sjálfum	yourself OI, yourself ON	skarlati	scarlet OI, scarlet ON
sjálfur	himself OI	skarlatsskikkju	scarlet-cloak OI, scarlet-cloak ON
sjáligastr	seen-like ON	skaut	hem OI, hem ON
sjám	we-see ON	skauti	fringes OI, fringes ON
sjást	see OI, see ON	skeið	sheathed-sword OI, sheathed-sword ON
sjau	seven ON		
sjáum	we-see OI	skein	shone OI, shone ON
sjáumk	see OI	skeindist	scratched OI, scratched ON
sjaunda	seven ON		
sjö	seven OI	skeljavík	Skeljavik (place) OI, Skeljavik (place) ON
sjóði	funds OI, funds ON		
sjóna	sjoni OI, sjoni ON	skemmtu	entertained OI, entertained ON
sjöunda	seven OI		
skaði	harm OI, harm ON	skikkjan	cloak OI, cloak ON
skæ	askew OI, askew ON	skikkju	cloak OI, cloak ON
skafta	Skafti (name) OI, Skafti's (name) OI, Skafti's (name) ON	skikkjuna	cloak OI, cloak ON
		skikkjunni	cloak OI, cloak ON
		skil	understand OI, understand ON
skafti	Skafti (name) OI, Skafti (name) ON	skildi	shield OI, shield ON
		skildinum	shield OI, shield ON
skal	shall OI, shall ON	skildu	separated OI
skálann	hut OI, hut ON	skilðu	knew ON, separated ON
skáld	poet OI, poet ON		
skáld-hrafn	Poet-Hrafn OI, Poet-Hrafn ON	skilist	understood OI
		skilizt	understood ON
skaldi	poet OI, poet ON	skilja	separate OI, separate ON, separated OI, separated ON
skáldmenn	poets OI		
skalk	shall ON		
skalla-grímssonar	son-of-Skalla-Grim (name) OI, son-of-Skalla-Grim (name) ON	skilnaði	separate OI, separate ON, separated OI, separated ON
		skilr	separated ON
skalt	shall OI, shall ON	skilur	separated OI
skaltu	shall OI, shall-you OI, shall-you ON	skinndregna	skinned OI, skinned ON
		skinnum	skins OI, skins ON
skamma	short OI, short ON	skip	ship OI, ship ON, ships OI, ships ON
skáney	Skaney (place) OI, Skaney (place) ON		
skapa	create OI, create ON	skipað	directed OI

178

Word List (Norse to English)

Norse	English
skipaði	directed OI, directed ON
skipat	directed ON
skipbroti	shipwreck OI, shipwreck ON
skipi	ship OI, ship ON, ships OI, ships ON
skipið	ship OI
skipinu	ship OI, ship ON
skipit	ship ON
skips	ship OI, ship ON, ships OI, ships ON
skipti	exchanges OI, exchanges ON
skiptust	exchanged OI, exchanged ON
skipuðu	ships OI, ships ON
skjöld	shield OI, shield ON
skjöldinn	shield OI, shield ON
skjótast	quickest OI, quickest ON
skjótt	quickly OI, quickly ON, swiftly OI
sköglar-tósta	Forest-Tostig (name) OI, Forest-Tostig (name) ON
skör	fragile OI, fragile ON
skora	challenged OI, challenged ON
skorað	challenged OI, scored OI
skorat	challenged ON
skorta	shortage OI, shortage ON
skortir	short OI, short ON
skörulega	boldly OI
sköruliga	boldly ON
skörum	Skarar (place) OI, Skarar (place) ON
skörungr	noble ON
skörungur	noble OI
skotlandsfjörðu	Scotlands-firths (place) OI, Scotland's-Firths (place) ON
skúii	Skuli (name) ON
skúlason	son-of-Skula (name) OI
skúli	Skuli (name) OI, Skuli (name) ON
skulir	shall OI, should OI, should ON
skulu	shall OI, should OI, should ON
skuluð	should OI, should ON
skulum	shall ON
skum	shall OI
skyldi	should OI, should ON
skyldir	should OI, should ON
skyldu	should OI, should ON
skylir	seek ON
skylmdust	shields OI
skylmðust	shields ON
slá	strike OI, strike ON
slétt	smoothed OI, smoothed ON
sléttir	smooth OI, smooth ON
sléttu	Slettu (place) ON, the-plains OI
sléttunni	the-plains OI, the-plains ON
slík	such OI, such ON
slíka	such OI, such ON
slíkar	silver ON, such OI
slíkr	such ON
slíks	such OI, such ON
slíkt	such OI, such ON
slíku	such OI, such ON
slíkur	such OI
slyppr	escapes ON
slyppur	escaped OI
smalamaðr	shepherd ON
smalamaður	shepherd OI
smalamann	shepherd OI, shepherd ON
smalamanninn	the-shepherd OI, the-shepherd ON
smátt	small OI, small ON
snarplega	sharply OI
snarpliga	sharply ON
snemma	early OI, early ON
snemmendis	around OI, around ON, early-age OI, precocious OI, precocious ON
snemnma	happened OI
snerist	turned OI, turned ON

Word List (Norse to English)

Norse	English
snorri	Snorri (name) OI
söðlaðir	saddled OI, saddled ON
söðul	saddle OI, saddle ON
sofnaði	slept OI, slept ON
sögðu	said OI, said ON
sögn	said OI, said ON
sögu	saga OI, saga ON
sögunni	saga OI, the-saga OI, the-saga ON
sólarroð	sunrise OI, sunrise ON
sólu	sun OI, sun ON
sömu	same OI, same ON
son	son OI, son ON
sona	son OI, son ON
sonar	son OI, son ON
sonr	son ON, son-of ON
sonu	sons OI, sons ON
sonum	son OI, sons OI, sons ON
sóta	sought OI, sought ON
sótt	sickness OI, sickness ON, sought OI, sought ON
sótti	attended OI, attended ON
sóttust	attended OI, attended ON, sought OI
spaka	wise OI, wise ON
spaki	wise OI, wise ON
spara	save OI, save ON, withold OI
spjóta	spear OI, spear ON
spjótinu	spear OI, spear ON
spöng	arch OI, arch ON
spott	ridicule OI, ridicule ON
spratt	sprang OI, sprang ON
spurði	asked OI, asked ON
spurðust	asked OI, asked ON
spyr	asked OI
spyrr	asked ON
stað	stand OI, stands ON
staðar	places OI, places ON
staddir	present OI, present ON, standing ON
staðfestu	established OI, established ON
stafir	stave OI, stave ON
stála	steel OI, steel ON
standa	stand OI, stand ON
starði	stared OI, stared ON
starfa	work OI, work ON
starfi	work OI, work ON
starfs	work OI, work ON
sté	stepped OI, stepped ON
stefið	stave OI
stefit	staved ON
stefna	agreement OI, agreement ON
stefni	summoned OI, summoned ON
steinari	steinar OI, steinar ON
steingrímsfirði	Steingrimsfjord (place) OI, Steingrimsfjord (place) ON
steinþór	Steinthor (name) OI
sterkr	strong ON
sterkum	strong OI, strong ON
sterkur	strong OI
stirð	stiff OI, stiff ON
stirðkveðið	stiff-spoken OI
stirðkveðit	stiff-spoken ON
stóð	stood OI, stood ON
stóðhross	stud-horses OI, stud-horses ON
stóðhrossa	stud-horses OI, stud-horses ON
stóðu	position OI, standing OI, standing ON
stofni	strain OI, strain ON
stofu	main-room OI, main-room ON, room OI
stökk	jumped OI, jumped ON
stökkða	drove ON
stökkti	drove OI
stolið	stole OI
stolit	stole ON
stóreignamaðr	large-property-man ON
stóreignamaður	large-property-man OI
stórort	large OI, large ON
stórra	great OI, great ON
stórráðu	ambitious OI, ambitious ON
stórum	great OI, great ON

Word List (Norse to English)

Norse	English
stræti	street OI, street ON
strengina	strings OI, strings ON
strútharalds	strutharald ON
strút-haralds	Strut-Harald's (name) OI
studdi	stood OI, stood ON
stúfinum	stump OI, stump ON
stúlkur	girls ON
stund	awhile OI, awhile ON, while OI, while ON
stundir	awhile OI, awhile ON
stundum	awhile OI, awhile ON
sturluson	son-of-Sturlu (name) OI
stýrimaðr	steersman ON
stýrimaður	steersman OI
stýrimanni	steersman ON
stýrimanninum	steersman OI
sú	so OI, that OI, that ON
suðr	south ON
suðrætt	the-south ON
suðreyjar	South-Islands (place) ON
suður	south OI
suðurátt	the-south OI
suðureyjar	South-Islands (place) OI
sull	boil OI, boil ON
sullr	boil ON
sullur	boil OI
súlu	columns OI, columns ON
sumar	summer OI, summer ON
sumarið	summer OI
sumarit	summer ON
sumarlangt	summer-long OI, summer-long ON
sumars	summer OI, summer ON
sumir	some OI
sumri	summer OI, summer ON
sundr	asunder ON
sundur	asunder OI
sundurgreinilegt	asunder-mixed OI
sunnan	south OI, south ON
svá	so ON, such ON
svaf	slept OI, slept ON
svanmærrar	swan-mares OI, swan-mares ON
svara	answer OI, answer ON
svaraði	answered OI, answered ON
svarar	answered OI, answered ON
svarra	answer OI, answer ON
svarta	black OI, the-black OI, the-black ON
svarteygr	black-eyed ON, black-eyes ON
svarteygur	black-eyed OI, black-eyes OI
svarti	the-black OI, the-black ON
svartr	black OI, black ON
sváru	swears OI, swears ON
svefni	sleep OI, sleep ON
svefninum	sleep OI, sleep ON
sveik	betrayed OI, betrayed ON
sveikstu	tricked OI
sveiktu	tricked ON
sveinn	boy OI, boy ON, Svein (name) OI, Svein (name) ON
sveinsson	son-of-Svein (name) OI, son-of-Svein (name) ON
sveitinni	party OI, party ON
sveittr	sweat ON
sveittur	sweat OI
sverð	sword OI, sword ON
sverða	sword OI, sword ON
sverði	sword OI, sword ON
sverðið	sword OI
sverðinu	sword OI, sword ON
sverðit	sword ON
sverð-rögnir	sword-reddened OI, sword-reddened ON
svertingr	Sverting (name) ON
svertingur	Sverting (name) OI
svía	Sweden (place) OI, Sweden (place) ON
svík	betray OI, betray ON
svikið	tricked OI
svikit	tricked ON
svíkja	betray OI, betray ON

Word List (Norse to English)

Norse	English	Norse	English
svipr	seemed ON	tali	talking OI, talking ON
svipur	seemed OI	taliðr	spoke-of OI, spoke-of ON
svíþjóð	Sweden (place) OI, Sweden (place) ON	tals	talk OI, talk ON
svíþjóðar	Sweden (place) OI, Sweden (place) ON	tekið	taken OI
		tekist	take OI
svíþjóðu	Sweden (place) OI, Sweden (place) ON	tekit	taken ON
		tekizt	take ON
svo	so OI, son-of-illugi OI, son-of-thorstein OI, such OI	tíðenda	news ON
		tíðendalaust	news-less ON
		tíðendi	news ON, tidings ON
svört	black OI, black ON	tíðinda	news OI
sýn	show OI, show ON	tíðindalaust	news-less OI
sýnast	appear OI, appear ON	tíðindi	news OI
sýndi	showed OI, showed ON	til	for OI, of OI, to OI, to ON, towards OI, towards ON, until OI, until ON
sýndist	seemed OI, seemed ON		
syni	son OI, son ON, son-of ON, sons OI		
		tilkoma	till-came OI
synir	sons OI, sons ON	tilkváma	till-came ON
sýnir	showed OI, showed ON	tíma	time OI, time ON, times OI, times ON
sýnist	seem OI, seem ON		
synja	refuse OI, refuses ON	títa	look ON
synjar	refuse OI, refuse ON	tíundaland	Tiundaland (place) OI, Tiundaland (place) ON
sýnt	seemed ON, showed OI, showed ON, shown OI		
		tjár	force OI, force ON
sýslar	work OI	tognum	extend OI, extend ON
sýslir	work ON	tók	took OI, took ON
systir	sister OI, sister ON	tóku	taken OI, took OI
systrasynir	cousins OI, cousins ON	tólf	twelve OI, twelve ON
systursynir	sister-sons OI, sister-sons ON	tólfta	twelve OI, twelve ON
		töluðu	talked OI, talked ON
		tölum	talk OI, talk ON
		tóm	time OI, time ON
		torfa	Torfi (name) OI, Torfi (name) ON, Torfi's (name) OI

T, t

Norse	English	Norse	English
tæmdist	came-into OI		
tæmðist	came-into ON	torveldlegur	difficult OI
tafli	board-games OI, board-games ON	torvelligr	difficult ON
		trautt	scarcely OI, scarcely ON
taka	take OI, take ON		
takast	take OI, take ON	tróðu	trod OI, trod ON
takið	take OI, take ON	trúða	trusted ON
tal	talk OI, talked OI, talked ON, talking OI, talking ON	trúði	trusted OI
		trúið	believe OI, believe ON
		tryggðum	loyalty OI, loyalty ON
tala	speak OI, speak ON, talk OI	tunga	tongue OI, tongue ON

Word List (Norse to English)

Norse	English	Norse	English
tungls	moon OI, moon ON	þat	it ON, so ON, that ON, that ON, the ON, this ON
tungu	tongue OI, tongue ON	þau	his OI, then OI, then OI, then ON, there OI, there ON, therefore OI, they OI, they OI, they ON
tungu-odds	Tunga-odd's (name) OI, Tunga-odd's (name) ON		
tungur	tongue OI, tongue ON		
túninu	the-field OI, the-field ON	þegar	as-soon-as OI, straightaway OI, straight-away OI, then OI, then ON, there ON
tvá	two ON		
tvau	two ON		
tveggja	two OI, two ON	þegjandi	silently OI, silently ON
tveir	two OI, two ON	þegns	citizen OI, citizen ON
tvo	two OI	þeim	that ON, their ON, them OI, them ON, then ON, these OI, they OI, they ON, those OI, those ON, to-them OI, with-them OI
tvö	two OI		
tyggja	chew OI, chew ON		
Þ, þ			
		þeima	them OI, them ON
þá	that OI, the OI, them OI, them ON, then OI, then ON, there OI, there ON, they OI, they ON, those OI, those ON	þeir	the OI, the ON, their OI, them OI, there OI, there ON, they OI, they ON, those OI
		þeír	they ON
það	it OI, that OI, the OI, this OI, to OI	þeira	their ON, theirs ON, there ON, they ON
þaðan	from-there OI, from-there ON, there OI	þeiri	there ON
þær	therefore OI, therefore ON	þeirra	of-them OI, their OI, theirs OI, they OI
þakkaði	thanked OI, thanked OI, thanked ON, thanked ON	þeirri	their OI, the-one OI
		þekkðist	took ON
þakkar	thanked OI, thanked ON	þekkjast	familiar OI, familiar ON
		þekktist	took OI
þangað	from-there OI, there OI, there OI	þengil	angel ON
þangat	from-there ON, there ON, there ON	þenna	that OI, that ON, then OI, then ON, these OI, those OI, those ON
þann	than OI, that OI, that OI, that ON, that ON, then OI, then OI, then ON, then ON, this OI, those ON	þér	to-you OI, to-you ON, you OI, you ON, yours OI, you-to OI
þar	their OI, then ON, there OI, there ON, they OI, they ON	þess	these OI, this OI, this ON
		þessa	this OI, this ON
		þessar	these OI, these ON
þarfleysi	needless OI, needless ON	þessi	these OI, these ON, this OI, this ON
		þessir	these OI, these ON
þás	then ON	þessu	this OI, this ON

Word List (Norse to English)

Norse	English	Norse	English
þetta	at-this OI, that OI, that ON, the OI, this OI, this ON	þórðr	Thord (name) ON
		þórður	Thord (name) OI
þéttan	dense OI, dense ON	þörf	need OI, need ON
þeys	dashing OI, dashing ON	þorfinnr	Thorfin (name) ON
		þorfinns	Thorfin (name) OI, Thorfin (name) ON
þið	you OI, you-two OI		
þig	you OI	þorfinnur	Thorfin (name) OI
þiggja	receive OI, receive ON	þorgerði	Thorgerd (name) OI, Thorgerd (name) OI, Thorgerd (name) ON, Thorgerd (name) ON
þiggr	accepted ON		
þiggur	accepted OI		
þik	you ON	þorgerðr	Thorgerd (name) ON
þín	your OI, your ON, yours OI, yours ON	þorgerður	Thorgerd (name) OI
		þorgils	Thorgils (name) OI, Thorgils (name) ON
þína	yours OI, yours ON		
þing	assembly OI, assembly ON	þorgilsstöðum	Thorglisstadir (place) OI, Thorglisstadir (place) ON
þingi	assembly OI, assembly ON		
		þorgrím	Thorgrim (name) OI, Thorgrim (name) ON, Thorgrim's (name) OI
þingið	assembled OI, assembly OI		
þinginu	assembly OI, assembly ON		
		þorgrímur	Thorgrim (name) OI
þingit	assembled ON, assembly ON	þórir	Thorir (name) OI, Thorir (name) ON
þings	assembly OI, assembly ON, the-assembly OI, the-assembly ON	þorkatli	Thorkel (name) OI, Thorkell (name) ON, Thorkel's (name) OI
		þorkell	Thorkel (name) OI, Thorkell (name) OI, Thorkell (name) ON
þingstöð	assembly-post OI, assembly-post ON		
þinn	yours OI, yours ON	þorkels	Thorkel (name) OI, Thorkell (name) ON
þinna	your OI, your ON	þorna	thorn OI, thorn ON
þinnar	yours OI, yours ON	þórnessþingi	Thorsnes-assembly (name) OI
þíns	yours OI, yours ON		
þínum	yours OI, yours ON	þórodda	Thorodd (name) OI, Thorodd (name) ON
þit	you ON		
þitt	your OI, your ON	þóroddr	Thorod (name) ON
þjónustu	service OI, service ON	þóroddsdóttur	daughter-of-Thorodd (name) OI, daughter-of-Thorodd (name) ON
þó	though OI, though ON, thought OI, thought ON		
		þóroddur	Thorodd (name) OI
þokka	charm OI, charm ON	þórorm	Thororm (name) OI, Thororm (name) ON
þola	endure OI, endure ON		
þór	Thor (name) OI, Thor (name) ON	þórormr	Thororm (name) ON
þórarinn	Thorarin (name) OI, Thorarin (name) ON	þórormur	Thororm (name) OI
		þórsnessþingi	Thorsnes-assembly (name) ON
þórði	Thord (name) OI, Thord (name) ON		

184

Word List (Norse to English)

Norse	English
þorstein	Thorstein (name) OI, Thorstein (name) ON
þorsteini	Thorstein (name) OI, Thorstein (name) ON
þorstein'i	thorstein ON
þorsteinn	Thorstein (name) OI, Thorstein (name) ON
þorsteins	Thorstein (name) OI, Thorstein (name) ON, Thorstein's (name) OI, Thorstein's (name) ON, Thorstein's (name) OI
þorsteinsson	son-of-Thorstein (name) OI, son-of-Thorstein (name) ON
þorvarði	Thorvard (name) OI, Thorvard (name) ON
þorvarðr	Thorvard (name) ON
þorvarður	Thorvard (name) OI
þótt	though OI, though ON
þótti	seemed OI, thought OI, thought ON
þóttist	thought OI, thought ON
þóttu	thought OI, thought ON
þóttumst	thought ON
þrá	desire OI, desire ON
þrættu	quarrelled OI, quarrelled ON
þramma	trammel OI, trammel ON
þrándheim	Trondheim (place) OI, Trondheim (place) ON
þrándheimi	Trondheim (place) OI, Trondheim (place) ON
þrándheims	Trondheim (place) OI, Trondheim (place) ON
þreifaði	felt OI, felt ON
þrem	three OI, three ON
þremur	three OI
þriði	third ON
þriðja	third OI, third ON
þriðji	third OI
þrigga	three OI
þriggja	three OI, three ON
þrír	three OI, three ON
þrjá	three OI, three ON
þrjár	three OI, three ON
þrjátigu	thirty OI, thirty ON
þrútnaði	swollen OI, swollen ON
þú	you OI, you ON
þundi	thunder OI, thunder ON
þungara	heavy OI, heavy ON
þungum	heavily OI
þunnum	heavily ON
þurfa	needed OI, needed ON
þuríðr	Thurid (name) ON
þuríður	Thurid (name) OI
þvá	wash ON
því	according OI, as OI, as ON, because OI, because ON, because-of ON, before OI, before ON, for OI, since OI, since ON, that OI, then OI, therefore OI, therefore ON, with OI
þvílíkan	therefore-like OI, what ON
þvílíkr	therefore-like ON
þvílíkur	such OI
þvít	to ON
þvo	wash OI
þýðask	attach ON
þýðast	attach OI, join ON, to-attach OI
þýddan	translated OI, translated ON
þykir	consider OI, seems OI, think OI
þykist	think OI
þykja	be-valued OI
þykkir	consider ON, seemed ON, seems ON, think ON
þykkist	think ON
þykkja	be-valued ON
þyngd	heavy OI
þyngð	heavy ON
þyrfti	need OI, need ON

U, u

Norse	English
ullr	Ullr (name) OI, Ullr (name) ON
um	about OI, about ON, for OI, in OI

Word List (Norse to English)

Norse	English
und	and OI, under OI, under ON
undan	away OI, under OI, under ON
undi	satisfied OI
unði	satisfied ON
undir	to OI, to ON, under OI
undirmál	under-speech OI, under-speech ON
undraðist	was-surprised OI, was-surprised ON
undu	under OI
unðu	won ON
ung	young OI, young ON
ungr	young ON
ungum	young OI, young ON
unna	love OI, love ON
unnandi	loved OI, loved ON
unnar	won OI, won ON
unni	love OI, love ON
unnið	deserved OI, won OI
unnit	deserved ON, won ON
unnviggs	down OI, down ON
upp	above OI, up OI, up ON, up-to-the-mountains OI
uppi	about OI, up OI, up ON
uppsala	Uppsala (place) OI, Uppsala (place) ON
urðu	became OI, became ON
utan	out OI, out-of OI
utanferðar	out-travel OI

Ú, ú

Norse	English
úr	from OI, out-of OI
úrskurðarmanns	ruling-person OI
úrskurðinn	ruling OI
út	back OI, back ON, back-from OI, back-from ON, from OI, out OI, out ON, out-of OI, out-of ON, outside OI
útan	out ON, out-of ON, to-out ON
útanferðar	out-travel ON
úti	out OI, out ON
útibúr	out-house OI, out-house ON
útkoma	back-came OI
útkváma	out-coming ON
útláts	out-let OI, out-let ON
útlöndum	other-lands ON

V, v

Norse	English
væn	fair OI, fair ON
væna	kind OI, kind ON
vænleik	beauty OI, likeness OI, likeness ON
vænleiks	good-looks OI, good-looks ON
vænn	handsome OI, handsome ON
vænstir	expected OI
vænu	kind OI, kind ON
væri	is ON, was OI, was ON, were OI, were ON, would-be OI, would-be ON
værir	be OI, be ON, would-be OI
væru	were OI
vafiðr	wrapped ON
vafiður	wrapped OI
vágr	opened ON
vakið	awoken OI
vakir	woke OI, woke ON
vakit	awoken ON
vaknaða	woke ON
vaknaði	awoke OI, awoke ON, awoken OI
valbrandssonar	son-of-Valbrand (name) OI, son-of-Valbrand (name) ON
valfell	Valfell (place) OI, Valfell (place) ON
valr	falcon ON
valrinn	falcon ON
valska	french OI, french ON
valur	falcon OI
valurinn	falcon OI
ván	hope ON, looked ON

Word List (Norse to English)

Norse	English
vandræðaskáld	troublesome-poet OI, troublesome-poet ON
vandræðaskáldi	troublesome-poet OI, troublesome-poet ON
vanhluta	of-parts OI, of-parts ON
vanhyggju	carelessness OI, carelessness ON
vann	won OI, won ON
vanvirða	disrespect OI, disrespect ON
vápn	weapon ON, weapons ON
vápnum	weapons ON
var	as OI, stayed OI, was OI, was ON, were OI, were ON, where OI
vár	be ON, spring ON
vara	wares OI, wares ON
varð	became OI, became ON, was OI, was ON, were OI
varðveislu	custody OI
varðveitt	preserved OI, preserved ON
varðveizlu	custody ON
várit	spring ON
várn	ours ON
varnaðr	wares ON
varnaður	wares OI
varr	where ON
várri	provisions ON
vart	hardly OI, hardly ON
várt	our ON, ours ON
váru	wares ON, was ON, were ON
várum	we ON
vas	was ON
vask	was ON
vaskasti	boldest OI, boldest ON
vasklegur	bold OI, boldly OI
vaskligr	bold ON
vaskr	bold ON
vaskur	bold OI
vatn	water OI, water ON
vatnanna	waters OI, waters ON
vatnið	waters OI
vatnit	lake ON
vatnsdal	Vatnsdal (place) OI, Vatnsdal (place) ON
vátta	testimony ON
vaxið	grown OI
vaxit	grown ON
vaxtar	build OI, build ON
veðr	weather OI, weather ON
veðrið	weather OI
veðrit	wind ON
veðrum	winds OI, winds ON
veg	fell OI, fell ON
vega	fight OI, fight ON
veggina	walls OI, walls ON
vegni	weigh OI, weigh ON
veislunni	feast OI
veist	know OI
veit	know OI, know ON
veita	grant OI, grant ON
veitat	provided OI, provided ON
veitti	granted OI, provided-for OI, provided-for ON, support OI, supported OI
veizlunni	feast ON
veizt	know ON
vel	well OI, well ON
vellir	fields OI, fields ON
veltr	depend ON
veltur	depend OI
venr	custom OI, custom ON
ver	were OI, were ON
vér	we OI, we ON
vera	be OI, be ON, being OI, be-it OI, be-it ON, to-be OI, to-be ON, was OI, was ON
veradal	Veradal (place) OI, Veradal (place) ON
verða	be OI, be ON, become OI, become ON, becoming ON, being OI, was OI, was ON
verðak	worth ON
verði	be OI, will-be OI, will-be ON
verðir	be OI, will-be ON

187

Word List (Norse to English)

Norse	English
verðr	became ON, worth ON
verður	became OI, worth OI
verið	been OI, had-been OI
verit	been ON, made ON
verkið	the-work OI
verkit	the-work ON
verkkaupi	spend OI, spend ON
verst	worst OI, worst ON
vestr	west ON
vestra	west OI, west ON
vestri	the-west OI, the-west ON
vestur	west OI
vetr	winter ON, winters ON
vetra	winters OI, winters ON
vetri	winter OI, winter ON
vetrinn	winter ON
vetrnáttum	winter-nights ON
vetrnóttum	winter-nights ON
vetrum	winters OI, winters ON
vetur	winter OI, winters OI
veturinn	winter OI
veturnáttum	winter-nights OI
veturnóttum	winter-nights OI
við	in OI, known OI, thereore OI, to OI, to ON, with OI, with ON, within ON
víða	widely OI, widely ON
víðara	wider OI, wider ON
viðskipti	exchanged OI, exchanged ON
vifja	willed ON
víg	killing OI, killing ON
víga-barði	Viga-Bardi (name) OI
viggs	slayers ON
vígsdöglinga	slayers-of-the-dead OI
vígur	spear-man OI
víkingr	viking ON
víkingrinn	viking ON
víkingur	viking OI
víkingurinn	viking OI
viku	week OI, week ON
vil	will OI, will ON, wish OI, wish ON
vilda	will ON
vildi	will OI, willed OI, willed ON, wished OI, wished ON
víldi	willed ON
vildir	will OI, will ON, willed OI, willed ON
vildu	wanted OI, wanted ON, willed OI, willed ON
vilhjálmr	William (name) ON
vilhjálmur	William (name) OI
vilið	will ON
vilja	will OI, will ON, willed OI, willed ON, wished OI
viljið	will OI
vill	will OI, will ON, wills OI, wish ON
villtu	will-you ON
vilt	like OI, will OI, wish OI
viltu	will-you OI
vina	friends OI, friends ON
vinátta	friendship OI, friendship ON
vináttu	friendliness OI, friendliness ON, friendship OI
vingan	friendship OI, friendship ON
vín-gefn	wine-given OI, wine-given ON
vini	friends OI, friends ON
vinir	friends OI, friends ON
vinkonu	girlfriend OI, girlfriend ON
vinn	win OI
vinnk	win ON
vinsæll	popular OI, popular ON
vinsælli	more-popular OI, more-popular ON
vinslitum	friendship OI, friendship ON
vinstri	left OI, left ON
virði	valued ON
virðing	honour OI, honour ON
virðingu	worthy OI, worthy ON
virðist	seemed OI, seemed ON, seems OI, seems ON
virðr	worth ON
virðulega	worthily OI

Word List (Norse to English)

Norse	English
virðuliga	worthily ON
virður	respect OI
virti	valued OI
vísað	turn OI
vísat	turn ON
vissak	know ON
vissi	knew OI, knew ON, know OI
vist	provisions OI, provisions ON
víst	certain OI, certain ON, certainly OI, certainly ON, know OI, know ON, known OI, surely OI, wise OI
vistar	surely ON
vistuðust	found-a-place OI, found-a-place ON
vísu	verse OI, verse ON
vísuna	verse OI, verse ON
vit	with OI, with ON
vita	know OI, know ON
vitir	know OI, know ON
vitja	visit OI, visit ON
vitjaði	visited OI, visited ON
vitr	wise ON
vitrastir	wisest OI, wisest ON
vitrastur	wisest OI
vitrustu	wisest OI, wisest ON
vitur	wise OI
vogur	opened OI
völlum	fields OI, fields ON
von	expected OI, hope OI, looked OI
vooru	were OI
vopn	weapon OI
vopnum	weapons OI
vor	provided OI, spring OI
vorið	spring OI
vorn	ours OI
vorri	provisions OI
vort	our OI
voru	there OI, wares OI, was OI, were OI
vorum	ours OI
vörusekkar	sacks ON, ware-sacks OI
vörusekkunum	ware-sacks OI, ware-sacks ON
vötn	waters OI, waters ON
votta	testimony OI
vöxt	growth OI, growth ON

Y, y

Norse	English
yðr	you ON
yðrum	your OI, your ON, yours OI, yours ON
yður	you OI, your OI, yours OI
yðvar	you OI, you ON
yðvarn	yours OI, yours ON
yfir	across OI, across ON, over OI, over ON
yfirbragð	complexion OI, complexion ON
yfirbragðslítið	little-appearance OI
yfirbragðslítit	little-appearance ON
yill	like ON
ykkr	you ON
ykkur	you OI
yngri	younger OI, younger ON
yrði	should OI, should ON
yrðu	be OI

Ý, ý

Norse	English
ý	be OI, be ON
ýfast	ruffled OI, ruffled ON
ýmisst	either ON
ýmist	either OI
ýmsum	various OI, various ON
ýta	pushed OI, pushed ON
ýti	out OI
ýtik	out ON

# Word List *(English to Norse)*

OI = Icelandic   ON = Old Norse

English	Norse	English	Norse

A, a

English	Norse
a	*á* OI, *á* ON, *einn* OI, *í* OI, *í* ON
able	*færim* ON, *færum* OI
able-to	*mega* OI, *mega* ON
about	*á* OI, *á* ON, *í* OI, *of* OI, *of* ON, *um* OI, *um* ON, *uppi* OI
above	*framar* OI, *framar* ON, *ofanverðan* OI, *ofanverðan* ON, *upp* OI
abusive	*níðskár* OI, *níðskár* ON
accepted	*þiggr* ON, *þiggur* OI
accomplished	*afreksmaðr* ON, *afreksmaður* OI
according	*því* OI
across	*yfir* OI, *yfir* ON
Adganes (place)	*agðanesi* OI, *agðanesi* ON
advanced	*heldur* OI
advantage	*hagvirki* OI, *hagvirki* ON
advice	*ráð* ON, *ráða* OI, *ráða* ON, *ráðum* OI, *ráðum* ON
advice-lies	*ráðlegast* OI, *ráðligast* ON
advise	*ráða* OI, *ráða* ON
advised	*ráða* ON, *ráði* OI, *ráði* ON, *ráðlegt* OI, *ráðligt* ON
afflictions	*forbæna* OI, *forbæna* ON
afraid	*hræðist* OI, *hræðumst* ON
after	*áðr* OI, *áðr* ON, *eftir* OI, *eftir* ON, *síðan* OI, *síðan* ON
aftermath	*eftirbátr* ON, *eftirbátur* OI
afterwards	*síðan* OI, *síðan* ON, *síðar* OI, *síðar* ON
against	*mótrunnr* OI
against-headland	*andness* OI, *andness* ON
against-running	*mótrunnr* ON
age	*aldr* ON, *aldur* OI
aggravating	*hríðgervandi* ON, *hríðgjörvandi* OI
agreed	*samdist* OI, *samðist* ON
agreement	*samið* OI, *samit* ON, *stefna* OI, *stefna* ON
ale-staff	*ölstafns* OI, *ölstafns* ON
all	*alla* OI, *alla* ON, *allan* OI, *allan* ON, *allar* OI, *allar* ON, *allir* OI, *allir* ON, *allr* OI, *allr* ON, *allra* OI, *allra* ON, *allri* OI, *allri* ON, *alls* OI, *alls* ON, *allt* OI, *allt* ON, *allur* OI, *öll* OI, *öll* ON, *öllu* OI, *öllu* ON, *öllum* OI, *öllum* ON
all-bloodied	*alblóðugr* ON
all-good	*allgóð* OI, *allgóð* ON
all-greatly	*allmjög* OI
all-heathen	*alheiðið* OI, *alheiðit* ON
all-mind	*alhugi* OI, *alhugi* ON
all-much	*allmikið* OI, *allmikit* ON
all-not-expected	*allóvænt* OI, *allóvænt* ON
allowed	*lét* OI, *létu* OI
all-prepared	*albúið* OI
all-promising	*allvænlegir* OI, *allvænligir* ON
all-ready	*albúinn* OI, *albúinn* ON
all-ruling	*allráðr* OI, *allráðr* ON
all-very	*allmjök* ON
all-weaponed	*alvápnaðir* ON, *alvopnaðir* OI
all-well	*allvel* OI, *allvel* ON
along	*eftir* OI, *fyrir* OI, *fyrir* ON, *lengi* OI, *með* OI
a-loud-man	*hávaðamaðr* ON, *hávaðamaður* OI
also	*og* OI
altogether	*allt* OI
always	*ávallt* OI, *ávallt* ON
am	*á* OI, *eg* OI, *em* OI, *em* ON
a-man	*maðr* ON, *maður* OI

Word List (English to Norse)

English	*Norse*	English	*Norse*
a-mark	*mörk* ON	arrange	*ráðast* OI
ambitious	*framgjarn* OI, *framgjarn* ON, *stórráðu* OI, *stórráðu* ON	arranged	*ráðast* ON
		as	*að* OI, *ás* OI, *ás* ON, *ási* OI, *ási* ON, *at* ON, *en* OI, *en* ON, *er* OI, *er* ON, *es* ON, *sem* OI, *sem* ON, *því* OI, *því* ON, *var* OI
ambitious-man	*metnaðarmaðr* ON, *metnaðarmaður* OI		
am-i	*emk* ON		
among	*í* OI, *með* OI	Asbjarnar (name)	*ásbjarnar* OI, *ásbjarnar* ON
among-advice	*meðalráð* OI, *meðalráð* ON	a-season	*missari* ON, *misseri* OI
ancestry	*ætt* OI	Asgerd (place)	*ásgerðr* ON, *ásgerður* OI
ancient	*fornum* OI, *fornum* ON	as-he	*er'hann* ON
and	*en* OI, *en* ON, *én* ON, *og* OI, *ok* ON, *ök* ON, *und* OI	ask	*bið* OI, *bið* ON
		asked	*bað* OI, *bað* ON, *beiddi* OI, *beiddi* ON, *biðr* ON, *biður* OI, *spurði* OI, *spurði* ON, *spurðust* OI, *spurðust* ON, *spyr* OI, *spyrr* ON
an-end	*enda* ON		
angel	*engil* OI, *þengil* ON		
anger	*ákafa* OI		
angry	*reiðr* ON, *reiður* OI		
another	*annað* OI, *annan* OI, *annan* ON, *annar* OI, *annarr* ON, *annarra* OI, *annarra* ON, *annat* ON, *öðru* OI, *öðru* ON	askew	*skæ* OI, *skæ* ON
		assembled	*þingið* OI, *þingit* ON
		assembly	*alþingi* OI, *alþingi* ON, *þing* OI, *þing* ON, *þingi* OI, *þingi* ON, *þingið* OI, *þinginu* OI, *þinginu* ON, *þingit* ON, *þings* OI, *þings* ON
answer	*svara* OI, *svara* ON, *svarra* OI, *svarra* ON		
answered	*segir* OI, *svaraði* OI, *svaraði* ON, *svarar* OI, *svarar* ON		
		assembly-post	*þingstöð* OI, *þingstöð* ON
any	*einhverju* OI, *einhverju* ON, *hvert* OI, *hvert* ON	assistance	*greiða* OI, *greiða* ON
		as-soon-as	*þegar* OI
anyone	*nökkurr* ON	asunder	*sundr* ON, *sundur* OI
appear	*sýnast* OI, *sýnast* ON	asunder-mixed	*sundurgreinilegt* OI
appears	*lízt* ON	as-vigourous	*íþróttar* OI, *íþróttar* ON
appreciated	*metinn* OI, *metinn* ON	at	*á* OI, *á* ON, *að* OI, *at* ON, *í* OI
arch	*spöng* OI, *spöng* ON		
are	*er* OI, *er* ON, *ert* OI, *ert* ON, *eru* OI, *eru* ON, *sért* OI, *séu* OI	athletic-man	*fimleikamaður* OI
		at-home	*heima* OI
		Atli (name)	*atla* OI, *atla* ON, *atli* OI, *atli* ON
are-we	*eru* OI		
are-you	*ertu* OI, *ertu* ON	attach	*þýðask* ON, *þýðast* OI
arm-good	*armgóða* OI	attempt	*reyna* OI, *reyna* ON
armour	*brynju* OI, *brynju* ON	attended	*sótti* OI, *sótti* ON, *sóttust* OI, *sóttust* ON
arms	*armi* OI, *armi* ON, *arms* ON, *fang* OI, *fang* ON		
		at-this	*þetta* OI
army	*her* OI, *herja* OI, *herja* ON, *herr* ON	Audun (name)	*auðun* OI, *auðun* ON, *auðuni* OI, *auðunn* ON
around	*áður* OI, *snemmendis* OI, *snemmendis* ON	Audun's (name)	*auðuni* OI, *auðuni* ON

191

Word List (English to Norse)

English	*Norse*	English	*Norse*
authority	*ráð* ON	beams	*geisli* OI, *geisli* ON
autumn	*hausti* OI, *hausti* ON, *haustið* OI, *haustit* ON	beaten	*barið* OI, *barit* ON
		beautiful	*fagrt* ON, *fagurt* OI, *fegurst* OI, *fögur* OI, *fríðar* OI, *fríðar* ON
average-head	*meðalkafla* OI, *meðalkafla* ON		
avoid	*hopa* ON, *opa* OI	beauty	*vænleik* OI
away	*brott* OI, *brott* ON, *brottu* OI, *brottu* ON, *fjarri* OI, *fjarri* ON, *undan* OI	became	*gerðist* OI, *gerðist* ON, *lagði* OI, *urðu* OI, *urðu* ON, *varð* OI, *varð* ON, *verðr* ON, *verður* OI
away-from	*frá* OI	because	*fyrir* OI, *því* OI, *því* ON
away-travel	*brottferðar* OI, *brottferðar* ON	because-of	*því* ON
		become	*orðið* OI, *oröit* ON, *verða* OI, *verða* ON
awhile	*stund* OI, *stund* ON, *stundir* OI, *stundir* ON, *stundum* OI, *stundum* ON	becoming	*kominn* OI, *kominn* ON, *verða* ON
		bed	*beð* ON
awoke	*vaknaði* OI, *vaknaði* ON	bed-closet	*lokrekkju* OI, *lokrekkju* ON
awoken	*vakið* OI, *vakit* ON, *vaknaði* OI	bedding	*beðr* OI, *beðr* ON
		be-done	*gera* ON
a-woman	*kona* OI, *kona* ON, *konu* OI	been	*verið* OI, *verit* ON
axe	*exar* OI, *öxar* ON	before	*áðr* ON, *áður* OI, *en* OI, *fyr* ON, *fyrir* OI, *fyrir* ON, *fyrr* OI, *fyrr* ON, *fyrri* OI, *fyrri* ON, *öndverðan* OI, *öndverðan* ON, *því* OI, *því* ON

B, b

English	*Norse*	English	*Norse*
baby-girl	*meybarn* OI, *meybarn* ON		
back	*áðr* OI, *áðr* ON, *áður* OI, *aftr* ON, *aftur* OI, *bak* OI, *bak* ON, *hryggja* OI, *hryggja* ON, *út* OI, *út* ON	behave	*lætur* OI
		be-heard	*hljóðs* OI, *hljóðs* ON
		behind	*eftir* OI
		behold	*líst* OI
back-came	*útkoma* OI	being	*vera* OI, *verða* OI
back-from	*út* OI, *út* ON	be-it	*vera* OI, *vera* ON
bad	*illa* OI	believe	*trúið* OI, *trúið* ON
badly	*illa* OI, *illa* ON	below	*neðan* OI, *neðan* ON
ban	*bann* OI, *bann* ON	bench	*bekk* OI, *bekk* ON
band	*herr* OI, *herr* ON	benefit	*kost* OI, *kost* ON
bane	*bani* OI, *bani* ON	benefit-happier	*gagnsæli* ON, *gagnsælli* OI
bastard	*bastarðr* ON, *bastarður* OI		
		Bergfinn (name)	*bergfinn* OI, *bergfinn* ON, *bergfinnr* ON, *bergfinnur* OI
battled	*börðust* OI		
battles	*orrostur* ON, *orustur* OI	berserker	*berserkrinn* ON
be	*gert* OI, *gerum* OI, *gört* ON, *værir* OI, *værir* ON, *vár* ON, *vera* OI, *vera* ON, *verða* OI, *verða* ON, *verði* OI, *verðir* OI, *ý* OI, *ý* ON, *yrðu* OI	beside	*hjá* OI, *hjá* ON

Word List (English to Norse)

English	Norse	English	Norse
best	*bazta* ON, *baztr* ON, *best* OI, *besta* OI, *bestu* OI, *bestum* OI, *bestur* OI, *bezt* ON, *bezta* ON, *beztu* ON, *beztum* ON, *flestra* ON, *mestir* ON	bloodied	*alblóðugur* OI, *blóði* OI, *blóðug* OI, *blóðug* ON, *blóðugr* ON, *blóðugur* OI
betray	*svík* OI, *svík* ON, *svíkja* OI, *svíkja* ON	blows	*höggum* OI, *höggum* ON
betrayed	*sveik* OI, *sveik* ON	blue	*bláar* OI, *bláar* ON
betrothed	*fastnaði* OI, *fastnaði* ON	blunts	*deyfir* OI, *deyfir* ON
better	*betr* ON, *betur* OI, *meiri* OI, *meiri* ON	board-games	*tafli* OI, *tafli* ON
between	*meðal* OI, *meðal* ON, *milli* OI, *milli* ON, *millim* ON, *millum* OI	boil	*sull* OI, *sull* ON, *sullr* ON, *sullur* OI
be-valued	*þykja* OI, *þykkja* ON	bold	*vasklegur* OI, *vaskligr* ON, *vaskr* ON, *vaskur* OI
beyond	*handan* OI, *handan* ON	boldest	*vaskasti* OI, *vaskasti* ON
bid	*bað* OI, *bæðir* OI, *bæðir* ON, *bauð* OI, *bauð* ON, *bauðst* OI, *bautt* ON, *beiða* OI, *beiða* ON, *beiddi* OI, *bið* OI, *bið* ON, *bíða* OI, *bíða* ON, *bíðit* OI, *bíðit* ON, *biðja* OI, *bjóða* OI, *bjóða* ON, *boð* ON, *boðið* OI, *boðit* ON	boldly	*skörulega* OI, *sköruliga* ON, *vasklegur* OI
		bond	*hlutvöndum* OI, *hlutvöndum* ON
		bone-flying	*beinflugu* OI, *benloga* ON
		booth	*búðar* OI, *búðar* ON, *búðartóftina* OI, *búðartóftina* ON
		booth-ruins	*búðartóftanna* OI, *búðartóftanna* ON
		booths	*búða* OI, *búða* ON
		booth-walls	*búðarveggir* OI, *búðarveggir* ON
bind	*binda* OI, *binda* ON	Bordeyri (place)	*borðeyri* OI, *borðeyri* ON
bird	*fugl* OI, *fugl* ON	bore	*bar* OI, *bar* ON, *bera* OI, *borða* OI, *borða* ON, *borið* OI, *fæddi* OI, *fæddi* ON
birds	*fuglar* OI, *fuglar* ON		
Bjorn (name)	*björn* OI, *björn* ON		
black	*svarta* OI, *svartr* OI, *svartr* ON, *svört* OI, *svört* ON		
		borg	*borgina* OI
black-eyed	*svarteygr* ON, *svarteygur* OI	Borg (place)	*borg* OI, *borg* ON, *borgar* OI, *borgar* ON, *borgina* ON
black-eyes	*svarteygr* ON, *svarteygur* OI	Borgafjord (place)	*borgarfirði* OI, *borgarfirði* ON
blame	*lasta* ON	Borgafjord-people (name)	*borgfirðinga* OI, *borgfirðinga* ON
blamed	*lasta* OI	born	*bera* OI, *bera* ON
bled	*blæddi* OI, *blæddi* ON	both	*báða* OI, *báða* ON, *báðir* OI, *báðir* ON, *bæði* OI, *bæði* ON, *hvorumtveggja* OI
blood	*blóð* OI, *blóð* ON, *blóði* OI, *blóði* ON		
blood-goslings	*blóðgögl* OI, *blóðgögl* ON	bothered	*nenna* OI, *nenna* ON
		bought	*keypti* OI, *keypti* ON

Word List (English to Norse)

English	*Norse*	English	*Norse*
bound	*bundnir* OI, *bundnir* ON, *bundu* OI, *bundu* ON	**C, c**	
bow	*lýtr* OI, *lýtr* ON	call	*heita* OI, *heita* ON, *kalla* OI, *kalla* ON
bowl	*knættit* OI, *knættit* ON	called	*heita* OI, *heita* ON, *heitir* OI, *heitir* ON, *heitit* ON, *heitit-* ON, *hét* OI, *hét* ON, *hétu* OI, *hétu* ON, *kallað* OI, *kallaði* OI, *kallaði* ON, *kallaðr* ON, *kallaður* OI, *kvaddi* OI, *kvaddi* ON
boy	*sveinn* OI, *sveinn* ON		
bravely	*fræknlega* OI, *fræknliga* ON		
breeches	*leistbrókum* OI, *leistbrókum* ON		
brennu	*brennu* OI, *brennu* ON		
bride	*brúðinni* OI, *brúðinni* ON, *brúðrin* ON, *brúðurin* OI		
bridegroom's	*brúðguma* OI, *brúðguma* ON	came	*kæmi* OI, *kæmi* ON, *kemr* ON, *kemur* OI, *kom* OI, *kom* ON, *koma* OI, *koma* ON, *kominn* OI, *komnir* OI, *komst* OI, *komst* ON, *komu* OI, *kómu* ON, *komust* OI, *kómust* ON
brightly	*brámáni* OI, *brámáni* ON		
brim	*brims* OI, *brims* ON		
bring	*færa* OI, *færa* ON, *færi* OI		
broad-axe	*breiðöxi* OI, *breiðöxi* ON	came-into	*tæmdist* OI, *tæmðist* ON
brother	*bróðir* OI, *bróðir* ON, *bróður* OI, *bróður* ON, *brúðr* OI, *brúðr* ON	can	*fær* OI, *fær* ON, *getr* OI, *getr* ON, *getur* OI, *kann* OI, *kann* ON
brother-in-law	*mags* OI, *mágs* ON	Canute (name)	*knút* OI, *knút* ON, *knútr* ON, *knútur* OI
brother-of	*bróðir* ON		
brothers	*bræðr* ON, *bræður* OI	care	*nenni* OI, *nenni* ON, *ræki* OI, *rækik* ON
brother's-son	*bróðurson* OI, *bróðursonr* ON	carelessness	*vanhyggju* OI, *vanhyggju* ON
brought	*brugðit* ON, *brugðu* OI, *brugðu* ON, *fæða* OI, *fæddist* OI, *færa* OI, *færa* ON, *færðr* ON, *færður* OI, *flutti* OI, *flutti* ON, *nær* OI	carried	*borið* OI, *borit* ON, *færð* OI, *færð* ON
		carry	*bera* OI, *bera* ON, *flyta* OI, *flytja* OI, *flytja* ON
		carry-out	*efna* OI, *efna* ON
brought-out	*brugðið* OI, *brugðit* ON	caught	*fengið* OI, *fengit* ON, *fengu* ON, *náði* ON
brow	*brúna* OI, *brúna* ON		
build	*vaxtar* OI, *vaxtar* ON	cause	*olli* OI, *olli* ON
bullying	*kúgan* OI, *kúgan* ON	caved-fish	*hrynfiski* OI, *hrynfiski* ON
burning	*fira* OI, *fira* ON		
burst	*brast* OI, *brast* ON	celebrated	*fagnað* OI, *fagnaði* OI, *fagnaði* ON, *fegnir* OI, *fegnir* ON
business	*mæla* OI, *mæla* ON		
but	*at* ON, *eða* OI, *eða* ON, *en* OI, *en* ON, *enn* OI, *og* OI	celebration-day	*affangadag* OI, *atfangadag* ON
		certain	*víst* OI, *víst* ON
but-for	*en* OI, *en* ON	certainly	*víst* OI, *víst* ON
by	*á* OI, *að* OI, *at* ON	challenged	*skora* OI, *skora* ON, *skorað* OI, *skorat* ON

194

Word List (English to Norse)

English	Norse	English	Norse
champion	*kappi* OI	come	*koma* OI, *koma* ON, *komi* OI, *komi* ON, *komið* OI, *kominn* OI, *komit* ON
character-reward	*bragarlaunum* OI, *bragarlaunum* ON		
charm	*þokka* OI, *þokka* ON		
chattered	*klakaði* OI, *klakaði* ON	come-in	*kominn* ON
cheek	*kinn* OI, *kinn* ON	comes	*kemr* ON, *kemur* OI, *komast* OI, *komast* ON
chew	*tyggja* OI, *tyggja* ON		
chief	*höfðingi* OI	come-together	*ættist* ON, *ættust* OI
chiefs	*höfðingjum* OI, *höfðingjum* ON	coming	*koma* OI, *koma* ON, *komið* OI, *komin* OI, *komin* ON, *kominn* ON
chieftancy	*höfðingjabragð* OI, *höfðingjabragð* ON		
chieftans	*höfðingja* OI, *höfðingja* ON	committed	*framið* ON, *framin* OI
		companion	*félagi* OI, *félagi* ON
child	*barn* OI, *barn* ON, *barni* OI, *barni* ON, *barnið* OI, *barnit* ON, *barns* OI, *barns* ON	companions	*förunautar* OI, *förunautar* ON, *förunautum* OI, *förunautum* ON
children	*barna* OI, *barna* ON, *börn* OI, *börn* ON, *börnum* OI, *börnum* ON	company	*félögum* OI, *félögum* ON, *liðinn* OI, *liðit* ON
		compensate	*bæta* OI, *bæta* ON
choice	*kostr* ON, *kostur* OI	compensation	*bæta* OI, *bætr* ON, *bætur* OI, *bóta* OI, *bóta* ON
christian	*kristið* OI, *kristit* ON		
chronic-illness	*krömdust* OI, *krömðust* ON	completely	*gerla* ON, *gjörla* OI
		completion	*lykðum* ON, *lyktum* OI
church	*kirkju* OI, *kirkju* ON	complexion	*yfirbragð* OI, *yfirbragð* ON
circle	*bauga* OI, *bauga* ON		
citizen	*þegns* OI, *þegns* ON	composition	*hlóð* OI, *hlóð* ON
claimed	*heimti* OI, *heimti* ON	consider	*litið* OI, *þykir* OI, *þykkir* ON
clays	*leirur* OI, *leirur* ON		
cleave	*kljúfa* OI, *kljúfa* ON	considering	*litit* ON
cleaved	*klauf* OI, *klauf* ON	contest	*kappmæli* OI, *kappmæli* ON
cloak	*skikkjan* OI, *skikkjan* ON, *skikkju* OI, *skikkju* ON, *skikkjuna* OI, *skikkjuna* ON, *skikkjunni* OI, *skikkjunni* ON	cooking-hut	*eldaskála* OI, *eldaskála* ON
		corpses	*hræ* OI, *hræ* ON
		corpse-scorer	*hræskæri* ON, *hræskærri* OI
close-to	*nær* OI	could	*mun* OI
clothed	*klæðum* OI, *klæðum* ON	council	*ráðsins* OI, *ráðsins* ON
		counsel	*ráð* OI
clothes	*búningi* OI, *búningi* ON, *klæðin* OI, *klæðin* ON	courage	*hugrekki* OI, *hugrekki* ON
		courteous	*kurteisi* OI, *kurteisi* ON
clothing	*klæði* OI, *klæði* ON	court-man	*hirðmaðr* OI, *hirðmaðr* ON, *hirðmaður* OI, *hirðmann* OI, *hirðmann* ON
cock	*göndlar* OI, *göndlar* ON		
cohabiting	*samvistum* OI		
colour	*lit* OI, *lit* ON		
colours	*litnar* OI, *litnar* ON	court-men	*hirðmönnum* OI, *hirðmönnum* ON
columns	*súlu* OI, *súlu* ON		

Word List (English to Norse)

English	Norse	English	Norse
cousins	*systrasynir* OI, *systrasynir* ON	death-blow	*banahögg* OI, *banahögg* ON
cover	*hylja* OI, *hylja* ON	death-day	*dauðdaga* OI, *dauðdaga* ON
create	*skapa* OI, *skapa* ON	decide	*ráða* OI
crippled	*örkumlaðan* OI, *örkumlaðan* ON	decided	*ráðinn* OI, *ræddi* ON, *ræddu* ON, *réð* OI, *réð* ON, *réðst* OI, *réðst* ON
crowded	*fjölmennir* OI, *fjölmennir* ON		
culture	*menning* OI, *menning* ON	decision	*ráða* OI
custody	*varðveislu* OI, *varðveizlu* ON	defeated	*sigraðr* ON, *sigraður* OI
		degree	*málgráðr* OI, *málgráðr* ON
custom	*siðvandi* OI, *siðvanði* ON, *venr* OI, *venr* ON	dejected	*hnipin* OI, *hnipin* ON
		delay	*seinka* OI, *seinka* ON
customs	*siðum* OI, *siðum* ON	delayed	*dvaldi* OI
cut-down	*höggvinn* OI, *höggvinn* ON	Denmark (place)	*danmörku* OI, *danmörku* ON
		dense	*þéttan* OI, *þéttan* ON

D, d

English	Norse	English	Norse
		depend	*veltr* ON, *veltur* OI
		depressed	*dapr* ON, *dapur* OI
Danish	*danir* OI, *danir* ON, *danskra* OI, *danskra* ON	descended	*ættaðr* ON, *ættaður* OI
		descendents	*ætt* OI, *ætt* ON
dashing	*þeys* OI, *þeys* ON	deserved	*unnið* OI, *unnit* ON
daughter	*dóttir* OI, *dóttir* ON, *dóttur* OI, *dóttur* ON	desire	*þrá* OI, *þrá* ON
		destroyer	*eyðanda* OI, *eyðanda* ON
daughter-of	*dóttir* OI, *dóttir* ON	determination	*einurð* OI, *einurð* ON
daughter-of-Bjorn (name)	*bjarnardóttir* OI, *bjarnardóttir* ON	determined	*ráðinn* OI, *ráðinn* ON
		deviation	*afbrigði* OI, *afbrigði* ON
daughter-of-Egil (name)	*egilsdóttur* OI, *egilsdóttur* ON	dew	*döggvar* OI, *döggvar* ON
daughter-of-Gnup (name)	*gnúpsdóttir* OI, *gnúpsdóttir* ON	did	*gerði* OI, *gerði* ON, *gerðu* OI, *gerðu* ON, *gerir* OI, *gerir* ON
daughter-of-Gunnar (name)	*gunnarsdóttur* OI, *gunnarsdóttur* ON		
		die	*látast* OI, *látast* ON
daughter-of-Thorodd (name)	*þóroddsdóttur* OI, *þóroddsdóttur* ON	died	*andaðist* ON, *dauðir* OI
		difficult	*erfitt* OI, *erfitt* ON, *torveldlegur* OI, *torvelligr* ON
daughters	*dætr* ON, *dætur* OI		
day	*dag* OI, *dag* ON, *daginn* OI, *daginn* ON, *dagr* OI, *dagr* ON, *degi* OI, *degi* ON	Dinge (place)	*dinga* OI, *dinga* ON
		Dingenes (place)	*dinganes* OI, *dinganes* ON
days	*daginn* OI, *daginn* ON	directed	*skipað* OI, *skipaði* OI, *skipaði* ON, *skipat* ON
dead	*dauðir* ON, *dauðr* ON, *dauður* OI, *örend* OI, *örend* ON		
		direction	*ætt* ON, *átt* OI
		directions	*ættum* ON, *áttum* OI
dealt	*deildi* OI, *deildi* ON	discussed	*ræddi* ON, *ræddu* OI
death	*dauða* OI, *dauða* ON, *fráfall* OI, *fráfall* ON	discussed-with	*ræddi* OI

196

Word List (English to Norse)

English	*Norse*	English	*Norse*
disrespect	*vanvirða* OI, *vanvirða* ON	duel	*hólm* OI, *hólm* ON, *hólmgöngu* OI, *hólmgöngu* ON, *hólminn* OI, *hólminn* ON, *hólminum* OI, *hólminum* ON, *hólms* OI, *hólms* ON, *hómgöngu* OI
districts	*hverfka* OI, *hverfkak* ON		
do	*fór* OI, *ger* OI, *gerið* OI, *gerið* ON, *gert* OI, *gert* ON		
dominated	*réð* OI		
done	*búin* ON, *gera* OI, *gert* OI, *gert* ON	duel-his	*hólmsins* OI, *hólmsins* ON
down	*hræpa* OI, *hræpa* ON, *niðr* ON, *niðri* OI, *niður* OI, *ofan* OI, *unnviggs* OI, *unnviggs* ON	duelling	*hólmganga* OI, *hólmganga* ON, *hólmgöngur* OI, *hólmgöngur* ON
dragged	*kippði* ON, *kippti* OI	duelling-man	*hólmgöngumaður* OI
drapa	*drápu* OI, *drápuna* OI, *drápuna* ON, *drápunnar* OI, *drápunnar* ON, *drápunni* OI, *drápunni* ON	dwelled	*dvaldi* OI, *dvalði* ON, *dvaldist* OI, *dvalðist* ON
		dwelling	*bæ* OI, *bæ* ON, *bænum* OI, *bænum* ON
		dylla	*dylla* OI, *dylla* ON
drapa-layer	*drápulag* ON		
drape-oneself	*lautsíkjar* OI, *lautsíkjar* ON		

E, e

English	*Norse*
draw	*dró* OI, *dró* ON
drawn	*brugðið* OI, *dregið* OI, *dregit* ON, *dregst* OI, *dregst* ON
dream	*draum* OI, *draum* ON, *drauminn* OI, *drauminn* ON, *draumr* ON, *draumur* OI, *dreymdi* OI
dreamed	*dreymdi* OI, *dreymði* ON
dreams	*drauma* OI, *drauma* ON, *draums* OI, *draums* ON, *draumum* OI, *draumum* ON
dreamt	*dreymt* OI, *dreymt* ON
drew	*brá* ON, *dregr* ON, *dregur* OI
drink	*drekka* OI, *drekka* ON
drive	*drifna* OI, *drifna* ON
driven	*drifinn* OI, *drifinn* ON
drove	*rak* OI, *rak* ON, *stökkða* ON, *stökkti* OI
Dublin (place)	*dyflinnar* OI, *dyflinnar* ON
each	*hvárir* ON, *hvárn* ON, *hvern* ON, *hvor* OI, *hvorir* OI, *hvorn* OI
each-other	*annars* OI, *annars* ON
eagerly	*ákafa* OI
eagerness	*ákafa* OI
eagle	*ari* OI, *ari* ON, *örn* OI, *örn* ON, *örninn* OI, *örninn* ON
Earl	*jari* ON, *jarl* OI, *jarl* ON, *jarli* OI, *jarli* ON, *jarlinn* OI, *jarlinn* ON, *jarls* OI, *jarls* ON
earldoms	*hjarls* OI, *hjarls* ON
earls	*jarla* OI, *jarla* ON
earl's	*jarls* OI, *jarls* ON, *jarlsins* ON
early	*öndverðan* OI, *öndverðan* ON, *snemma* OI, *snemma* ON
early-age	*snemmendis* OI
earth	*jörð* OI, *jörð* ON
earthed	*jarðaðr* ON, *jarðaður* OI
east	*austan* OI, *austan* ON, *austr* ON, *austur* OI

Word List (English to Norse)

English	Norse	English	Norse
eastern	*austr* ON	England (place)	*england* OI, *england* ON, *englandi* OI, *englandi* ON, *englands* OI, *englands* ON
easterner	*austmaðr* ON		
easterners	*austmenn* OI, *austmenn* ON		
eastern-man	*austmaðrinn* ON, *austmaður* OI, *austmaðurinn* OI, *austmanni* ON, *austmanninn* OI, *austmanninn* ON	England's (place)	*englands* OI, *englands* ON
		Englands-Sea (place)	*englandshaf* OI, *englandshaf* ON
		England-voyage	*englandsfar* OI, *englandsfar* ON
east-wind	*austanvindr* OI, *austanvindr* ON	enjoy	*njóta* OI, *njóta* ON
		enjoyed	*gaman* OI, *gaman* ON
edge	*egg* OI	enjoyment	*gaman* OI, *gaman* ON
Egil (name)	*egill* OI, *egill* ON, *egils* OI, *egils* ON, *egli* OI	enraged	*allæfr* ON, *allæfur* OI
		entertained	*skemmtu* OI, *skemmtu* ON
eighteen	*átján* OI, *átján* ON	equal	*jafnan* OI, *jafnan* ON, *jafnmikit* ON, *jafnoka* OI, *jafnoka* ON
Einar (name)	*einar* OI		
Eindridi (name)	*eindriði* OI, *eindriði* ON		
Eir (name)	*eir* OI, *eir* ON	equal-aged	*jafnaldrar* OI, *jafnaldrar* ON
either	*hvárt* ON, *hvergi* ON, *hvort* OI, *ýmisst* ON, *ýmist* OI	equally	*jafnan* OI, *jafnan* ON, *jafnræði* OI, *jafnræði* ON, *jafnræðis* OI, *jafnræðis* ON, *jafnröskr* OI, *jafnröskr* ON
either-side	*hvárirtveggju* ON, *hvárntveggja* ON, *hvárstveggja* ON, *hvárumtveggja* ON, *hvorirtveggju* OI, *hvorstveggja* OI		
		equally-beautiful	*jafnfagrt* ON, *jafnfagurt* OI
		equally-long	*jafnlangir* OI, *jafnlangir* ON
either-way	*hvorntveggja* OI, *hvorstveggja* OI	equal-man	*jafnmenni* OI, *jafnmenni* ON
embers	*glóðspýtis* OI, *glóðspýtis* ON	equal-many	*jafnmargir* OI, *jafnmargir* ON
embrace	*faðmlagsins* OI, *faðmlagsins* ON, *fangs* OI, *fangs* ON	equal-much	*jafnmikið* OI
		Erik (name)	*eirík* OI, *eirík* ON, *eiríki* OI, *eiríki* ON, *eiríkr* OI, *eiríkr* ON, *eiríks* OI, *eiríks* ON, *eiríkur* OI
end	*enda* OI, *endr* OI, *endr* ON, *hætt* OI, *hætt* ON		
ended	*andaða* OI, *andaða* ON, *andaðist* OI, *andaðist* ON, *enda* ON, *endast* OI, *endast* ON, *lauk* OI, *lauk* ON, *lokið* OI, *lokit* ON	Erik's (name)	*eiríks* OI, *eiríks* ON
		errand	*erendi* ON, *erindi* OI
		escaped	*slyppur* OI
		escapes	*slyppr* ON
		especially	*einkar* OI, *einkar* ON
ending	*enda* OI	established	*staðfestu* OI, *staðfestu* ON
ends	*lýkr* ON, *lýkur* OI		
endure	*þola* OI, *þola* ON	estate	*föðurleifð* OI, *föðurleifð* ON
engaged	*réð* OI		
engaged-woman	*festarkona* OI, *festarkona* ON		

Word List (English to Norse)

English	Norse	English	Norse
Ethelred (name)	*aðalráð* OI, *aðalráð* ON, *aðalráði* OI, *aðalráði* ON, *aðalráðr* OI, *aðalráðr* ON, *aðalráður* OI	fair	*fagra* OI, *fagra* ON, *fagrt* ON, *fegrst* ON, *fögr* ON, *fögru* OI, *fögru* ON, *væn* OI, *væn* ON
Ethelred-Gift (name)	*aðalráðsnaut* OI, *aðalráðsnaut* ON	fair-colour	*litfagra* OI, *litfagra* ON
Ethelred-given (name)	*aðalráðsnaut* OI	fairest	*fegrst* ON
evening	*kveldi* OI, *kveldi* ON, *kveldið* OI, *kveldit* ON	fairness	*fagra* ON
event	*atburðr* ON, *atburður* OI	fair-wind	*byr* OI, *byr* ON
events	*atburðum* OI, *atburðum* ON	falcon	*valr* ON, *valrinn* ON, *valur* OI, *valurinn* OI
eventually	*síðir* OI, *síðir* ON	fall	*falli* OI, *falli* ON
everyone's	*allra* OI	fallen	*fallnir* OI, *fallnir* ON
everything	*hvívetna* OI, *hvívetna* ON	falling	*fall* OI, *fall* ON
everywhere	*hvervetna* OI, *hvervetna* ON	fame	*frægð* OI, *frægð* ON
except	*nema* OI	familiar	*þekkjast* OI, *þekkjast* ON
exchanged	*skiptust* OI, *skiptust* ON, *viðskipti* OI, *viðskipti* ON	family	*ætt* OI
exchanges	*skipti* OI, *skipti* ON	famous	*frægir* OI, *frægir* ON
excitement	*örva* OI, *örva* ON	far-away	*fjarkominn* OI, *fjarkominn* ON
expected	*vænstir* OI, *von* OI	fare	*fari* ON
expenses	*gjalda* OI, *gjalt* OI, *gjalt* ON	fared	*fór* OI, *fór* ON
experience	*raunir* OI, *raunir* ON	farm	*bæ* OI, *bæjar* OI, *bæjar* ON, *bóndi* ON
experienced	*reyndr* ON, *reyndur* OI	farmer	*bónda* OI, *bónda* ON, *bóndi* OI, *bóndi* ON, *bóndum* ON
extend	*tognum* OI, *tognum* ON	farmers	*bóndum* OI
extremely	*ákafa* OI, *ákafa* ON, *ákaflega* OI, *ákafliga* ON	farmer's-son	*bóndason* OI, *bóndason* ON
eyelids	*hvarma* OI, *hvarma* ON	farmer's-sons	*bóndasonum* OI
eyes	*augu* OI, *augu* ON, *augum* OI, *augum* ON, *eygr* ON, *eygur* OI	farmyard	*hlaðið* OI, *hlaðinu* OI, *hlaðinu* ON, *hlaðit* ON
Eyolf (name)	*eyjólfr* ON, *eyjólfur* OI	father	*faðir* OI, *faðir* ON, *feðr* ON, *föður* OI, *föður* ON
Eyri (place)	*eyri* OI	father-and-son	*feðgum* OI, *feðgum* ON
		fathers	*faðir* OI, *feður* OI
		fearlessly	*öruggum* OI, *öruggum* ON
		feast	*veislunni* OI, *veizlunni* ON
		fee	*féið* OI
		feed	*fæða* OI
		fee-gifts	*fégjöfum* OI, *fégjöfum* ON
		fee-loan	*fjárlánið* OI, *fjárlánit* ON
		fee-servant	*féhirði* OI, *féhirði* ON, *féhirðir* ON, *féhirslumaður* OI

F, f

English	Norse
face	*andliti* OI, *andliti* ON
faced	*hjörþeys* OI, *hjörþeys* ON

Word List (English to Norse)

English	Norse
feet	*fæti* OI, *fætr* ON, *fætrna* ON, *fætur* OI, *fæturna* OI, *fótrinn* ON, *fóturinn* OI
fell	*féll* OI, *fell* ON, *felldi* OI, *felldi* ON, *féllu* OI, *fellu* ON, *veg* OI, *veg* ON
fellow	*drengja* OI, *drengja* ON, *drengr* ON, *drengur* OI
felt	*þreifaði* OI, *þreifaði* ON
fens	*fen* OI, *fen* ON
festagramr	*festargramr* ON
festargram	*festargram* OI, *festargram* ON
Festargramur (place)	*festargramur* OI
feud	*rógi* OI, *rógi* ON
few	*allfá* OI, *allfá* ON, *fá* OI, *fá* ON, *fám* OI, *fám* ON, *fátt* OI, *fátt* ON
field	*alvangs* OI, *alvangs* ON
fields	*vellir* OI, *vellir* ON, *völlum* OI, *völlum* ON
fight	*berðist* ON, *berðust* OI, *berimst* ON, *berjast* OI, *berjast* ON, *berjumst* OI, *vega* OI, *vega* ON
finally	*loks* OI, *loks* ON
find	*finn* OI, *finn* ON, *finna* OI, *finna* ON, *fund* OI
fine	*ágætr* ON, *ágætur* OI
fire	*hyrjar* OI, *hyrjar* ON
first	*fyrst* OI, *fyrst* ON
five	*fimm* OI, *fimm* ON, *fimmta* OI, *fimmta* ON
flame	*flaum* OI, *flaum* ON
flesh	*hölds* OI, *hölðs* ON
flew	*fljúga* OI, *fljúga* ON, *fló* OI, *fló* ON, *flugu* OI, *flugu* ON
flokk	*flokk* OI, *flokk* ON, *flokkr* ON, *flokkur* OI
flood	*flóða* OI, *flóða* ON
flood-deer	*flóðhyrs* OI, *flóðhyrs* ON
flying	*fljúga* OI, *fljúga* ON, *fló* ON
folk	*fólka* OI, *folka* ON
follow	*fylgja* OI, *fylgja* ON
followed	*fylgdi* OI, *fylgði* ON
followers	*fjölmenni* OI, *fjölmenni* ON, *fylgjur* OI, *fylgjur* ON, *hirðmanna* OI, *hirðmanna* ON
following	*fylgir* OI, *fylgir* ON
fool	*fól* OI, *fól* ON
foot	*fæti* OI, *fæti* ON, *fótrinn* ON
foot's	*fótarins* OI, *fótarins* ON
foot-striking	*fóthöggva* OI, *fóthöggva* ON
for	*er* OI, *er* ON, *fyr* ON, *fyri* OI, *fyrir* OI, *fyrir* ON, *því* OI, *til* OI, *um* OI
force	*tjár* OI, *tjár* ON
foremost	*öndvegi* OI, *öndvegi* ON
Forest-Tostig (name)	*sköglar-tósta* OI, *sköglar-tósta* ON
forgive	*fyrirgefa* OI, *fyrirgefa* ON
for-her	*hennar* OI
forsake	*ásaka* OI, *ásaka* ON
fortune	*auður* OI
foster	*fæða* ON
foster-brother	*fóstbróðir* OI, *fóstbróðir* ON
fostered	*fæddist* OI, *fæddist* ON
fought	*berðist* ON, *börðust* OI, *börðust* ON
found	*fann* OI, *fann* ON, *fengið* OI, *fundist* OI, *fundizt* ON, *fundust* OI, *fundust* ON
found-a-place	*vistuðust* OI, *vistuðust* ON
four	*fjögur* OI, *fjögur* ON, *fjórum* OI, *fjórum* ON
fragile	*skör* OI, *skör* ON
free	*frítt* OI, *frítt* ON
french	*valska* OI, *valska* ON
friendliness	*vináttu* OI, *vináttu* ON
friends	*vina* OI, *vina* ON, *vini* OI, *vini* ON, *vinir* OI, *vinir* ON
friendship	*vinátta* OI, *vinátta* ON, *vináttu* OI, *vingan* OI, *vingan* ON, *vinslitum* OI, *vinslitum* ON
fringes	*skauti* OI, *skauti* ON

Word List (English to Norse)

English	Norse	English	Norse
from	*af* OI, *at* ON, *frá* OI, *frá* ON, *fram* OI, *fram* ON, *frammi* OI, *frammi* ON, *ór* ON, *úr* OI, *út* OI	girls	*meyjar* OI, *meyjar* ON, *meyjarnar* OI, *stúlkur* ON
from-here	*héðan* OI	give	*gá* OI, *gá* ON, *gæfið* ON, *gæfuð* OI, *gef* OI, *gef* ON, *gefa* OI, *gefa* ON, *gefið* OI, *gefið* ON, *gefr* OI, *gefr* ON, *gifta* OI, *gjaforð* OI, *gjaforð* ON
from-like	*framlega* OI, *framliga* ON		
from-now	*fresti* OI, *fresti* ON		
from-saying	*frásagnar* OI, *frásagnar* ON		
from-there	*frá* OI, *þaðan* OI, *þaðan* ON, *þangað* OI, *þangat* ON	give)	*fæða* OI
		give-birth	*fæða* OI, *fæða* ON
		give-birth)	*fæða* ON
full	*fullu* OI, *fullu* ON	give-birth-to	*fæðir* OI, *fæðir* ON
full-men-most	*fjölmennast* OI, *fjölmennast* ON	given	*gaf* OI, *gaf* ON, *gefin* OI, *gefin* ON
funds	*sjóði* OI, *sjóði* ON	given-name	*nökkvi* OI, *nökkvi* ON
		glad	*gleði* OI, *gleði* ON

G, g

English	Norse	English	Norse
		gladder	*glaðara* OI, *glaðara* ON
		gladly	*gjarna* OI, *gjarna* ON
		gleam	*bliks* OI, *bliks* ON
Galti (name)	*galti* OI, *galti* ON	Gleipnisvellir (place)	*gleipnisvellir* OI, *gleipnisvellir* ON
gave	*fékk* OI, *gaf* OI, *gaf* ON, *gifti* OI, *gifti* ON, *henti* OI	glistens	*glæstrar* OI, *glæstrar* ON
Geatland (place)	*gautland* OI, *gautland* ON	glorious	*dýrlegra* OI, *dýrligra* ON
Geatlanders	*gautar* OI, *gautar* ON	Gnup (name)	*gnúps* ON
Geirny (name)	*geirný* OI, *geirný* ON	Gnup's (name)	*gnúps* OI
generations	*ætt* OI	go	*fara* OI, *fari* OI, *fari* ON, *fer* OI, *fer* ON, *gakk* OI, *gakk* ON, *ganga* OI, *ganga* ON, *gangið* OI, *gangið* ON, *gekk* OI
gently	*blíðlega* OI, *blítt* OI, *blítt* ON		
get	*fá* OI, *fá* ON, *fám* OI, *fám* ON, *fékk* OI, *fenga* ON, *fengi* OI, *fengir* OI, *fengir* ON, *hlýtr* OI, *hlýtr* ON		
		god	*goð* ON, *guð* OI
		god-drew	*guðbrá* OI
giants	*randgálkn* OI, *randgölkn* ON	godord	*goðorð* OI, *goðorð* ON
		god's	*guðs* OI
gift	*gefa* OI, *gifta* OI, *gifta* ON, *gjöfina* OI, *gjöfina* ON	goes	*gekk* ON, *gengr* ON
		going	*eg* OI, *fara* ON, *fari* ON, *farið* OI, *farit* ON, *ganga* OI, *gangim* ON, *gengi* OI, *gengu* OI, *gengu* ON, *göngu* OI, *göngu* ON, *göngum* OI
gifts	*gjafar* ON, *gjafir* OI, *gjálfri* OI, *gjalfri* ON, *gjöfli* OI, *gjöfli* ON, *gjöfum* OI, *gjöfum* ON		
Gilsbakka (place)	*gilsbakka* OI, *gilsbakka* ON		
Gilsbakki (place)	*gilsbakka* OI	gold	*gull* OI, *gull* ON
girl	*mær* OI, *mær* ON, *mey* OI, *mey* ON	golden	*gullmens* OI, *gullmens* ON
girlfriend	*vinkonu* OI, *vinkonu* ON		

Word List (English to Norse)

English	*Norse*	English	*Norse*
gold-ring	*gollhring* ON, *gullhring* OI, *gullhring* ON, *gullhringa* OI, *gullhringa* ON	grip	*grepp* OI, *greppa* OI, *greppa* ON, *greppi* OI, *greppi* ON, *greppr* OI, *greppr* ON
gone	*fært* OI, *fært* ON, *farit* ON	gripped	*grípa* OI, *grípa* ON
good	*góð* OI, *goð* ON, *góð* ON, *góða* OI, *góða* ON, *góðan* OI, *góðan* ON, *góðar* OI, *góðar* ON, *góðr* ON, *góðra* OI, *góðra* ON, *góðri* OI, *góðri* ON, *góðu* OI, *góðu* ON, *góðum* OI, *góðum* ON, *góður* OI, *gott* OI, *gott* ON	ground	*fold* OI, *fold* ON
		group	*bekkinum* OI, *bekkinum* ON, *liði* OI, *liði* ON, *liðið* OI, *liðit* ON
		grown	*vaxið* OI, *vaxit* ON
		growth	*vöxt* OI, *vöxt* ON
		guested	*gistu* OI, *gistu* ON
		Gufua (place)	*gufárós* OI, *gufuárósi* OI, *gufuárósi* ON
		guide	*leiðtoga* OI, *leiðtoga* ON
good-looks	*vænleiks* OI, *vænleiks* ON	guides	*leiðtoga* OI, *leiðtogana* OI, *leiðtogana* ON, *leiðtogar* OI, *leiðtogar* ON
got	*fékk* OI, *fekk* ON, *fengu* OI, *fengu* ON, *gekk* OI, *hlaut* OI, *hlaut* ON, *náði* OI		
		gums	*góma* OI, *góma* ON
go-we	*göngum* OI, *göngum* ON	Gunnar (name)	*gunnar* OI, *gunnar* ON
grant	*veita* OI, *veita* ON	Gunnlaug (name)	*gunniaugr* ON, *gunnlagi* OI, *gunnlaug* OI, *gunnlaug* ON, *gunnlaugi* OI, *gunnlaugi* ON, *gunnlaugr* OI, *gunnlaugr* ON, *gunnlaugs* OI, *gunnlaugs* ON, *gunnlaugur* OI
granted	*veitti* OI		
great	*mikið* OI, *mikil* OI, *mikill* OI, *mikill* ON, *mikinn* OI, *mikinn* ON, *mikit* ON, *miklir* OI, *miklu* OI, *stórra* OI, *stórra* ON, *stórum* OI, *stórum* ON		
greatest	*mestr* ON, *mestur* OI		
great-issue	*mikilræði* OI, *mikilræði* ON	Gunnlaug's (name)	*gunnlaugi* OI, *gunnlaugi* ON, *gunnlaugs* OI, *gunnlaugs* ON
greatly	*mikið* OI, *mikit* ON		
greeted	*kveða* OI, *kveða* ON, *kvöddu* OI, *kvöddu* ON	Gunnlaug's-gift (name)	*gunnlaugsnaut* OI, *gunnlaugsnaut* ON
Grenjar (place)	*grenjum* OI, *grenjum* ON		

H, h

English	*Norse*
grey	*grám* OI, *grám* ON, *grár* OI, *grár* ON
grey-call	*grásíma* OI, *grásíma* ON
grey-hair	*hæru* OI, *hæru* ON
Grim (name)	*grími* OI, *grími* ON, *grímr* ON, *grímur* OI
Grimstungur (place)	*grímstungum* OI, *grímstungum* ON
Grindavik (place)	*grindavík* OI, *grindavík* ON
had	*átti* OI, *átti* ON, *áttu* OI, *áttu* ON, *hafa* OI, *hafa* ON, *hafði* OI, *hafði* ON, *hafi* OI, *hafi* ON, *hefði* OI, *hefði* ON, *hefir* OI, *hefir* ON, *hefnt* OI, *hefnt* ON, *höfðu* OI, *höfðu* ON

Word List (English to Norse)

English	Norse	English	Norse
had-been	*hafði* OI, *verið* OI	have-come	*kominn* OI
hair	*hár* OI, *hár* ON	have-you	*hafðu* ON
Hakon (name)	*hákon* OI, *hákon* ON	having	*hafa* ON
half	*hálfa* OI, *hálfa* ON, *hálft* OI, *hálft* ON, *hálfum* OI, *hálfum* ON	hawk-from	*haukfránn* OI, *haukfránn* ON
hall	*sal* OI, *sal* ON	he	*hann* OI, *hann* ON, *hans* OI, *hans* ON, *hinn* OI, *hinn* ON, *honum* OI, *honum* ON, *hrafn* OI, *sér* OI, *sik* ON, *sinn* OI
Hallfred (name)	*hallfreðar* OI, *hallfreðar* ON, *hallfreði* OI, *hallfreði* ON, *hallfreðr* ON, *hallfreður* OI		
		head	*höfuð* OI, *höfuð* ON
		headland	*nes* OI, *nes* ON, *nesi* OI, *nesi* ON, *nesinu* OI, *nesinu* ON
hand	*handa* OI, *handa* ON, *hendi* OI, *hendi* ON, *hendinni* OI, *hendinni* ON, *hendr* ON, *höfuð* OI, *höfuð* ON, *hönd* OI, *hönd* ON	headlands	*andnesjum* OI, *andnesjum* ON
		head-wound	*höfuðsárið* OI, *höfuðsárit* ON
handled	*höldr* OI, *hölðr* ON	hear	*heyra* OI, *heyra* ON, *heyrðið* ON, *heyrðuð* OI
hands	*handan* OI, *hendur* OI, *höndum* OI, *höndum* ON	heard	*frétti* OI, *frétti* ON, *heyrði* ON, *hjá* OI
handsome	*vænn* OI, *vænn* ON	hears	*heyri* OI
happened	*snemnma* OI	heath	*heiði* OI, *heiði* ON
happily	*blíðliga* ON	heather-lands	*lyngs* OI, *lyngs* ON
hard	*harðr* ON, *harður* OI, *hörða* OI, *hörða* ON	heath-slayings	*heiðarvíg* OI, *heiðarvíg* ON
hardest	*harðasti* OI, *harðasti* ON	heaven	*himni* OI, *himni* ON
		heavily	*þungum* OI, *þunnum* ON
hardly	*vart* OI, *vart* ON		
hardy	*harðlyndr* ON, *harðlyndur* OI	heavy	*þungara* OI, *þungara* ON, *þyngd* OI, *þyngð* ON
hardy-much	*herðimikill* OI, *herðimikill* ON	heed	*gaum* OI, *gaum* ON
harm	*skaði* OI, *skaði* ON	held	*hafði* OI, *hann* OI, *heldr* ON, *heldur* OI, *hélt* OI, *helt* ON
has	*er* OI, *er* ON, *hafa* OI, *hafa* ON, *hár* OI, *hárr* ON, *hefir* OI, *hefir* ON		
		Helga (name)	*helga* OI, *helga* ON, *helgu* OI, *helgu* ON
haughty	*rembist* OI, *remb-ist* ON	helmet	*hjálmi* OI, *hjálmi* ON, *hjálminum* OI, *hjálminum* ON
have	*eiga* OI, *eiga* ON, *fá* OI, *fá* ON, *fár* OI, *fár* ON, *hafa* OI, *hafa* ON, *hafðu* OI, *hafi* OI, *hafi* ON, *hafið* OI, *hafið* ON, *hef* OI, *hefði* OI, *hefði* ON, *hefi* OI, *hefi* ON, *hefir* OI, *hefir* ON, *hefk* ON, *höfum* OI, *höfum* ON	help	*duga* OI, *duga* ON, *fullting* OI, *fullting* ON
		helpless	*hlífarlaus* OI, *hlífarlauss* ON
		hem	*skaut* OI, *skaut* ON
		Heming (name)	*hemingr* ON, *hemingur* OI
have-become	*orðinn* OI, *orðinn* ON	hence	*heðan* ON

Word List (English to Norse)

English	Norse
her	*hana* OI, *hana* ON, *hennar* OI, *hennar* ON, *henni* OI, *henni* ON, *hon* ON, *sér* OI, *sér* ON, *sína* OI, *sína* ON
here	*hann* OI, *hér* OI, *hér* ON, *hingað* OI, *hingat* ON
Hermund (name)	*hermund* OI, *hermund* ON, *hermundr* ON, *hermundur* OI
hero	*hildingr* ON
hers	*hennar* OI, *hennar* ON, *sína* OI, *sína* ON, *sinn* OI, *sínum* OI, *sínum* ON
herself	*sér* ON
hiding	*leyna* OI, *leyna* ON
high	*hávar* OI, *hávar* ON
hills	*fjöllin* OI, *fjöllin* ON
hilt	*hjöltunum* OI, *hjöltunum* ON
hilt-chewed	*hjaltugguðum* OI, *hjaltugguðum* ON
him	*hann* OI, *hann* ON, *hans* OI, *hans* ON, *hánum* ON, *honum* OI, *honum* ON, *sér* OI, *sér* ON, *sig* OI, *sik* ON
himself	*sér* OI, *sér* ON, *sig* OI, *sik* ON, *sjálfr* OI, *sjalfr* ON, *sjálfr* ON, *sjálfur* OI
himself-to	*sér* OI
his	*hans* OI, *hans* ON, *hinni* OI, *honum* OI, *honum* ON, *sér* OI, *sín* OI, *sín* ON, *sína* OI, *sína* ON, *sinn* OI, *sinn* ON, *sinnar* OI, *sinnar* ON, *sinni* OI, *sinni* ON, *síns* OI, *síns* ON, *sínu* OI, *sínum* OI, *sínum* ON, *sitt* OI, *sitt* ON, *þau* OI
Hitdardal-champion (name)	*hítdælakappi* OI
Hjalli (name)	*hjalla* OI, *hjalla* ON
Hjardarholt (place)	*hjarðarholt* OI, *hjarðarholt* ON
Hlidarendi (place)	*hlíðarenda* OI
Hlínar (place)	*hlínar* OI, *hlínar* ON
hoard	*hoddum* OI, *hoddum* ON
hoard-warrior	*hoddstríðandi* OI, *hoddstríðandi* ON
hoe	*pál* OI, *pál* ON
hold	*halda* OI, *heldur* OI
Holtavarda-Heath (place)	*holtavörðuheiði* OI, *holtavörðuheiði* ON
home	*heim* OI, *heim* ON, *heima* OI, *heima* ON, *heiman* OI, *heiman* ON
home-invitation	*heimboðs* OI, *heimboðs* ON
home-travel	*heimferðar* OI, *heimferðar* ON
home-way	*heimleiðis* OI, *heimleiðis* ON
honour	*heiðr* ON, *sæmd* OI, *sæmð* ON, *virðing* OI, *virðing* ON
hope	*ván* ON, *von* OI
horse	*hest* OI, *hest* ON, *hesti* OI, *hesti* ON, *hestr* ON, *hestur* OI
horses	*hross* OI, *hross* ON, *hrossa* OI, *hrossa* ON, *hrossin* OI, *hrossin* ON
hostility	*fjandskapar* OI, *fjandskapar* ON
hot	*heitt* OI, *heitt* ON
house	*bús* ON, *haus* OI, *haus* ON, *húsin* OI, *húsin* ON
housekeeper	*húskarli* OI, *húskarli* ON
house-man	*heimamaðr* ON, *heimamaður* OI
house-roof-ridge	*húsmæninum* OI, *húsmæninum* ON
housewife	*húsfreyja* OI, *húsfreyja* ON, *húsfreyju* OI, *húsfreyju* ON
how	*hve* OI, *hvé* ON, *hverju* OI, *hverju* ON, *hvern* OI, *hvern* ON, *hversu* OI, *hversu* ON
how-so	*hversu* OI, *hversu* ON
Hrafn (name)	*hrafn* OI, *hrafn* ON, *hrafni* OI, *hrafni* ON, *hrafns* OI
Hrafn's (name)	*hrafni* OI, *hrafns* OI, *hrafns* ON

Word List (English to Norse)

English	Norse	English	Norse
Hraunhofn (place)	*hraunhöfn* OI, *hraunhöfn* ON	Ilugi (name)	*illuga* ON, *illugi* ON
Hraunsdal (place)	*hraunsdal* OI, *hraunsdal* ON	in	*á* OI, *að* OI, *at* ON, *í* OI, *í* ON, *in* ON, *inn* OI, *inum* ON, *um* OI, *við* OI
Hreduvatn (place)	*hreðuvatns* OI, *hreðuvatns* ON	incapable	*ófær* OI, *ófærr* ON
Hrutafjord (place)	*hrútafirði* OI, *hrútafirði* ON, *hrútafjarðar* OI, *hrútafjarðar* ON	inclined	*hneigði* OI, *hneigði* ON
		indecent	*ógerla* ON, *ógjörla* OI
humble	*hógværr* ON	Ingibjorg (name)	*ingibjargar* OI, *ingibjörgu* OI, *ingibjörgu* ON
hundergar's	*húngerðar* OI, *húngersar* ON		
Hungerd (place)	*húngerðar* OI, *húngerðar* ON, *húngerðr* ON, *húngerður* OI	Ingibjorg's (name)	*ingibjargar* OI, *ingibjargar* ON
		inheritance	*arfi* OI, *arfi* ON, *arfr* ON, *arfur* OI, *föðurleifð* OI
hurt	*sárt* OI	inside	*innan* OI, *innan* ON, *innar* OI, *innar* ON
husband	*bónda* OI, *bónda* ON	instep	*ristinni* OI, *ristinni* ON
hut	*skálann* OI, *skálann* ON	intend	*ætla* OI, *ætla* ON, *ætlar* OI, *ætlar* ON
Hvammsfjord (place)	*hvammsfirði* OI, *hvammsfirði* ON	intended	*ætlað* OI, *ætlaði* OI, *ætlaði* ON
Hvitarsida (place)	*hvítársíðu* OI, *hvítársíðu* ON	intended-maiden	*festarmeyjar* OI, *festarmeyjar* ON
		intended-woman	*heitkona* OI
		in-the-end	*enda* OI
		into	*í* OI, *í* ON

I, i

i	*eg* OI, *ek* ON, *mér* OI, *mér* ON	invitation	*boð* OI, *boðið* OI, *boðinu* OI, *boðinu* ON, *boðsins* OI, *boðsins* ON
Iceland (place)	*íslandi* OI, *íslandi* ON, *íslands* OI, *íslands* ON	invite	*býðr* ON
Icelander	*íslandi* OI, *íslandsmaður* OI, *íslendingar* OI, *íslendingar* ON, *íslendingr* ON, *íslendingrinn* ON, *íslendingur* OI, *íslendingurinn* OI, *íslenskra* OI, *íslenzkr* ON, *íslenzkra* ON	invited	*bað* OI, *bauð* OI, *bauð* ON, *bauðk* ON, *beiddist* OI, *beiddist* ON, *boðið* OI
		ireland	*írlandi* OI, *írlandi* ON
		iron-claws	*járnklær* OI, *járnklær* ON
		is	*er* OI, *er* ON, *í* OI, *væri* ON
		island	*eyri* OI, *eyri* ON
		islands	*eyjunum* OI, *eyjunum* ON
if	*ef* OI, *ef* ON	is-she	*hún* OI
ill	*illa* OI, *illa* ON, *illr* OI, *illr* ON, *illt* OI, *illt* ON	it	*á* OI, *at* ON, *hann* OI, *hann* ON, *það* OI, *þat* ON
Illuga (name)	*illuga* ON	it-goes	*gengur* OI
Illuga's (name)	*illuga* ON		
Illugi (name)	*illuga* OI, *illugi* OI		
Illugi's (name)	*illuga* OI		
Illugi's (name)	*illuga* OI, *illuga* ON		

J, j

Word List (English to Norse)

English	*Norse*	English	*Norse*
Jofrid (name)	*jófríðar* OI, *jófríðar* ON, *jófríði* OI, *jófríði* ON, *jófríðr* ON, *jófríður* OI	kinsmen	*frænda* OI, *frændaafli* ON, *frændi* OI, *frændr* ON, *frændum* OI, *frændum* ON, *frændur* OI
join	*þýðast* ON	Kjartan (name)	*kjartan* OI, *kjartans* OI, *kjartans* ON
journey	*færi* OI, *færi* ON, *ferð* OI, *ferð* ON	knee	*kné* OI, *kné* ON
journeyed	*fór* OI	knelt	*hné* OI
joyed	*gaman* OI	knew	*kenndi* OI, *kenndi* ON, *skilðu* ON, *vissi* OI, *vissi* ON
jule	*jóla* OI, *jólin* OI		
jumped	*hraut* OI, *hraut* ON, *stökk* OI, *stökk* ON	knorrs	*knörru* OI, *knörru* ON
		know	*kenna* OI, *kenna* ON, *kunnig* OI, *kunnig* ON, *veist* OI, *veit* OI, *veit* ON, *veizt* ON, *vissak* ON, *vissi* OI, *víst* OI, *víst* ON, *vita* OI, *vita* ON, *vitir* OI, *vitir* ON

K, k

English	*Norse*	English	*Norse*
keep	*halda* OI, *halda* ON		
kept	*keyptu* OI, *keyptu* ON		
kill	*drepa* OI, *drepa* ON		
killed	*drap* OI, *drap* ON	known	*kann* OI, *kunnig* ON, *við* OI, *víst* OI
killing	*víg* OI, *víg* ON		
kind	*væna* OI, *væna* ON, *vænu* OI, *vænu* ON	Kollsvein (name)	*kollsveinn* OI
kindar	*kindar* OI	Kollsveinn (name)	*kollsveinn* OI, *kollsveinn* ON
king	*kontmgs* ON, *konung* OI, *konung* ON, *konungi* OI, *konungi* ON, *konunginn* OI, *konunginn* ON, *konungr* ON, *konungs* OI, *konungs* ON, *konungur* OI, *siklingr* OI	Kormlod (name)	*kormlaðar* OI, *kormlaðar* ON
		Kungalf (name)	*konungahellu* OI, *konungahellu* ON
		kvaran	*kvarans* OI
		kvarans	*kvárans* ON
		Kvaran's (name)	*kvarans* OI, *kvárans* ON
king-descendents	*konungmanna* OI, *konungmanna* ON		

L, l

English	*Norse*
kingdom	*ríki* OI, *ríki* ON, *ríkinu* OI, *ríkinu* ON, *ríkr* ON, *ríkur* OI
kings	*konungar* OI, *konungar* ON
king's	*konungs* OI
king's-gift	*konungsnaut* OI, *konungsnaut* ON
kinship	*frændsemi* OI, *frændsemi* ON
kinsman	*frænda* OI, *frænda* ON, *frændi* OI, *frændi* ON

English	*Norse*
Lade (place)	*hlaðir* OI, *hlaðir* ON, *hlöðum* OI, *hlöðum* ON
laden	*hlaðbúinn* OI, *hlaðbúinn* ON
laid	*lá* ON, *lagðak* ON, *lagði* OI, *lagði* ON, *lagið* OI, *lagit* ON, *leiddr* ON, *lét* OI, *létu* ON
lake	*vatnit* ON
land	*land* OI, *land* ON, *landi* OI, *landi* ON, *landið* OI, *landit* ON

Word List (English to Norse)

English	Norse
lands	*landa* OI, *landa* ON, *lands* OI, *lands* ON, *löndum* OI, *löndum* ON
Langa (place)	*langá* OI, *langá* ON
Langvatnsdal (place)	*langavatnsdal* OI, *langavatnsdal* ON
large	*stórort* OI, *stórort* ON
large-property-man	*stóreignamaðr* ON, *stóreignamaður* OI
last	*síðast* OI, *síðast* ON
late	*síð* OI, *síz* ON
later	*fresti* OI, *seinir* OI, *seinir* ON, *síð* OI, *síð* ON, *síðar* OI, *síðar* ON
later-ready	*síðbúnir* OI, *síðbúnir* ON
laughed	*hló* OI, *hló* ON
law	*lög* OI, *lög* ON, *lögum* OI, *lögum* ON
law-assembly	*lögréttu* OI, *lögréttu* ON
law-man	*lögmaðr* ON, *lögmaður* OI
law-rock	*lögbergi* OI, *lögbergi* ON, *lögbergs* OI, *lögbergs* ON
lawspeaker	*lögsögn* OI, *lögsögu* ON, *lögsögumaðr* ON, *lögsögumaður* OI
law-speaker-man	*lögsögumaðr* ON
lawspeaking	*lögspeki* OI, *lögspeki* ON
Laxdardal (place)	*laxdæla* OI, *laxdæla* ON
lay	*lá* OI, *lægi* OI, *lægi* ON, *læt* OI, *læt* ON, *lætr* ON, *lagði* OI, *legði* ON, *leggi* OI, *leggja* OI, *leggja* ON, *lét* OI, *lét* ON
layer	*lag* OI
laying	*lá* OI, *lá* ON, *lagðir* OI, *lagðir* ON, *lénur* OI, *lénur* ON
lay-out	*láta* OI
leader	*höfðingi* OI, *höfðingi* ON
learned	*fróðum* OI
leave	*láta* OI, *láta* ON, *orlof* OI
leaving-prepared	*brottbúningi* OI, *brottbúningi* ON
led	*leiddi* OI, *leiddi* ON, *leiddur* OI
leek	*lauka* OI, *lauka* ON
left	*létu* OI, *létu* ON, *vinstri* OI, *vinstri* ON
leg	*fótinn* OI, *fótinn* ON, *leggi* OI, *leggi* ON
legal-settlement	*lögskilum* OI, *lögskilum* ON
Leiruvog (place)	*leiruvág* ON, *leiruvog* OI, *leiruvogum* OI
less	*laus* OI, *minna* OI, *minna* ON, *minni* OI, *minni* ON, *minnr* ON, *minnur* OI
less-brave	*óröskari* OI, *óröskvari* ON
let	*lætur* OI, *lát* OI, *lát* ON, *láta* OI, *láta* ON, *látum* OI, *látum* ON, *lét* OI, *lét* ON, *léti* OI, *léti* ON
lets	*lætr* OI, *lætr* ON
letting	*láta* OI
let-us-be	*gerum* OI, *gerum* ON
Levanger (place)	*lifangr* ON, *lifangri* OI, *lifangri* ON, *lifangur* OI
Leysingastadir (place)	*leysingjastöðum* OI, *leysingjastöðum* ON
life	*líf* OI, *líf* ON
light	*létt* OI, *létt* ON, *ljósjarpr* ON, *ljósjarpur* OI, *ljósum* OI
lights	*ljósum* OI, *ljósum* ON
light-warrior-god	*lýsi-gunnar* OI, *lýsi-gunnar* ON
like	*líka* OI, *líka* ON, *líkar* OI, *líkar* ON, *líkr* ON, *líkur* OI, *líst* OI, *vilt* OI, *yill* ON
liked	*líka* OI, *líka* ON
likely	*líklegast* OI, *líklegt* OI, *líkligast* ON, *líkligt* ON
likeness	*vænleik* OI, *vænleik* ON
likewise	*eins* OI, *eins* ON
limp	*haltr* ON, *haltur* OI
limping	*haltr* ON, *haltur* OI
linden	*lind* OI, *lind* ON
linen	*hörvi* OI, *hörvi* ON, *líns* OI, *líns* ON
linns	*linns* OI, *linns* ON
listen	*hljóð* OI, *hljóð* ON, *hlýða* OI, *hlýða* ON, *hlýddið* ON, *hlýdduð* OI

207

Word List (English to Norse)

English	*Norse*	English	*Norse*
little	*lítið* OI, *lítil* OI, *lítil* ON, *lítit* ON, *litla* OI, *litla* ON, *litlu* OI, *litlu* ON, *lítt* OI, *lítt* ON	low	*lágt* OI, *lágt* ON, *lágu* OI, *lágu* ON
		lower	*óæðra* OI, *óæðra* ON
		loyalty	*tryggðum* OI, *tryggðum* ON
little-appearance	*yfirbragðslítið* OI, *yfirbragðslítit* ON	luck	*happs* OI, *happs* ON
little-need	*lítilþörf* OI, *lítilþörf* ON	lure	*lokka* OI, *lokka* ON
live	*bús* OI, *lífi* OI, *lífi* ON	lying	*lá* ON
lived	*bjó* OI, *bjó* ON, *bjuggu* OI, *bjuggu* ON		

M, m

English	*Norse*
loaded	*hlaðbúna* OI, *hlaðbúna* ON
loan	*láni* OI, *láni* ON
local-leader	*hersis* OI, *hersis* ON
lodgings	*ranna* OI, *ranna* ON
London-town (place)	*lúndúnaborg* OI, *lundúnaborg* ON, *lundúnabryggjur* OI, *lundúnabryggjur* ON
long	*lengi* OI, *lengi* ON, *löngum* OI, *löngum* ON
longer	*lengr* ON, *lengur* OI
look	*líta* OI, *títa* ON
looked	*horfði* OI, *horfði* ON, *leit* OI, *leit* ON, *sá* OI, *sá* ON, *ván* ON, *von* OI
looked-after	*mannaforráð* OI, *mannaforráð* ON
looks	*horfir* OI, *horfir* ON
loop	*lykkju* OI, *lykkju* ON
loose	*laus* OI, *lausan* OI
loosed	*laust* OI, *laust* ON
lord	*herra* OI, *herra* ON
lose	*lauss* ON
loss	*líflát* OI, *líflát* ON
lost	*laus* OI, *lausan* OI, *lausan* ON, *lauss* ON, *laust* OI, *laust* ON
lot	*hlut* OI, *hlut* ON, *hluta* OI, *hluta* ON
love	*ann* OI, *ann* ON, *ást* OI, *ást* ON, *ofrást* ON, *ofurást* OI, *unna* OI, *unna* ON, *unni* OI, *unni* ON
loved	*unnandi* OI, *unnandi* ON
lovely-eyes	*ástaraugum* OI, *ástaraugum* ON

English	*Norse*
made	*gerði* OI, *gerði* ON, *verit* ON
maiden	*mær* OI, *meyjar* OI
main-room	*stofu* OI, *stofu* ON
make	*ger* OI, *ger* ON, *gerðu* OI, *gerðu* ON
man	*karl* OI, *karl* ON, *karlmaður* OI, *kon* OI, *kon* ON, *maðr* ON, *maður* OI, *mann* OI, *mann* ON, *manna* OI, *manna* ON, *manni* OI, *manni* ON, *mannni* OI
man's	*manna* ON
man-door	*karldurum* ON, *karldyrum* OI
manly	*mannaða* OI, *mannaða* ON
man-ring	*mannhringr* ON, *mannhringur* OI
man's	*manna* OI, *manns* OI, *manns* ON
many	*karlmaðr* ON, *manna* OI, *marga* OI, *margar* OI, *margar* ON, *margir* OI, *margir* ON, *margr* ON, *margs* OI, *margt* ON, *margur* OI, *mart* OI, *menn* OI, *miklu* OI, *mjög* OI, *mörg* OI, *mörg* ON
many's	*margs* ON
mares	*merum* OI, *merum* ON
mark	*mörk* OI, *mörk* ON
marks	*merkr* ON, *merkur* OI, *mörkum* OI, *mörkum* ON

Word List (English to Norse)

English	*Norse*	English	*Norse*
marriage	*eiga* OI, *kvángast* ON, *mægðar* OI, *mægðar* ON	men-comparing	*mannjöfnuð* OI, *mannjöfnuð* ON
marriage-proposal	*bónorðið* OI, *bónorðit* ON, *kvánbæna* ON, *kvánbænum* ON, *kvonbæna* OI, *kvonbænum* OI	men-equal	*menrýris* OI, *menrýris* ON
		mentioned	*nefndi* OI, *nefndir* OI, *nefndir* ON
married	*átt* OI, *átt* ON, *átti* OI, *átti* ON, *fékk* OI, *gift* OI, *gift* ON, *kvángaðr* ON, *kvongaður* OI	mercy	*grið* OI, *grið* ON, *griðin* OI, *griðin* ON
		merry	*kátir* OI, *kátir* ON
		messengers	*sendimenn* OI
marry	*kvongast* OI	met	*fundist* OI, *fundust* OI, *hitti* OI, *hitti* ON, *mætti* OI, *mætti* ON, *mættust* OI, *mættust* ON, *móti* OI
matter	*mál* OI, *mál* ON, *mála* OI, *mála* ON, *málið* OI, *málit* ON, *máls* OI, *máls* ON		
		metal-missile	*málmflaug* OI, *malmflaug* ON
matters	*mál* OI, *málin* OI, *málin* ON	metals	*málma* OI, *malma* ON
		mid	*mitt* OI, *mitt* ON
mature	*rosknaðr* ON, *rosknaður* OI	middle	*mundangs* OI, *mundangs* ON
may	*má* OI, *má* ON, *mætti* ON, *mátti* OI, *mátti* ON, *mega* OI	Midfjorder-Skeggi's (name)	*miðfjarðar-skeggja* OI, *miðfjarðar-skeggja* ON
		might	*mátt* ON, *máttu* OI
maybe	*ef* OI	mind	*hygg* OI, *hykk* ON, *sinni* ON
me	*mér* OI, *mér* ON, *mig* OI, *mik* ON, *mín* OI, *mín* ON		
		mind-mood	*skaplyndi* OI
meanwhile	*meðan* OI, *meðan* ON	mine	*mér* OI, *mig* OI, *mín* OI, *mín* ON, *mína* OI, *mína* ON, *mínar* OI, *mínar* ON, *minn* OI, *minn* ON, *minnar* OI, *minnar* ON, *míns* OI, *míns* ON, *mínu* OI, *mínu* ON, *mínum* OI, *mínum* ON, *mitt* OI, *mitt* ON
measure	*mætr* OI, *mætr* ON		
measured	*alin* OI, *alin* ON, *alnar* OI, *alnar* ON		
medium-narrow	*miðmjór* OI, *miðmjór* ON		
meet	*fund* OI, *fund* ON, *fundi* OI, *mætast* OI, *mætast* ON, *mót* OI, *mót* ON, *móti* OI, *móti* ON		
		mockery	*háð* OI, *háð* ON
		moderate	*hógvær* OI
meeting	*fund* OI, *fund* ON, *fundi* OI, *fundi* ON	moderate-man	*hófsmaðr* ON
		modest	*hófsmaður* OI
meet-we	*mættimst* ON, *mættumst* OI	Móði (name)	*móði* OI, *móði* ON
		money	*aura* OI, *fé* OI
Melrakkasletta (place)	*melrakkaslèttu* OI, *melrakkaslèttu* ON	month	*mánaði* ON, *mánuði* OI
		mood	*skaplyndi* OI
men	*gumna* OI, *gumna* ON, *maðr* ON, *mann* OI, *mann* ON, *manna* OI, *manna* ON, *manni* OI, *manni* ON, *menn* OI, *menn* ON, *mönnum* OI	moon	*tungls* OI, *tungls* ON
		more	*fleiri* OI, *fleiri* ON, *meir* OI, *meir* ON, *meira* OI, *meira* ON, *meiri* OI
men-choice	*mannval* ON	more-effective	*hallkvæmri* OI, *hallkvæmri* ON
men-choices	*mannval* OI		

Word List (English to Norse)

English	Norse	English	Norse
more-famous	*frægri* OI, *frægri* ON	named	*heiti* OI, *heitik* ON, *heitir* OI, *heitir* ON, *hét* OI, *hét* ON, *nafn* OI, *nefndi* ON, *nefndir* OI, *nefndir* ON, *nefndist* OI, *nefndist* ON, *nefndr* ON, *nefndum* OI, *nefndum* ON, *nefndur* OI
more-popular	*vinsælli* OI, *vinsælli* ON		
morning	*mogun* OI, *moguninn* OI, *morgin* ON, *morgininn* ON, *morgun* OI, *morguninn* OI, *morguns* OI, *morguns* ON		
Mosfell (place)	*mosfelli* OI, *mosfelli* ON, *mosfells* OI, *mosfells* ON	namesake	*nafni* OI, *nafni* ON
		near	*hjá* OI, *nær* OI, *nær* ON
most	*flesta* OI, *flesta* ON, *flestra* OI, *mest* OI, *mest* ON, *mesta* OI, *mesta* ON, *mesti* OI, *mesti* ON, *mestir* OI, *mestri* OI, *mestri* ON, *mestu* OI, *mestu* ON	neared	*næði* OI, *næði* ON
		nearer	*nær* ON
		near-kin	*náfrændi* OI, *náfrændi* ON
		need	*þörf* OI, *þörf* ON, *þyrfti* OI, *þyrfti* ON
		needed	*þurfa* OI, *þurfa* ON
most-beauty	*fegurst* OI	needless	*þarfleysi* OI, *þarfleysi* ON
most-visible	*sjálegastur* OI	negotiate	*semja* OI, *semja* ON
mother	*móðir* OI, *móðir* ON, *móður* OI, *móður* ON	neither	*hvárigum* ON, *hvárki* ON, *hvárrgi* ON, *hvergi* OI, *hvergi* ON, *hvorgi* OI, *hvorigum* OI, *hvorki* OI
mountain	*fjalla* OI, *fjalla* ON		
moved	*fluttist* OI, *fluttu* OI, *fluttu* ON		
much	*mikið* OI, *mikil* OI, *mikil* ON, *mikill* OI, *mikill* ON, *mikilli* OI, *mikilli* ON, *mikit* ON, *mikla* OI, *mikla* ON, *miklu* OI, *miklu* ON, *mjög* OI, *mjök* OI, *mjök* ON	never	*aldrei* OI, *aldri* ON
		new	*nýju* OI, *nýju* ON, *nýstr* OI, *nýztr* ON
		newcomer	*nýlundu* OI, *nýlundu* ON
		newly-taken	*nýtekið* OI, *nýtekit* ON
		news	*fregna* OI, *fregna* ON, *frétt* OI, *frétt* ON, *tíðenda* ON, *tíðendi* ON, *tíðinda* OI, *tíðindi* OI
murder-running	*morðrunnr* OI, *morðrunnr* ON		
must	*mun* OI		
my	*mig* OI, *mín* OI, *mín* ON, *minn* OI, *minn* ON, *mínum* OI, *mínum* ON, *mitt* OI	news-less	*tíðendalaust* ON, *tíðindalaust* OI
		next	*annað* OI, *annat* ON, *næst* OI, *næst* ON, *naustu* OI
Myrar (place)	*mýramanna* OI		
Myrar-folk (name)	*mýramanna* OI, *mýramanna* ON	next-to	*næst* OI, *nauztu* ON
		Nidaros (place)	*niðaróss* OI, *niðaróss* ON
myself	*mér* ON		
myself-to	*mér* OI	night	*nætti* OI, *nátt* OI, *nátt* ON, *nóttina* OI, *nóttina* ON

N, n

		nights	*nætr* ON, *nætur* OI, *nátta* OI, *nátta* ON, *náttum* OI, *náttum* ON
name	*nafn* OI, *nafn* ON	Njal's (name)	*njáls* OI, *njáls* ON

Word List (English to Norse)

English	Norse	English	Norse
Njörun (name)	njörun OI, njörun ON	of	á OI, á ON, að OI, af OI, af ON, at ON, ef OI, frá OI, í OI, í ON, of OI, og OI, ór ON, til OI
no	ekki ON, engi OI, engum ON		
noble	ættar OI, ættar ON, gims OI, gims ON, göfgir OI, göfgir ON, skörungr ON, skörungur OI	offer	boðit ON, býð OI, býð ON, býður OI
		offered	bauð OI
		of-men	manna OI
none	eigi OI, eigi ON, enga ON, engar ON, engi OI, engi ON, engra ON, engu ON, öngar OI, öngra OI, öngu OI, öngum OI, öngvar OI	of-parts	vanhluta OI, vanhluta ON
		often	oft OI, oft ON
		of-the-dead	döglinga ON
		of-them	þeirra OI
		of-words	orðið OI, orðit ON
nor	né OI, né ON	Olaf (name)	ólaf OI, óláf ON, ólafi OI, óláfi ON, óláfr ON, ólafs OI, óláfs ON, ólafur OI, óleifi OI, óleifi ON
Norduradal (place)	norðrárdal ON, norðurárdal OI		
north	norðan OI, norðan ON, norðr ON, norður OI		
Northman	norðmaðr ON, norðmaður OI	Olaf's (name)	ólafs OI, óláfs ON
		old	gamall OI, gamall ON
Norway (place)	noreg OI, nóreg ON, noregi OI, nóregi ON, noregs OI, nóregs ON	oldest	ellstr ON, elstur OI
		Olfus (name)	ölfusi OI, ölfusi ON
		on	á OI, á ON
norwegian	norrænn OI, norrænn ON	once	eitt OI, eitt ON, sinni OI, sinni ON
Norwegian-men	noregsmenn OI, nóregsmenn ON, noregsmönnum OI, nóregsmönnum ON	one	annar OI, ein OI, ein ON, eina OI, eina ON, einhvern OI, einn OI, einn ON, einnhvern OI, einnhvern ON, einni OI, einni ON, eins OI, eins ON, einu OI, einu ON, einum OI, einum ON, eitt OI, eitt ON, í OI sitt ON
not	ei OI, eigi OI, eigi ON, ekki OI, ekki ON, engi OI, né OI, né ON, nú OI, önga OI		
not-fighting	óvígr ON, óvígur OI		
nothing	ekki OI, ekki ON, engu ON	one's	
		only-spoken	eintalað OI, eintalat ON
not-spoken	ómælt OI, ómælt ON	Onund (name)	önund OI, önund ON, önundar OI, önundar ON, önundi OI, önundi ON, önundr ON, önundur OI
nourishes	elr OI, elr ON		
now	nú OI, nú ON		

O, o

English	Norse	English	Norse
		Onund's (name)	önundar OI
		Onund's-sons (name)	önundarsynir OI, önundarsynir ON
obedient	hlýðisamt OI, hlýðisamt ON	open	opið OI
obey	hlýða OI	opened	opit ON, vágr ON, vogur OI
		opening	gat OI, gat ON

Word List (English to Norse)

English	Norse	English	Norse
opportunity	*færi* OI, *færi* ON	out-travel	*utanferðar* OI, *útanferðar* ON
opposite	*gegnt* OI, *gegnt* ON	over	*ofan* OI, *ofan* ON, *yfir* OI, *yfir* ON
or	*eða* OI, *eða* ON	over-turned	*hnekkði* ON, *hnekkti* OI
Orkney (place)	*orkneyja* OI, *orkneyja* ON	own	*eig* OI, *eig* ON, *eiga* OI, *eiga* ON
Orkney-islands (place)	*orkneyjar* OI, *orkneyjar* ON	owned	*eiga* OI, *eiga* ON, *eignum* OI, *eignum* ON
Orkneys (place)	*orkneyjum* OI, *orkneyjum* ON	Oxarar (place)	*öxarár* OI, *öxarár* ON
Ornolfsdal (place)	*örnólfsdal* OI, *örnólfsdal* ON	Oxararholm (place)	*öxarárhólmi* OI, *öxarárhólmi* ON
Osvif's (name)	*ósvífrs* ON, *ósvífs* OI		
other	*aðra* OI, *aðra* ON, *aðrir* OI, *aðrir* ON, *annarra* OI, *annarra* ON, *annars* OI, *annars* ON, *annat* ON, *hinnar* OI, *hitt* OI, *hitt* ON, *kostur* OI, *öðru* ON, *öðrum* OI, *öðrum* ON		

P, p

English	Norse
paid	*galt* OI, *galt* ON, *greiddu* OI, *greiddu* ON
painful	*meinn* OI, *meinn* ON
part	*hlutr* ON, *hlutur* OI
party	*sveitinni* OI, *sveitinni* ON
pass	*líða* OI, *líða* ON
passage	*fari* OI
passed	*leið* OI, *leið* ON, *liðið* OI, *liðin* OI, *liðin* ON, *liðinn* ON, *liðit* ON, *liðnar* OI, *liðnar* ON, *liðnir* OI, *liðnir* ON, *liðu* OI, *liðu* ON
pay	*fá* OI, *fé* OI, *gjalda* OI, *gjalda* ON
peace-land	*friðland* OI, *friðland* ON
peacock	*pá* OI
peacock's	*pá* ON
peacock's	*pá* OI
people	*alþýðu* OI, *alþýðu* ON, *fólk* OI, *fólk* ON, *manna* OI, *manna* ON, *menn* OI, *menn* ON, *mönnum* OI, *mönnum* ON
placed	*lág* OI, *lág* ON
places	*staðar* OI, *staðar* ON
platform	*palli* OI, *palli* ON
played	*leikist* OI, *leikizt* ON, *lékum* OI, *lékum* ON
pledged	*heitið* OI

English	Norse
other-lands	*útlöndum* ON
others	*aðrir* OI, *aðrir* ON, *hin* OI, *hin* ON, *öðrum* OI, *öðrum* ON
other-side	*öðrumegin* OI
otherwise	*ella* OI, *ella* ON, *öðru* OI
ounces	*aura* OI, *aura* ON
our	*okkarri* OI, *okkarri* ON, *okkr* ON, *okkra* OI, *okkra* ON, *várt* ON, *vort* OI
ours	*okkrir* OI, *okkrir* ON, *okkur* OI, *sinni* OI, *sinni* ON, *várn* ON, *várt* ON, *vorn* OI, *vorum* OI
out	*á* OI, *á* ON, *í* OI, *út* OI, *út* ON, *utan* OI, *útan* ON, *úti* OI, *úti* ON, *ýti* OI, *ýtik* ON
out-coming	*útkváma* ON
out-house	*útibúr* OI, *útibúr* ON
out-let	*útláts* OI, *útláts* ON
out-of	*af* OI, *af* ON, *ór* ON, *úr* OI, *út* OI, *út* ON, *utan* OI, *útan* ON
out-of-mind	*afhuga* OI, *afhuga* ON
outside	*út* OI
outstanding	*afbragð* OI, *afbragð* ON
outstanding-man	*afarmenni* OI, *afarmenni* ON

Word List (English to Norse)

English	Norse	English	Norse
poem	*kvæði* OI, *kvæði* ON, *kvæðið* OI, *kvæðinu* OI, *kvæðinu* ON, *kvæðit* ON, *kvæðum* OI, *kvæðum* ON	prime-grown	*frumvaxta* OI, *frumvaxta* ON
		privately	*sér* ON
		procedure	*atferli* OI, *atferli* ON
poem-repay	*bragarlaunum* OI	promised-woman	*heitkona* OI, *heitkona* ON
poem's-reward	*kvæðislaunum* OI, *kvæðislaunum* ON	promising	*allvænlegur* OI, *allvænligr* ON, *efnilegir* OI, *efniligir* ON
poet	*skáld* OI, *skáld* ON, *skaldi* OI, *skaldi* ON	proof	*mark* OI, *mark* ON
Poet-Hrafn	*skáld-hrafn* OI, *skáld-hrafn* ON	proposal	*bónorð* OI, *bónorð* ON, *bónorðið* OI
poetry	*brag* OI, *brag* ON	propose	*biðja* OI, *biðja* ON, *fastna* OI, *fastna* ON, *kvánbænar* ON, *kvonbænar* OI, *ráð* OI
poets	*skáldmenn* OI		
point	*hlunns* OI, *hlunns* ON		
point-given	*odd-gefnar* OI, *odd-gefnar* ON		
		proposed-to	*bað* OI
point-of-sword	*blóðrefillinn* OI, *blóðrefillinn* ON	propose-to	*biðja* ON
		prospects	*efni* OI, *efni* ON
point-reddener	*oddrjóð* OI, *oddrjóð* ON	provided	*veitat* OI, *veitat* ON, *vor* OI
poor	*félítill* OI, *félítill* ON, *félitlir* OI, *félitlir* ON	provided-for	*veitti* OI, *veitti* ON
popular	*vinsæll* OI, *vinsæll* ON	provisions	*várri* ON, *vist* OI, *vist* ON, *vorri* OI
position	*stóðu* OI		
postponed	*frestaðist* OI, *frestaðist* ON	pushed	*ýta* OI, *ýta* ON
praise	*mæra* OI, *mæra* ON	put	*setti* OI, *setti* ON
praised	*lofaði* OI, *lofaði* ON, *lofnar* OI, *lofnar* ON		

Q, q

English	Norse
pray	*bæðir* OI
prayer	*bæna* OI, *bæna* ON
precocious	*snemmendis* OI, *snemmendis* ON
quarrelled	*þrættu* OI, *þrættu* ON
quay	*bryggjur* OI, *bryggjur* ON
prepare	*búa* OI, *búa* ON
queen	*drottningar* OI, *dróttningar* ON
prepared	*albúinn* OI, *albúit* ON, *bjó* OI, *bjó* ON, *bjóst* OI, *bjóst* ON, *bjuggu* OI, *bjuggu* ON, *bjuggust* OI, *bjuggust* ON, *búast* OI, *búast* ON, *búið* OI, *búin* OI, *búinn* OI, *búinn* ON, *býst* OI, *býst* ON
quick	*bráðger* OI, *bráðgerr* ON
quickest	*skjótast* OI, *skjótast* ON
quickly	*bráðlega* OI, *hvatra* OI, *hvatra* ON, *skjótt* OI, *skjótt* ON
quiet	*fátalaðr* ON, *fátalaður* OI
preparing	*búnir* OI
present	*fyrir* OI, *staddir* OI, *staddir* ON

R, r

English	Norse
preserved	*varðveitt* OI, *varðveitt* ON
priest	*presti* OI, *presti* ON, *prestur* OI
rage	*gný* OI, *gný* ON
raiding	*herjuðu* OI, *herjuðu* ON, *hernað* OI, *hernað* ON

Word List (English to Norse)

English	Norse	English	Norse
ran	*hljóp* OI, *hljóp* ON, *hljópu* ON, *hlupu* OI, *renndi* OI, *renndi* ON	returning	*aftr* ON
		reward	*launa* OI
		rewarded	*launaði* OI, *launaði* ON
ranks	*hergerðandi* OI, *hergerðandi* ON	rich	*auðigr* ON, *auðigur* OI, *auðr* ON
Rannveig (name)	*rannveig* OI, *rannveig* ON	rich-man	*auðmaðr* ON, *auðmaður* OI
rather	*heldr* ON, *heldur* OI, *helst* OI, *helzt* ON	ride	*ráð* OI, *ríða* OI, *ríða* ON
Raudamel (name)	*rauðamel* OI, *rauðamel* ON	ridge	*egg* OI, *egg* ON
		ridicule	*spott* OI, *spott* ON
readied	*bjóst* OI, *bjóst* ON	riding	*riðu* OI
ready	*búnir* OI, *búnir* ON	right	*hægr* OI, *hægr* ON, *hægri* OI, *hægri* ON
readying	*búnir* ON	righting	*rétting* OI, *rétting* ON
receive	*þiggja* OI, *þiggja* ON	ring	*hringinum* OI, *hringinum* ON
received	*fagnaði* OI, *fangi* OI, *fangi* ON, *fekksk* ON, *fékkst* OI	ring-endurance	*hringþollr* OI, *hringþollr* ON
red	*rauð* OI, *rauð* ON, *rauðan* OI, *rauðan* ON	rings	*hringa* OI, *hringa* ON
		rising	*risnir* OI, *risnir* ON
reddened	*roðið* OI, *roðinn* OI, *roðinn* ON, *roðit* ON	risk	*hætta* OI, *hætta* ON
refuse	*synja* OI, *synjar* OI, *synjar* ON	river	*ána* OI, *ána* ON, *ánni* OI, *ánni* ON
refuses	*synja* ON	robber-man	*ránsmaðr* ON, *ránsmaður* OI
rejected	*hafnaði* OI, *hafnaði* ON	rode	*réð* OI, *réð* ON, *réðst* OI, *réðst* ON, *réðu* OI, *réðu* ON, *reið* OI, *reið* ON, *ríða* OI, *ríða* ON, *ríðr* ON, *riðu* OI, *riðu* ON, *ríður* OI
relatives	*ættmanna* OI, *ættmanna* ON		
relieved	*feginn* OI, *feginn* ON		
religion	*átrúnaði* OI, *átrúnaði* ON		
reluctance	*seinlega* OI, *seinliga* ON	roof-ridge	*mæninum* OI, *mæninum* ON
remaining	*eftir* OI, *eftir* ON	room	*stofu* OI
remembered	*man* OI, *man* ON, *munat* OI, *munat* ON, *mundi* OI, *munði* ON	rose	*freyddi* OI, *freyddi* ON, *risu* OI, *risu* ON
repaid	*launað* OI, *launat* ON	round	*runna* OI, *runna* ON
repay	*launa* OI, *launa* ON, *selja* OI	ruffled	*ýfast* OI, *ýfast* ON
		ruled	*réð* OI, *réð* ON
repent	*iðrast* OI	ruling	*órskurðinn* ON, *ráðið* OI, *ráðit* ON, *úrskurðinn* OI
reserved	*fálátr* ON, *fálátur* OI		
resolute	*einart* OI, *einart* ON	ruling-person	*órskurðarmanns* ON, *úrskurðarmanns* OI
resolved	*reynd* OI, *reynd* ON		
respect	*virður* OI	run	*hlaupinn* OI, *hlaupinn* ON, *renni* OI, *renni* ON
rested	*hvíldi* OI, *hvíldi* ON		
retain	*geyma* OI, *geyma* ON	ruthless	*óvæginn* OI, *óvæginn* ON
return	*aftr* OI, *aftr* ON		
returned	*áður* OI, *aftr* ON, *aftur* OI, *fluttist* ON		

Word List (English to Norse)

English	*Norse*	English	*Norse*
S, s		saturday-night	*laugarkveld* OI, *laugarkveld* ON
sacks	*sekkana* OI, *sekkana* ON, *vörusekkar* ON	save	*spara* OI, *spara* ON
sad	*daprlig* ON, *dapurleg* OI, *döpr* ON, *döpur* OI	saw	*sá* OI, *sá* ON, *ságu* OI, *ságu* ON, *sáu* OI, *sé* ON
saddle	*hnakk* OI, *hnakk* ON, *söðul* OI, *söðul* ON	say	*mælt* OI, *mælt* ON, *sé* OI, *segi* OI, *segi* ON, *segir* OI, *segja* OI, *segja* ON
saddled	*söðlaðir* OI, *söðlaðir* ON	saying	*kvað* OI, *kvað* ON, *kváðu* OI, *kváðu* ON, *segið* OI, *segið* ON
sadness	*fæð* OI, *fæð* ON		
saga	*sögu* OI, *sögu* ON, *sögunni* OI	scarcely	*trautt* OI, *trautt* ON
said	*kvað* OI, *kvað* ON, *kvaðst* OI, *kvaðst* ON, *kváðust* OI, *kváðust* ON, *kvæði* OI, *kveðst* OI, *kveðst* ON, *mæl* OI, *mæl* ON, *mælt* OI, *mælt* ON, *mælti* OI, *sagði* OI, *sagði* ON, *sagðir* OI, *sagðir* ON, *sagt* OI, *sagt* ON, *segir* OI, *segir* ON, *sögðu* OI, *sögðu* ON, *sögn* OI, *sögn* ON	scarlet	*skarlati* OI, *skarlati* ON
		scarlet-cloak	*skarlatsskikkju* OI, *skarlatsskikkju* ON
		scholar	*fræðimaður* OI
		scored	*skorað* OI
		Scotlands-firths (place)	*skotlandsfjörðu* OI
		Scotland's-Firths (place)	*skotlandsfjörðu* ON
		scratched	*skeindist* OI, *skeindist* ON
		sea	*haf* OI, *haf* ON, *hafi* OI, *hafi* ON
sail	*sigla* OI, *sigla* ON	seas	*sævar* OI, *sævar* ON
sailed	*sigla* OI, *sigla* ON, *sigldi* OI, *sigldi* ON, *sigldu* OI, *sigldu* ON, *siglir* OI, *siglir* ON	seat	*aðsetu* OI
		second	*annar* OI, *annarr* ON, *öndri* OI, *öndri* ON
sails	*sigldi* OI, *sigldi* ON	second-time	*annað* OI, *annat* ON
sake	*sakar* ON, *sak-ar* ON, *sakir* OI	secrecy	*leynd* OI, *leynd* ON
		secret	*leynt* OI, *leynt* ON
sake-less	*saklausa* OI, *saklausa* ON	see	*raun* OI, *raun* ON, *sé* OI, *sé* ON, *sék* ON, *sér* OI, *sér* ON, *sérð* OI, *sésk* ON, *sést* OI, *séumk* ON, *sjá* OI, *sjá* ON, *sjást* OI, *sjást* ON, *sjáumk* OI
same	*sama* OI, *sama* ON, *samira* OI, *samira* ON, *sömu* OI, *sömu* ON		
same-like	*sæmilega* OI, *sæmiliga* ON		
same-lying	*samlagar* OI, *samlagar* ON	seeing	*sér* OI
		seek	*skylir* ON
sank	*hné* OI, *hné* ON	seem	*sýnist* OI, *sýnist* ON
sat	*sat* OI, *sat* ON, *sátu* OI, *settist* OI, *settist* ON	seemed	*svipr* ON, *svipur* OI, *sýndist* OI, *sýndist* ON, *sýnt* ON, *þótti* OI, *þykkir* ON, *virðist* OI, *virðist* ON
satisfied	*undi* OI, *unði* ON		
saturday-afternoon	*laugaraftan* OI, *laugaraftan* ON	seems	*þykir* OI, *þykkir* ON, *virðist* OI, *virðist* ON

215

Word List (English to Norse)

English	Norse	English	Norse
seen	sá ON, sénar OI, sénar ON	sharp	hvöss OI, hvöss ON
seen-like	sjáligastr ON	sharply	snarplega OI, snarpliga ON
self-example	sjálfdæmi OI, sjálfdæmi ON	she	hana OI, hana ON, henni OI, hon ON, honum ON, hún OI
sell	sel OI, sel ON, selja OI, selja ON	sheathed-sword	skeið OI, skeið ON
send	senda OI, senda ON	sheep	kindar ON
sending-men	sendimenn OI, sendimenn ON	she-is	hún OI
sent	sendi OI, sendi ON	shelter	selja OI, selja ON
separate	skilja OI, skilja ON, skilnaði OI, skilnaði ON	shepherd	smalamaðr ON, smalamaður OI, smalamann OI, smalamann ON
separated	skildu OI, skilðu ON, skilja OI, skilja ON, skilnaði OI, skilnaði ON, skilr ON, skilur OI	shield	röndum OI, röndum ON, skildi OI, skildi ON, skildinum OI, skildinum ON, skjöld OI, skjöld ON, skjöldinn OI, skjöldinn ON
serpent	iðrask ON, orma ON, orms OI, orms ON		
serpent-days	ormdags OI, ormdags ON	shields	skylmdust OI, skylmðust ON
serpent's-bed	ormabeð OI		
serpent-tongue	ormstunga OI, ormstunga ON, ormstungu OI	ship	skip OI, skip ON, skipi OI, skipi ON, skipið OI, skipinu OI, skipinu ON, skipit ON, skips OI, skips ON
serpent-tongue's	ormstungu OI, ormstungu ON		
Serpent-Tongue's (name)	ormstungu ON	ships	skip OI, skip ON, skipi OI, skipi ON, skips OI, skips ON, skipuðu OI, skipuðu ON
servant	húskarl OI, húskarl ON		
service	þjónustu OI, þjónustu ON		
set	seti OI, seti ON, sett OI, sett ON	shipwreck	skipbroti OI, skipbroti ON
settle	boðs OI, boðs ON	shock-thorn	höggþyrnis OI, höggþyrnis ON
settled	bjuggu ON, búið OI, búit ON	shone	skein OI, skein ON
settlement	sætt OI, sætt ON	short	skamma OI, skamma ON, skortir OI, skortir ON
settling-people	búandmönnum OI		
seven	sjau ON, sjaunda ON, sjö OI, sjöunda OI	shortage	skorta OI, skorta ON
shakes	hristar OI, hristar ON		
shall	mun OI, munt OI, munt ON, munu OI, munu ON, skal OI, skal ON, skalk ON, skalt OI, skalt ON, skaltu OI, skulir OI, skulu OI, skulum ON, skum OI		
shall-you	skaltu OI, skaltu ON		

Word List (English to Norse)

English	Norse	English	Norse
should	*mun* OI, *mun* ON, *muna* OI, *muna* ON, *mundi* OI, *mundu* OI, *mundu* ON, *muni* OI, *muni* ON, *munt* OI, *munt* ON, *muntu* OI, *munum* OI, *munum* ON, *mynda* ON, *myndi* ON, *skulir* OI, *skulir* ON, *skulu* OI, *skulu* ON, *skuluð* OI, *skuluð* ON, *skyldi* OI, *skyldi* ON, *skyldir* OI, *skyldir* ON, *skyldu* OI, *skyldu* ON, *yrði* OI, *yrði* ON	sixty	*sextigu* OI, *sextigu* ON
		sjoni	*sjóna* OI, *sjóna* ON
		Skafti (name)	*skafta* OI, *skafti* OI, *skafti* ON
		Skafti's (name)	*skafta* OI, *skafta* ON
		Skaney (place)	*skáney* OI, *skáney* ON
		Skarar (place)	*skörum* OI, *skörum* ON
		Skeljavik (place)	*skeljavík* OI, *skeljavík* ON
		skinned	*skinndregna* OI, *skinndregna* ON
		skins	*skinnum* OI, *skinnum* ON
		Skuli (name)	*skúii* ON, *skúli* OI, *skúli* ON
		slander	*háðvörum* OI, *háðvörum* ON, *rógi* OI, *rógi* ON
shovel	*reku* OI, *reku* ON		
show	*sýn* OI, *sýn* ON		
showed	*sýndi* OI, *sýndi* ON, *sýnir* OI, *sýnir* ON, *sýnt* OI, *sýnt* ON	slayers	*viggs* ON
		slayers-of-the-dead	*vígsdöglinga* OI
		sleep	*svefni* OI, *svefni* ON, *svefninum* OI, *svefninum* ON
shown	*sýnt* OI		
sickness	*sótt* OI, *sótt* ON		
Sigrid (name)	*sigríðar* OI, *sigríðar* ON	sleeves	*ermar* OI, *ermar* ON
Sigtrygg (name)	*sigtryggr* OI, *sigtryggr* ON, *sigtryggur* OI	slept	*sofnaði* OI, *sofnaði* ON, *svaf* OI, *svaf* ON
Sigurd (name)	*sigurðar* OI, *sigurðar* ON, *sigurðr* ON, *sigurður* OI	Slettu (place)	*sléttu* ON
		small	*lítið* OI, *smátt* OI, *smátt* ON
Sigvalda (name)	*sigvalda* OI, *sigvalda* ON	smell	*lykt* OI, *lykt* ON
silently	*þegjandi* OI, *þegjandi* ON	smooth	*sléttir* OI, *sléttir* ON
		smoothed	*slétt* OI, *slétt* ON
silk-beard	*silkiskegg* OI, *silkiskegg* ON	Snorri (name)	*snorri* OI
silver	*silfrs* ON, *silfurs* OI, *slíkar* ON	so	*sá* OI, *sá* ON, *samir* OI, *samir* ON, *sé* OI, *sé* ON, *sem* OI, *sem* ON, *sú* OI, *svá* ON, *svo* OI, *þat* ON
silver-inlay	*sifurrekna* OI, *silfrrekna* ON		
since	*sem* OI, *síðan* OI, *síðan* ON, *síðar* OI, *síðar* ON, *því* OI, *því* ON	sold	*seldi* OI, *seldi* ON
		solve	*leysa* OI, *leysa* ON
		some	*nakkvar* OI, *nokkuð* OI, *nokkurir* OI, *nökkurir* ON, *nökkut* ON, *sumir* OI
sink	*hníga* OI, *hníga* ON		
sister	*systir* OI, *systir* ON		
sister-sons	*systursynir* OI, *systursynir* ON	somebody's	*einhverjum* OI, *einhverjum* ON
sit	*siti* ON, *sitið* ON, *sitja* OI, *sitji* OI, *sitjið* OI	something	*nokkuð* OI, *nökkut* ON
		something-of	*nökkurr* ON
sitting	*sátu* OI, *sátu* ON, *sitja* OI, *sitja* ON	somewhat	*nakkvað* OI, *nokkur* OI, *nökkut* ON
six	*sex* OI, *sex* ON	some-what	*nokkuð* OI, *nökkut* ON

217

Word List (English to Norse)

English	*Norse*	English	*Norse*
son	*son* OI, *son* ON, *sona* OI, *sona* ON, *sonar* OI, *sonar* ON, *sonr* ON, *sonum* OI, *syni* OI, *syni* ON	son-of-Skalla-Grim (name)	*skalla-grímssonar* OI, *skalla-grímssonar* ON
		son-of-Skula (name)	*skúlason* OI
		son-of-Sturlu (name)	*sturluson* OI
son-in-law	*mági* OI, *mági* ON	son-of-Svein (name)	*sveinsson* OI, *sveinsson* ON
son-of	*sonr* ON, *syni* ON	son-of-thorstein	*svo* OI
son-of-Edgar (name)	*játgeirsson* OI, *játgeirsson* ON	son-of-Thorstein (name)	*þorsteinsson* OI, *þorsteinsson* ON
son-of-Egil (name)	*egilsson* OI, *egilsson* ON, *egilssonar* OI, *egilssonar* ON, *egilssyni* OI, *egilssyni* ON	son-of-Valbrand (name)	*valbrandssonar* OI, *valbrandssonar* ON
		sons	*sonu* OI, *sonu* ON, *sonum* OI, *sonum* ON, *syni* OI, *synir* OI, *synir* ON
son-of-Eyvind (name)	*eyvindarson* OI, *eyvindarson* ON		
		soon	*bráðlega* OI, *bráðliga* ON, *brátt* OI, *brátt* ON
son-of-Hafur-Bjarni (name)	*hafr-bjarnarson* ON, *hafur-bjarnarson* OI	sorely	*óðgjarn* OI, *óðgjarn* ON
son-of-Hakon (name)	*hákonarson* OI, *hákonarson* ON	sought	*sóta* OI, *sóta* ON, *sótt* OI, *sótt* ON, *sóttust* OI
son-of-Hallkel (name)	*hallkelsson* OI, *hallkelsson* ON	sound	*hljóð* OI, *hljóð* ON
son-of-Hardar's (name)	*harðarsonar* OI, *harðarsonar* ON	south	*suðr* ON, *suður* OI, *sunnan* OI, *sunnan* ON
son-of-Hlífar (name)	*hlífarsonar* OI, *hlífarsonar* ON	South-Islands (place)	*suðreyjar* ON, *suðureyjar* OI
son-of-Hlodvi (name)	*hlöðvisson* OI, *hlöðvisson* ON	space	*bil* OI, *bil* ON
		spares	*eirir* OI, *eirir* ON
son-of-Hoskuld (name)	*höskuldssonar* OI, *höskuldssonar* ON	speak	*máls* OI, *máls* ON, *tala* OI, *tala* ON
son-of-Hrosskel (name)	*hrosskelssonar* OI, *hrosskelssonar* ON	speaking	*mæltu* OI
		spear	*spjóta* OI, *spjóta* ON, *spjótinu* OI, *spjótinu* ON
son-of-illugi	*svo* OI		
son-of-Illugi (name)	*illugason* OI, *illugason* ON	spear-man	*vígur* OI
		spear-sister	*oddfeimu* OI, *oddfeimu* ON
son-of-Kallak (name)	*kallaksson* OI, *kjallaksson* ON	spell	*galdrs* OI, *galdrs* ON
son-of-Kolbein (name)	*kolbeinsson* OI, *kolbeinsson* ON	spend	*verkkaupi* OI, *verkkaupi* ON
son-of-Kveld-Ulf (name)	*kveld-úlfssonar* OI, *kveld-úlfssonar* ON	spirit-mother	*hugmóðr* OI, *hugmóðr* ON
son-of-Molda-Gnup (name)	*molda-gnúpssonar* OI, *molda-gnúpssonar* ON	spoke	*kvað* OI, *kvaðst* OI, *kvaðst* ON, *mælt* OI, *mælti* OI, *mælti* ON, *mæltu* OI, *mæltu* ON
son-of-Olaf (name)	*ólafsson* OI, *ólafssonar* OI, *óláfssonar* ON		
		spoken	*mælt* OI, *mælt* ON
son-of-Onund (name)	*önundarson* OI, *önundarson* ON, *önundarsonar* OI	spoke-of	*taliðr* OI, *taliðr* ON
		sport	*leik* OI, *leik* ON
		sprang	*spratt* OI, *spratt* ON
son-of-Sel-Thori (name)	*sel-þórisson* OI, *sel-þórisson* ON	spread	*rakti* OI

218

Word List (English to Norse)

English	Norse	English	Norse
spring	*vár* ON, *várit* ON, *vor* OI, *vorið* OI	strings	*strengina* OI, *strengina* ON
stallions	*hestar* OI, *hestar* ON	strong	*sterkr* ON, *sterkum* OI, *sterkum* ON, *sterkur* OI
stand	*stað* OI, *standa* OI, *standa* ON	strongest	*hraustasti* OI, *hraustasti* ON
standing	*staddir* ON, *stóðu* OI, *stóðu* ON	struck	*hjó* OI, *hjó* ON, *hoggið* OI, *höggvit* ON
stands	*stað* ON	strutharald	*strútharalds* ON
stared	*starði* OI, *starði* ON	Strut-Harald's (name)	*strút-haralds* OI
startled	*bilt* OI, *bilt* ON	stud-horses	*stóðhross* OI, *stóðhross* ON, *stóðhrossa* OI, *stóðhrossa* ON
stave	*stafir* OI, *stafir* ON, *stefið* OI		
staved	*stefit* ON	stump	*stúfinum* OI, *stúfinum* ON
stayed	*haldit* ON, *var* OI		
staying	*haldið* OI	subject	*mál* OI
steel	*stála* OI, *stála* ON	such	*háttar* OI, *háttar* ON, *slík* OI, *slík* ON, *slíka* OI, *slíka* ON, *slíkar* OI, *slíkr* ON, *slíks* OI, *slíks* ON, *slíkt* OI, *slíkt* ON, *slíku* OI, *slíku* ON, *slíkur* OI, *svá* ON, *svo* OI, *þvílíkur* OI
steersman	*stýrimaðr* ON, *stýrimaður* OI, *stýrimanni* ON, *stýrimanninum* OI		
steinar	*steinari* OI, *steinari* ON		
Steingrimsfjord (place)	*steingrímsfirði* OI, *steingrímsfirði* ON		
Steinthor (name)	*steinþór* OI	summer	*sumar* OI, *sumar* ON, *sumarið* OI, *sumarit* ON, *sumars* OI, *sumars* ON, *sumri* OI, *sumri* ON
stepped	*sté* OI, *sté* ON		
stiff	*stirð* OI, *stirð* ON		
stiff-spoken	*stirðkveðið* OI, *stirðkveðit* ON	summer-long	*sumarlangt* OI, *sumarlangt* ON
still	*enn* OI, *enn* ON, *kyrrt* OI, *kyrrt* ON	summoned	*stefni* OI, *stefni* ON
stole	*stolið* OI, *stolit* ON	sun	*sólu* OI, *sólu* ON
stood	*stóð* OI, *stóð* ON, *studdi* OI, *studdi* ON	sunrise	*sólarroð* OI, *sólarroð* ON
storm	*dyn* OI, *dyn* ON	support	*veitti* OI
straightaway	*þegar* OI	supported	*veitti* OI
straight-away	*þegar* OI	supposing	*ætlan* OI, *ætlan* ON
strain	*stofni* OI, *stofni* ON	surely	*víst* OI, *vistar* ON
stream	*lækjar* OI, *lækjar* ON	surprisingly	*furðu* OI, *furðu* ON
street	*stræti* OI, *stræti* ON	Svein (name)	*sveinn* OI, *sveinn* ON
strength	*afl* OI, *afl* ON, *afli* OI, *afli* ON, *afls* OI, *afls* ON	Sverting (name)	*svertingr* ON, *svertingur* OI
stretched	*seildist* OI, *seildist* ON	swan	*álft* OI, *álft* ON, *álftin* ON
strike	*höggva* OI, *höggva* ON, *slá* OI, *slá* ON	swan-mares	*svanmærrar* OI, *svanmærrar* ON
striking	*hjör* OI, *högg* OI, *högg* ON, *höggva* OI	swears	*sváru* OI, *sváru* ON
		sweat	*sveittr* ON, *sveittur* OI
striking-down	*hugreifum* OI, *hugreifum* ON	swede	*sænski* OI, *sænski* ON

Word List (English to Norse)

English	*Norse*	English	*Norse*
Sweden (place)	*svía* OI, *svía* ON, *svíþjóð* OI, *svíþjóð* ON, *svíþjóðar* OI, *svíþjóðar* ON, *svíþjóðu* OI, *svíþjóðu* ON	tenant	*landseti* OI, *landseti* ON
		tenants	*landseta* OI, *landseta* ON
		test	*freistaðim* ON, *freistuðum* OI
sweet-swallower	*ljúfsvelgs* OI, *ljúfsvelgs* ON	tested	*reynt* OI, *reynt* ON
swiftly	*skjótt* OI	testimony	*vátta* ON, *votta* OI
swollen	*þrútnaði* OI, *þrútnaði* ON	than	*að* OI, *at* ON, *en* OI, *en* ON, *sem* ON, *þann* OI
sword	*hjörva* OI, *hjörva* ON, *hjörvi* OI, *hjörvi* ON, *mæki* OI, *mæki* ON, *sverð* OI, *sverð* ON, *sverða* OI, *sverða* ON, *sverði* OI, *sverði* ON, *sverðið* OI, *sverðinu* OI, *sverðinu* ON, *sverðit* ON	thanked	*þakkaði* OI, *þakkaði* ON, *þakkar* OI, *þakkar* ON
		that	*á* OI, *á* ON, *að* OI, *af* OI, *ák* ON, *at* ON, *att* OI, *en* OI, *en* ON, *er* OI, *ér* OI, *er* ON, *ér* ON, *sá* ON, *sem* OI, *sem* ON, *sú* OI, *sú* ON, *þá* OI, *það* OI, *þann* OI, *þann* ON, *þat* ON, *þeim* ON, *þenna* OI, *þenna* ON, *þetta* OI, *þetta* ON, *því* OI
sword-reddened	*sverð-rögnir* OI, *sverð-rögnir* ON	the	*á* OI, *að* OI, *er* OI, *er* ON, *hið* OI, *hin* OI, *hina* OI, *hinn* OI, *hinnar* OI, *hinni* OI, *hins* OI, *hinum* OI, *í* OI, *in* ON, *ina* ON, *inn* ON, *innar* ON, *inni* ON, *ins* ON, *it* ON, *sem* OI, *þá* OI, *það* OI, *þat* ON, *þeir* OI, *þeir* ON, *þetta* OI

T, t

English	*Norse*	English	*Norse*
take	*færa* OI, *færa* ON, *fari* OI, *taka* OI, *taka* ON, *takast* OI, *takast* ON, *takið* OI, *takið* ON, *tekist* OI, *tekizt* ON		
taken	*nema* OI, *nema* ON, *nemr* OI, *nemr* ON, *tekið* OI, *tekit* ON, *tóku* OI	the-assembly	*þings* OI, *þings* ON
		the-berserker	*berserkrinn* ON, *berserkurinn* OI
taking	*nema* OI, *nema* ON	the-best	*best* OI
talented-people	*atgervismenn* OI	the-birds	*fuglarnir* OI, *fuglarnir* ON
talk	*tal* OI, *tala* OI, *tals* OI, *tals* ON, *tölum* OI, *tölum* ON	the-black	*svarta* OI, *svarta* ON, *svarti* OI, *svarti* ON
talked	*ræddi* OI, *tal* OI, *tal* ON, *töluðu* OI, *töluðu* ON	the-dream	*drauminum* OI, *drauminum* ON
talking	*tal* OI, *tal* ON, *tali* OI, *tali* ON	the-eagle	*örninn* OI
		the-eagles	*ernirnir* OI, *ernirnir* ON
taught	*kenndi* OI, *kenndi* ON, *kennt* OI, *kennt* ON	the-farmer	*bónda* OI
		the-field	*túninu* OI, *túninu* ON
temper	*skaplyndi* OI, *skaplyndi* ON	the-gift	*gjöfina* OI
temperament	*skapferði* OI, *skapferði* ON, *skaplyndi* OI	the-good	*goða* OI, *goða* ON
		the-headland	*nesin* OI, *nesin* ON
temperamental	*skapfelligr* ON, *skapfelligur* OI	the-house	*húsin* OI

Word List (English to Norse)

English	*Norse*	English	*Norse*
their	þar OI, þeim ON, þeir OI, þeira ON, þeirra OI, þeirri OI	these	þeim OI, þenna OI, þess OI, þessar OI, þessar ON, þessi OI, þessi ON, þessir OI, þessir ON
theirs	sín OI, sín ON, sinn ON, sinna OI, sinna ON, sinni OI, sinni ON, sínu OI, sínu ON, sínum OI, sínum ON, þeira ON, þeirra OI	the-sea	haf OI, haf ON
		the-shepherd	smalamanninn OI, smalamanninn ON
the-land	landinu OI, landinu ON	the-sky	lofti OI, lofti ON
them	sinni OI, sinni ON, þá OI, þá ON, þeim OI, þeim ON, þeima OI, þeima ON, þeir OI	the-south	suðrætt ON, suðurátt OI
		the-swan	álftin OI, álftinni OI, álftinni ON
the-moors	mýrunum OI, mýrunum ON	the-way	háttað OI, háttat ON
the-mountains	fjöllunum OI, fjöllunum ON	the-west	vestri OI, vestri ON
		the-work	verkið OI, verkit ON
themselves	sér OI, sér ON, sjálfra OI, sjálfra ON	they	senn OI, senn ON, sinn OI, sinn ON, þá OI, þá ON, þar OI, þar ON, þau OI, þau ON, þeim OI, þeim ON, þeir OI, þeir ON, þeír ON, þeira ON, þeirra OI
then	á OI, at ON, en OI, en ON, enn ON, er OI, er ON, hinn OI, inn OI, inn ON, síðan OI, síðan ON, sinn OI, sinn ON, þá OI, þá ON, þann OI, þann ON, þar ON, þás ON, þau OI, þau ON, þegar OI, þegar ON, þeim ON, þenna OI, þenna ON, því OI		
		things	hluti OI, hluti ON
		think	hygg OI, hygg ON, þykir OI, þykist OI, þykkir ON, þykkist ON
		third	þriði ON, þriðja OI, þriðja ON, þriðji OI
		thirty	þrjátigu OI, þrjátigu ON
the-one	þeirri OI	this	að OI, í OI, sig OI, sinni OI, sinni ON, sitt OI, það OI, þann OI, þat ON, þess OI, þess ON, þessa OI, þessa ON, þessi OI, þessi ON, þessu OI, þessu ON, þetta OI, þetta ON
the-plains	sléttu OI, sléttunni OI, sléttunni ON		
there	hingat ON, þá OI, þá ON, þaðan OI, þangað OI, þangat ON, þar OI, þar ON, þau OI, þau ON, þegar ON, þeir OI, þeir ON, þeira ON, þeiri ON, voru OI		
		this-man	manninum OI, manninum ON
thereafter	síðan OI	Thor (name)	Þór OI, Þór ON
therefore	fyrir OI, fyrir ON, þær OI, þær ON, þau OI, því OI, því ON	Thorarin (name)	Þórarinn OI, Þórarinn ON
		Thord (name)	Þórði OI, Þórði ON, Þórðr ON, Þórður OI
therefore-like	þvílíkan OI, þvílíkr ON	Thorfin (name)	Þorfinnr ON, Þorfinns OI, Þorfinns ON, Þorfinnur OI
thereore	við OI		
the-saga	sögunni OI, sögunni ON		

Word List (English to Norse)

English	Norse
Thorgerd (name)	þorgerði OI, þorgerði ON, þorgerðr ON, þorgerður OI
Thorgils (name)	þorgils OI, þorgils ON
Thorglisstadir (place)	þorgilsstöðum OI, þorgilsstöðum ON
Thorgrim (name)	þorgrím OI, þorgrím ON, þorgrímur OI
Thorgrim's (name)	þorgrím OI
Thorir (name)	þórir OI, þórir ON
Thorkel (name)	þorkatli OI, þorkell OI, þorkels OI
Thorkell (name)	þorkatli ON, þorkell OI, þorkell ON, þorkels ON
Thorkel's (name)	þorkatli OI
thorn	þorna OI, þorna ON
Thorod (name)	þóroddr ON
Thorodd (name)	þórodda OI, þórodda ON, þóroddur OI
Thororm (name)	þórorm OI, þórorm ON, þórormr ON, þórormur OI
Thorsnes-assembly (name)	þórnessþingi OI, þórsnessþingi ON
thorstein	þorstein'i ON
Thorstein (name)	þorstein OI, þorstein ON, þorsteini OI, þorsteini ON, þorsteinn OI, þorsteinn ON, þorsteins OI, þorsteins ON
Thorstein's (name)	þorsteins OI, þorsteins ON
Thorstein's (name)	þorsteins OI
Thorvard (name)	þorvarði OI, þorvarði ON, þorvarðr ON, þorvarður OI
those	þá OI, þá ON, þann ON, þeim OI, þeim ON, þeir OI, þenna OI, þenna ON
though	þó OI, þó ON, þótt OI, þótt ON
thought	hugði OI, hugði ON, hugðumk ON, hugðumst OI, hyggi OI, hyggi ON, þó OI, þó ON, þótti OI, þótti ON, þóttist OI, þóttist ON, þóttu OI, þóttu ON, þóttumst ON
threat	hót OI, hót ON, ógn OI, ógn ON
three	þrem OI, þrem ON, þremur OI, þrigga OI, þriggja OI, þriggja ON, þrír OI, þrír ON, þrjá OI, þrjá ON, þrjár OI, þrjár ON
through	gegnum OI, gegnum ON
thunder	þundi OI, þundi ON
Thurid (name)	þuríðr ON, þuríður OI
tidings	tíðendi ON
till-came	tilkoma OI, tilkváma ON
time	tíma OI, tíma ON, tóm OI, tóm ON
times	tíma OI, tíma ON
Tiundaland (place)	tíundaland OI, tíundaland ON
to	á OI, á ON, að OI, af OI, at ON, att ON, er OI, er ON, í OI, í ON, it ON, það OI, þvít ON, til OI, til ON, undir OI, undir ON, við OI, við ON
to-attach	þýðast OI
to-be	vera OI, vera ON
together	saman OI, saman ON, samt OI, samt ON
together-staying	samvistum OI, samvistum ON
to-going	atgöngu OI, atgöngu ON
to-hand	hendi OI, hendi ON
to-her	hana OI, hennar OI, hennar ON
to-him	honum OI, honum ON
to-him-of	honum ON
to-know	kunna OI, kunna ON
told	sagt OI, segir OI
to-me	mér OI, mér ON
tongue	tunga OI, tunga ON, tungu OI, tungu ON, tungur OI, tungur ON
took	færði OI, færði ON, nam OI, nam ON, námu OI, námu ON, þekkðist ON, þekktist OI, tók OI, tók ON, tóku OI

Word List (English to Norse)

English	Norse
took-land	*nam* OI, *nam* ON
took-to	*lagði* OI, *lagði* ON
to-out	*útan* ON
to-propose	*festa* ON, *festi* OI
Torfi (name)	*torfa* OI, *torfa* ON
Torfi's (name)	*torfa* OI
to-running	*atgangi* OI, *atgangi* ON
to-seat	*atsetu* ON
to-settle	*búið* OI, *búit* ON
to-the-king	*konungi* OI
to-them	*þeim* OI
to-travel	*fara* OI
towards	*til* OI, *til* ON
toyed	*leiki* OI, *leiki* ON
to-you	*þér* OI, *þér* ON
trading-men	*kaupmenn* OI, *kaupmenn* ON, *kaupmennina* OI, *kaupmennina* ON, *kaupmönnum* OI, *kaupmönnum* ON
trading-men's	*kaupmannanna* OI, *kaupmannanna* ON
trading-posts	*kaupstefna* OI, *kaupstefna* ON
trading-station	*kaupstað* OI, *kaupstað* ON
traditions	*sið* OI, *sið* ON
trammel	*þramma* OI, *þramma* ON
transferred	*fluttr* ON, *fluttur* OI
translated	*þýddan* OI, *þýddan* ON
travel	*far* OI, *far* ON, *fara* OI, *fara* ON, *farar* OI, *farar* ON, *farið* OI, *farim* ON, *farit* ON, *ferðar* OI, *ferðar* ON, *fóru* OI, *fóru* ON, *förum* OI
travel-away	*brottferðar* OI
travel-goods	*fararefna* OI, *fararefna* ON, *fararefni* OI, *fararefni* ON
traveling	*fara* OI, *fara* ON
travelled	*farið* OI, *farit* ON, *fer* OI, *fór* OI, *fór* ON, *fóru* OI, *fóru* ON
travelling	*fara* ON, *farinn* OI, *farinn* ON, *ferðarinnar* OI, *ferðarinnar* ON, *ferðina* OI, *ferðina* ON, *ferðinni* OI, *ferðinni* ON
travelling-man	*farmaðr* ON, *farmaður* OI
treasure	*grepp* ON, *gripi* OI, *gripi* ON
treasured	*gersemi* OI, *gersimi* ON
tree	*runnr* OI, *runnr* ON
trick	*brigð* OI, *brigð* ON, *prettum* OI, *prettum* ON
tricked	*bregðr* ON, *bregður* OI, *sveikstu* OI, *sveiktu* ON, *svikið* OI, *svikit* ON
tried	*reynd* OI
triumphs	*sigreynir* OI, *sigreynir* ON
trod	*tróðu* OI, *tróðu* ON
Trondheim (place)	*þrándheim* OI, *þrándheim* ON, *þrándheimi* OI, *þrándheimi* ON, *þrándheims* OI, *þrándheims* ON
troublesome-poet	*vandræðaskáld* OI, *vandræðaskáld* ON, *vandræðaskáldi* OI, *vandræðaskáldi* ON
true	
true	
true	
true	
true-knowledge	*sannfróðr* OI, *sannfróðr* ON
trunk	*bol* OI, *bol* ON
trusted	*trúða* ON, *trúði* OI
truth	*sannendum* ON, *sannindum* OI
Tunga-odd's (name)	*tungu-odds* OI, *tungu-odds* ON
tunic	*kyrtil* OI, *kyrtil* ON, *kyrtli* OI, *kyrtli* ON
turn	*vísað* OI, *vísat* ON
turned	*snerist* OI, *snerist* ON
turned-out	*reyndist* OI, *reyndist* ON
twelve	*tólf* OI, *tólf* ON, *tólfta* OI, *tólfta* ON

Word List (English to Norse)

English	*Norse*	English	*Norse*
two	*tvá* ON, *tvau* ON, *tveggja* OI, *tveggja* ON, *tveir* OI, *tveir* ON, *tvo* OI, *tvö* OI	used	*nýtti* OI
		usually	*jafnan* OI, *jafnan* ON

U, u

V, v

English	*Norse*
ugliest	*ljótastir* OI
ugly	*ófagrt* ON, *ófagurt* OI
ugly-nose	*nefljótr* ON, *nefljótur* OI
Ullr (name)	*ullr* OI, *ullr* ON
undecided	*óráðinn* OI, *óráðinn* ON
under	*und* OI, *und* ON, *undan* OI, *undan* ON, *undir* OI, *undu* OI
under-speech	*undirmál* OI, *undirmál* ON
understand	*skil* OI, *skil* ON
understood	*skilist* OI, *skilizt* ON
un-fellow-like	*ódrengilega* OI, *ódrengiliga* ON
unfolded	*rakði* ON, *rekði* ON, *rekti* OI
unfriendly	*óvingjarnlega* OI, *óvingjarnliga* ON
unhealthily	*óþínslega* OI, *óþínsliga* ON
unknown	*ókunnum* OI, *ókunnum* ON, *óvit* OI, *óvit* ON
un-marked-like	*ómerkilegur* OI, *ómerkiligr* ON
un-needed	*óþurft* OI, *óþurft* ON
un-peace	*ófriðar* OI, *ófriðar* ON
unrest	*ólæti* OI, *ölteiti* ON
un-settled	*óráðinn* OI
until	*fyrr* OI, *til* OI, *til* ON
unwise	*óráðinn* OI
up	*upp* OI, *upp* ON, *uppi* OI, *uppi* ON
upper	*efsta* OI, *efsta* ON
Uppsala (place)	*uppsala* OI, *uppsala* ON
up-to-the-mountains	*upp* OI
us	*okkr* ON, *okkur* OI, *oss* OI, *oss* ON
use	*nýta* OI, *nýta* ON, *nytjar* OI, *nytjar* ON, *nýtti* OI, *nýtti* ON

English	*Norse*
vacation	*orlof* OI, *orlof* ON, *orlofs* OI, *orlofs* ON
Valfell (place)	*valfell* OI, *valfell* ON
valid	*gildir* OI, *gildir* ON
valleys	*dalnum* OI, *dalnum* ON
valued	*virði* ON, *virti* OI
vanity	*hégóma* OI, *hégóma* ON, *hégómi* OI, *hégómi* ON
various	*ýmsum* OI, *ýmsum* ON
Vatnsdal (place)	*vatnsdal* OI, *vatnsdal* ON
vehemence	*ofsi* OI, *ofsi* ON
venomous-sting	*naðrstunga* OI, *naðrstunga* ON
Veradal (place)	*veradal* OI, *veradal* ON
verse	*vísu* OI, *vísu* ON, *vísuna* OI, *vísuna* ON
very-little	*alllitlu* OI, *alllitlu* ON
victorious	*sigrsæla* ON, *sigursæla* OI
victory	*sigrs* ON, *sigurs* OI
Viga-Bardi (name)	*víga-barði* OI
viking	*víkingr* ON, *víkingrinn* ON, *víkingur* OI, *víkingurinn* OI
visit	*vitja* OI, *vitja* ON
visited	*vitjaði* OI, *vitjaði* ON
voyage	*ferðum* OI, *ferðum* ON

W, w

English	*Norse*
wait	*bíða* OI, *bíða* ON
waited	*beið* OI, *beið* ON
waited-end	*beiðendum* OI, *beiðöndum* ON
walk	*ganga* OI, *ganga* ON
walked	*gekk* OI, *gekk* ON, *gekkst* OI
walls	*veggina* OI, *veggina* ON
wanted	*vildu* OI, *vildu* ON

Word List (English to Norse)

English	Norse
war	*her* OI
wares	*vara* OI, *vara* ON, *varnaðr* ON, *varnaður* OI, *váru* ON, *voru* OI
ware-sacks	*vörusekkar* OI, *vörusekkunum* OI, *vörusekkunum* ON
warm	*hlýra* ON, *hlýrra* OI
warrior	*gramr* OI, *gramr* ON, *grams* OI, *grams* ON, *gunnar* OI, *gunnar* ON, *kappi* OI, *kappi* ON
war-swift	*gunnbráðs* OI, *gunnbráðs* ON
war-twig	*gunnsproti* OI, *gunnsproti* ON
wary	*hafna* OI, *hafnar* ON
was	*að* OI, *at* ON, *er* OI, *er* ON, *eru* ON, *es* ON, *gerist* OI, *gerist* ON, *'s* ON, *væri* OI, *væri* ON, *var* OI, *var* ON, *varð* OI, *varð* ON, *váru* ON, *vas* ON, *vask* ON, *vera* OI, *vera* ON, *verða* OI, *verða* ON, *voru* OI
was-called	*heitaðist* OI, *heitaðist* ON, *hét* OI
wash	*þvá* ON, *þvo* OI
was-named	*hét* OI, *hét* ON
was-surprised	*undraðist* OI, *undraðist* ON
water	*vatn* OI, *vatn* ON
waters	*vatnanna* OI, *vatnanna* ON, *vatnið* OI, *vötn* OI, *vötn* ON
waves	*bárur* OI, *bárur* ON
ways	*megin* ON
we	*okkr* OI, *okkr* ON, *várum* ON, *vér* OI, *vér* ON
wealth	*auðs* OI, *auðs* ON, *fé* OI, *fé* ON, *féið* OI, *féit* ON, *fjár* OI, *fjár* ON, *fjáreign* OI, *fjáreign* ON
wealth-provides	*auðveitir* OI, *auðveitir* ON
wealthy	*auðigr* ON, *auðigs* OI, *auðigs* ON
weapon	*vápn* ON, *vopn* OI
weapons	*vápn* ON, *vápnum* ON, *vopnum* OI
we-are	*eru* OI
weather	*veðr* OI, *veðr* ON, *veðrið* OI
wedding	*brúðlaup* OI, *brúðlaup* ON, *brúðlaupi* OI, *brúðlaupi* ON
wedding-feast	*brúðlaupinu* OI, *brúðlaupinu* ON
week	*viku* OI, *viku* ON
weep	*gráta* OI, *gráta* ON
weigh	*vegni* OI, *vegni* ON
welcome	*fagna* OI, *fagna* ON
welcomed	*fagnat* ON
well	*allvel* OI, *heil* OI, *heil* ON, *heilastr* ON, *heilastur* OI, *með* OI, *vel* OI, *vel* ON
went	*færðu* OI, *færðu* ON, *farið* OI, *farit* ON, *fékk* OI, *fer* OI, *ferr* ON, *fór* OI, *fór* ON, *fóru* OI, *gekk* OI, *gekk* ON, *gengi* ON, *gengu* OI, *gengu* ON, *gengust* OI, *gengust* ON, *kom* OI
wept	*grét* OI, *grét* ON
were	*er* OI, *er* ON, *eru* OI, *eru* ON, *væri* OI, *væri* ON, *væru* OI, *var* OI, *var* ON, *varð* OI, *váru* ON, *ver* OI, *ver* ON, *vooru* OI, *voru* OI
we-see	*sjám* ON, *sjáum* OI
west	*vestr* ON, *vestra* OI, *vestra* ON, *vestur* OI
what	*er* OI, *hvað* OI, *hvat* ON, *hverja* OI, *hverja* ON, *hverninn* OI, *hverra* OI, *hverra* ON, *þvílíkan* ON
when	*en* ON, *er* OI, *er* ON
where	*er* OI, *hvaðan* OI, *hvaðan* ON, *hvar* OI, *hvar* ON, *hvárr* ON, *hvor* OI, *sem* OI, *var* OI, *varr* ON
whether	*hvárt* ON, *hvort* OI

225

Word List (English to Norse)

English	Norse	English	Norse
which	*er* OI, *er* ON, *es* ON, *hvern* OI, *hvernig* ON, *hvers* OI, *hvers* ON, *hvor* OI, *sem* OI, *sem* ON	winter-nights	*vetrnáttum* ON, *vetrnóttum* ON, *veturnáttum* OI, *veturnóttum* OI
while	*en* OI, *er* OI, *með* OI, *meðan* OI, *meðan* ON, *stund* OI, *stund* ON	winters	*vetr* ON, *vetra* OI, *vetra* ON, *vetrum* OI, *vetrum* ON, *vetur* OI
while-formed	*hríðmundaðar* OI, *hríðmundaðar* ON	wise	*fróðir* OI, *fróðra* OI, *fróðra* ON, *spaka* OI, *spaka* ON, *spaki* OI, *spaki* ON, *víst* OI, *vitr* ON, *vitur* OI
white	*hvíti* OI, *hvíti* ON, *hvítr* ON, *hvítum* OI, *hvítum* ON, *hvítur* OI		
who	*er* OI, *er* ON, *es* ON, *hver* OI, *hverjum* OI, *hverjum* ON, *hverr* ON, *sem* OI	wisest	*vitrastir* OI, *vitrastir* ON, *vitrastur* OI, *vitrustu* OI, *vitrustu* ON
		wish	*vil* OI, *vil* ON, *vill* ON, *vilt* OI
whose	*hver* OI, *hver* ON	wished	*vildi* OI, *vildi* ON, *vilja* OI
why	*hví* OI, *hví* ON	with	*er* OI, *með* OI, *með* ON, *því* OI, *við* OI, *við* ON, *vit* OI, *vit* ON
wicked	*illa* OI		
widely	*víða* OI, *víða* ON		
wider	*víðara* OI, *víðara* ON	within	*við* ON
widow	*ekkja* OI, *ekkja* ON	withold	*spara* OI
wife	*heitkonu* OI, *heitkonu* ON, *kona* OI, *kona* ON, *konu* OI, *konu* ON, *kvánar* ON, *kvonar* OI	without	*ómegð* OI, *ómegð* ON
		with-them	*þeim* OI
		woke	*vakir* OI, *vakir* ON, *vaknaða* ON
will	*mun* OI, *vil* OI, *vil* ON, *vilda* ON, *vildi* OI, *vildir* OI, *vildir* ON, *vilið* ON, *vilja* OI, *vilja* ON, *viljið* OI, *vill* OI, *vill* ON, *vilt* OI	woman	*kona* OI, *kona* ON, *konu* OI, *konur* OI, *rýgr* OI, *rýgr* ON
		women	*konur* OI, *konur* ON
		won	*unðu* ON, *unnar* OI, *unnar* ON, *unnið* OI, *unnit* ON, *vann* OI, *vann* ON
will-be	*verði* OI, *verði* ON, *verðir* ON		
willed	*vifja* ON, *vildi* OI, *vildi* ON, *víldi* ON, *vildir* OI, *vildir* ON, *vildu* OI, *vildu* ON, *vilja* OI, *vilja* ON	wonderful	*ágætum* OI, *ágætum* ON
		word	*orð* OI, *orðið* OI, *orðit* ON
William (name)	*vilhjálmr* ON, *vilhjálmur* OI	worded	*orðið* OI, *ort* OI, *ort* ON, *orta* OI, *orta* ON, *ortir* OI, *ortir* ON, *ortr* ON, *ortur* OI
wills	*vill* OI		
will-you	*villtu* ON, *viltu* OI		
win	*vinn* OI, *vinnk* ON	words	*orð* OI, *orð* ON
wind	*veðrit* ON	work	*starfa* OI, *starfa* ON, *starfi* OI, *starfi* ON, *starfs* OI, *starfs* ON, *sýslar* OI, *sýslir* ON
winds	*veðrum* OI, *veðrum* ON		
wine-given	*vín-gefn* OI, *vín-gefn* ON		
winter	*vetr* ON, *vetri* OI, *vetri* ON, *vetrinn* ON, *vetur* OI, *veturinn* OI	worst	*verst* OI, *verst* ON
		worth	*verðak* ON, *verðr* ON, *verður* OI, *virðr* ON

Word List (English to Norse)

English	*Norse*	English	*Norse*
worthily	*virðulega* OI, *virðuliga* ON	yours	*okkrir* OI, *okkrir* ON, *þér* OI, *þín* OI, *þín* ON, *þína* OI, *þína* ON, *þinn* OI, *þinn* ON, *þinnar* OI, *þinnar* ON, *þíns* OI, *þíns* ON, *þínum* OI, *þínum* ON, *yðrum* OI, *yðrum* ON, *yðr* OI, *yðvarn* OI, *yðvarn* ON
worthy	*virðingu* OI, *virðingu* ON		
would	*mun* OI, *mundi* OI, *mundu* OI, *mundu* ON, *munu* ON, *myndi* ON		
would-be	*mundu* ON, *væri* OI, *væri* ON, *værir* OI		
wound	*benja* OI, *benja* ON, *særimsk* ON, *særumst* OI, *sár* OI, *sára* OI, *sára* ON, *sárr* ON	yourself	*sér* ON, *sjálfum* OI, *sjálfum* ON
		you-to	*þér* OI
		you-two	*þið* OI
wound-eager	*sárfíkinn* OI, *sárfíkinn* ON	yule	*jól* OI, *jól* ON, *jóla* ON, *jólin* OI, *jólin* ON
wounded	*sár* OI, *sár* ON, *sárr* ON, *sárt* ON	yule-invitation	*jólaboð* OI, *jólaboð* ON
wounds	*sár* OI		
wound-sickles	*bensigðum* OI, *bensigðum* ON		
wound-vulture	*sárgammr* OI, *sárgammr* ON		
wrapped	*vafiðr* ON, *vafiður* OI		
wrestling	*glímu* OI, *glímu* ON, *glímur* OI, *glímur* ON		
wronged	*skarðan* OI, *skarðan* ON		
wrote	*orti* OI, *orti* ON		

Y, y

English	*Norse*
yes	*já* OI, *já* ON
yesterday	*gær* OI, *gær* ON
yet	*enn* OI
you	*þér* OI, *þér* ON, *þið* OI, *þig* OI, *þik* ON, *þit* ON, *þú* OI, *þú* ON, *yðr* ON, *yður* OI, *yðvar* OI, *yðvar* ON, *ykkr* ON, *ykkur* OI
young	*ung* OI, *ung* ON, *ungr* ON, *ungum* OI, *ungum* ON
younger	*yngri* OI, *yngri* ON
your	*þín* OI, *þín* ON, *þinna* OI, *þinna* ON, *þitt* OI, *þitt* ON, *yðrum* OI, *yðrum* ON, *yður* OI

www.ingramcontent.com/pod-product-compliance
Lightning Source LLC
Chambersburg PA
CBHW051404070526
44584CB00023B/3281